# TRANSCULTURAL CINEMA

*David MacDougall*

# TRANSCULTURAL CINEMA

*Edited and with an Introduction by Lucien Taylor*

PRINCETON UNIVERSITY PRESS   PRINCETON, NEW JERSEY

*Library of Congress Cataloging-in-Publication Data*

MacDougall, David.
Transcultural cinema / David MacDougall ; edited and
with an introduction by Lucien Taylor.
p.     cm.
Filmography: p.
Includes bibliographical references and index.
ISBN 0-691-01235-0 (cloth : alk. paper).—
ISBN 0-691-01234-2 (pbk. : alk. paper)
1. Motion pictures in ethnology. 2. Documentary films.
I. Taylor, Lucien. II. Title.
GN347.M33   1999          98-21197
305.8′002′08—dc21

# Contents

# Illustrations

# Preface

THIS BOOK brings together many of the essays I have written on documentary and ethnographic film in recent years. Some were written for particular occasions or because someone asked me to, but most I wrote because I wanted to or needed to. Much of this writing was done as a kind of counterweight to the experiences of filmmaking, for making films generates countless questions that the films themselves can address only indirectly.

Some of these essays have grown out of my sporadic attempts to take stock of documentary and ethnographic film, if only to reassure myself that either had a future. In others I have tried to take a closer look at matters that seem so self-evident they are almost never talked about. Still others concern questions I have struggled with for years in filmmaking but that may finally be unanswerable. In addressing them, I share Dai Vaughan's belief that it is important to make the effort, even if one arrives at only an incomplete understanding. Those essays may provoke little more than a shock of recognition for those who have been over the same ground.

Where there are direct links with films, I have tried to state them clearly. The indirect links are harder to pinpoint and run deeper, for nearly everything here has its origins in the implications formal, philosophical, and personal—of filmmaking practice. That includes, inseparably, the viewing of other people's films and my decades-long conversations with other filmmakers and writers. If there are further connections with filmmaking, they lie in the shape of the essays and my reasons for writing them. Films are made for other people to see, but they are also made simply so that they will exist, for the sake of what one cares about. These essays sometimes have a similar purpose, in seeing whether certain things can be put into words. They also borrow from my belief that filmmaking should be a process of exploration, rather than a way of stating what you already know. For this reason they do not always lay out their conclusions at the beginning, nor do they always follow the most direct path.

When Lucien Taylor, in a moment of generosity, offered to edit this book, I could imagine no one more appropriate or better suited to do it. More than anyone, it was he who encouraged me to keep writing these pieces during the years he was editor of *Visual Anthropology Review*. In selecting and helping me revise them, he has been a stimulating and painstaking editor, with a discerning eye for the weak connection, the lapse in logic, the inaccurate word. Where the essays have improved, he deserves most of the credit, and where they have not, the responsibility—through ignorance or obstinacy—lies with me. Others who have read drafts and given me valuable criticism include Patsy Asch, Leslie Devereaux, Christopher Gregory, Gary Kildea, Peter Loizos, Bill Nichols, Nicolas Peterson, and Judith MacDougall, who as my partner in life and filmmaking for over twenty-five years has, more than anyone, made this writing possible. If Judith ever felt I misrepresented our ideas or experiences, she has been kind enough never to discourage my attempts, and she has often helped me to reexamine my ideas and express them more clearly.

There are several others to whom I am particularly grateful, who as teachers or pioneers renewed my interest and determination at crucial moments. I count among these Colin Young, for his incisive thinking about film; James Blue, for his contagious passion for it; Jean Rouch, who made me conscious of new possibilities in filmmaking; and Dai Vaughan, who in his film editing and film writing provided a consummate model.

In the end, though, I am most thankful to several of the people I have filmed, for what they have shown me of the unaccountable courage, kindness, and grace of human beings. In recognition of that, I dedicate this book to them.

*Canberra*
*July 1998*

# TRANSCULTURAL CINEMA

# Introduction

LUCIEN TAYLOR

ALONG WITH Robert Flaherty and Jean Rouch, David and Judith MacDougall belong to that rare breed of filmmakers who have contributed appreciably to both documentary and ethnographic film traditions. But while the MacDougalls' films are well enough known, David MacDougall's writing is perhaps less so. His essays have of necessity been occasional, composed in interludes from filmmaking, and prompted by particular problems of the day. They do, however, coalesce around two abiding preoccupations. On the one hand, he fears for the fragile future of the documentary, all the more so in this age of spectacle and simulation. And on the other, he reflects on the respective qualities of images and texts, or more particularly ethnographic films and anthropological writing. These twin concerns in turn coalesce into two sets of principles: one for a reinvigorated documentary, a documentary that is more deeply invested in reality, and another for a revitalized visual anthropology. This latter not only reveals rather different aspects of the world from written anthropology, but is also quite at odds with reigning conceptions of what a "visual" anthropology should be.

Along the way, the book also essays nothing less than an outright reevaluation of documentary, and the relation of documentary observation both to participation (with one's subjects) and representation (of one's subjects). Such an endeavor pits MacDougall against prevailing orthodoxies in filmmaking, film criticism, and anthropology alike. So we should not be seduced by the understated style of his prose, or the inflections of certain essays, into failing to recognize that his intent is revisionist, and to the hilt. For if an observational approach to documentary is now almost universally deprecated, MacDougall urges us to think twice about what is at stake. In doing so, he takes another look at the relationship between documentary and the world, and also between fact and fiction. At first sight this reassessment of the observational might seem to reflect no more than a willful eccentricity on his part, but what emerges in these essays is that he is *anything but* a dyed-in-the-wool observational filmmaker, of the "spy-in-the-sky" variety that has been so painstakingly picked to pieces by the critics. For, as in fact we should already know from the MacDougalls' films, an observational approach to documentary exists not in contradistinction to participatory or "reflexive" propensities, but rather as their consummation. What becomes incontrovertibly clear in this book is that if observation is not, in the end, participatory and self-reflective, then it is not human.

This book is organized in three parts. While there is some seepage between them, part 1 brings together recent writing by MacDougall on the subjectivity of film-viewing and filmmaking, and on potentially non-word-based forms of "knowing" in anthropology. Part 2 includes his periodic assessments of the field of visual anthropology, and addresses specific questions that arise in it (such as style, authority and collaboration, and subtitling). And part 3 contains essays that are devoted more broadly to documentary cinema, particularly to issues of ontology and phenomenology in film. The final essay, "Transcultural Cinema," is in many ways a capstone to the book as a whole, in which his anthropological and cinematic concerns come together in their most definitive formulation yet.

## Rethinking Observational Cinema

It is indeed only superficially paradoxical to remark that David MacDougall is at once the keenest critic of observational filmmaking and one of its most consummate practitioners. "Observational cinema" is of course one label among many for that documentary film style—or rather that cluster of styles including Direct and vérité, each marked by the signatures of their makers, sharing little more than a family resemblance—that developed on the back of the invention of portable synchronous sound in the early 1960s. The implications of the new technology were various, and it is a measure of their significance that we are still wrestling with them today. For one thing, sync sound enabled documentarians to film individuals and interactions in informal settings in a way that had not previously been possible without recourse to studio dramatization, with its intrinsic fictionalization. The result was a shift in documentary from the depiction of the public to the private, and hence from the general to the particular, and (what is construed as) the typical to the unique. In short, a plethora of personal experience was opened up as a subject for documentary, one that Jean Rouch, Richard Leacock, the Maysles, and the MacDougalls would all, in their own ways, exploit.

Additionally, pre-sync sound documentaries had as a rule relied quite heavily on third-person commentary, either to contextualize the footage, and so render it intelligible, or explicitly to elaborate an argument by the film-maker. But when spectators were able to watch film subjects speaking in their own words and more or less in their own time—for observational filmmakers typically incorporate the long takes that other editors cut short—commentary came to seem an unnecessary hindrance, an encumbrance that served less often to clarify the meaning of a scene than to circumscribe it, and thereby to constrict it. Moreover, whereas earlier expository films tended to conflate the voice of the *filmmaker* with the voice of the *film*, and that, in turn, with voices *in* the film, in observational films the variety of voices—of the filmmaker, the film-as-text, and the subjects in the film—is more legible. Indeed, in retaining traces of the filmmaking encounter, observational films are in certain regards the most avowedly authored form of documentary. Furthermore, as MacDougall emphasizes at a number of points in his essays, the experience of viewing observational films is an active one of making sense out of the scenes passing before your eyes, and as such it is rather more demanding than being fed the filmmaker's point-of-view through a voice-over sound track. Some would go on to make the case that to the extent that it is demanding it is also empowering, for the spectators and subjects alike, since they are both given a different kind of freedom and authority within the film. But if that is so, it is a freedom that is not to the liking of all viewers, and it is surely in large part because of the demands observational cinema places on viewers that, at least outside the confines of ethnographic film circles and a handful of resilient aficionados, it is all but dead today.

In the mainstream—which is to say, as standard television fare over an ever greater swath of the earth's surface—the observational filmmaking of the 1960s and early 1970s has since given way to a style that relies principally on interviews, intercut with archival or actuality footage. As MacDougall reminds us (in "Film Teaching and the State of the Documentary," chapter 11), although the interview is a stepchild of the same sync sound technology that initially paved the way for observational filming, the two are typically quite different in spirit, with the interview-based documentary harking back to the earlier expository style that observational filmmakers had sought to supersede. In the standard interview setting, subjects are invited to *say* what they think or do, to reflect on their experiences after the fact, while observational filmmakers, like ethnographers, are more interested in what people *actually* do, in experience itself as it is lived. To be sure, saying and doing are not altogether distinct from one another, and phenomenologists have a tendency to forget that reflecting on one's life is an integral part of living it. Likewise, performances staged for the camera may have affinities with those that people put on for themselves—and the performers may be no less true to themselves for it. (One has only to think of the MacDougalls' film *Photo Wallahs* (1991) for evidence of that.)

But if the distinctions here are far from absolute, they are no less crucial for it. Certainly observational cinema typically cares far more for people getting on with their lives than telling you about them, and for performances that are an integral part of the fabric of social life and not enacted especially for the camera. However, in the hands of its most exacting adherents, such as the MacDougalls, it also illuminates the relationship between the two. For even the most self-effacing camera is still present as a structuring absence, and it is the nature and extent of its structuration that the best observational filmmakers manage to express. Moreover, although the interview might seem to be enabling for the filmmakers' subjects, it is really empowering for filmmakers themselves, who are able to conceal their own editorial point of view, and their own discursive voice, behind the testimony of their subjects. Interviews, carefully chopped and chosen, may also have the concision and precision of the voice-over favored by expository documentary, and as such, they return us to a style that is as much—if not more—about saying as it is about showing. It is a style which, like much else in Western culture, prefers the word over the image. To the contrary, for all of observational cinema's freeing up of subjects to speak in their own words, its signal importance was that it bid viewers to look as much as to listen. And in this it returned documentary to one of its initial imperatives: to open our eyes to the world, and in so doing, to restore us to it.

Among experimental documentary filmmakers, by contrast, observational filmmaking has for the most part been supplanted by one of two other styles, each of which seeks to remedy certain of its weaknesses. On the one hand, there has been a resurgence of what in Britain goes by the name of "do-cudrama," a style—or rather, here again, a miscellany of styles—that extends at least as far back as Georges Méliès' 1902 film of Edward VII's coronation, in which actuality shots of Westminster Abbey commingle with a Parisian reconstruction of the same event. Docudrama interweaves the documentary and the dramatic, sometimes self-consciously, sometimes not. To some degree its resurgence is surely due to the fact that observational filmmakers' efforts to shift the focus of documentary from the public to the private could never be any more than partially successful. For just as the past—other than what is stored in archives and attics, or evoked in memories and mementos— is inherently inaccessible to documentary (with implications that MacDougall probes in "Films of Memory," chapter 12), and just as there are objective conditions and incidents of civil unrest that would occasion either the destruction of the camera or the injury of its operator, so too there are moments of personal and interpersonal intimacy in which people will not remain oblivious or indifferent to the camera, or which many filmmakers would hesitate to intrude upon. That is to say, there are situations in which a truly documentary eye would either violate or destroy the object it had set out to record. Stylized dramatization, or reenactment that highlights its own semiotic status as performance rather than passing itself off as "realism," is one possible response to this predicament. But duplicitous or disguised dramatization, that is intended to be viewed as spontaneous and non-acted, is unfortunately much more common. Most of what passes for "reality" footage on television, and indeed for documentary anywhere, is of this genre. Whether shot with the polish and remove of classical fiction or deploying what we might call a neo-observational aesthetic (wobbly camera, poor lighting, indecipherable dialogue, and the like) as evidence of its own "authenticity," it in fact sublimates the real behind a simulation of its own fashioning. Historically, the depiction of subjects reenacting their lives for, but without acknowledging, the camera, has of course been accepted as part and parcel of the fabric of "documentary," and in this respect much docudrama is pre-observational in spirit, even if its resurgence is post-observational in its historical moment. As the hybrid and heterogeneous admixture of fact and fiction that it is, the genre naturally faces problems of its own. Directors of docudrama often justify their endeavors by reminding us that fact and fiction ineluctably bleed into one another in all filmmaking (and, for that matter, all representation). However, docudrama in general tends to subordinate fact to fiction, as well as to leave the distinction between the two unarticulated even as it plays on it.

The second style that seems to have succeeded the observational in the independent filmmaking community (and increasingly the mainstream) is the autobiographical: the first-person diaristic film essay. In view of his early appeal (in "Beyond Observational Cinema," chapter 4) for a more "participatory" filming style to offset the desire for authorial invisibility that he saw as latent within an observational approach, MacDougall cannot in the end—somewhat ironically, given his own inclinations—shirk his responsibility here. That said, the MacDougalls' signatures to their own films are often autobiographical: if this is most patently so in *Link-Up Diary* (1987) and *A Wife among Wives* (1981), their own first-person presence is nonetheless a quiet feature of all their films. In its own way too, autobiographical documentary is a response to the fact that there remain vast areas of our emotional life which are either inaccessible to nonfiction film or whose representation in third-person documentary would raise profound ethical and epistemological problems. A first-person approach represents one logical consummation of cinéma vérité. It injects a salutary degree of subjectivity into documentary, and provocatively blurs the boundary between subject and object, as well as between social actor and filmic actor. However, like vérité itself, it tends to conflate the filmic and the pro-filmic, and so to deflect attention away from what one might awkwardly call the "extra-cinematic" life of its subjects—those aspects of their lives that are not exclusively a function of their representation on film. In fact, cinéma vérité, by characterizing itself as the truth *of* cinema, rather than truth revealed by the cinema, went so far as to define the question of the relationship between the filmic and the pro-filmic out of bounds.

Largely, if by no means entirely, against the grain of these dominant documentary trends, David and Judith MacDougall have since the 1970s doggedly continued to refine their own unmistakable style. It is a style that has come to influence a whole generation of ethnographic filmmakers, even as it has continued to evolve—for even the most superficial comparison of their African and Australian films shows that their filmmaking has done anything but stand still. The most important of their early films are the two trilogies they shot among pastoral peoples in East Africa. These were among the first ethnographic films to translate indigenous dialogue with subtitles rather than dubbed voice-over, retaining thereby the auditory qualities of the original speech. If David MacDougall has since had reason to question the consequences of subtitling (see "Subtitling Ethnographic Films," chapter 7), their initial accomplishments need still to be appreciated. In particular, by translating speech for foreign viewers, subtitles would seem to have been instrumental in convincing many Westerners that non-Westerners *had* intellectual lives at all. The MacDougalls' first trilogy was shot in 1968 among the Jie in the Karamoja District of Uganda, and consists of two short films (*Nawi* [1970], *Under the Men's Tree* [1972]) and the 70-minute *To Live with Herds* [1972], a look at life in a homestead during a harsh dry season, and the rather sour relationship between the Jie and the local government. Their second trilogy was shot in 1974 among the Turkana of northwestern Kenya, and consists of three features: *The Wedding Camels* (1977), about a fraught negotiation of bridewealth before a wedding; *Lorang's Way* (1979), a subtle portrait of a self-possessed but vulnerable man who reflects on his life and the fragile future of his culture; and *A Wife among Wives* (1981), an exploration of the ways that some Turkana see marriage and polygyny.

The laconic style of the MacDougalls' films shares neither the palpable provocation of cinéma vérité (which, in retrospect, appears as much as a forebear of the expository interview as of the first-person film) nor the blue pencil of Direct Cinema, which typically confined its attention to intrinsically suspenseful situations and notable personalities (be they celebrities or eccentrics). But it is a style that is difficult in the end *not* to label "observational," if only because its powers of observation are at once so unwavering and self-evidently partial. Again, this does not mean that it is not participatory, for if it is anything it is that; nor does it mean that it is not reflexive, for it is that too. Indeed the contemporary predeliction to reproach observational cinema for its "plain style" and its naive "realism," or to construe its gaze as distant or distantiating, as akin to that of a voyeur or a surveillant, has in many ways got the wrong end of the stick. For the truth is more nearly the opposite. Even as the MacDougalls highlight their own status as "outsiders," their films are remarkable for their affecting intimacy with their subjects.

It is true that their later films about political resistance and cultural regeneration among indigenous Australians (such as *Familiar Places* [1980], *Takeover* [1980], *Three Horsemen* [1982], *Stockman's Strategy* [1984], *Collum Calling Canberra* [1984], and *Link-Up Diary* [1987]) would be more directly collaborative. They were made at the initiative of the communities themselves, involved subjects in the editing, and experimented with nonsynchronous first-person voice-over—"interior commentary," MacDougall calls it—as they grappled with the allusive speech and reticence of their subjects. However, if their African films are less directly collaborative, they are still overtly dialogical, and with both their subjects and their viewers. Far from portraying the world from an absolute standpoint outside human experience, or objectifying their subjects with a dispassionate view from afar, they draw near to them.

As MacDougall explains in "Unprivileged Camera Style" (chapter 9), in both their shooting and editing style, they sought to tie viewers (physically and psychologically) to their own limited perspective as they were filming. Indeed, in the attention of their films to telling detail, their regard for idiosyncratic nuances of emotion and behavior, their fidelity to the unhurried tempo of real time, their unobtrusive self-consciousness about the filmmakers' presence, and their preference for a series of interconnected vignettes over the creation of a synthetic single narrative—in these ways and more, they have a stylistic rigor and an aesthetic precision that could almost be characterized as classical. If André Bazin and Siegfried Kracauer marveled at film's "redemption" of physical reality—its revelation of the natural world—one is tempted to say that in the MacDougalls' films we can but marvel at the redemption of everyday lived experience.

At the crudest level, the MacDougalls' refusal of the cut-away, the match-cut, and the "suturing" together of shots from different camera angles into a seamless diegetic whole, does not so much conform to the plain style of realism as it actively contests it. To be blunt about it, there is nothing either *plain* or *realist* about their work, or about much observational cinema. (I am talking, of course, about the films themselves, not about the expressions of intent that filmmakers may make on their behalf, which are another matter altogether.) The MacDougalls' films register in innumerable ways their interactions with the world, and in so doing bring reality and representation into pointed juxtaposition. They throw the rules of realism into relief as often as they abide by them. In doing so, they actively (if implicitly) militate against the semantic self-sufficiency toward which realism, in its display of a diegesis of its own making, intrinsically inclines. In short, the MacDougalls' films undertake both an interrogation of style and an exploration of the world. And it is this sense of the residual possibilities open to an observational approach, both in the rendering of human existence and in reflecting upon the interplay between reality and representation, that is at the heart of MacDougall's concerns in the essays in this volume.

This is not based on a misplaced desire to rescue observational cinema as a genre, or even as a style—which, had it not already been recuperated by the fiction film, would now, in mimicry of its former self, most likely make itself felt as parody. Nor is it a denial that there are as many inferior observational films as there are any other: an observational approach no more acts as a surety of truth, or social significance, than any slavish application of "scientific method" does of discovery. It is, rather, an appreciation of the observational as a dimension or *potentiality* of film, of film *per se*. It would perhaps be more accurate to refer to this as the *documentary* dimension of *all* film, that which films going under the rubric of "documentary" should accentuate. More precisely, it is that aspect of the medium which, as an apparent record of its object, seeks to resist its incorporation into a discourse of the filmmaker's fabrication. As Dai Vaughan once remarked, "documentary always exceeds its makers' prescriptions. . . . If it did not, ethnographic films might as well be made in the studio with actors."[1] But in an age when we have very nearly forgotten what "documentary" means—when producers refer to almost any actuality image that does not feature an on-screen presenter or a talking head as "vérité," and ever more often a voice-over forewarns us what a talking head will say for fear we shall misconstrue the talking head itself—in such an age this would probably only muddy the waters further.

If the essays here come together as a political project at all, it is to rescue the documentary from its deathbed. This might appear grandly ambitious, or else merely perverse, in that, at least if film festivals are any indication, it would seem that more documentaries are being made today than ever before. But they are for the most part documentaries that have forgotten how to look, that shy away from exploring everyday experience, and that limit themselves to subjects deemed to be of immediate "topicality." All of which has contributed to documentary, as a concept, being progressively evacuated of content, to its conflation with journalism, and to its infusion with the pieties that typically accompany either advocacy or reproof. Contrarily, MacDougall wishes to reclaim documentary as an arena of engagement with the world, one that actively confronts reality, and that in so doing is transformed into a mode of inquiry in its own right.

But how exactly might documentary "confront" reality? How should, or could, it engage with the world? The vast mass of films purveyed as documentary belong fairly and squarely in the domain of journalism. This is most obviously so in terms of their content, for they are almost exclusively oriented to the public and the "political." But it is also true in respect to both their style and their narrative structure, which tends to resemble that of a newspaper article. MacDougall, on the other hand, sees the domain of the documentary as akin to that of the novel, both in regard to content (an interest in the personal, the domestic, the reflective) and in regard to form. His film *Tempus de Baristas* (1993) depicts the sympathy and rapport among three Sardinian mountain shepherds. In its texture and structure, it is perhaps the most overtly novelistic of the MacDougalls' films, but the affinity with the novel is evident in them all.

## Film and Text

David MacDougall's writing is that of a dedicated filmmaker, in the sense that it yokes theory to practice, and is replete with experiences and insights that could only ever come to one as a filmmaker. There are also affinities between his writing and his filmmaking—for his essays are as apparently without artifice, as unassuming almost, as his films. Instead of declaring their essence to you at the outset, they tend rather to draw you in gradually and disclose their drift over their course. It comes then as something of a surprise to learn of his insistence on *discontinuities* between images and texts—first and foremost, quite simply as objects, and secondarily as discourses—for it is a recurring theme in many of his essays. Film, he contends, is no more a text than culture is. If that sounds more or less unexceptionable today (though it didn't when he first wrote it), he goes on to propose a succession of arguments that are at a definite angle to the prevailing currents in visual anthropology, in particular the tendency to propose in its stead an anthropology of visual culture or communication. In "Visual Anthropology and the Ways of Knowing" (chapter 2) and "Transcultural Cinema" (chapter 13), MacDougall maintains that film is less a communicative act than a form of commensal engagement with the world, and one that implicates subject, spectator, and filmmaker alike. This is a process that favors experience over explanation, and which proceeds more by implication than demonstration. Furthermore, as Roland Barthes had already alerted us, the significance of its imagery at some point resists linguistic, or even metalinguistic, translation. Certainly no one in this post-Bazinian age could claim that film is unadulterated ontological revelation, but neither then is it a completely conventionalized system of signification. Against those who wish it were, or that it should be made to be, MacDougall suggests that many of film's most arresting properties are precisely those that obstinately refuse to submit to semiotic decoding.

There is another theme that looms large in these essays, one that follows on very much from the first. This is the peculiar potential that film offers for rendering human experience and subjectivity, together with its array of attendant problems. It is explored, *inter alia*, in "The Subjective Voice in Ethnographic Film" (chapter 3). For film is at once particular and general, both in ways that text is not: it is particular in its indexical attachment to its object and in its depiction of the individual person, but it is general in the indiscriminate fashion in which it portrays the physical continuities of the world and (in the sound film) in its coupling of image, action, and word. Text is both particular and general too, of course, but in very nearly opposite ways: in and of themselves, its signs are about as differentiated as you can get without turning them into algebra, but in their relationship to their referents, they are (as a rule) quintessentially arbitrary and abstract. In part because of its sweeping depiction of detail and consequent inclusion of "noise" side by side with the "signal," film has tended to reveal a rather different world from text (expository text, especially), and this alone, to MacDougall's mind, has been reason enough to precipitate the pervasive anthropological aversion to the filmic.

To some degree, MacDougall upholds a homology between life and film, on the one hand, and film and text, on the other. (There are other homologies too that crop up here and there in the essays that follow, and they are just as provocative: in "The Fate of the Cinema Subject" (chapter 1) he proposes that photography (or a freeze frame) is to film, as film and photography are to life, and in "When Less is Less" (chapter 10) that long takes are to short takes as are rushes to a finished film.) MacDougall suggests that just as the fullness of life inherently exceeds our evocation of it on film, so too film, with its analogical relationship and materially causative association with the world, no less surely oversteps the reach of our textual representations. These parallel arguments infuse his writing in turn with two related sensibilities. On the one hand, a sense of loss, or melancholia, as he ruminates on the myriad ways in which film both fixes its subjects in shadows of their former selves, and inevitably encroaches on their liberty and autonomy. And on the other, a sense both of possibility and of love—the possibility for film to create a shared field of consciousness linking subjects, filmmaker, and spectators, and the love he feels for his subjects flowing on from his recognition (in James Agee's unforgettable phrase) of their "immeasurable weight in actual existence."

## Self and Other

Explictly in these essays, as implicitly in his films, David MacDougall suggests that filmmakers and their subjects are not entirely separate or autonomous entities. Certainly they have their own perspectives and priorities, and (in "Whose Story Is It?," chapter 6) he takes pains to point out the manifold forms of authorship and meaning that films may encompass. Indeed, MacDougall's growing recognition of the differences between filmmakers and subjects—and not just in a cross-cultural context—lies behind his shift from proposing a "participatory" form of filmmaking (in "Beyond Observational Cinema," chapter 4) to his later call, on the tail of their series of Australian films, for an "intertextual" approach (in "Complicities of Style," chapter 5). He does not advocate intertextuality as an end in itself, nor does he mean by it the making of films that tip their hat to other films (as all films do, to varying degrees, whether wittingly or unwittingly). He means rather that films should seek to divulge, in both style and substance, the "multiple voices" that contribute in different ways to their formation. But if he insists that the various voices are distinct, and that filmmakers should not hoodwink themselves into pretending otherwise, his larger point (which he develops most explicitly in "The Fate of the Cinema Subject," chapter 1) is that the positions and indeed the dispositions of filmmakers and subjects alike are *inscribed*—quite literally, in the physical sense of inscription, which is as much index as sign— in the films that ensue from their collective encounter.

In a film, MacDougall contends, filmmaker and subject are bound up with each other, as inextricably, in the end, as the self is with the world. Needless to say, this is so ethically as well as aesthetically, for what are aesthetics if not an expression of a filmmaker's ethics? Here he brings elements of Merleau-

Ponty's phenomenology to bear on his argument, which he prefers to the more agonistic vision of Sartre's existential humanism. Merleau-Ponty had proposed substituting his own dyad, the Visible and the Invisible, for Sartre's Being and Nothingness, on the grounds that the invisible is not a *negation* or a contradiction of the visible but simply its *secret sharer*. This is something that MacDougall too wishes to underscore. The recognition that the visible and the invisible overlap with one another—or, in Lacan's words, that "[t]hat which makes us conscious institutes us at the same time as *speculum mundi*"[2]—and that they refer not so much to different entities as to different *aspects* of entities, has potentially far-reaching implications for the role of the visual within traditionally word-oriented disciplines such as the human sciences. Merleau-Ponty had remarked of Sartre's analytic of Being and Nothingness that it was of a seer "who forgets that he has a body . . . who tries to force the passage toward pure being and pure nothingness by installing himself in pure vision,"[3] a characterization that we might also recognize as pertaining to the totalizing vision of the functionalist anthropologist. To the contrary, MacDougall proposes that both subject and spectator are embodied, as is the filmmaker, and that they are so in the very *flesh* of the film. Moreover, whereas Sartre had suggested that we experience the "otherness" of others as both absolute and horrendous, thus conceiving of alterity as epistemologically abominable (a conception that he would seem to have bequeathed to many a documentary critic, with their emphasis on the "objectification" of uninformed subjects at the mercy of opportunistic filmmakers), MacDougall notes that it need be nothing of the sort. In this he goes a long way toward resolving the moral hand-wringing that has characterized much recent reflection on the relationship between Self and Other, and especially anthropologist and informant (or filmmaker and subject).

For if, as Sartre declared, there is no substantial selfhood—if, that is to say, the notion of an autonomous interior life is nothing but an illusion—then, by the same token, alterity is anything but absolute. Put another way, the Self is no more inviolable than the Other is inalienable. Far from it, in fact: Self and Other, fragmentary and partial as they are, are mutually constitutive, coexisting in a shared, if shifting, field of consciousness. Neither (*pace* Lacan) is the subject wholly split in itself, nor (*pace* Sartre) is there any complete rupture between Self and Other. To the contrary, as MacDougall emphasizes, individual experience presupposes a plurality of subjectivities, in ourselves and others, and *these do not detract from our selfhood so much as they actively contribute to it*. In film as in life, our conception of ourselves as well as of the world is intricately related to our conception of others. Other people's subjectivities are their own, to be sure, but they also inhabit the same world as we do, and this cohabitation is a source of commonalities—between individuals and by extension, says MacDougall, between groups—as much as it is of differences.

Here too the implications are clear, both for the human sciences and the study of film. In the first place, and in a radical move, MacDougall extends the phenomenology of film from its *reception* to its *production*: as a film-maker he is uniquely situated to talk not so much about what his films mean to their viewers, but about how he and his subjects experience the act of making them. Additionally, once we acknowledge that the subject is *both* seen and seer—which is not to say seen *before* seer, as in Lacan's curiously unreciprocal account of the preexistent gaze, unseen but imagined in the field of the Other—we can no longer understand documentary to present a unidirectional spectacle of its subjects to its spectators. And neither can we construe it as refusing to reciprocate the spectators' stare. For spectators do not merely see the subjects, they are also seen by them, albeit through the prism— MacDougall would go so far as to say, the *posture*—of the filmmaker's vision, the contours of which are in turn no less surely seen by both. He thus recasts the problem of Self and Other as, in his own words, "a set of reciprocal relations in which film, when all is said and done, plays only a very small part."

## A *Visual* Anthropology

If this is not the place to rehearse the anthropological accomplishments of the MacDougalls' films, neither should we overlook that they have grown out of periods of fieldwork as extended as those customarily undertaken with a view to producing written monographs. Nor should we disregard the fact that in their pervasive orientation to the transmission of culture they are anthropological from top to toe. One could, in fact, deploy the MacDougalls' films as litmus tests for anthropological concerns of the day. There are clear parallels between the content of their East African films and that of written Africanist anthropology of the period—in their portrayal of the postcolonial perturbations of newly independent states, their attention to the politics and economics of bridewealth, and their concern with issues of marriage and polygyny more broadly. Their Australian films of the late 1970s gave us an intimation of the explosion of ethnographic interest in resistance to structures of inequality that would occur during the 1980s, as well as in the affirmation and transformation of indigenous cultural identities during the 1990s. And their exploration in *Photo Wallahs* (1991) of photographic practices and performances in the Himalayan hill station of Mussoorie is clearly (again, in terms of content, at least) as consistent with conventional anthropological expectations as is David's inquiry into male gender identity and the construction of the emotions among Sardinian shepherds in *Tempus de Baristas* (1993).

We may also be tempted to take for granted the MacDougalls' films' various innovations with the norms of anthropological representation—their resistance to the myopic allure of the "ethnographic present," their attendance to individual embodied experience, their openly dialogical and reflexive turns, and their efforts at collaboration, to name a few—but we should not forget that these "experiments" with form all preceded by quite a while the general tendencies of written anthropology. For, if certain qualities of the MacDougalls' films are now, with the benefit of hindsight, lauded for having been ahead of their time, these are the very same qualities that, in flouting the strictures of structural-functionalism, were cause for the depreciation of their work by anthropologists back in the 1970s. And so the question naturally arises as to whether these essays too may be fated to be received as anthropological apostasy today and canonized tomorrow.

For one thing, MacDougall's consideration of the differences between images and text (in "Ethnographic Film: Failure and Promise," chapter 8), as well as his emphasis on both the performative properties and the analogical aspect of film (in "Visual Anthropology and the Ways of Knowing," chapter 2), are at an angle to those who advocate a specifically filmic form of ethnography but in fact proceed by conceiving of images *as if* they were texts, or by reducing images to their paralinguistic or propositional properties. Moreover, whereas the tendency among those seeking to legitimate or institutionalize visual anthropology has been to belittle differences between film and text—or to reiterate the truism that an ethnographic film may reflect as much local knowledge or anthropological interpretation as a written monograph—MacDougall would not wish to see a "visual anthropology" come into institutional being at the cost of divesting itself of its distinguishing feature, which is to say, its *visuality.*

Indeed, a striking feature of the contemporary spate of interest in visual anthropology—so striking, in a sense, that it seems to have gone unremarked—is that it claims the visual, not as its *medium* of analysis, but as its *object.* In other words, it masquerades as "visual" anthropology, but in fact displaces a *truly* visual anthropology by a call for enlarged anthropological attention *to* the visual. Although MacDougall has no quarrel with this *in principle*—a visual anthropology and an anthropology of the visual are no more incompatible with one another than they are one and the same—he may well *in practice.* For it is quite possible that the emerging visual anthropology will keep ethnographic film even more firmly relegated to the margins of things than it already is, and than, in MacDougall's book, it need be.

No one would contest that in the anthropological study *of* the visual, ethnographic film should take its due place alongside other visual dimensions of the human world—other film genres, most immediately, but also photography and painting, art, advertisements and architecture, the mass media, and any other manifestations of what, in an older discourse, we used to call "material culture." However, the danger is that this orientation occlude, whether by design or by default, an anthropology that is in and of itself visual. Moreover, while certain visual dimensions of culture may be amenable to their representation in words, visual culture as a whole surely *cries out* for its representation in visual media. This is likely to be far less unfaithful to its object than is interpreting (and so translating) the visual verbally. Additionally, if visual anthropology is concerned not only with the "vidistic environment," in Sol Worth's phrase (with, that is, visual symbolic forms) but also with the phenomenology of visual experience *tout court*—and since the "meaning" of symbolic forms is indissociable from our subjective apprehension of them, how could it not be?—then it is difficult to deny that the prosthetic eye of the camera has an inherent unfair advantage over our pens and keyboards. If indeed the written anthropology of the visual succeeds in stealing the thunder of a constitutively rather than merely incidentally visual anthropology, it will be hard not to ascribe this to intellectual intimidation. For as MacDougall attests, a truly visual anthropology poses a considerably greater challenge to current academic practice than verbal analysis of the visual. By the same token, it also presents far greater possibilities for the future development of anthropology, and MacDougall would not wish to see these squandered.

In fact, in its present constitution the anthropology of the visual suffers from a certain laxity of definition, and on at least three counts. In the first place, it would be hard to overestimate the significance of the senses, and of them sight, to the experience of fieldwork per se. And while it is unhappily the case that sensory experience is largely snuffed out of the ensuing ethnography, fieldwork is of course a hallmark of anthropology in general, not an emerging subdisciplinary speciality requiring a proprietary prefix, "visual."

Secondly, the visible is itself imbricated with the invisible, through and through, as is sight with the other elements of the human sensorium. At the most general level, visuality—the manifestation of visual experience in all its cultural and historical modalities—is clearly inseparable from sociality: so much so, indeed, that it is hard to conceive of any aspect of anthropology that could not at a stretch be brought within the purview of the new subdiscipline. After all, even kinship, that most abstract and amorphous of concepts, is made manifest in behavior, and language too has its visible moments of enunciation, its kinesics and proxemics, not to mention its graphic signs. In short, the emerging visual anthropology is very nearly omnisubsumptive, which logically leads one to wonder to what extent it really is new or, for that matter, necessary. Moreover, if it remains intent on keeping the visual at arm's length—as an object rather than a medium of anthropology—then it will end up not by recuperating but by recoiling from the visual, and in recoiling from it, repressing it. MacDougall's essays present a sustained argument against this possibility, but at the same time offer clear evidence of its danger. They also, in making the case for ethnographic film (and, by implication, photography), turn on its head the visual-nonvisual hierarchy that is at play in the anthropology of the visual. For while the material signifier of ethnographic film—film itself—may be constitutively visual (it is usually also aural and often verbal too), the world that it expresses—its diegesis, or signified—may be no more than incidentally visual. Since ethnographic film explores lived experience through its inscription in bodies, gestures, and looks, this is exactly what one would expect. At its best, ethnographic film gives equal ontological weight to the visible and the invisible. In the anthropology of the visual, on the other hand, it is the scope of the *signified* that is constitutively visual—a curiously self-defeating delimitation, in view of the fact that the visual and the nonvisual are each saturated with the other.[4]

Thirdly, there is, certainly, a large flurry of excitement about visual culture across the humanities and the human sciences, one that has come to be called a visual "moment." Partly this is due to the prevailing sense of exhaustion with the earlier linguistic turn—represented most obviously by deconstruction and post-structuralism—and a recognition that the opacity and ambiguity of the visual are sources of possibility in their own right, rather than deficiencies that are best remedied by their reduction into expository prose. In this regard, the conditions are surely ripe for a renewed appreciation of ethnographic film. But it is just as surely a response to the staggering preponderance of the visual in the modern world, the magnitude and nature of which we are barely beginning to scratch the surface of. In many ways we have passed from a Debordian society *of* the spectacle to a situation in which society functions quite simply *as* spectacle. "Reality TV," fixated on the socially taboo and the legally criminal, and often availing itself of a neo-observational aesthetic, is one symptom of this. Network news, with its melodramas, performances, and endless advertisements for itself, is fast becoming another. But they are symptoms of a mediatization of society that is as immaterial and invisible as it is material and visible, and which is now so thoroughgoing that it threatens to eclipse any possibility of representation. Max Horkheimer wrote, "As their telescopes and microscopes, their tapes and radios become more sensitive, individuals become blinder, more hard of hearing, less responsive, and society more opaque, hopeless, its misdeeds . . . larger, more superhuman than ever before," and this was a while *before* the dawn of digital video, cyberspace, and virtual reality.[5] The hypermediatization of society is thus, if paradoxically, inimical to the development of documentary. It has brought into being a situation that any documentary worthy of the name seeks to resist, however vainly, and in full knowledge that it may end up being recycled as raw material in the simulation of an other "reality" deprived of all happenstance and, for want of a better word, actuality. While anthropologists of the visual can be more serene than documentary filmmakers in the knowledge that their own representations are less likely to feed back into the system in quite the same way, they cannot claim the mass media or the "spectacularization" of society as their own particular province, for these transformations are naturally occupying others in the human sciences and the humanities just as much.

## Reflexivity Redefined

If MacDougall's writing on film (quite aside from his own filmmaking practice) represents a countercurrent to prevailing trends in visual anthropology, it is not restricted to that alone. For these essays now spell out for us, as indeed his films already exemplify, a more refined conception of reflexivity than has been articulated to date, whether by scholars in the human sciences or film theorists. In many ways it follows on from his observational approach to filmmaking, and his complementary recognition that documentary's evocation of a sense of being-in-the-world is itself a form of physical and social engagement with that world, and moreover an engagement in which subject, filmmaker, and spectator all participate. For rather as a spectator may discern that the relationship between subject and filmmaker is one, not of absolute alterity, but rather of shifting intersubjectivity, a documentary also contains an infinity of indications about the epistemological and political forces that constrain its representation.

If the opening of *A Wife among Wives* (1981) provides a memorable example of a straightforward kind of reflexivity, in "Visual Anthropology and the Ways of Knowing" (chapter 2) MacDougall develops a more nuanced notion, in which reflexivity is registered, whether intentionally or not, in the very style and structure of a film—not then, or not simply, in the returned look, the microphone boom breaking the frame, the camera operator in the mirror, and such like, but in intricacies of texture and subtleties of gesture that appear willy-nilly throughout the body of a film. They are integral to the film itself, and are inscribed in nuances of detail—in what is in frame one moment but not the next, in what is said as well as what goes unsaid, in the movement or the stasis of the frame, in the camera's proximity to or distance from a subject, in a pan or a tilt. Reflexivity of this order is at once implicit in the film and utterly intrinsic to it. It is neither a meta-commentary anterior to the work itself nor a detached baring-of-the-device—neither a self-conscious moment of *mise-en-abyme* nor an explicit putting into play of Brechtian "alienation effects." As a concept, it thus goes beyond the formalist notion of defamiliarization, or intertextuality, since it also addresses, through the very form of the film, the social nature of representation itself.

If the reflexivity that MacDougall is mapping out for us may yet be considered anti-illusionistic—and I believe it can—that is simply because its anti-illusionism is an inherent offshoot of its methodological self-scrutiny, which, at least in the MacDougalls' case, is both rigorous and sensitive. For such reflexivity—"deep reflexivity," one is inclined to call it—is not simply an aesthetic strategy; it is also an ethical position. But that does not mean that it can be articulated in any way outside the "performance" of the film itself. For deep reflexivity is neither antithetical to reality nor an explicit critique of realism. To the contrary, MacDougall demonstrates that reflexivity and reality coexist within representation, and are not, finally, separable from each other. We should be careful therefore to distinguish it both from the rhetorical reflexivity that is currently all the rage in anthropology, which aims at face value, at least to some degree, to subvert its own authority, and from the nominally "epistemic" reflexivity of Bourdieu, which seeks contrarily to shore up the epistemological solidity of sociology. One of the implications of MacDougall's model is that it saddles spectators with as much responsibility as filmmakers. Reflexivity is thus located as much in the domain as the viewer, or the reader, as it is of the filmmaker. This is of course exactly as it should be. For it is logically ludicrous to imagine that filmmakers have the wherewithal to inform us for once and for all how they influenced the pro-filmic in rendering it on film. (It is also sociologically naive to suppose that they should have the requisite sincerity.) If "deep reflexivity" thus impels us to look more closely at the fabric and the framework of films, it also surely places similar demands on us when reading written works.

## Beyond Culture

In the final essay of the book, "Transcultural Cinema" (chapter 13), MacDougall winds up by taking on what is perhaps, at least in the American tradition, the core concept of anthropology itself—that of "culture." He contends that ethnographic films do not simply traverse cultural boundaries—that much we know—they also *transcend* them. And in so doing, they call them into question. We noted above that if film and text are both particular and general, they are so in very different ways. Film succeeds in being both particular and general in its unique relationship to lived experience, which is at once embodied in the originary acts of seeing, hearing, and moving we see on the screen, *and* deployed as the mediating structures of the film's discourse. Film, uniquely, evokes experience through the *re-presentation* of experience. And the "shock" of film's transculturality, MacDougall suggests, is that *through* its particularity it evokes the *universality* of human experience—experience, in a word, that transcends cultural boundaries. Film reveals not only the intersubjective field of consciousness linking Self and Other, but also the gradual modulations and commonalities of experience between different cultural groups. In consequence he believes that film may put new heart into the anthropology of consciousness, extend it beyond its orientation to altered states of consciousness to consciousness per se—"everyday" consciousness—and attend all the while to the interplay between the conscious and the unconscious.

We would be off the mark in taking MacDougall's position to be either a false universal*ism* or an abstract humanism of the "Family of Man" variety. It is simply an insistence on the fact that while cultural differences are real, they are neither immutable nor absolute. His position is, however, to be distinguished from the "postmodernist" fetishization of frontiers and borders, because he does not see the porosity of boundaries as exclusively (or predominantly) a contemporary phenomenon, or even in the end as a matter of geography. He contends that wherever "cultural boundaries" are drawn up, they may still be overridden by similarities between individuals that are of greater social significance than any of their professed cultural differences. I suspect this is an argument that we anthropologists will have some difficulty assimilating. However, MacDougall's emphasis on universal aspects of human experience, many of them stemming from the brute fact of embodiment, receives strong support from recent developments in cognitive science, and particularly connectionism. In fact, his orientation to universality should not be "shocking" to us at all, for it used to be very much a leaning of anthropology as a whole—the notion that the familiarization of the unfamiliar engendered a reciprocal relativization of the familiar and taken-for-granted, that inquiry into the Other also informed the Self, and that studies of cultures-in-particular were in the end the study of culture-in-general, and so on. But it is a perspective that we have let slide in our attentiveness to difference and our exaggerated insistence that cultural construction goes "all the way down."

If the implicit, or the ensuing, concept of culture here construes it as something like "the 'dress' of the social situation," as Edmund Leach once memorably put it, I don't think that MacDougall would argue that the American concept of "culture" be dethroned and replaced by the British "society," or even "social structure." I think rather that he is simply urging anthropologists to undertake a more intense interrogation of "culture" than we have attempted to date. It does not go far enough to recognize that culture is contested as well as consensual, and that cultures are neither internally homogenous nor neatly separable from one another. That is no longer in doubt. (What is peculiar is that it should ever have been.) We should also proceed beyond the presumption that we may satisfactorily substitute for "culture" concepts like "discourse" or "practice," or even Bourdieu's neologism "habitus." Perhaps, indeed, we should stop searching for a substitute altogether.

In short, MacDougall's essays make plain that we need to rethink the contribution that culture makes to both lived experience and personal identity, and admit that it may be rather less than is in our immediate professional interests to admit. They also establish that we need to reevaluate the respective significance of culture and nature, even as the spectacularization of society—a phenomenon, needless to say, that is eminently cultural—may be assuming a hitherto unimaginable intensity. For the brute fact is that just as film gives equal time to the uncoded as well as the coded, it also gives equal time to nature and culture. This too has surely been another cause for anthropologists' apprehensions about film, but it is assuredly one that we should discount. The presence of the natural alongside the cultural also lends the medium a potentially interdisciplinary quality, one that we could profitably exploit. How surprising it would be if ethnographic film were to lead the way in reconciling anthropology with its cognate disciplines, separated as they now are by little more than institutional inertia!

In the process of rethinking the place of culture, we may have occasion to reflect upon the implications of the fact that whereas written anthropology has tended to foreground culture, ethnographic film, with its evocation of the particular, its orientation to the individual, and its affinity for narrative, has not. This it shares, of course, with life itself, where the coloration that culture provides to experience rarely rises explicitly to the fore as a subject for reflection in its own right. Moreover, in film as in life, commonalities of consciousness between individuals may be more salient than their cultural differences. And if indeed they are more significant in their experience, it is only logical that we should also accord them more prominence in our theory. MacDougall makes no bones about the fact that, in thus relegating—or, as we may prefer to say, restoring—culture to the phenomenological background, ethnographic film may be considered to be, in certain regards, "pre-anthropological." It is also, in defying all efforts to transmute it into expository prose, decidedly post-hermeneutic. Whether, in the end, ethnographic film will additionally turn out to be post-anthropological, or alternatively anthropology will allow itself to become, in certain regards, "post-cultural," we shall have to wait and see.

## Notes

1. "The Aesthetics of Ambiguity," in *Film As Ethnography*, ed. Peter Ian Crawford and David Turton (Manchester. Manchester University Press, 1992), p. 114.

2. This is a liberal translation of Lacan's sentence, "Ce qui nous fait conscience nous institue du même coup comme *speculum mundi*" (in "La schize de l'oeil et du regard," *Le séminaire de Jacques Lacan*, ed. Jacques-Alain Miller [Paris: Éditions du Seuil, 1973], p. 71). The awkwardness of the original ("Ce qui nous fait conscience . . ." as opposed to "ce qui nous rend conscient") is presumably meant to emphasize that subjective consciousness in no way precedes objecthood in the eyes of others.

3. Maurice Merleau-Ponty, *The Visible and the Invisible*, ed. Claude Lefort, trans. Alphonso Lingis (Evanston, Ill.: Northwestern University Press, 1968), p. 77

4. I am using the word "signified" in its, by now customary, colloquial sense, as more or less analogous to "referent," rather than the mental representation thereof, which is what de Saussure meant by it.

5. Max Horkheimer, *Dawn and Decline: Notes 1926-1931 and 1950-1969*, trans. Michael Shaw (New York: Seabury Press, 1978), p. 162.

# PART ONE

# CHAPTER ONE

# The Fate of the Cinema Subject

A PERSON I HAVE filmed is a set of broken images: first, someone actually seen, within touch, sound, and smell; a face glimpsed in the darkness of a viewfinder; a memory, sometimes elusive, sometimes of haunting clarity; a strip of images in an editing machine; a handful of photographs; and finally the figure moving on the screen, of cinema itself. It is Mataki, Logoth, Losike, Lorang, Arwoto, Francis, Geraldine, Ian, Sunny, Jaswant, Miminu, Franchiscu, Pietro. Each name lifts my spirits but also disturbs me. Film gives us the bodies of those we have filmed, yet those same bodies dissipate or are transformed before our eyes. I want to try to grasp the sense of this—if not to find the person among the phantoms, then perhaps to find some reasons for my puzzlement. If images lie, why are they so palpable of the life between us? I want to look, sometimes sidelong, at the spaces between the filmmaker and the subject: of imagery and language, of memory and feeling. These are spaces charged with ambiguity, but are they not also the spaces in which consciousness is created?

## James Agee's Despair

> And so in this quiet introit, and in all the time we
> have stayed in this house, and in all we have sought,
> and in each detail of it, there is so keen, sad, and pre-
> cious a nostalgia as I can scarcely otherwise know; a
> knowledge of brief truancy into the sources of my
> life, whereto I have no rightful access, having paid no
> price beyond love and sorrow.
> —*James Agee*[1]

James Agee has perhaps best expressed the passion and uncertainty of documentary—the "effort to perceive simply the cruel radiance of what is" (Agee and Evans, 1960: 11). Throughout the great and overwrought work that he produced with Walker Evans, his self-reproach and despair at the inadequacy of his writing surges up like an obsession. Some undetermined logic links the work to the fate of its subjects. Knowing that "words cannot embody," he still desperately means them to. If he persists it is because he has stumbled upon a mystery. He fears the blunting of our sensibilities, and his own. He is at war

1. A sharecropper family, Alabama, 1936. Photograph by Walker Evans from *Let Us Now Praise Famous Men* (1960 edition).

with language and with all representation that dares to speak for the lives upon which it trespasses. His anger and turmoil are those of someone who has been moved by both art and life but can no longer see where they meet. In the end he can only write, "somehow I have lost hold of the reality of all this, I scarcely can understand how" (p. 414).

At times in his collaboration with Evans, Agee seems to find solace in the photographs, a grip on reality that the writing misses. In photography, he observes, much of the difficulty of words, perhaps especially their "inability to communicate simultaneity with any immediacy," is "solved from the start." Yet it is "solved so simply . . . that this ease becomes the greatest danger against the good use of the camera" (pp. 236–37). Indeed, the camera's misuse has "spread so nearly universal a corruption of sight that I know of less than a dozen alive whose eyes I can trust even so much as my own" (p. 11).[2] In this broad indictment, Agee is no doubt thinking of Margaret Bourke-White's photographs in *You Have Seen Their Faces*, which both he and Evans considered an outrage.[3] But even a photographer like Evans makes a perilous bargain with images, as a writer makes with words. [Figure 1.]

During his career Agee wrote film criticism and screenplays and made two documentary films with Helen Levitt, *In the Street* (1945–46) and *The Quiet One* (1948). He was to discover that films bring together the concreteness of photographs with the fluidity of language, but with no lessening of the attendant risks of inadequacy and corruption. Indeed, in articulating their shots and sequences, films take on much of the clumsiness of language. Can documentary filmmakers, then, be any more sanguine about their work than Agee or Evans were about theirs? Does the mixture of photography, movement, and editing make film any more truthful than writing? How many filmmakers could maintain this and still look their subjects in the eye?

If some documentary filmmakers seem complacent about their work, many others, I suspect, are engaged in a secret struggle with their films: with the immediacy that hides a hundred evasions, with the luck that looks like forethought, with the skill that produces its predictable effects. Perhaps most keenly they feel the stifling domestication of film, which by its naming and cosseting of life shields viewers from the very things they are meant to discover. This struggle produced in Agee a streak of cruelty toward himself and his audience, as it did in Baudelaire and Artaud and filmmakers such as Franju and Buñuel. This emerges partly in an onslaught on the senses, and in a taunting of conventional writing. But one finds it also expressed more humbly in gaps and puzzled silences, and a calculated bluntness that reminds one of the practice of Indian temple carvers, who would strike off a toe or finger from a figure rather than risk the anger of the gods.

## Compound Visions

Film is the only method I have to show another just
how I see him.
—*Jean Rouch*[4]

*First premise: The filmmaker can never see the film as others see it.* This is easily overlooked, for films are more easily thought of as concrete works than as complex crossing-points of thoughts and feelings. As an object, a film may be fixed on a piece of celluloid, but to its viewers it is neither fixed nor even whole. It may be remembered for no more than a half dozen scenes out of a hundred, and those scenes may be different for every half dozen people who see it. It may be admired for a variety of socially consecrated reasons and yet actually be valued for quite different ones.

The filmmaker's response is in many ways the reverse of that of other viewers. For the filmmaker, the film is an extract from all the footage shot for it, and a reminder of all the events that produced it. It reduces the experience onto a very small canvas. For the spectator, by contrast, the film is not small but large: it opens onto a wider landscape. If the images evoke for the filmmaker a world that is largely missing, in the spectator they induce endless extrapolations from what is actually seen. The spectators glimpse a world opened rather than limited by the rectangular frame of the image. Like literature, the film's effect is to stimulate a work of their own imaginations. But for the filmmaker the same images only reaffirm that the subject existed. Instead of imagining, there is remembering; instead of discovery, there is recognition; instead of curiosity, there is foreknowledge and loss. To be sure, the filmmaker's remembered world is also partly imagined, but it may be years before the filmmaker, looking at the film, is able to see this.

Most people see a film only once, and so, as in Zeno's paradox of the runner who never arrives, they never actually see it. Viewing a film for the first time is a continuous unfolding that is only complete when one reaches the end. At any point one knows only what has gone before, never what is to come. Thus, throughout the viewing of a film, it remains incomplete; but once it is over, it is gone, to be grasped in its entirety only in memory. Even as the film progresses, its effect is not to coalesce step by step into a single entity, for its meanings are constantly in flux, altered by the addition of each new scene. Viewing it is more like a journey through a series of rooms, in which one is never sure where one has been before. A second or subsequent viewing, however, is fundamentally different from the first. As with a poem or novel, each part takes its place in the remembered work as a whole. Yet even here the work is never quite what one expected: some things have been misremembered, and one is struck by the things that went unnoticed before.

For a viewer, the structure of a film, in the absence of any alternatives, is something given, but for the filmmaker it is the structure that survives after a series of conscious and unconscious rearrangements and amputations. The film has finally come to *this*. It may have found a certain form and been saved from its worst blunders, but in the process it has sacrificed the many other films that were always latent in the rushes. A film sustains a hundred deaths and a hundred-and-one rebirths, but its last birth prepares a death of its own. The same images that come alive for the spectator are now already for the filmmaker gradually becoming *representative*. They may be the preferred images (although there are always regrets for things left out, defeated by the film's logic), but they are also only extracts from the more varied view of the subject that exists in the rushes. The scenes have begun to lose something even as they emerge for the viewers charged with a first-time freshness and promise. To the filmmaker, they look increasingly like film, not life.

There is, nevertheless, a countercurrent to this, like a reversed polarity, in certain responses of the filmmaker. A few shots that are perhaps of no more than passing interest to the casual viewer resonate with a special significance: a day remembered, an object actually handled, some characteristic of a person that is particularly cherished. Films thus confirm the compound qualities that Gilbert Lewis has remarked upon in paintings: "that what the artist tried to put

in his painting—the perceptions, feelings, thoughts that lay behind his work—
. . . [are] always more than any particular beholder does draw from it; and yet
. . .the ideas, impressions and feelings that the painting calls forth from the
beholder always go beyond what the artist intended" (1980: 38). Here, writ
large, is Roland Barthes's *punctum*: "It is what I add to the photograph and
*what is nevertheless already there*" (1981: 55).

*Second premise: The subject is part of the filmmaker, the filmmaker part of
the subject.* In this may be found one of the causes of the confusion that many
filmmakers feel in the presence of their films. The film subject has a multiple
identity—as the person who exists outside the film, in his or her own being; as
the person constructed through interaction with the filmmaker; and as the person constructed once again in the viewers' interactions with the film. We can
say that in the last two cases, the film subject is the product of a kind of
*investiture*: it is what is added to the person that is already there, even if by
"there" we mean only in the film's traces. More to the point, it is what is
already there *in the filmmaker and viewer*. We have certain ways of being
human, but they are made concrete largely through their presence and reaffirmation in others. To the filmmaker, then, image-making is largely a form
of extension of the self toward others, rather than a form of reception or appropriation.[5] The film subject comes into being through a process of identification and sensing—what might be called *ostention*, applying Michael
Polanyi's concept of "tacit knowledge" (1966). This is knowledge we cannot
"tell" in the abstract; it is knowledge we can only convey by showing—by
expressing our relation to it in a manner that allows others to enter into a
similar relation to it.[6] Film is deictic: the act of making a film is a way of
*pointing out* something to oneself and to others, an active shaping of experience. We reach out to others with our senses as a sort of probe (in films,
through the extension of the camera) and make sense of them through what
we contain in ourselves. Our knowledge is transposed, or displaced, toward
them, so that it appears to be *of* them. We are using our bodies and cameras as
kindred instruments, in somewhat the sense that Marcel Mauss meant when
he wrote of the "techniques du corps" (Mauss 1973).

This kind of vision, however, is beset by inconsistencies. The filmmaker
sees the subject framed in two radically different ways: first through the
viewfinder of the camera and later through the images on the film. The first
view, although it may resemble the film image, is ontologically different from
it, and different again from the image as it will seem, cut shorter and surrounded by other images, in the finished film. It takes place in an ephemeral
zone in which life has yet to accumulate meaning and a future. The subject
moves in and out of the miniature frame of the viewfinder, breathing the same
air as the filmmaker and surrounded by the same objects and sounds. They
await the same things—a door opening, unexpected arrivals and departures,
the coming of night. In these moments, the subject's existence and the film-

maker's are closely interwoven. To speak of the film subject at all is to speak of this shared space, willed with such intensity into the camera. It is so distant from the film that follows, and yet so instrumental in it, as to seem hallucinatory at the time. Film, filmmaker, and subject are drawn together in a fusion from which they are destined to be forced apart.

This comingling is compounded by the spectator's vision. A film that I make results from my immediate engagement with the world, and I am its first viewer. The spectator, coming upon the film as a second viewer, becomes entangled in my vision and my intention. There is an intimation of the subject's life beyond the film, but always infused with myself. Later on I may look at the film with an audience, and I may then have the curious experience of viewing myself viewing.

The spectator is, although indirectly, linked to the film subjects through the filmmaker's vision, since this is never independent of what it sees. At every moment the filmmaker's vision is defined and constituted in relation to its surroundings. The film subjects themselves, in their responses to the world, affect the filmmaker's way of seeing them. The filmmaker's subjectivity is thus variable, sometimes standing apart, sometimes joining with the subjectivity of others at the moment of filming, always ebbing and flowing. For this reason the filmmaker, seated with others watching the film, is influenced by their subjectivity and at times experiences their very different way of seeing it.

## The Fugitive Subject

> [Shot] 392 MS. from the shore below. Antoine descends a huge open stairway. He reaches the beach and runs towards the sea. The camera tracks back with him. The tide is out and the beach is long and flat. He is alone. He reaches the surf and walks into the water; it circles around his shoes and he looks down, surprised. He turns and walks in the water parallel to the beach. Taking a look over his shoulder at the sea, he turns back to the shore. The camera approaches him and the shot freezes into a still—Antoine Doinel, the sea behind him.
> —*From a post-production script of* Les Quatre cents coups[7]

The closing freeze-frame of Truffaut's film is perhaps too well known, often remembered only for having prompted a cinematic cliché. Yet the scene presents us with a moment of cinematic complexity, in which it is possible to read an invisible writing of pleasure and pain. It is as much about film as about life: about the contact with life that films create and the sense of loss

2. Jean-Pierre Léaud / Antoine Doinel in *Les Quatre cents coups* (1959).

they also engender. It touches upon the relations between ourselves and all persons in films, both fictional and documentary.

This freeze-frame activates several levels of our consciousness. By freezing the moving image it returns film to the status of still photography, from which cinema was born. Seized out of the flow of events, the photograph excludes us from the film and bears us away from the story like passengers on a train, leaving someone behind on a station platform (precisely the older cinematic convention that this image replaces). The character's life in the film may go on, but *for us* it must stop, to be replaced by a memorial image, like the snapshot of a loved one. [Figure 2.] Such a transformation of the cinematic into the photographic confronts us with the essential contradiction of photography— its intimation of life perceived in a present that is simultaneously past. It produces the effect of living unknowingly *within a photograph* up until the very moment it is taken, a sensation perhaps only comparable to awakening suddenly from a dream. That is the initial, disturbing effect of Truffaut's ending.

Considered a few moments later, the photograph takes on a different aspect. As it recedes into the past it becomes an increasingly poignant emanation *from* the past—the figure of Antoine Doinel pinned helplessly against the sea, his unknown future before him. The scene repeats in a different key an earlier scene in the film in which he is spread-eagled against the wall of the Rotor at the fun fair. Thus within a few seconds we experience both the arresting shock and the retrospective sadness of photography.

That might be all if this were a documentary film. Because it is fiction a further shift occurs, a transformation of *Les Quatre cents coups* from fiction *into* documentary. For although the freeze-frame interrupts the story of the character, Antoine Doinel, it also interrupts (and, in effect, sets in motion) the story of the actor, Jean-Pierre Léaud. In calling attention to a reality outside the narrative, Truffaut refers us from the character back to the actor who plays his part. The connection is all the more pointed because both character and actor are adolescents, poised at a moment from which everything must change. The music slows, like a clock running down, and seemingly with it the fiction loses its force. Jean-Pierre Léaud the actor is discovered within the film, his unknown future before him. We are released by a fade-out into our actual surroundings—perhaps the cinema where we have seen the film or (since a cinema is still a liminal world) into the streets around it. The transformations of the sequence have progressively shifted us out of the narrative of Antoine into the uncertainty of his future, out of the flow of cinema and into the stasis of photography, out of the present tense of the photograph and into its presence-as-past, out of the signified (the character) and into its signifier (the actor), out of the world of the cinema and into quotidian life.

Films such as this (we might add to it Chris Marker's *La Jetée* [1964] and Jean Eustache's *Les Photos d'Alix* [1979]) readdress the cinema as photography and cross the axis of photography with the axis of life. Photography distresses us by its inability to bridge the gap between the *now* of its presence as image and the *then* of its presence as living subject. In looking at photographs we may feel the desire, always unfulfilled, to enter their world—that moment when the picture was taken, always hovering on the verge of animation but never achieving it. Similarly, we may want a film to continue beyond its end-

such as in Vertov's film → the stark contrast between the still and the moving image)

ing—as if, by reanimating the frozen image of Doinel/Léaud, he could be brought back from the world of the dead.[8] Truffaut's freeze-frame suggests that he seeks in cinema an answer to still photography's premonitions of death, but also perhaps an answer to the passage of fugitive life.

In fiction films, the characters seem to slip away into the past. More disturbingly, the subjects of documentary slip away into the future, like impatient children before a portrait painter. Films stand still, but their subjects move on. Less than two years after Robert Flaherty filmed Allakariallak (better known as Nanook), he learned he had died of starvation on a hunting trip. While researching a book on Flaherty, Alan Marcus found the boy of *Louisiana Story* (1948), now in his fifties, cooking food on a barbecue in the heart of Louisiana.[9] If film adds movement and transiency to still photography, it has never resolved the deeper transiency of the subjects escaping from the work. Even as a film is being shot, its subjects are in transition, moving toward a future that the film cannot contain.

## The Displaced Eye

> How alive they are! They have their whole lives be-
> fore them; but also they are dead (today), they are
> then *already* dead (yesterday).
> —*Roland Barthes*[10]

Freeze-frames reproduce an event familiar to all filmmakers: seeing an editing machine stopped, with a film image suddenly arrested on its viewing screen. Visitors glancing into cutting rooms are as likely to see frozen images as moving ones. Dziga Vertov plays with this stopping and starting in *The Man with the Movie Camera* (1928), in a sequence doubtless well known to Truffaut. For the filmmaker, such a suspension of motion reproduces in miniature the larger suspension of life that a film as a whole imposes on its subjects. The few hundred feet of a film create, in effect, one large freeze-frame. Even before editing the film, this has become apparent to the filmmaker while viewing the rushes; but it may be apparent very much earlier. For many filmmakers it is in fact most keenly felt at the very moment of filming. It casts a shadow over the relationship with the subjects—a premonition of the dissolution to which every film is subject.

Such experiences are the result of a displaced vision that is rarely available to film audiences themselves. It involves an awareness of the living presence of the subject in the presence (or anticipation) of its illusion, and it produces a kind of grief. This may even include a measure of disgust at cinema itself. But whereas grief is often tempered by time and acceptance, this grief is situated at the very point of separation: at the tearing apart of the signifier from its object. Such an emotion finds its concrete expression in the contradictions of the filming equipment, for while a camera is always an instrument framing the present, the film it contains is always an instrument of the past.

This separation is progressively exacerbated and transformed by time, as the film comes further adrift from the present tense of filming. A new present tense intervenes: the present tense of viewing the footage itself. There are, as we know, those moments in life when we see with terrible clarity what we are about to lose, and understand its importance. Such moments are spread throughout the process of filmmaking. The sense of intimacy, of drawing closer to the grain of one's subjects, develops in the very same structure as the loss of contact with them. The film footage becomes an emblem of this contradiction—an object of magical properties.

Looking through the viewfinder of a camera and handling the footage of those one has filmed are both acts of intense and intimate inspection. The first is vivid and pitched at a high level of expectation. The future is unknown: the filmmaker and subjects are bound together in a common present, awaiting each fresh turn of events. Film editing, by contrast, is solitary and deliberate. It involves constant and often wearisome repetitions over extended periods of time. Gradually the filmmaker comes to know the footage in all its details. Every word and gesture of the people filmed assumes an added weight, in the knowledge of what will become of them, but also in its quintessential rightness. In shots seen over and over again, people behave uncannily as they must—as they were destined to behave. One sees in each person the perfection of qualities of which they have little consciousness themselves. There is a sense of undeserved privilege, of being witness to moments in people's lives of transitory grace. The world of a film-in-the-making has a preternatural stillness, illuminated by the sort of light found only in certain dreams, from which one wakes to grayness and desolation. It is permeated by an awareness of its own passing.

The attentiveness of the filmmaker to the subjects, that begins with the making of the film, inevitably shifts toward the images themselves, in a relation that cannot be reciprocated. It produces an increasing intimacy, but a one-way intimacy that is always in danger of fetishizing its objects. The film subjects can have no contact with the filmmaker comparable to the filmmaker's covert contact with them. Whatever their relationship outside the film, the film necessarily intervenes and inserts itself between them. The sense of immediacy created by watching the footage—its never-ending present tense, the sense of everything happening *now*—has the further effect of bizarrely distorting the historical continuum within which the filmmaker and subjects exist. There is the confusing sense of a widening gulf, for although the film subjects' presence is constantly evoked by the footage, so is their absence.

Studying old photographs, including one by André Kertész of a schoolboy identified only as Ernest ("It is possible that Ernest is still alive today: but where? how? What a novel!"),[11] Roland Barthes was struck by a similiar separation. Here, in the apparition of a past moment in the present, was the compound intimation of "that is" and "that-has-been," which he called photography's *noeme* of Time. Unlike still photographs, film is founded on the resurrection of time passing. In its animation of movement and sound, it suspends for a few minutes the closure of photography. But for the filmmaker, this physical and temporal "now-ness" is accompanied by a reciprocal sense of stillness, for each shot has no destination, no consequence, beyond the next cut. In the end, film clearly has no more dominance over time, no more power to recall life, than the frozen images of photographs. Indeed, it offers the semblance of life only to snatch it away. This might properly be called cinema's *noeme* of Loss.

Is it surprising then that filmmakers should so often regard their films as empty shells, and find the viewing of them painful? Each is undercut by the widening fissure between the time it was made and the time of viewing. Even before the film is completed its subjects have subtly changed and are experiencing things quite unforeseen at the time of filming. This knowledge eats away at the foundations of the encapsulated world the film portrays, in which the uncertainties of the future were distant and at least shared ones. For this fragmentation of its world, the film itself has no remedy. As more time elapses, the lives presented on the screen will become increasingly spectral. They will begin to float in a disconnected, legendary past, perhaps acquiring a new aura of value (like the image of a long-lost friend), but for the filmmaker this is little consolation. Whatever freshness and complicity with life the images once had, they will now offer something more palliative, like memory itself.

Predictably, one of the most unsettling experiences for a filmmaker is coming face to face with the people in the film after a period of separation. This usually happens after a bout of intensive film editing. Through constant viewing, the subjects have become both more familiar and yet indistinct, like friends one writes to over the years but rarely sees. In the editing room, the filmmaker has been able to call them up like phantoms by switching on a machine, but then comes the moment of greeting them in person. During this meeting, after warm exchanges, there is often an impression—made all the more disturbing for being forbidden—of seeing the subjects as the ghosts of themselves. Sometimes, it is true, the present moment dominates, making the *film* seem remote and artificial. More often the film remains stubbornly vivid in the mind, making the subjects seem like usurpers.

What is distressing is not any awkwardness in meeting the subjects again but the reversal involved in their seeming to have become less real than their images on film. They would undoubtedly find this odd, but such feelings are generally kept from them. They cannot know how closely they have been watched, or what importance they have assumed in the filmmaker's imagination. If the filmmaker expects a return of such feelings, he or she will be disappointed. The film creates no corresponding intimacy. If anything, it leads to a certain self-consciousness and reserve on the part of the subjects, for having arrested a particular period in their lives. Their memories of the filmmaker, on the other hand, will, like most memories, consist of only a few sharp images picked out against a quickly fading background.

Such moments expose the fundamental craziness of documentary filmmaking. Many filmmakers abandon documentary altogether. Some move quickly from one film to another, terminating their relationships with their subjects as soon as a film is completed. A few others go to a great deal of trouble to maintain the relationships created while filming, or to reestablish them on a new basis. Although some films lead to lifelong friendships, the film itself tends to stand in the way of this. It has the potential to disturb—by exposing the subjects to their neighbors, and by exposing the filmmaker's view of them to them. By fixing its subjects irrevocably in the past, a film encroaches on their subsequent freedom and identity. The knowledge of this may lead the filmmaker to further acts of expiation or redress.

## The Stars Grow Old

> My movie is born first in my head, dies on paper; is
> resuscitated by the living persons and real objects I
> use, which are killed on film but, placed in a certain
> order and projected onto a screen, come to life again
> like flowers in water.
> —Robert Bresson[12]

Some filmmakers respond to the closure of past films by reactivating the filming process. There has been a proliferation of documentary sequels and series, including such films as N!ai, The Story of a !Kung Woman (1980) (John Marshall's biographical film, incorporating footage shot over a 28-year period), Children of Fate (1992)[13] (an updating of a film made thirty years before), the Seven Up series[14] (conducting interviews with the same people every seven years), and among ethnographic films, the Mursi, Hamar, and New Guinea trilogies.[15] In these efforts to film people again or repeatedly, we can often see the need to render a kind of justice.

What are we to make of Madame L'Eau (1992), the most recent of Jean Rouch's major films about the cohort of friends who once called themselves Dalarou?[16] The film returns to past people and places, but in fact it does not seem to be a film in search of the past. On the contrary, it seems like an effort to undo the past and rekindle the association of this aging group of men. Is it

Rouch's way of refusing the envelopment of previous films, of cinema it-self—if only by making another film? There is of course no final escape from such a chain of revisitations; but a series of films spaced over many years at least calls attention to the intervening spaces, much as a jump cut calls atten-tion to missing footage. Each new film makes amends for the portrayals and betrayals of past films. Each buys time and puts off the final reckoning.

This is perhaps an impulse peculiar to documentary. Sequels in fiction films merely extend a work of the imagination, sometimes to capitalize on an earlier success or snatch a character from an uncertain fate, as Truffaut did in later films about Antoine Doinel. The documentary filmmaker has a different set of relationships with the world. The difference between documentary and fiction, as Bill Nichols observed in 1991, is that the documentary subject has an exis-tence independent of the film—a point made even more passionately by James Agee fifty years earlier:

> It is that he exists, in actual being, as you do and as I do, and as no character of the imagination can possibly exist. His great weight, mystery, and dignity are in this fact. . . . Because of his immeasurable weight in actual existence, and because of mine, every word I tell of him has inevitably a kind of immediacy, a kind of meaning, not at all necessarily "superior" to that of imagination, but of a kind so different that a work of the imagination (however intensely it may draw on "life") can at best only faintly imitate the least of it. (Agee and Evans 1960: 12)

In an early film by Rouch, *Bataille sur le grand fleuve* (1951), we come upon a scene of a young man playing in the water with a baby hippopotamus. He kisses the hippo on the nose, and there is a clear bond of affection between them. It is a scene of some tenderness, all the more so because it is offset by the violent scenes of hippopotamus hunting in the same film. Although parts of the film sweep us up in group emotions, here for the first time in Rouch's work we are drawn into the orbit of an individual personality. In viewing this scene we have an impression, as perhaps Rouch did himself, of a story left unfinished. The young man is Damouré Zika, later to become the "star" of *Jaguar* (1954–67), *Cocorico, Monsieur Poulet* (1974), and *Madame L'Eau*.

A return to the site of an earlier film is like returning to the scene of a crime. Something has very often been neglected, misrepresented, or left unfinished. John Marshall is clear about this in explaining his change of approach in later films about the Ju/'hoansi in southwestern Africa. "My first film, *The Hunters*, was shot in 1952–53. The reality of what I was seeing while the men were hunting was far less important to me than the way in which I was shooting and interpreting the reality to reflect my own perceptions. . . . If I had used the rules of filming I use today, *The Hunters* would have appeared as a slowly expanding series of events rather than a narrow story" (1993: 36). Elsewhere, Marshall describes certain kinds of filmmaking explicitly as killing "by myth" (pp. 19–21). Films can have untold consequences, but all spring from their

3. From *Au Hasard, Balthazar* (1966).

initial, presumptuous act. The real "crime" of representation is representation itself. It is no coincidence that some people fear photography as a theft of the soul, or that some religions forbid the making of human effigies. By freezing life, every film to some degree offends against the complexity of people and the destiny that awaits them.

If this causes some documentary filmmakers to turn to fiction, it causes many viewers of fiction to find the characters there less interesting than the actors who play them. The popularity of movie stars derives in large part from the enigma of what they withhold of their private lives, which the withholding implicitly guarantees. In film after film they appear as "themselves" and in doing so create a continuum between life and film, unlike those actors who disappear into a particular role. This was always the appeal of the star: the reassurance that beyond the role was the reality of a life. Stars thus outwit the cinema, traversing each film in turn and inviting the audience to take a disproportionate interest in what lies outside it.

Robert Bresson's films are perhaps the antithesis of theatrical films and therefore come round upon the star system of Hollywood from the opposite direction. Bresson's unknown actors—or "models," as he calls them—are like the mirror-images of the stars. Instructed simply to speak the words of the text, and not permitted to "act," they bring together the filmic and nonfilmic worlds. In Bresson's fiction, the living person, the found actor, continues obliviously to project an autonomous self on the screen, so that despite all the artifice of cinema some residue persists. In his films Bresson struggles toward meanings in excess of any story or consideration of "character," preferring rather to wander intentionally into those areas of "obtuse" meaning that Barthes (1977b) describes as beyond "culture, knowledge, information," beyond the narrative and the symbolic. There is thus an affinity between the star system and the use of non-actors. Each circumvents the mimetic conventions of theater and searches for qualities that deny the closure of cinema. In Bresson's case, the search reaches its apogee in the use of a donkey as the central figure in *Au Hasard, Balthazar* (1966). [Figure 3.] Here is the perfect non-actor, who can have no understanding of the film and whose "dumb" acquiescence is therefore an exact equivalent of his role as the silent bearer of a fate meted out by human beings. Balthazar's Calvary provides a metaphor for a cinema suffering under the tyranny of its own circumscriptions of meaning.

Time and the persistence of the self are the subversive forces in film. Documentary sequels and the star system more surely refute the finality that images create than any portrayal of change contained in the films themselves. Films trap the subjects before them, but the subjects continually slip out from beneath the images they leave behind on film. New films temporarily restore the congruence of image and subject. New images thus return extracinematic credibility to the cinema. By making sequels, Truffaut keeps alive the intertwined destinies of his chosen character and actor, from child to adult, holding the separation of art and life in abeyance. In *Jaguar* a smiling Damouré jokes with a pretty girl on the banks of the Niger, in perfect continuity with his earlier friendship with the baby hippopotamus. As a robed senior man in *Madame L'Eau* he smiles with similar tenderness at his Dutch friends. Jean Gabin grows from a heavy-eyed young lover in *Le Quai des brumes* (1938) to a pouchy-eyed gangster cooking dinner for an old friend in *Touchez-pas au grisbi* (1953). To the public it is important to see that, like themselves, the stars grow old.


## Betrayal by "Character"

If I could do it, I'd do no writing at all here. It would
be photographs; the rest would be fragments of cloth,
bits of cotton, lumps of earth, records of speech,
pieces of wood and iron, phials of odors, plates of
food and excrement. . . . A piece of the body torn out
by the roots might be more to the point.
—*James Agee*[17]


The film image has two seemingly incompatible properties: it evokes the absent human body but then, in its absence, opens it up to more intense scrutiny (and violence) than if it were physically present. Indeed, it is because of its immateriality that the body can be treated with such abandon. It can be enlarged, cut into separate pieces, and gazed upon in minute detail. We see people in films as we rarely see them within the physical and social confines of daily life. This odd duality of extreme absence and extreme presence reflects back upon the viewer. We watch films both at a distance and in close-up. We remain disengaged even as our awareness of sensory detail is sharpened. As Susan Buck-Morss (1994) puts it, the film viewer's body is both anaesthetized and hypersensitized. Because complete involvement would result in a kind of overload, it is the element of absence from the scene on both counts that enables the cinema to function as an extension of perception and thought.

Both the language of distance and the language of proximity serve the filmmaker's purpose, but the violence they do to the film subject is also a primary source of the filmmaker's distress. The transformations that take place in the portrayal of the film subject are complex, and not always a matter of conscious intent. Filmmakers often watch helplessly as the figures on the screen take on characteristics quite different from themselves in life. This process requires the viewer's complicity and therefore unites the viewer and filmmaker in a common, if fluctuating, subjectivity. Although the filmmaker is inherently barred from the perspectives of other viewers, he or she always tries to grasp them vicariously. By trial and error—by adding, removing, and shifting the position of material—the filmmaker observes how the balance of elements is altered and how small changes affect the way in which the film subject is gradually shaped.

Film editing involves the elimination of certain kinds of material in the interests of other material, dictated both by the film's length and its overall intentions. Of the complex elements of personality and behavior originally perceived by the filmmaker, only a few will have been registered in the filming, and of these only a few will survive in the finished film. The result might be called a sketch, except that a sketch suggests a rough and manifestly incomplete portrait. But unlike sketching, a few vivid scenes in a film convincingly present us with a person as a whole. Agee's own writing constantly reproached him with its inadequacy to render the "weight, mystery and dignity" of the living person—*a piece of the body torn out by the roots might be more to the point.* Film appears to give us the body, and some of its dignity. But to the filmmaker, who can see it in all its inevitable reduction and deformity, the illusion of wholeness can seem as great a reproach.

Much of the deformity can be traced to the film's intentions. As Dai Vaughan points out bluntly, the difference between film and reality is that "film is about something, whereas reality is not" (1985: 710). There is a tension in filmmaking between portraying people as complex, often ambiguous individuals and as representatives of particular social roles. Some filmmakers attempt to show their subjects in a dialectical relationship with the political and social structures that surround them, whereas for others social analysis means treating individuals, to the exclusion of other qualities, as exemplars of larger forces in conflict. Although the filmmaker may resist this process, the film subject is thereafter defined and overdetermined by it. It is not always the filmmaker's zeal that reduces a person to a narrow role, but a kind of internal field that is set up in the film once its initial coordinates have been set, and which acts upon the subject like a magnet. Individuals acquire a polarity and then seem drawn toward one pole or the other.

Most filming is guided by an analysis that gives priority to certain aspects of each person filmed. The next stage, the editing, involves constructing a semblance of the person using only a fraction of the footage available. These scenes must compete with the other needs of the film, including its expository, narrative, and thematic concerns. Some scenes may be considered so crucial to the film's argument that they are retained at the expense of those that present more subtle insights into the film's subjects. Peripheral characters are often cut out entirely, unless they appear inadvertantly with the protagonists. The aesthetic qualities of shots may or may not play a role, depending upon the importance attached to the look or ambience of the film, and this may further limit how individuals are presented. Repetitions are routinely eliminated, even though there is no such thing as true repetition. The benefits of this winnowing are a clarification of the dominant lines and relationships of the film. Its casualties are the nuances that appear once and nowhere else.

Documentary filmmakers exercise varied strategies for portraying their subjects. Some choose to emphasize selected aspects of personality or behavior as functional elements in the film; others try to suggest a more rounded image in miniature—the difference, in effect, between a caricature and a portrait. But

chievement of a portrait is always a matter of degree, for there is no
objective measurement of the self. The filmmaker is bound by what is expressed and expressible in the footage. Even then, the "person," as such, only
exists in the abstract sense of a particular set of interactions and constructions.
The filmmaker may try to suggest this indeterminacy rather than present the
person as a fixed "character" but is inevitably opposed by the finality of the
film. Filmmakers watch in sorrow as one aspect after another of a subject's
complexity is sacrificed to the film's required length or thematic priorities.
Entire dimensions of a known person are as casually lopped off as fingers or
toes—here, in one short moment, the knowledge of a language; there, a love
of poetry, a turn of phrase, or a sense of humor.

Few filmmakers become reconciled to this process. The experience of editing a film is full of tensions and contradictions. There is a will toward clarity
and coherence, but this is resisted by an opposing will toward the unexpected
and indeterminate. People in actual life are constantly improvising, but as the
film subject becomes more simply and crudely delineated, there is less evidence of this human creativity. The filmmaker observes the hardening shell of
a film persona, replacing the living person. There is both simplification and
atrophy.

A different kind of reduction results from the way the subject is positioned
in the film. In Frederick Wiseman and John Marshall's *Titicut Follies* (1967)
there is an emblematic image. It is the close-up of the blinking, cigarette-
smoking doctor as he first appears conducting a psychiatric interview.[18] The
shot proves that this man existed. But this is also a certain *kind* of man, a
character created not by a script but by framing and editing, and as recognizable as any of the conventional figures of the *commedia dell'arte*. As surely as
in a fiction film, he has been cast for a part. It is the part of the mad doctor—
half-comic, half-villainous, usually foreign, often Germanic, engaged in ne-
crophilic or apocalyptic activities. He is the close cousin of a string of other
mad doctors, stretching from Frankenstein and Jekyll to Caligari, Moreau,
Mabuse, and Strangelove. Here he appears as an ironic figure in the inverted
carnival world of the Bridgewater "follies," crazier than the madmen he is
supposed to cure. He further suggests another theme never far from the surface in many of Wiseman's films, the theme of the Nazi death camps. At one
point he is seen clumsily tube-feeding an emaciated inmate, joking and drop-
ping cigarette ash into the feeding tube. There is an implied link here with Dr.
Mengele and, more obliquely, Dr. Werner von Braun, mentioned in the rant-
ings of another inmate.

What is the relation between this grotesque figure and the person who
served as its model? It is difficult to say. Based on the evidence of the film he
is as much a creation of Western history and literature as of Wiseman and
Marshall. Through "casting" they have breathed new life into an archetype,
using a kind of cinematic shorthand. Like the non-actors who appear in Eisenstein's and Pudovkin's films, much of his potency as a character rests on his

obliviousness of himself as a type, his lack of self-parody. The world has enough self-parody of its own—he has only to fit its requirements.

The doctor's case suggests that characters drawn from life can gravitate—in the audience's view, as much as in the filmmaker's—toward certain predetermined positions in a dramatic and moral field. Hayden White (1980) has observed that narrative itself presupposes and articulates a moral order. Narrative conventions prefigure the moral ground of both the documentary and fictional film. The resulting polarities are felt not only in archetypal characters but in the organization of the film itself. Indeed, the dictates of structure are sometimes so powerful that they overcome the effects of a person's appearance or the audience's sympathies. An unlikely character may become a hero simply by being placed in the hero's position. This possibility is played upon repeatedly in the inversions of folk tales, where what one appears to be (a frog, a Cinderella) is not one's true identity. Such hidden valences in the patterning of human relationships tend to support Aristotle's identification of character with action rather than personality. At the level of narrative, action becomes the determining feature of character, since it is what the characters (or social actors—or *actants*, to use Griemas's term) do, or have the potential to do, that fixes them in dramatic constellations—often in mutually defining pairs such as oppressor/oppressed, lover/loved one, donor/recipient, hunter/hunted, etc. Filmmakers utilize these structures, but they are also at the mercy of them.

In Dennis O'Rourke's *"Cannibal Tours"* (1987), the film's construction as a series of juxtapositions implacably casts Sepik River villagers and European tourists as polar opposites. O'Rourke's positioning of the camera as passive friend of the villagers and active investigator of the tourists places him and most viewers in opposition to the tourists, despite his ex post facto claims that "we" and he are no different from them. In the films Wiseman made after *Titicut Follies*, workers in schools, hospitals, and other institutions are always in danger of being conflated with the institution itself, despite Wiseman's efforts to preserve this distinction. When I filmed Mr. Owor, an Assistant District Commissioner in Uganda in 1968 (in *To Live with Herds* [1972]), I was conscious of positioning him as an instrument of government policies, but I was not prepared for the extent to which this reduced him as a human being to a set of postcolonial mannerisms. He was in fact much more sympathetic to the plight of the Jie than the film suggests to many viewers, even though signs of this are not altogether absent from the film. When he appears in the film, he steps into a kind of trap. In dramatic terms, he is the "external antagonist," the oppressor.

These instances suggest that the placement of persons within dramatic and ideological structures may be more important than other factors in shaping viewers' perceptions of them. Also important are the directly physical effects of filmic representation. These are still not well understood but have yielded a body of Hollywood folklore. It is believed that film images emphasize some

characteristics of appearance and personality and suppress others, often in unpredictable ways. This lies behind the casting director's faith in screen tests
and the supposed ability of some producers to pick an actor with star qualities
out of a crowd of equally promising candidates. Filming people produces a
variety of forms of abstraction, despite realist conventions and the modelling
of photography on human vision. The immediate readability of a face as a face
tends to make the subtler effects of photographic abstraction go unnoticed. In
addition to the changes produced by lenses and film stocks, the conditions of
film viewing create further perceptual and psychological effects. The very size
of a projected image, and its positioning above the eyeline of the viewers, are
part of this. When people meet movie stars for the first time, they often remark
that they seem smaller than they had imagined them.

In sensing that their subjects are transformed in films, filmmakers show
their awareness of these varied effects, even if they cannot always explain
why they occur. However, a further effect—of *mythification*—appears to run
counter to the more general principle of reduction. Filmmakers usually feel
their films present a faithful but reduced image of their subjects rather than a
substitution or deception. But in the process of mythification, the film subject
seems not to be reduced but rather in some way monstrously augmented.

The theme of the double or the impostor is one of recurring fascination in
the cinema, in such films as *The Scapegoat* (1959), *The Face of Another*
(1966), *The Return of Martin Guerre* (1982), *Sommersby* (1993), and *Olivier
Olivier* (1992). To documentary filmmakers, the figures in their films sometimes appear to be just such impostors. It is this doubling, this sense of the
figures on the screen being appropriated by the stories of themselves, that
transforms the unique and flexible personality into the more limited figure of
legend or myth. A legend (from *legere*) is what is "read"—that which has
been foretold. It has been abstracted from the intricacies of life and held up as
a model. Such a realization is perhaps even responsible for the ironic under-
tone in James Agee's celebration of ordinary people as "famous men."

Mythification presents the paradox of a reduction produced by enlarge-
ment. The mythic figure in cinema is not unlike the human face on a movie
screen, at once both immaterially thin and larger than life. Its origins can often
be traced to the earliest stages of filmmaking, when a subject is singled out for
attention. As the film progressively frames its subject, it begins to cut away its
surroundings proportionately, just as a close-up eliminates all of the body but
a hand or a face. Increasingly condensed into itself, the figure looms larger
and more isolated from its environment than ever, unlike minor characters
who extend more fully and inconsequentially into the world around them.
Even the greater screen time devoted to the subject, which should contribute
to a more fully developed portrait, feeds rather than reverses this increasingly
constricted monumentality. In this way ordinary human beings are replaced
by their oversized doubles, like faces on a cinema billboard.[19]

The making of mythic figures in documentary often begins with the filmmaker's choice of a subject with special qualities—someone who already seems larger than life. Such persons may well have a strong sense of their own public image and work to maintain it. They may be dramatically outgoing or quite the opposite: reserved but seemingly possessed of an inner strength. Often these qualities are reproduced in their physical appearance, which comes to stand in both a metaphorical and indexical relationship to them. Their counterparts are to be found everywhere among the stars of fictional cinema.

Usually filmmakers choose such subjects more knowingly than innocently, but in either case they can be caught in a trap of their own devising. What initially attracted them to the subject may well turn out to be all there is to see: a public personality who fills a certain role but has little to offer beyond it. In choosing Tiger King for *Man of Aran* (1934), or Ta'avale for *Moana* (1926), Robert Flaherty perhaps hoped for the multidimensionality of Nanook but got much less. In *Jaguar*, the flamboyance of Damouré overshadows the characters of Lam and Illo, who sometimes suggest a complexity that he lacks. By choosing their subjects in imitation of the heroic figures of fiction, filmmakers may find they have sacrificed documentary opportunities for something that fiction does much better.

Some documentary subjects fit the patterns of popular myth so well that much of their own identity is immediately erased. It is difficult to see the two aspiring basketball players of *Hoop Dreams* (1994) without referring unconsciously to actual sports heroes such as Jackie Robinson (in real life or the 1950 movie), or to fictional ones such as Sylvester Stallone's character in *Rocky* (1976) and its sequels. The protagonists of the Maysles' film *Salesman* (1969) are identified by their nicknames ("The Badger," "The Gipper," "The Bull," etc.), fitting them into a schema of stock personalities.[20] Many documentaries about artists, writers, and scientists give their subjects only enough latitude as individuals to fit the films' heroic needs. Films about such historical figures as Roosevelt, MacArthur, Churchill, and Martin Luther King are usually overwhelmed by their myths. It is all but impossible to see anything but the persona, for everything serves it, even fresh revelations (such as those about Kennedy and J. Edgar Hoover), which either fail to surprise or seem merely to provide the exceptions that prove the rule.

A greater problem is faced by filmmakers who, unlike those who aim to create mythic characters, try to film people who are found to be remarkable within the contexts of ordinary life. Part of what makes these people remarkable, in fact, is that they make no claim to special status. Their qualities are those we come upon unexpectly, and indeed exceed what we have any right to expect. When making a film about such a person, it is painful to see their qualities petrify into something given—to be taken for granted just because the person is the subject of a film. There is a sense of betrayal. The person seems devoured by his or her attributes as a "subject," finally becoming no more than the incarnation of them. It is impossible to "discover" such a person in a film as one discovers someone in life.

In this way, even film subjects who do not fit pre-existing stereotypes disappear into a typicality created by their framing. Little has been written about this phenomenon by filmmakers, although anecdotally many note that their subjects become more schematic as they are progressively centered by the film.[21] Resisting this may often only wrap a larger aura of myth around them. While we were editing the "Turkana Conversations" films, it was disconcerting to see how Lorang, a senior man among other senior men, receded inside the carapace of his role. The person we knew possessed a formidible presence, but he was also fallible and often perplexed, as the films show. To give a fuller sense of his interior life we quoted certain of his observations, but these quotations, instead of bringing us closer to him, tend instead to take on the qualities of prophecy. We also wanted to see Lorang through the double prism of history and friendship, but because the viewer can only guess at the friendship, it is the public figure, the figure of legend, who emerges more forcefully. Lorang perhaps met too fully the requirements of the films for them to suggest his autonomous life. In Jorge Preloran's *Imaginero* (1969) one has a similarly condensed and essentialized vision of Hermogenes Cayo, despite Preloran's careful attention to the humble details of his life.

Eighteen years later, while filming *Tempus de Baristas* (1993), I found myself alternately inviting and resisting these effects. On the one hand, I wanted to show the three protagonists as I saw them through the camera and as I felt them to be, richly and uniquely, in themselves—perhaps through the qualities of film, as no one had seen them before. At the same time I feared that they would then emerge as mere "film subjects" rather than the more mysterious and complex people I knew them to be. While filming, I was always aware of this dilemma, searching both for what was characteristic of them and yet for what might unaccountably break through it. [Figures 4 and 5.]

## To the Quick

> When bread is baked some parts are split at the surface, and these parts which thus open, and have a certain fashion contrary to the purpose of the baker's art, are beautiful in a manner, and in a peculiar way excite a desire for eating.
> —*Marcus Aurelius*[22]

> Content is a glimpse of something, an encounter like a flash.
> —*Willem de Kooning*[23]

People filmed, whether famous actors or bystanders caught anonymously by the camera, have qualities in common with the characters of novels and plays. Framed, incorporated into a film's economy, and released to the imaginations

4. Pietro Balisai Soddu, during the filming of *Tempus de Baristas*, 1992.

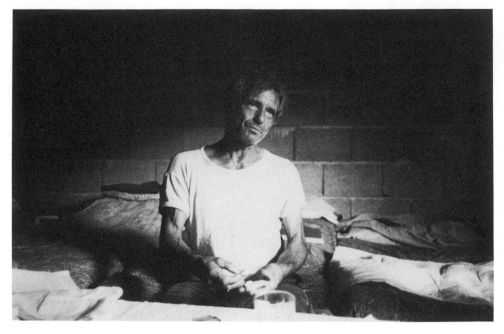

5. Franchiscu Balisai Soddu, during the filming of *Tempus de Baristas*, 1992.

of their viewers, they become objects of meaning and portent. But as images seen by the eye, they have also a phenomenological existence as substantial as our glimpses of actual persons, and can certainly affect us as much. We cannot reduce these images altogether to "meaning," like words on a page. They attest to someone seen by the filmmaker, and they link us to that person through the filmmaker's vision.

Films constantly invite us to look through and beyond them for the traces of such links. In fiction films we inspect the faces of actors, or seize upon certain objects, or examine the details of streets which, although we have never been there, seem strangely familiar. The enticement is perhaps even greater in documentary, where this oblique kind of looking comes closest to mimicking the filmmaker's own troubled glance. Documentary filmmakers commit what Paul Henley once called "the sin of Heisenberg," forever interfering with what it is they seek. This is not only because, as in particle physics, the process of filming transforms its object, but because the representation of anything is by definition the creation of something different. Documentary can thus only succeed by becoming part of its object, fusing itself with it, creating a new reality. It may then succeed in spite of itself, like a damaged eye that sees objects only in its peripheral vision.

Filmmakers reach beyond the nameable and containable. It is the physical world underlying signification that provides the motive power of documentary and much of fiction film. Film seeks to retrieve certain abandoned habits of our prelinguistic life, the perceptions which as children were part of our bodily awareness of others and the physical world. It thus regenerates a form of thinking through the body, often affecting us most forcefully at those junctures of experience that lie between our accustomed categories of thought.[24]

This challenge to the logic and hegemony of words has contributed to what W.J.T. Mitchell has called "the pictorial turn" in Western thinking. Films have forced a reexamination of knowledge constituted in writing and have suggested alternative ways of expressing sensory and social experience. Less obviously, films also challenge pictorial representation itself, on which they depend. Like earlier historical challenges to the authority of words, the challenge to the image arises from similar contradictions within visual representation. Film images easily become as anodyne as words; and although they attract us, they simultaneously cut us off from the world of their referents. In their redoubling of human vision, images underscore human separateness. It is this most precisely descriptive side of film, its literally senseless illusion of the physical, that mocks us, not its social or literary meanings, which we can dismiss or accept at our will. In their struggle with the various forms of reduction produced by images, filmmakers seek for what breaks unexpectedly and inexplicably through the seams of cinematic convention. Only by denying representation, by breaking through its plausibility, does film contrive to heal the wound that cinema creates and restore the viewer to the world. Here one arrives at the unspoken core of documentary, its justification for some and the danger it holds for others.

For many filmmakers, then, documentary is not just a way of representing the real but of touching within themselves and others something more fleeting and more precious. This contact, when it occurs, is almost always produced under what Barthes calls the "alibis" of art or science, although it is rarely acknowledged as the object of either. We may glimpse it in a few frames out of a thousand, or a few seconds in an entire film. It is that moment in a shot or sequence that gives it its life, without which (to put it conversely) it would be tautological, no more than "itself." It is what we wait for when watching a film a second time, as we wait for certain moments in music. It may lie in a gesture, a look, in the catch of a voice, a puff of smoke, or a distant sound that animates a landscape. This moment may be regarded as what is quintessentially *filmic* in film. As Barthes puts it: "The filmic is that in the film which cannot be described, the representation which cannot be represented. The filmic begins only where language and metalanguage end" (1977b: 64). The "filmic" may in fact be seen as a refutation of film, half-hidden within the envelopment of filmic representation. Not even "a signifier without a signified,"[25] it is rather an *unsignified*. It is the tacit part of our film experience, which allows us to "inhabit" the filmic environment. It is our sensory response to the content of film.

Our bodies provide certain metaphors for what films do. People frequently

*Handwritten margin notes:* TRANSCENDENTALISM → filmic

*Handwritten right margin:* Those moments in film like life, that are true or truly real

*Handwritten bottom:* A sudden break in the monotony of the phantasmagoria that is physical reality

speak of going to the heart of the matter, which in documentaries usually means arriving at some useful social observation or description. In considering the "filmic," however, it is perhaps more appropriate to speak of going *to the quick*. In English "the quick" has in fact a constellation of meanings. It is that which is tender, alive, or sensitive beneath an outer protective covering; that which is most vulnerable; the exposed nerve of our emotions; that which moves or touches us; which is transient, appearing only in a flash; which renews, fertilizes or "quickens" with life; which is liquescent like quicksilver: molten, bright, avoiding the touch, spilling away, changing form; that which, like quicklime or quicksand, devours, dissolves and liquifies; that which has a quality of alertness or intelligence, as of a child to learn. Our immediate impression of the quick is of an uncovering, or revelation. We experience it as a sudden exposure, a contrast between dull and sensitive surfaces.

The quick not only provides an analogy for film experience but has a physical basis in the filmmaker's vision. Just as the quick implies the touching of surfaces, so the filmmaker's gaze touches—and is touched by—what it sees. A film can thus be said to look and to touch. The association between sight and touch has a long history. It appears in early Egyptian and Renaissance emblems and is a feature of Descartes's and Berkeley's models of the senses. In Berkeley's view, seeing in depth was only possible because of the accompanying sense of touch, a crossing of the axes of optics and haptics (Gandelman 1991). This is borne out by descriptions of certain blind people who, upon recovering their sight in adulthood, are unable to recognize objects until they can touch them, or feel models of them (Sacks 1995b). Recently, the senses have been reconceived not simply as separate faculties capable of some form of synaesthetic translation, but as *already* interconnected—in fact, as the entire perceptive field of the body. Thus Hans Jonas, in discussing the perception of form, argues that "blind men can 'see' by means of their hands, not because they are devoid of eyes but because they are beings endowed with the general faculty of 'vision' and only happen to be deprived of the primary organ of sight" (1966: 141–42).[26] Luria's mnemonist, S., had complex synaesthetic responses to the world, suggesting that he experienced to a hypertrophic degree sensory processes common to us all (Luria 1968: 21–29).[27] Vivian Sobchack, following Merleau-Ponty, declares: "The senses are different openings to the world that cooperate as a *unified system* of access. The lived-body does not have senses. It is, rather, sensible. It is, from the first, a perceptive body" (1992: 77).[28]

Filmmaking requires interactions of the body with the world in registering qualities of texture and shape, which do not exist abstractly or independently of such encounters. The world is not apart from, but around and *within* the filmmaker and viewer. Touching is not a one-way process but reciprocal, in the sense that an equal pressure is applied to what is touched and what is touching. This recalls Polanyi's characterization of the senses as a probe that links us to others. Similarly, Merleau-Ponty (1992: 93) implicitly criticizes the residual Cartesianism of Sartre's account of double sensation (one hand touching the other) for maintaining an absolute separation of the body as either perceiver or perceived, rather than allowing for an ambiguous alternation of these roles.[29] A further ambiguity surrounds the separation of the senses; for although seeing and touching are not the same, they originate in the same body and their objects overlap, so that most of what can be seen can also be touched. In this convergence, touch and vision do not become interchangeable but share an experiential field. Each refers to a more general faculty.[30] I can touch with my eyes because my experience of surfaces includes both touching and seeing, each deriving qualities from the other.

## The Second Self

> The spark caught in his eye's pupil gives significance
> to his whole person.
> —*Robert Bresson*[31]

> That expressive instrument called a face can carry an
> existence, as my own existence is carried by my
> body.
> —*Maurice Merleau-Ponty*[32]

To what can we attribute the identification with others that is so fundamental to the film-viewing experience? Clearly, it derives partly from complex responses to the human face. "Our work," said Ingmar Bergman, "begins with the human face. . . . The possibility of drawing near to the human face is the primary originality and the distinctive quality of the cinema."[33] Responses to the face begin in early infancy and may even result from an innate mechanism of recognition in the brain. In film, such responses are strongly evoked by close-ups, which bring the viewer into a position of unusual physical intimacy with the film subject. The subject is given (gives *itself*) to the viewer, inviting particular emotions of commitment and potential exchange. Without the human face, much of what matters to us in films would vanish.

The face is a primary site of the "quick." It is the site of individuality—a uniquely recognizable group of features, the stamp of the self. Compared to the face, other parts of the body are relatively interchangeable.[34] When identities are to be concealed in photographs, it is the face that is covered, and often only the eyes. The face is also the site of expression, signalling emotional states and the recognition of others. It is where we look for signs of intelligence and comprehension. It is the theater of the body, registering the inner life of its owner in biologically and culturally predetermined ways.[35]

Within the face, the eyes are the apotheosis of the quick, the most alive and sensitive parts of the body, seemingly afloat in liquid and protected by the dry outer covering of the lid. The lid is the eye's instrument of revelation.[36] (The veiling of women, like a second lid, reinforces the face and eyes as a site of the quick, to be hidden and protected, and made an object of desire.) The eyes are therefore the part of the body most carefully watched for disjunctions between social performance and inner feeling. Next, the hands are most often studied for such clues (as in poker games). It is appropriate that the fingerprint, the other unique mark of individuality, should be found at the most sensitive extremities of touch, and that we should call the flesh beneath the fingernail "the quick." The human voice, another imprint of identity (now recognized in the "voice print"), is a further site of the quick. In listening to voices, our differentiation of the senses begins to blur. Voices have textures, as though perceived tactilely and visually. Produced by our bodies, they are distinctive physical manifestations of ourselves. Like our eyes, they can be "covered" by closing our lips—but also by language, which is how civilization imposes its laws on the animal sounds we make.[37]

Our film experience relies upon our assuming the existence of a parallel sensory experience in others. If our attraction to the "quick" can be said to have a *destination*, it is the consciousness of others (the sense they have of being themselves). It is through this that our own sense of self is defined and confirmed. The link between the known body (the filmmaker, the viewer) and a broader sense of self—the sense that others (the film subjects) have of themselves (and others)—is thus implicit in documentary's preoccupation with the real. Sight and touch are linked to consciousness, in the broadest sense. To touch the quick in others is to touch it in ourselves. We reaffirm our identity not only through others' responses to us, nor merely by seeing ourselves *as* others (as in Lacan's account), but in the light of others' equivalent consciousness.

This may explain Agee's awe in the face of the "weight, dignity, and mystery" of the living person. Documentary demands that another's separate consciousness be acknowledged. Whatever the descriptive function of a film, it must register its subjects' consciousness of being, the quick in them, a consciousness that we can only assume to be like our own by a leap of faith. Very occasionally films glimpse this through the overlayerings of conventional behavior, like live flesh through dead tissue. It appears in the artless responses of others, not unlike slips of the tongue that reveal a subtext with which we are complicit. This phenomenon of physical communion is described by Merleau-Ponty in the following terms:

> No sooner has my gaze fallen upon a living body in process of acting than the objects surrounding it immediately take on a fresh layer of significance: they are no longer simply what I myself could make of them, they are what this other pattern of behaviour is about to make of them. . . . I say that it is another person,

a second self [*un second moi-même*], and this I know in the first place because this living body has the same structure as mine. I experience my own body as the power of adopting certain forms of behaviour and a certain world, and I am given to myself merely as a certain hold upon the world: now, it is precisely my body which perceives the body of another person, and discovers in that other body a miraculous prolongation of my own intentions, a familiar way of dealing with the world. Henceforth, as the parts of my body together comprise a system, so my body and the other person's are one whole, two sides of one and the same phenomenon, and the anonymous existence of which my body is the ever-renewed trace henceforth inhabits both bodies simultaneously. (1992: 353–54)

This resonance of bodies, verging on the ineffable in Merleau-Ponty's account (which also ignores specific cultural, class, and sexual variations), nevertheless suggests a synchrony between viewer and viewed that recovers the prelinguistic, somatic relation to others of infancy, a capacity that still remains accessible to us in adulthood. We make contact with others not by interpreting the meaning of their conduct, but by imitating what Merleau-Ponty calls a much more generalized *postural schema*. This he likens to "a 'postural impregnation' of my own body by the conducts I witness" (Merleau-Ponty 1964a: 118).[38] Such experiences often involve a third term that is the common object of these subjectivities. This means that in viewing a film the viewer is usually responding not only to the content of images (the postures of the subjects, for example) but also to the postural schema of the film itself, embodying the filmmaker. The viewer's response is thus one of double synchrony with the film subject and filmmaker, the first partly mediated by the second.

Intimations of a "second self" in others are reflexive in that they touch *us* to the quick, but this can only occur when they break through (but without necessarily dispersing) the double surface of filmic *depiction* (its denotation) and filmic *significance* (its further symbolic and connotative meanings) to what Barthes calls *signifiance*. Breaking through the first (depiction) might appear an impossibility, since the images of people we see in a film are but a kind of photochemical imprinting. It is only through the viewer's body that the filmic image is restored to its referent. This occurs through the viewer's sharing of a common field with the filmmaker and film subjects, common referents in the world. The viewer "fills" or replenishes the image with his or her own bodily experience, inhabiting the absent body represented on the screen. In Merleau-Ponty's view, such responses may even encompass inanimate objects through what he calls an *équivalent interne*. "Things have an internal equivalent in me; they arouse in me a carnal formula of their presence" (1964b: 164). By reversing T. S. Eliot's concept, we might characterize this as an instance of a *subjective* correlative.

For the filmmaker, the camera is the primary instrument of engagement with others, and the resulting footage is secondary. One looks through the viewfinder at those with whom one shares a physical space, and then (later) at the film. Each experience modifies the other. The camera is used with an expectation of what the footage will look like, but also, in a sense, in defiance of it. The special conditions of filmmaking—of an almost preternatural awareness of the subjects—lead one to invest one's vision with an intensity that must exceed the bounds of any resulting film. This may account for Rouch's intoxicated "ciné-transe" and for the complete absence of fear that many filmmakers report while filming in dangerous situations. The "quick" is finally a metaphor for the film itself—a product of this heightened consciousness.

If the quick (like Barthes's "obtuse" meaning) is "indifferent to the story and to the obvious meaning" (Barthes 1977b: 61), then it survives in most films under false pretenses. It has little to do with the representation of reality, or with the information that documentaries purvey, or with the moral universe within which they make pronouncements on our conduct. It *may* have something to do with aesthetics, although this too is easily corrupted. The quick is more like what W.J.T. Mitchell, in the context of art history, has called the "deep inside" of representation,[39] allowing the viewer brief access to something pretextual: the filmmaker's relation to the subject. But is the quick the pretext for the film, or the other way round?

## An Economy of Consciousness

> More and more I love it of them, the being in them,
> the mixing in them, the repeating in them, the decid-
> ing the kind of them every one is who has human
> being.
> —*Gertrude Stein*[40]

> You illuminate him and he illuminates you. The light
> you receive from him is added to the light he receives
> from you.
> —*Robert Bresson*[41]

Filmmaking acts like a lens, concentrating the emotions of everyday experience. Many films are in fact declarations of love, if we could but see it. This may take the form of an attachment to a particular social and cultural milieu, as is found in Rouch's films, or be directed toward particular individuals, as in Preloran's. It may be freely acknowledged or expressed indirectly, transferred or sublimated into exploring the relationships of the subjects themselves. Like Agee's passionate vision, it sometimes reaches to the quick of its subjects, as a kind of caress.

Filmmakers' attitudes toward their subjects contain the attributes of other relationships, ranging from indifference and dislike to the protectiveness of a parent, from the admiration of a friend to the attentiveness of a lover. Such feelings are registered in the selection of images and in the nuances of their treatment. Documentary filmmakers are not oblivious to beauty, but their attraction to the real is, as Barthes says of the obtuse meaning, "no respecter of the aesthetic" (1977b: 59). It prefers the quick to the beautiful. As in Kant's view of the sublime, whatever aesthetic pleasure it produces is undercut by the pain of reason, and it is therefore sometimes savage or ironic in its expectation of loss.

If one loves the people in one's films, it is not only for themselves. The subjects of a film reflect a larger world of consciousness of which one is a part. This, in Merleau-Ponty's view, creates an inevitable narcissism. "Since the seer is caught up in what he sees, it is still himself he sees: there is a fundamental narcissism of all vision" (1968: 139). As Christian Metz puts it, "the spectator *identifies with himself,* with himself as a pure act of perception (as wakefulness, alertness): as the condition of possibility of the perceived and hence as a kind of transcendental subject, which comes before every *there is*" (Metz 1982: 49). These descriptions of absorbtion in the self require some qualification, however. The filmmaker's attraction to the film subject also depends significantly upon the differences of others. We do not claim another's consciousness unconditionally, as Merleau-Ponty would have it, or *derive* our sense of consciousness from it. Rather, filming others celebrates the common experience of consciousness, including the very differences between us. We do not see others as vessels or mirrors, capable of receiving or reflecting our feelings, but as points of reference. We do not expect others to experience the world exactly as we do; and indeed there would be little fascination in them if they did.[42]

As a number of writers have recently argued, unitary theories of psychological or political appropriation and control may be insufficient to explain the complexities of either fiction films or documentaries.[43] The gaze of filmmakers and spectators is neither uniform nor unvarying, nor can it be defined by single perspectives of gender, age, or culture. Explanations of the gaze based on male heterosexuality are not only partial and exclusionary, but rely upon a narrow conception of visual and sensory pleasure, not to mention narrow constructions of maleness and sexuality. The complex subjectivities involved in making and viewing documentary films give salience to Susan Sontag's (1966: 14) call for an erotics (as opposed to a hermeneutics) of art.[44] In particular, they draw attention to that substratum of film experience that places nonlinguistic sensory experience in radical opposition to filmic depiction, representation, and "meaning." This parallels Barthes's association of the obtuse or "third" meaning in film with the erotic character of *figuration.* We must, he writes, "distinguish between *figuration* and *representation.*"

> Figuration [he continues] is the way in which the erotic body appears (to whatever degree and in whatever form that may be) in the profile of the text. For example: the author may appear in his text (Genet, Proust), but not in the guise of

direct biography (which would exceed the body, give a meaning to life, forge a destiny). Or again: one can feel desire for a character in a novel (in fleeting impulses). Or finally: the text itself, a diagrammatic and not an imitative structure, can reveal itself in the form of a body, split into fetish objects, into erotic sites. All these movements attest to a *figure* of the text, necessary to the bliss of reading. Similarly, and even more than the text, the film will *always* be figurative (which is why films are still worth making)—even if it represents nothing. (1975: 55–56)

Our consciousness provides the immediate stage upon which our known and unconscious desires are played out, but we ask questions about it for which there are no definitive answers. Where are the boundaries between another consciousness and my own? Why am I not the other experiencing self, and the other not me? If we belong to the same phenomenon, why separately and not jointly? Are we perhaps simultaneously—but independently—touching parts of a single, unified field?

Film provides an analogy for such a unified field. Although it is only one of the many arenas of consciousness, it is distinct from most others in an important respect. Many activities such as communal labor, song, dance, and ritual have an intersubjective dimension in that they imply the sharing of a common experience. They are also interactive, since the participants' actions are partly shaped by their responses to the actions of others. But these activities are ephemeral and leave little trace of the actual encounters. Filming, by contrast, produces an object in which the filmmaker's interaction with the film subject is explicitly inscribed. Rather than simply running their course, their experiences intersect permanently in the fabric of the film. In the end, each stands exposed to the other in a new way. For many documentary filmmakers, what is finally most important about film, apart from communicating with the viewers, is that it provides a way of communicating with the subjects—a way for each to show the other what otherwise cannot be shown, in a statement that is irrevocable.

[1998]

## Notes

1. From *Let Us Now Praise Famous Men* (Agee and Evans 1960: 415).

2. In an interesting parallel to this, Susan Sontag writes: "I should argue, contrary to McLuhan, that a devaluation of the power and credibility of images has taken place no less profound than, and essentially similar to, that afflicting language" (1969: 21).

3. William Stott quotes Evans on Erskine Caldwell's and Margaret Bourke-White's book (1937) as "a double outrage: propaganda for one thing, and profit-making out of both propaganda and the plight of the tenant farmers. It was morally shocking to Agee and me" (1973: 222).

4. From "The Camera and Man" (Rouch 1975: 99).

5. I am aware this differs from the currently widespread view that making images

means taking something from the subject, which may then be used as a source of symbolic power and control. While not altogether rejecting that possibility, I believe it oversimplifies the filmmaker-subject relationship and is based upon the misleading ethnocentric metaphor: "knowledge is extraction." It also evinces a mounting Western fear of vision as dangerous, invested with a magical potency.

6. This may become clearer from the following passage: "All descriptive sciences study physiognomies that cannot be fully described in words, nor even by pictures. But can it not be argued, once more, that the possibility of teaching these appearances by practical exercises proves that we can tell our knowledge of them? The answer is that we can do so only by relying on the pupil's intelligent co-operation for catching the meaning of the demonstration. Indeed, any definition of a word denoting an external thing must ultimately rely on pointing at such a thing. This naming-cum-pointing is called 'an ostensive definition'; and this philosophic expression conceals a gap to be bridged by an intelligent effort on the part of the person to whom we want to tell what the word means. Our message had left something behind that we could not tell, and its reception must rely on it that the person addressed will discover that which we have not been able to communicate" (Polanyi 1966: 5–6).

7. This is from the version prepared with Marcel Moussy (Truffaut and Moussy 1969: 152–55).

8. Truffaut in fact did this, taking Antoine from the beach and continuing his story in *Antoine et Colette* (the first episode of *L'Amour à vingt ans* [1962]), *Baisers volés* (1968), *Domicile conjugale* (1970) and *L'Amour en fuite* (1979). This history of sequels has its documentary counterpart, as is discussed later in this essay.

9. Personal communication, November 24, 1994.

10. From Barthes's *Camera Lucida* (1981: 96).

11. A Parisian schoolboy named Ernest, photographed by André Kertész in 1931 (Barthes 1981: 83).

12. From his *Notes on Cinematography* (Bresson 1977: 7).

13. This film explores the fate of several people filmed by Robert Young and Michael Roemer in their film *Cortile Cascino* of 1961—and borrows extensive footage from it. It was made by Robert Young's son and daughter-in-law, Andrew Young and Susan Todd.

14. Made by Michael Apted, and including such films as *Seven Plus Seven* (1970) and *21* (1978).

15. These series include "In Search of Cool Ground," the Mursi Trilogy by Leslie Woodhead and David Turton, comprising *The Mursi* (1974), *The Kwegu* (1982), and *The Migrants* (1985); the *Hamar Trilogy* by Joanna Head and Jean Lydall, comprising *The Women Who Smile* (1990), *Two Girls Go Hunting* (1991), and *Our Way of Loving* (1994); and the three New Guinea films by Bob Connolly and Robin Anderson, *First Contact* (1982), *Joe Leahy's Neighbours* (1988), and *Black Harvest* (1992).

16. Dalarou was the name of the "production company" for *Cocorico, Monsieur Poulet*, signifying Damouré, Lam, and Rouch. In 1994 I heard Rouch pointedly refer to the group as "Dalarouta" in order to include Tallou. Since *Madame L'Eau*, Rouch has released another film of Damouré alone, speaking about AIDS in his role as a health worker in Niamey, Niger: *Damouré parle du SIDA* (1994).

17. From *Let Us Now Praise Famous Men* (Agee and Evans 1960: 13).

18. Dr. Ross, described as a "junior physician" at the Massachusetts Correctional Institution at Bridgewater (Anderson and Benson 1991: 47).

19. The forces of reduction in polished and coherent works sometimes lead one to

turn with gratitude to less sophisticated films and books (home movies, war memoirs), in which useless details abound, people simply appear and disappear, and the most harrowing events are reported unexpectedly and laconically. This effect of understatement and artlessness is sometimes imitated, for example by filmmakers such as Buñuel, or in the writing of Hemingway and Paul Bowles.

20. However, in an interesting reversal, the makers of *Soldier Girls* (1981) attempt to undermine the view they have previously built up of Sergeant Abing, the archetypal, unfeeling drill instructor, and Private Alves, who plays dumb to get out of the army.

21. E. M. Forster, in *Aspects of the Novel* (1927), noted that the protagonists of nineteenth-century novels often became atrophied toward the end, as if they had already fulfilled their purpose.

22. From *The Meditations*, III, 2. This is from the George Long translation of 1862 (Antoninus 1891: 85), which in this passage seems to capture a level of meaning missing from several more modern translations.

23. Cited by Susan Sontag as an epigraph to her essay, "Against Interpretation" (1966: 14).

24. The filmmaker Dusan Makavejev once remarked (I have forgotten the occasion) that we are unable to acknowledge many of the commonplace experiences of daily life, in part because there are no words in our language for them but also because they violate the social categories that our language upholds, such as the sharp distinction between the sexual and nonsexual. In which category, he asked, do we place the uncanny, sensuous touch of a child's hand on our face? In *Let Us Now Praise Famous Men*, Agee does not disown his physical attraction to many of his subjects—men, women, and children—an acknowledgment considered unseemly at the time.

25. From his essay, "The Third Meaning" (1977b: 61).

26. Even physiologically, the senses appear to share a common ground. Oliver Sacks points out that the cerebral cortex is malleable, developing to exploit those parts of the sensory spectrum available to it. "It has been well established that in congenitally deaf people (especially if they are native signers) some of the auditory parts of the brain are reallocated for visual use. It has also been well established that in blind people who read Braille the reading finger has an exceptionally large representation in the tactile parts of the cerebral cortex. And one would suspect that the tactile (and auditory) parts of the cortex are enlarged in the blind and may even extend into what is normally the visual cortex" (1995b: 132).

27. Temple Grandin reports a similar case of an autistic man for whom "sound came through as color, while touching his face produced a soundlike sensation" (1995: 76).

28. Sobchack goes on to quote Merleau-Ponty's *Phenomenology of Perception* to the effect that the "body is, not a collection of adjacent organs, but a synergetic system, all the functions of which are linked together in the general action of being in the world" (Sobchack 1992: 78).

29. M. C. Dillon discusses this critique in *Merleau-Ponty's Ontology* (1988: 139–50).

30. Merleau-Ponty takes this even further: "Therefore there are not the senses, but only consciousness" (1992: 217).

31. From *Notes on Cinematography* (Bresson 1977: 44).

32. From *Phenomenology of Perception* (Merleau-Ponty 1992: 351).

33. Quoted by Gilles Deleuze in *Cinema 1: The Movement-Image* (1986: 99). Like Bergman, Deleuze adopts the characteristically Western view of the face as the primary register of emotion, treating the close-up as the archtypal form of what he calls the affection-image (pp. 87–91).

34. In terms of their individual distinctiveness, the external genitals probably occupy a position intermediate between faces and such body parts as arms or legs. In some societies where men and boys often go naked (such as among East African pastoralists) it is not uncommon for nicknames to be based upon their appearance. Yet, as Lucien Taylor has pointed out to me, the covering of body parts, and any sense of shame associated with them, seems to have little to do with their individuality, for in most societies faces are generally open to inspection and the genitals are not, lying in fact at opposite ends of the spectrum of public accessibility.

35. In Western literature the face is a stage upon which whole dramas of the life of the intellect and the emotions are enacted for others. Consider the following characteristic passage from Tolstoy's *War and Peace*: "There was only one expression on her agitated face when she ran into the drawing-room- -an expression of love, of boundless love for him, for her, for all that was near to the man she loved; an expression of pity, of suffering for others, of passionate desire to give herself completely to the task of helping them. It was plain that Natasha's heart at that moment held no thought of self, or of her own relations with Prince Andrei. Princess Maria with her sensitive intuition saw all this at the first glance, and with sorrowful relief wept on her shoulder. . . . She felt that no question or answer could be put into words. Natasha's face and eyes would have to tell her all more clearly and with profounder meaning" (1982: 1157).

36. The genitals, which juxtapose dry outer coverings with the more sensitive, moist parts of the body's interior, share much with the eye, and become interchangeable with it in such works as Bataille's *Histoire de l'oeil* (Story of the Eye). The vulnerability and associations of the eyes and sexual organs with the interior of the body are underlined in Buñuel and Dali's film *Un Chien andalou* (1929) and in such practices as circumcision. Among the Dowayo, according to Nigel Barley, the contrast between wet and dry is the explicit justification for circumcision. Removal of the foreskin is considered a way of "drying out" boys to make them more distinct from women (1983: 80–81).

37. Roland Barthes, in "The Grain of the Voice," in *Image-Music-Text*, contrasts this sensory texture, an extension of the body, to music as language: "The 'grain' of the voice is not—or is not merely—its timbre; the *signifiance* it opens cannot better be defined, indeed, than by the very friction between the music and something else" (1977a: 185). In *The Pleasure of the Text* he observes that "the *grain* of the voice . . . is an erotic mixture of timbre and language" (1975: 66). "The articulation of the body, of the tongue, not that of meaning, of language" is to be found most easily in the cinema. "In fact, it suffices that the cinema capture the sound of speech *close up*" (1975: 66–67).

38. In this regard see also Csordas's related idea of "somatic modes of attention" in diagnosis and healing (1993).

39. In "Interdisciplinarity and Visual Culture" (Mitchell 1995: 542).

40. From *The Making of Americans* (Stein 1934: 211).

41. From *Notes on Cinematography* (Bresson 1977: 41).

42. The fascination in fact lies in the tension between the familiar and the unfamil-

iar, in the liberating resistance to our own limitations set up by the unfamiliar. This response may be seen as connected to our emotions more generally if we accept the inhibition theory of emotion of William James and others. See Solomon (1984), Dewey (1894), Paulhan (1930: 13–34), Pribram (1970). This becomes the basis of Leonard Meyer's (1956) theory of emotion in music. It can also be seen as fundamental to emotional responses to film in Gilles Deleuze's concept of the shot as containing a suspended, or inhibited intention (Deleuze 1986: 65). (See also Mitchell's discussion of resistance in photographs, referred to in note 44.) In Lacan's terms, life in the Symbolic world inhibits our ways of engaging with experience and may create a pressing need to recover the immediacy of our prelinguistic life.

43. See, for example, Jameson (1983), de Lauretis (1984; 1987), Renov (1993), Mayne (1993), Nichols (1994a), and Williams (1995).

44. Since Sontag's essay, there have been a number of attempts to explore documentary in experiential terms rather than as social history or via textual exegesis, notably by Bill Nichols in *Ideology and the Image* (1981) and *Representing Reality* (1991) and, more recently, by Michael Renov. In an important article, Renov (1993) discusses four "modalities of desire" that motivate documentary filmmakers, in which one may discern some of the motivations I have been discussing here. However, I believe more remains to be said about the difference between desiring to express, represent, or explain the real and desiring to reach out to it with the camera. From a somewhat different angle, W.J.T. Mitchell takes up Barthes's concept of "resistance" in relation to Jacob Riis's photographs of slum-dwellers, but he discusses this primarily as a locus of opposition to interpretation rather than as one of sensory experience (Mitchell 1994: 281–87).

# CHAPTER TWO

# Visual Anthropology and the Ways of Knowing

Today one should react to the utterance of "That's
not anthropology" as one would to an omen of intellectual death.
—*Dell Hymes[1]*

## Visible Culture and Visual Discourse

THERE IS mounting interest today in visual anthropology, even if no one
knows quite what it is. Its very name is an act of faith, like a suit of clothes
bought a little too large in the hope that someone will grow into it. In fact, the
term covers a number of quite different interests. Some conceive of visual
anthropology as a research technique, others as a field of study, others as a
teaching tool, still others as a means of publication, and others again as a new
approach to anthropological knowledge.

One apparent reason for the recent interest in visual anthropology is renewed interest in the visual itself. This may be part of what W.J.T. Mitchell
has called the "pictorial turn" in critical thinking, in reaction to the intense
linguistic focus of post-war structuralism, poststructuralism, deconstruction,
and semiotics (1994: 11–33). A second reason is the widespread questioning
within anthropology of the adequacy, forms—and even the possibility—of
ethnographic description. Finally, there is the emergence in anthropology of a
new range of subjects involving the body, such as the role of the senses and
emotions in social life, and the cultural construction of gender and personal
identity. In these areas, visual representation may be seen as offering an appropriate alternative to ethnographic writing.

A further reason also suggests itself, but it implies a more radical shift in
the ways that anthropologists think about their discipline. It was foreshadowed in a prescient essay of Edward Sapir published in 1934. Sapir not only
drew attention to the uncomfortable gap between cultural and psychological
explanations of human behavior but also questioned the undue reliance anthropologists placed upon the concept of culture in understanding the experience of the individual.

> If we made the test of imputing the contents of an ethnological monograph to a
> known individual in the community which it describes, we would inevitably be
> led to discover that, while every single statement in it may, in the favorable case,

be recognized as holding true in some sense, the complex of patterns as described cannot, without considerable absurdity, be interpreted as a significant configuration of experience, both actual and potential, in the life of the person appealed to. (1949a: 593)

Sapir went on to urge greater attention to "the more intimate structure of culture" (p. 594), comparing it to living speech, in contrast to the more formal, quasi-grammatical systems that may be derived from it. Today's interest in visual anthropology may arise from a similiar dissatisfaction felt by anthropologists with the disjunction between their encounters with living people and the terms in which they often feel constrained to write about them.

In thinking about anthropology, we are inclined to forget that it is created as much in the insights of fieldwork as in the writing and reading of texts. One might even say there are two anthropologies—one amply expressed in the literature and one largely unexpressed. The two perceptions are not necessarily in conflict, but they are so different in the qualities they apprehend, and yet so closely intertwined, as to create some perplexity about anthropology itself in the mind of the researcher. The first is the anthropology of culture viewed as ordered, limiting, and pervasive. It is largely concerned with the consensual and systemic continuities in people's lives. The second is the anthropology of culture viewed as fertile, elaborative, and liberating. It sees culture as more restricted in its influence upon individuals, providing rather the means by which they weave meaning and a sense of self into more broadly shared characteristics of social life. Its starting point, and its concern, is how culture is lived by those who, in the end, embody it and re-create it for themselves. It is likely to emphasize precisely those features that the first anthropology strips away.

Anthropologists may thus be inclined to ask: Is there a process available to anthropology that proceeds not only outward from the matrix of life but goes back inside it again to the experiencing subject? Is there an anthropology that can concern itself with the meaning of bearing a culture—with the intricate texture of experience, and its interweaving of the customary and personal—or must such endeavors always belong to the province of literature? Sapir held that individual and social approaches to behavior involve much the same areas of human experience but cannot in the end be synthesized. Instead they form alternatives, each with its own perspective and measure of truth (1949b: 544–45). This second anthropology—this "more intimate structure of culture"— may thus provide one of the grounds for the visual anthropology of the future.

Recent interest in visual anthropology has two further sources. One is the increased attention now being paid by anthropologists to varied forms of visual culture (including film, video, and television), popular image production (for example, local still photography, sign painting, and posters), and much that was formerly studied under the rubric of the anthropology of art. These visual expressions often form strands in larger cultural systems that Barthes described as "braids" of different codes. Through such interconnections visual anthropology can play a part in the study of much in human society that is nonvisual.

A second source of interest in visual anthropology lies in the possibility of visual forms (especially film and video) becoming a recognized *medium* of anthropology—a means of exploring social phenomena and expressing anthropological knowledge. Development along this second axis of visual anthropology has potentially more far-reaching consequences, for instead of simply adding to anthropology's fields of study, it poses fundamental challenges to anthropological ways of "speaking" and knowing. It reflects the changing climate of thinking about anthropological representation itself. It also expresses a will to address the impasse that has long paralyzed visual anthropology in its relation to anthropological writing. For although there has been growing interest among anthropologists in studying visible culture, use of the visual media within the discipline has, as Jay Ruby observed over twenty years ago (1975: 104) remained largely marginalized to record-making and didactic functions.

Such a step is not a matter of a simple progression. There is no smooth continuity from knowledge produced through prose to knowledge produced through images. First, anthropological ideas must be examined in relation to the processes that have produced them. This means questioning the implications of anthropology's dominant orientation toward the verbal, and simultaneously exploring understandings that may be available and communicable only in nonverbal form. It means conceiving of an image-and-sequence-based anthropological thought as distinct from a word-and-sentence-based anthropological thought. A number of obvious questions arise. How has the visual figured in the intellectual history of anthropology, and what assumptions and institutions have encouraged or discouraged attention to it? How have previous conventions of research and writing shaped categories of anthropological knowledge? Are there inherent contradictions between generating written and visual texts, involving such basic anthropological issues as description, theory-formation, and verification? If so, there may well be an *inverse* relation between the two ways of approaching society and culture—but an inversion that can be productive. In the end, visual anthropology may need to define itself not at all in the terms of written anthropology but as an alternative to it, as a quite different way of knowing related phenomena.

## The Troubling Visual

It is here, in these vague regions of knowledge, that
the coming of Photography, or the mere idea of it,
acquires remarkable and specific importance for it introduces into these venerable disciplines a new con-

dition, perhaps a new uncertainty, a new kind of rea-
gent whose effects have certainly not as yet been
sufficiently explored.
—*Paul Valéry*[2]

From the beginning, the visual has both fascinated and troubled anthropologists, like a horse that is both beautiful and unridable. The visual evokes the
myriad concerns of anthropology, and yet it can remain frustratingly uncom-
municative about them. But even if, as Roland Barthes said, a photograph is a
message without a code, photographic images can nevertheless be fashioned
into codes that are at once vividly concrete and yet ambiguous, engaging the
intellect and imagination in both controlled and uncontrollable ways.

The history of the visual in anthropology has not followed a simple course,
but reveals itself as two streams flowing in opposite directions. Early enthusiasm for the visual was linked to a confidence in the expressiveness of the
physical world that has since diminished, while an interest in the visual as a
pathway to nonvisual aspects of human experience has gradually grown. In
the meeting of these two streams, their contrary assumptions have created
confusion and, in some cases, a kind of paralysis. This view is only partly at
odds with Pinney's (1992b) that although the visual has triumphed in the
world as the apotheosis of scrutiny, knowledge, and control (he cites Rorty
[1980] and of course Foucault), there has (according to a second history) been
a progressive disenchantment with photography in anthropology—that its
presumptive " 'truth' here appears to be in retreat" (p. 83). This disenchantment, even distrust, is also part of my argument, but I attribute it less to photography's self-defeating obscurity than to its potency, which Pinney elsewhere ascribes to an overabundance of meanings (1992a: 27). But Pinney's
emphasis is on photography, not film. There are, as he acknowledges (1992b:
90), significant ontological differences between the two and differences in
their histories. Indeed, in contrast to photography, the cinema has emerged as
modernity's eloquent literature of the *non*visual. The potential of cinema, as
ethnographic film, has thus attracted the attention of the same post-Malinowskian anthropologists for whom the photograph has become increasingly
opaque.

Anthropologists have remained perplexed about what to do with the visual,
although they have nevertheless made recurrent, tentative uses of it, often in
ways (record-making and teaching, for example) that have tended to contain
rather than develop its challenge to the thinking of the discipline. This is consistent with Kuhn's description of "normal science" (1962), which does not
easily open itself to elements that interrupt its discourse. Ironically, the visual
has often been rendered invisible and transparent to anthropology—by being
regarded as mere optical copy or artistic indulgence—precisely because it
threatens shifts in its paradigms of too great an order. To those oriented to-

ward verbal texts, visual discourses often appear to be jumbled, formless. As Robbe-Grillet observed: "A new form always seems to be more or less an absence of any form at all, since it is unconsciously judged by reference to consecrated forms" (cited by Carpenter, in Carpenter and Heyman 1970: 21).

Descriptions in early anthropological writing, as in early travel literature, were often vividly visual, a feature seized upon and elaborated by Frazer in *The Golden Bough*. This commitment to evoking the visual in words continued in some later ethnographic writing, as in the famous opening of Firth's *We, the Tikopia*, Evans-Pritchard's writing on the Nuer,[3] and certain more recent ethnographies.[4] Illustrations were also a prominent feature of early ethnological monographs: their pages are filled with line drawings and engravings (often based on photographs) of implements, hair-styles, body ornamentation, and indigenous architecture. Photography itself made an early appearance in the cataloguing of human types and occupations (as early as 1851 in India [Pinney 1990: 261]), in the techniques of anthropometry (Edwards 1990; Spencer 1992), and in published ethnographies. W.H.R. Rivers's *The Todas* of 1906 contains 76 photographs, and the Seligmanns' *The Veddas* published in 1911 has 119. Chronophotography and the films of Félix-Louis Regnault, A. C. Haddon, Walter Baldwin Spencer, and Rudolf Pöch are now well known to visual anthropologists, and these virtually coincided with the invention of cinema. It is also important to remember that in addition to such image-making, which presented other societies to the public at one remove, early anthropology also emphasized the elaborate visual display of objects in museums and, to a lesser extent, of actual people imported from remote societies. Family groups from many cultures were exhibited in the Anthropology Hall of the World's Columbian Exposition of 1893 in Chicago, which Franz Boas helped to organize and for which he imported a Kwakiutl group (Hinsley 1991).

From about 1930 onwards there was a notable decline in the use of photographs in anthropology, the famous Bali project of Gregory Bateson and Margaret Mead perhaps being the exception that proved the rule. That experiment produced no immediate imitators, in part because the war years soon followed, but also very possibly because it did not go far enough in devising a new intellectual framework for visual anthropology. Bateson and Mead had divergent approaches (Bateson and Mead 1977) and according to Bateson's description of their methods, Mead's written notetaking generally took interpretive precedence over the photographic material (Bateson and Mead 1942: 49–50). The most obvious decline in the use of the visual was in the gradual disappearance of photographs from anthropological monographs, first noted by de Heusch (1962: 109). Some possible reasons for this have been advanced by Pinney, including the desire to avoid contamination from the exoticism of travel photography, the movement away from the massive technical facticity of evolutionary ethnographies toward greater abstraction, and the triumph of fieldwork, which had in effect replaced the photographic plate with the anthropologist's own long exposure to the anthropological object (Pinney 1992b: 81–82).

Certainly other reasons can be found as well, also tied to shifts in anthropology's intellectual history. Much that had given photography its initial impetus—anthropometry, "salvage" anthropology, and the emphasis upon material culture and ritual—was being replaced in the 1930s by an emphasis upon structural functionalism and psychoanalytic approaches to culture. Mead's insight in championing photography was in recognizing that it could record informal social interactions as well as formal ceremonies and technology, but her use of it never extended to the kind of investigative use that Bateson envisaged. Another shift was the decline (except in the Third Reich) of studies of racial types, such as the photographically illustrated *The Racial Characteristics of the Swedish Nation* of 1926.

As earlier reasons for "visualizing" anthropology declined, new reasons were emerging on quite a different basis. The value of photography and film to anthropology had at first been tied to appearance. It was believed that visual knowledge told the story of mankind: the emergence of civilization out of savagery, the evolution of the races, and the diffusion of cultural traits from one part of the world to another. The visual also provided a way of consolidating anthropological knowledge in a demonstrable way. Museums were perhaps necessary in establishing anthropology's discursive domain, in the physical absence of those remote peoples who were its ostensible subjects. There was also the motive of urgency. As colonial incursions wiped out people, languages, and cultures, photography gave to salvage anthropology an illusion of physical preservation. Like the collecting of oral texts and anecdotal information, it was felt that whatever could be recorded today might eventually—like the Rosetta Stone—become a key to understanding the cultural diversity of the past.

The renewal of interest in the visual was tied not to appearance but to the imagination. In this transition, the work of the Harvard-Peabody expeditions to the Kalahari can be seen as a kind of fulcrum. Laurence Marshall, who financed the expeditions, was encouraged by the Peabody Museum director, J. O. Brew, to record the technology of "wild Bushmen" as a "window on the Pleistocene" (Anderson and Benson 1993: 136). This was in accord with earlier conceptions of anthropological photography. According to John Marshall, "My father thought truth could be discovered by objective methods in any field" (p. 26). Marshall gave his son a spring-wind Bell & Howell camera, Kodachrome film, a 1929 edition of *Notes and Queries on Anthropology* as a shooting script, and told him to film technology. John Marshall began doing this conscientiously but soon turned to filming episodes of social interaction. The turning point was a kind of epiphany, when he discovered that while he was exhaustively filming the making of a carrying net "knot by knot," his classificatory sister had gone into the bush, had a baby, and returned with it (Marshall 1993: 35–36). Further to the north, Jean Rouch's career had followed a similar pattern. Beginning with the filming of technology and ritual, he very soon turned his attention to the social and psychological contexts of hunting, initiation, and possession.

Marshall's and Rouch's approach differed radically from most other approaches to visual anthropology. Their aim was to register human relationships that in many cases were evident only by inference from the visible. For this purpose it was no longer sufficient for film to record appearances; it was necessary to construct a filmic discourse. The result was not a piece of data to be analyzed later. It required the engagement of the viewer in an imaginary geographical and social space created by the film. Thus it can fairly be said of Rouch's and Marshall's films that their anthropological achievement lies not primarily in ethnographic content of the sort that can be summarized or duplicated in anthropological writing, nor even in a physical evocation of people and places that writing could scarcely achieve, but in cinematically created understandings of the emotions, intellect, desires, relationships, and mutual perceptions of the participants. When we are in the midst of the hippopotamus-hunt with Ayorou fishermen in *Bataille sur le grand fleuve* (1951), the technology of hippopotamus hunting is of very much less anthropological weight than the collective enterprise of the hunting as a social institution.

This kind of communication (although communication is too narrow a term for it) has remained largely unrelated to anthropological expectations of film until very recently. Ethnographic films have been viewed, as George Marcus points out, primarily as supplemental and naturalistic, not capable of fundamentally altering anthropologists' conceptions of their objects of study, and as case studies for assimilation into written anthropology's existing projects of classification (1990: 2). This view has been reinforced by the reticence of some ethnographic filmmakers and the willingness of many others to be pigeon-holed as visionaries, artists, or educators. However, a generation of anthropologists has now grown up with a different view of film and its possibilities. Their lives have been been deeply touched by the narrative cinema, and they have witnessed the emergence of a variety of new documentary forms. As a result, they have little patience with the arrogance and intellectual poverty of the traditional educational film or the sterility of much research footage. These are very often the same anthropologists who are simultaneously questioning the authority of anthropological texts—their blind spots and elisions, their claims to speak for others, their concepts of ethnographic reality. They know that the fictional cinema is capable of producing complex constructions of the social experience of individuals, and they recognize that in many cases it deals with exactly those subjects that anthropology has seemingly failed to take up.

Visual forms are thus attracting the attention of those anthropologists interested in the limitations and potential of anthropological texts, as well as those studying a variety of emergent social and cultural subjects. Their interests include (among other things): memory, the emotions, the senses, time and duration, the uses of space, the clustering of cultural phenomena, the shaping of personality, gender, posture and gesture, the cross-cutting complexity of social interactions, the making of emotional environments (of fear, of sexuality), the relation of solitude to sociality, the construction of self, the definition of childhood and other stages of life, and more generally the transmission and creative elaboration of culture. In some cases the attraction is not only to the possibility of new lines of approach but to the new forms of understanding offered by alternative means of expression. Thus Marcus encourages anthropologists to reconsider cinematic montage as a way of representing "the simultaneity and spacial dispersion of the contemporary production of cultural identity" (p. 9).

It can be argued that much of the past resistance to the visual in anthropology was due not to indifference, as Mead maintained some years ago (1975), but to a sense of unease and even danger, a danger perceived on two fronts. One of these is that the visual is too open to misinterpretation; the other is that it is too seductive. The photograph, as Pinney puts it, "contains too many meanings" (1992a: 27). Whatever its "obvious" meaning (what Barthes called the *studium*), there is too much *excess* meaning and, as distinct from written description, too many unintended sites of connotation. The photograph is also too engaging, for it draws the viewer into an interpretive relationship that bypasses professional mediation. One is tempted to compare this state of affairs to that preceding the Reformation, when to propose an unmediated relationship with God was to commit a heresy.

A significant contrast between the written and the visual in anthropology may therefore lie not in their very great ontological differences, nor even in their very different ways of constructing meaning, but in their *control* of meaning. Anthropology's project, like that of much literary criticism, has been to find homogeneities in its objects of study, and one of its ways of achieving this has been to strip these objects of what it regards as idiosyncrasies and irrelevant detail. Anthropology "makes sense" partly through elimination, but at a cost recognized in Geertz's advocacy of "thick description." In a sense, *translation* is always to anthropology's advantage, for it channels data through the keyhole of language, producing a condensation of meaning and leaving most of the data behind. Photography, film (and now video) construct meanings, as it were, on the other side of the keyhole, for photographic images, however heavily coded in diverse ways, also contain analogues (rather than translations) of vision. If they were somehow to pass through the keyhole they would, as Barthes says, stubbornly drag their referents with them (1981: 5–6). Films construct their arguments physically out of their primary data. Written anthropology comes closest to this when it deploys indigenous verbal texts as the building blocks of its own arguments.

What makes visual representation problematic for anthropology are its analogue and uncoded properties. These arise first of all from the co-presentation of centered and peripheral details in the same frame—in the case of a film, of "figure" and "ground" when the figure is designated through implication by the surrounding shots. Figure in this sense corresponds to what would be the primary denotation of a verbal description of the image, accompanied by other levels of intended meaning. Here, along with its visual detail on an informational level are the connotations that form its symbolic content. But the ground is there as well, offering a range of further details, not consciously intended, that may lead anywhere, challenging meaning because they are unexplained. They are open to interpretation, as mere fragments or as mistaken signifiers, and they are also potential distractions from the author's purpose.

This field is sufficiently available and uncontrolled to pose certain threats to anthropological discourse. Let us take a hypothetical example based on past practice, at the risk of it being argued that such an example has no parallels in the present. It was once a common aim of anthropology to make records of rituals as they would have been performed before European contact. Suppose, then, that a ritual is being filmed, and at the climactic moment a ritual leader appears in a T-shirt bearing the words "I am a sex addict" (I recently saw such a T-shirt). To the traditionalist the conceit of "authenticity" would have been irretrievably broken, both by the anachronism of the shirt and the probable risibility of any audience seeing the film. A written description could easily "frame out" such an image, but although filmmakers do in fact often frame things out, in this case, with the ritual leader so central to the event, a film would have difficulty in doing so. It may be argued that such intrusive elements are in fact salutary correctives to a lost cause, but this hardly disposes of the possibility that in a more sophisticated film some other kind of intervention might create a similar distraction or pose a similar threat to the anthropologist's intended subject.

The threat implicit in analogue representation is the threat of undesired or unexplained (and therefore uncontrolled) content and, by extension, the "misreading" of it. Photographers and filmmakers, of course, continually confront this possibility and do control many aspects of how audiences interpret images, by means of selection, framing, and contextualization. However, images seem to have a life of their own, and people are capable of responding to them in a wide variety of ways. Several studies suggest that audiences tend to interpret films ethnocentrically, even when this runs counter to the filmmakers' purpose.[5] Thus ethnographic films and photographs may be considered dangerous in ways that written descriptions are not. They may first of all be thought dangerous to those they portray, since the anonymity of the subjects

is less easily preserved. Perhaps more controversially, they are often perceived as dangerous to their viewers as well. This implies on one level that the
uninitiated (such as university students) should be protected from potential
misunderstandings for their own or the common good. But it also implies that
visual materials should be regarded as dangerous in a more abstract sense, to
"knowledge." This accusation can rebound upon their authors, who may be
held to be "irresponsible" (Moore 1988: 3). From such a perspective the onus
falls upon the filmmaker to control any potential misinterpretations of the material—not upon the viewer to be a better interpreter of it.

These issues are not clear-cut and involve questions of degree. They im-
pinge upon debates about intellectual and academic freedom and public responsibility, upon the right to be wrong or hold unpopular beliefs, the right to
depict others, and upon questions of clear and present danger, such as shouting "fire" in a crowded theater. When does making an ethnographic film become equivalent to shouting "fire"? Was Rouch's portrayal of Hauka possession and dog-eating in *Les Maîtres fous* (1955) such a case, as was maintained
by many critics at the time? (Fulchignoni and Rouch 1981: 16; Stoller 1992:
151–53).

My point here is to isolate certain characteristics of visual representation,
but these inevitably bear upon the place of the visual in anthropology and
visual anthropology itself. The question of control and mediation contains
within it the much larger question of the relation of audiences to the content of
different media. For example, one can perhaps speak of the "recipient" of
written anthropological information, as the object of a communication, but it
is more difficult to speak of the recipient of visual images. The relationship
has different qualities and may even be said to be of a different order. I wish
here to underscore the exploratory response demanded by visual works, to
which I shall return later. Image-based media such as film and video rely extensively upon the principle of discovery—the discovery of relationships between images, linked not only by their proximity but by their resonances. This
is a different principle from the declarative linking of ideas in expository writing, although there are some resemblances, such as in the use of camera
movement. (Films are of course verbal as well, and contain verbal resonances.) Cinematic montage, unlike "elephant trunk-to-tail" expository construction, inserts the viewer rather than the author into the gaps between its
shots and sequences. The author is present, often very strongly, but only by
inference. In oversimplified terms, it could be said that to a great extent in
these media the viewer is given the subjects but creates the predicates. It is the
viewer who discovers connections within a network of possibilities structured
by the author. The viewer may make other discoveries too, just as a reader of
poetry (or of a rich ethnographic description) may discover meanings of
which the writer is not consciously aware. Contrary to the assumption that
film viewers are passive, this produces a highly interactive and interpretive

relationship to visual works, qualitively different from interpreting expository texts which, at least in the past, primarily involved assessing the implications of assertions.

The exploratory faculty in turn calls forth the imaginative faculty. Much of the film experience has little to do with what one sees: it is what is constructed in the mind and body of the viewer. Films create a new reality in which the viewer plays a central role, or at least is invited to do so. Thus, much of the meaning of sophisticated ethnographic films lies in how their theories and insights are embedded in their structures. Some viewers may initially be unable to interpret such films, even though they are adept enough at interpreting more abstract structures in other situations or the complex symbolic systems of other societies. Others may refuse to do so on the grounds that such meanings are either arbitrary or irrelevant or unquantifiable. Anthropologists who express these objections typically regard photographs and films from an ethnographically realist perspective.

Hastrup (1992: 9) has described her failure to photograph an Icelandic ram exhibition at which "the air was loaded with sex and . . . the exhibition was literally and metaphorically a competition of sexual potence." She concludes that "the nature of the event could not be recorded in photography. . . . While one can take pictures of ritual groves and of the participants in the ritual, one cannot capture their secret on celluloid. This has to be told." This sounds like giving up on photography too easily. Even accepting that in this setting Hastrup was in a difficult position, the key to the failure seems to lie in the words "capture . . . on celluloid," for if that indeed is where the process of photography stops, then it is understandable that the pictures fail to express what she would have wished. Although Hastrup clearly understands metaphorical meaning, photography here has been conceived apart from the imagination. One can envisage photographs by André Kertész or Brassaï or Danny Lyon expressing just such meanings as Hastrup hoped to record.

Other examples are not hard to find. Maurice Bloch remarked to an interviewer in 1988 that

> ethnographic film is a jolly good idea if they [sic] can be used as data which is incorporated in teaching. . . . What ethnographic film— and especially the ethnographic films which are being made at the moment—are trying to do is give the idea that if you just stare at people, if you just hear their words out of context, you've learnt something about them. This idea that ethnographic film speaks for itself is what is wrong. The kind of thing one tries to teach in anthropology is, if you just stare at exotic scenes and listen to the things that people are saying without knowing anything about these people, you understand less about them than if you have never seen them or heard them. (Houtman 1988: 20)

Bloch goes on to speak of the constructed character of ethnography, but seems not to understand the constructed character of films. The prevailing assumption here seems to be that a film is no more than arbitrarily joined together slices of life. This is a serious misconception even in relation to how avowedly "realist" films must be interpreted.

Paralleling this, but somewhat more puzzling, in view of the explicitly constructed character of the work, are the now familiar reactions to Gardner's *Forest of Bliss* (1985) as "a jumble of incomprehensible vignettes" (Ruby 1989: 11), and a film that "evokes the intense frustration of initial incomprehension" (Parry 1988: 4) and, astonishingly, a film that "we are left to figure . . . out for ourselves from the images" (Moore 1988: 1). Anthropological writing usually tells us what it is about, but films expect us to find out. To object to a film because of this is to ignore a crucial aspect of its discourse. *Forest of Bliss* is a complex work, but by no means as demanding as *Masques dogons* or *The Waste Land*. Whatever doubts as to its anthropological value (and here I think the author's disavowal of anthropological intent should be taken in the same spirit as Robert Frost's disavowal of symbolic intent) it would seem essential to "read" the work before coming to such conclusions. These critics seem reluctant to engage with the film on the level of its own construction, or for what it might have to give them. Indeed, there is little analysis of its construction. They either castigate it for the sin of distortion by omission (for which any delimited work is fair game) or (in Moore's case) construct a reading that seems wilfully obtuse. Interestingly, the film is simultaneously accused of having *no* meaning and the *wrong* meaning. But its real sin is perhaps to affront anthropology. To occupy an ideal ethnographer's position "and then to refuse to convert it into the currency of the discipline" is, as Mary Louise Pratt observes in another case, "a monumental betrayal" (1986: 30–31). Such people are likely to be "disciplined."

The *Forest of Bliss* debate exhibits more mistrust than Bloch's blanket dismissal of film. The objections to the film are somehow out of scale with its presumed faults. Gardner is taken personally to task, but its "scandal" and the threat it poses lie, it seems to me, in its use of an uncompromising form of cinematic discourse. Bloch objects to "mere film" (to use Adam Kendon's term) being presented as knowledge, but *Forest of Bliss* can hardly be accused of that. Nor can its alleged aesthetic failings logically be construed as an affront to science. This might be any film that, like alien tissue, invaded the body of anthropology.

What is it in the anthropological organism that excites the vigilance of these antibodies? There are, to be sure, the free-floating signifiers that escape from explanation or control. But there is another level of meaning that escapes even from the realm of connotation, what Barthes calls the third or "obtuse" meaning: "meaning [that] appears to extend outside culture, knowledge, information" (1977: 55). This property of the photographic image is perhaps always more present in cinema than in still photography because it exists in contradiction to the regimes of meaning that are always more pronounced in cinema. It resides in the materiality of the image: that part of it which, as Kristin Thompson notes, fails to participate in the creation of either narrative or symbol (1986: 131). This *excess* creates a fundamental psychological disturbance in all human endeavors to construct schemata of the world. It is nevertheless the source of much of the fascination of photographic media, and a contributor to the underlying erotics and aesthetics of both art and science. Barthes describes this as *figuration*, in contrast to *representation*, for it traverses the grain of significance. "Film," he writes, "will *always* be figurative (which is why films are still worth making)—even if it represents nothing. Representation, on the other hand, is *embarrassed figuration*, encumbered with other meanings than that of desire: a space of alibis (reality, morality, likelihood, readability, truth, etc.)" (1975: 56). Is film then not also an embarrassment to one more alibi, that of anthropology?

## Film and Anthropological Knowledge

> The trouble with Ptolemaic astronomy was not that it was wrong but that it was sterile—there could be no real development until Galileo was prepared to abandon the basic premiss that celestial bodies must of necessity move in perfect circles with the earth at the centre of the universe. We anthropologists likewise must re-examine basic premises and realize that English language patterns of thought are not a necessary model for the whole of human society.
> —*Edmund Leach*[6]

Disciplines tend to grow to fit the niches of greatest opportunity and least expressive difficulty. They also tend to define themselves in opposition to what they are not, thus sealing themselves against some forms of change. This process is coupled with shifts in historical consciousness. Just as visuality suited and reinforced nineteenth-century anthropology's project of collecting and cataloguing the world, the word-orientation of more recent times has encouraged an emphasis upon language, beliefs, kinship, and the less visible aspects of economic and political life. Consequently, anthropological knowledge has grown as a lop-sided organism. At various times anthropology has relegated to other fields (such as psychology and moral philosophy) those issues that have raised potential intellectual contradictions for it. Like Bourdieu's defenders of class decorum, it has protected itself by notions of what it *forbids itself* to be. Debates about the ethics of anthropology, challenging the humanist doctrine of cultural relativism, emerged most notably under the stimulus of the Vietnam War. Only comparatively recently have the senses and emotions been viewed as cultural constructions or, in the case of emotions, as social agents (Lyon 1995). Previously, these were "not anthropology." Similarly, in promoting anthropology as a science, some anthropologists have reacted with suspicion to approaches that challenged concepts of scientific method or scientific language, often branding these as "fiction" or "art." (Rouch's response, characteristically, was to declare his films "science fiction.")

It has been said that the main consequence of postmodern provocations in anthropology has not been so much to stimulate new ways of writing as new ways of reading (Tyler and Marcus 1987: 277). Presented antithetically, these choices pose a difficulty, for I wish to argue both cases. The self-consciousness of anthropology has indeed altered the way in which anthropological works are read. It has shifted the frame of reference outwards, replacing assumptions about the unproblematical transparency of writing with a new sensitivity to language, voices, and relationships—between writers and readers, texts and their objects. This has placed demands upon anthropologists to engage with works in more complex ways. At the same time, the new-found experimentation and heteroglossia of anthropology, and the parallel discourses of indigenous, minority, and diasporic peoples, have opened anthropology to different ways of thinking and speaking (Ginsburg 1994; Nichols 1994b; Ruby 1991). Structures from the cinema and literature offer still further models (montage and narrative, for example). Some of these have been available for a very long time but have remained outside the definition of anthropological concerns. Ethnographic filmmaking has been a primary demonstration of this.

In a seminal paper of 1975, Jay Ruby asked: "Is an ethnographic film a filmic ethnography?" The terms in which the question was put focused attention on whether it was or was not but tended to elide questions of whether it could or should be. Nevertheless, the paper took a major step toward expressing explicitly what had been only a vague article of faith before: that film could perform a role in anthropology analogous to ethnographic writing, but in cinematic terms. A film could, in effect, present cultural patterns and account for them within a theoretical framework. In the paper he proposed some basic criteria for scientific ethnography and held that these should be no less applicable to films than to writing. He concluded that few films fulfilled these criteria.

Ruby's conception helped define visual anthropology at a crucial period in its history. How applicable is this definition today? Ruby made certain assumptions about film and anthropology that derived from the semiotic theory of Sol Worth (1969; 1981a). One was that film and anthropology were primarily engaged in transmitting messages about culture (Worth specified "behavior" [1981a: 77]), an orientation in accord with communications theory of the time). In his early writings Worth was explicit about what he meant by filmic communication: "I shall mean," he wrote, "the *transmission* of a *signal, re-*

*ceived* primarily through *visual receptors, coded* as *signs*, which we treat as *messages* by *inferring meanings* or *content* from them. The film will be said to communicate to the extent which the viewer infers what the maker implies" (Worth 1969: 43, original emphasis). Although Worth later revised his thinking somewhat to give more space to metaphorical forms of communication (Gross 1981: 30–31), his approach, like Christian Metz's in his earlier works, tended to stress the denotative systems of film.

Ruby's view of anthropological and filmic communication in 1975 was in accord with this linguistic model. Ethnographic filmmaking was described as a process of description within a theoretical framework that produces statements about culture, which are to be inferred by an audience. However, ethnography since then has changed dramatically and is now conceived of as having many more alternatives—for example, explorations of complex networks of cultural meanings (what might be called "dispersed gestalts") and descriptions of the social reality of specified social actors. Works of ethnography today may contain an analysis that does not finally result in a set of formal assertions or conclusions. Indeed, it may be conceived of as neither a message nor a representation, but as a record of engagement with a different culture. Just as there are many anthropologies, so there are many ethnographies. Despite this shift, one problem not fully accounted for in the 1975 description is that while it is possible for a written ethnography to present an overall picture of cultural patterns in a community, a film can only present specific instances and imply some generality for them. Written ethnography lends itself far better to the making of summary statements. Filmic ethnography, by contrast, tends to draw attention to *relations*. Writing can give theoretical causal explanations, but a film can only suggest causal relationships within a given context.

The clearest link with semiotic theory was perhaps Ruby's most restrictive criterion for filmic ethnography: its use of "a distinctive lexicon—an anthropological argot" (1975: 107). This argot is further defined as "a specialized visual anthropological lexicon" (p. 109), a narrower but more accurate use of the term than Worth's "grammars of argot" (Worth 1965: 18). Its recommendation derives from the observation that anthropological writing uses distinctive terminology whereas nonanthropological writing does not. But what is puzzling about this is that although anthropology may use certain technical terms, these are by no means untranslatable into standard English, and in any case anthropological and nonanthropological writing manifestly use a common language. Their varieties of language are vastly closer than written ethnography is to filmic discourse. Nor is the use of anthropological argot any guarantee of anthropological value—it can be used by anyone, and anthropological works of great value can certainly be written without it. (One is tempted to say, the best aspire to.) Anthropological terms are often a convenient shorthand and a badge of professionalism, but no more than that. The real question here is whether it is appropriate to speak of film being capable of an argot at all, even if it made any professional difference. Anthropology uses terminology to express concepts, but filmic concepts are expressed not through terms but through constructions. Anthropology may be lexical, but film is not.[7] If there is anthropological expertise to be found in ethnographic films, it will not be found in an argot but in the anthropological understanding that informs them.

Ruby's crucial—and still valid—point is that visual anthropology must learn to make *anthropological* films rather than films *about anthropology* (1975: 109). All too many ethnographic films fall into the second category. They refer to anthropology but make no original contribution to anthropological knowledge. Some are skillful popularizations of anthropological ideas, such as many in the *Disappearing World* series (see Singer 1992; Turton 1992), but they are not finally anthropological in their objectives. A useful method for distinguishing between the anthropological film and the film about anthropology, I would suggest, is to assess whether the film attempts to cover new ground through an integral exploration of the data or whether it merely *reports on* existing knowledge. Films about anthropology, by and large, employ the conventions of teaching and journalism; anthropological films present a genuine process of inquiry. They develop their understandings progressively, and reveal an evolving relationship between the filmmaker, subject, and audience. They do not provide a "pictorial representation" of anthropological knowledge, but a form of knowledge that emerges through the very grain of the filmmaking.

At no time does Ruby draw a simple equation between written and filmic works. In a 1994 article he asks: "What can pictorial images convey that words cannot? How do film images mean? This is a question fundamental to all visual/pictorial studies and at the very heart of visual anthropology" (1994: 166). But underlying such questions, what kind of knowledge is considered acceptable to anthropology? Is it only knowledge "recognized as contributing to the mainstream of our profession"? (Ruby 1989: 11). If so, the history of ideas suggests that the probing of new possibilities is often incompatible with mainstream academic approval. The *doxa* is more likely to want visual anthropology to confirm what it already does than do something quite different. Visual anthropology, like other emerging anthropologies, may need to conceive of a "radical ethnography." Unfortunately, a bare description of ethnographic criteria can give us very little idea of what cultural patterns might emerge more clearly from being treated visually, or how that treatment might necessarily depart from the methods evolved in writing. Nor are "criteria for evaluation uniquely suited to a pictorial representation of anthropological knowledge" (Ruby 1989: 9) likely to emerge in the abstract; they will only develop through the making and intelligent "reading" of new works. To go further we need to enlarge upon the fundamental question. What can images convey that may lead to new knowledge, and when is such knowledge relevant to anthropology?

One consequence of post-structuralist film theory and the rethinking of representation in anthropology has been to shift our attention from denotation to connotation. Films are more often understood to involve different readings at different levels, and in different contexts. They are less often conceived in the terms of communications theory but rather as a process of constructing new realities, as in Rouch's films (Stoller 1992: 193). Works become sites of meaning-potential rather than sets of meanings sent and received, or the outside world seen through representations. Stephen Tyler considers it necessary to break the whole ideology of representational signification in anthropological discourse, advocating "evocation" that produces an understanding rather than an anthropological object (1987: 206–8). We no longer think so confidently of speaking about or for others, but rather, as Ruby (1991) puts it (paraphrasing Trinh T. Minh-ha), of "speaking with, or speaking alongside." Yet the observer can never be fully disengaged from the observed: in the work, subject and object are bound up with one another.

This binding has partly to do with the filmmaker's own physical presence in the film—a presence of the same order as that of the subjects. In their materiality photographic images have an immediacy absent in written texts, and although this is often evoked in descriptive prose it is uncommon in anthropological writing. There are certainly verbal equivalents to the photographs of concentration camps that struck Susan Sontag with the force of a physical encounter (1977: 19–20). I know of a description in Nicholas Gage's book *Eleni* (1982) that I would not willingly read again and can scarcely bear to think of. But this form of verbal description, even of a much less intense kind, is of secondary importance in most anthropological writing. It is also fundamentally different from photographic imagery. Bill Nichols cites the extraordinary revulsion of some Norwegian schoolchildren to a particular ethnographic film ("some were found vomiting, one crying") as an indication of film's power to reach directly to bodily and emotional experience, circumventing intellectual understanding (1994a: 76). The human face also has great prominence in films, but there is still much that we do not know about psychological, cultural, and neuropsychological responses to the face, despite continuing interest from a variety of perspectives.[8]

The kind of knowledge we have of the analogue contents of films, as opposed to what we derive from written texts, can be usefully compared to Bertrand Russell's (1912) distinction between *knowledge by acquaintance* and *knowledge by description*. Although our understanding is always influenced by context (the immediate "framing" of what we see, and what we already know), and although seeing a photographic image differs from seeing its referent, films present us with some of the characteristics of acquaintance that verbal descriptions do not. Russell includes in knowledge by acquaintance the direct awareness of sense-data, memory, introspection (that is, our awareness of being aware, through thought and emotion), and, more problematically, self. It excludes physical objects but includes "universals," or abstract concepts, such as "whiteness, diversity, brotherhood." Russell does not explicitly say that knowledge by description is what we acquire from language, but rather that it is what we know from a distance, which allows us "to pass beyond the limits of our private experience." Nevertheless, I think language is what is meant here.

It can certainly be argued that films only permit knowledge at a distance (and therefore only by description) but Russell's distinction presents an interesting parallel to the specificity of objects in films (the sense-data of them) in contrast to the generality of the language that stands for them in written texts. Without attempting to press the comparison further, the concept of acquaintance is at least useful in distinguishing some of the more experiential qualities of films from the more abstractly coded ones: a person's face from the words the person is speaking; the texture of a bird's feathers from the idea of a bird as a cultural symbol of hope or resurrection.

An indication of these two kinds of knowledge, and the quite different domains they occupy, can be gained from an account that the filmmaker Gary Kildea gives of an exchange he had with Clifford Geertz in 1989. Kildea had been giving a public presentation of some footage from his work-in-progress, *Valencia Diary* (1992), filmed on the island of Mindanao in the Philippines.

> As the lights went up there was a call for questions. Probably to break the embarrassing silence more than anything else, Geertz raised his hand. He said that despite having been shown many interesting personalities and events in and around the village, he'd been left wondering about some of the most basic facts about it—its population, for example. I fended off the question, saying that it was, after all, just a work in progress, but I do remember feeling uneasy that I didn't even know what the population was. In the entire nine month "fieldwork" period it had never once occurred to me to ask. On reflection I realized that I should have answered: "Why offer statistics as an indicator of scale when a single wide shot reveals—all at once—*that* village in all its specificity; a village of *that* size.[9]

What is the status of such expressions of experiential knowledge in anthropology? Kildea argues that "it's not a question of redundancy of information but of the mixing up of incompatible 'judgements' on the world. Whereas it behooves an anthropologist in the field to take [a] census, it behooves a filmmaker to make meaning at the level of perceived phenomena." Nichols, although not an anthropologist, argues that evoking an embodied knowledge may legitimately be another way of being anthropological, and that film may assist in this (1994a: 74–75). Anthropological theory does not pay much attention to re-creating knowledge by acquaintance, although this is obviously a key aspect of fieldwork. There are few arguments that the knowledge of the anthropological audience should derive from anything but description, although empathy is often implied as a useful and desirable adjunct. Ruby's statement that "we are scholars who are producing anthropological knowledge" (1989: 9) suggests that this knowledge is indeed a kind of product, or in postmodern terms "cultural capital," that might exist even if it were not being experienced by anyone. Pinney, as noted earlier, has suggested that the anthropologist in the field has often been viewed as a kind of photographic plate, to be "exposed" to the subject and developed later for the benefit of the anthropological audience (1992b: 81–82). Marilyn Strathern describes the Malinowskian anthropologist, in contrast to the earlier tradition of armchair anthropologists, as a self-conscious emissary and broker between subject and audience. "The audience was required to connive in its distance from the anthropologist's subject matter. Meanwhile the anthropologist moved between the two. His proximity to the culture he was studying became his distance from the one he was addressing, and vice versa. This, *tout court*, is how the modern(ist) fieldworker has imagined him- or herself ever since" (1987: 261).

There is, however, an undercurrent, an implication, in recent anthropological writing, that just as the anthropologist must insert him- or herself experientially in the process of fieldwork, so the audience must be inserted into the production of the work. This is a perception with a close affinity to the cinema. New concepts of anthropological knowledge are being broached in which meaning is not merely the outcome of reflection upon experience but necessarily *includes* the experience. In part, then, the experience *is* the knowledge. Such knowledge cannot survive the translation process: it is *relational* rather than an object in itself. Michael Jackson argues (with reference to Ludwig Binswanger and Merleau-Ponty) that "meaning should not be reduced to a sign which, as it were, lies on a separate plane outside the immediate domain of an act" (1989: 122). Thus many cultural institutions (ritual, in particular) should not be understood primarily as communicating specific symbolic or social messages. Their meaning resides as much, or more, in their performance. Bloch (1974: 181–82; 1986) stresses the conjunction of statement and action in ritual, and the importance of the illocutionary act in ritual language. Gilbert Lewis observes:

> We allow or expect a latitude, variety or complexity in the interpretation of ritual meaning which is different from what we would expect of language. To speak of ritual communicating messages as language does is to suppose to be resolved a series of special problems which are not [resolved]. . . . We cannot yet perceive what entities in ritual would be remotely parallel to lexical or phonemic units or discern stable rules governing their combination when some message is to be transmitted. (1980: 32)

But how can such meaning become accessible to an anthropological audience? Can what Jackson calls "body praxis"—culturally significant somatic behavior of posture and gesture—be meaningful except in terms of concrete acts in specific contexts? Can emotion be understood as a cultural or social phenomenon except in relation to specific dramatic scenarios? In discussing ritual, Jackson makes very much the same point as Gilbert Lewis, arguing that "it is probably the separateness of the observer from the ritual acts which makes him think that the acts refer to or require justification in a domain beyond their actual compass." He continues:

> For these reasons it is imperative to explore further what Wittgenstein called "the environment of a way of acting" and accept that understanding may be gained through seeing and drawing attention to connections or "intermediary links" within such an environment, rather than by explaining acts in terms of preceding events, projected aims, unconscious concerns, or precepts and rules. (1980: 126)

This tendency questions and begins to shift, even reverse, the conventional relation between data and anthropological theory. Or rather, it tends to bind theory more closely to data, suggesting that anthropological ideas must at times be articulated *through* data. The corollary of this is that as such ideas become more embodied they become more closely allied to the "second" anthropology, Sapir's anthropology of "the more intimate structure of culture." This anthropology is no less valid than the first, for just as there is truth in general conclusions that may only with "some absurdity" be applied to individuals, there are more intimate anthropological truths that can only with some absurdity be developed into general statements. This roughly reflects the orientations of written and filmic works, which in the first case tend toward the inductive and in the second toward the empirical. If Malinowskian anthropology stressed distance between the audience and the ethnographic object, and the similarities between them, post-Malinowskian anthropology is able once again to stress both closeness and difference (Strathern 1987).

These latter forms of knowledge require a direct acquaintance with social moments, physical environments, and the bodies of specific social actors. It is in these relations that film is of most value to anthropology. While anthropological writing is effective in speaking about human cultures in general, film, like the imaginative arts, can say much about how individuals live within (and transmit) a "culture." In the process, it can define cultural phenomena that exist primarily in relational terms themselves: for example, concepts of gender or class that significantly define themselves in contrast to alternatives: to what they arc *not*. The distinctive characteristic of relational knowledge is that the meaning exists in the sum, not in the parts. Film is capable of presenting complex networks of images within which a variety of ambiguous cultural constructions and resonances are understood (sexual, ideological, hierarchic) but which are never explicitly acknowledged, or which recur in different combinations. Objects of symbolic consequence in one context often appear in another with only a lingering shading of their other meanings. This coexistence of the said and unsaid is a powerful force in every society. Furthermore, perhaps only through identification with social actors is it possible to gain an adequate understanding of social ambiguity. The portrayal in narratives of specific human relationships and of the pressures of conflicting cultural imperatives can provide an anthropological perception of society in a phenomenological sense, rather like recognizing distinctive chords, the symptoms of an illness, or the valences of molecular structures. This suggests that film can act as a kind of performative anthropology.

Yet film is not confined to the immediate, anecdotal level of anthropological understanding. The proto-language which is cinema operates through the uttering of its referents, the uttering of the body. But this utterance may occur within a shot, across a juxtaposition of shots, or across the overarching structure of an entire work. Film is cumulative, in the sense that it builds up understandings through an accretion of scenes, often bringing a particular pattern to the surface retrospectively in a moment of crystallization. This may be observed when a social ambiguity that has long been a source of tension is actually seen to be tested.

Anthropologists have tended to define knowledge not in terms of acquaintance, but description. "Cultural description" is a phrase widely used in North American anthropology to define the anthropologist's task. Philippe Descola, citing Lévi-Strauss (and reflecting a very French anthropological perspective), has divided the discipline into three "steps": ethnography, ethnology, and anthropology. He characterizes ethnography as primarily collection, ethnology primarily analysis and comparison, and anthropology (a rare activity) a philosophical project of "making sense of general problems of social life" (Knight and Rival 1992: 9). We might classify the products of these steps when they reach the anthropological audience (now narrowing the first term somewhat) as: *descriptive knowledge* (the factual domain), *structural knowledge* (the domain of relations) and *explanatory knowledge* (the domain of theory). What we find missing from this list, from the realm of "knowledge by acquaintance," is *affective knowledge* (the domain of experience). We must look for it elsewhere, perhaps catching a glimpse of it in ancillary works such as Lévi-Strauss's *Tristes Tropiques* (1974) or Paul Rabinow's *Reflections on Fieldwork in Morocco* (1977).

In filmic discourse, explanatory knowledge (theory) resides primarily in the structures of editing, but Gilles Deleuze provides us with a theory of cinema that is helpful in understanding how the film shot incorporates the three other categories of knowledge. Deleuze divides the "movement-image" (the shot) into three aspects which, like Descola's three steps, are not mutually exclusive but cumulative. Each is dependent upon those before it. The *perception-image* is that aspect (he calls it an "avatar") that distinguishes the shot from undifferentiated perception, and which by the subtraction created through framing eliminates other objects and perspectives. We may see a resemblance here to the eliminating power of anthropological selection and translation. This has a fundamentally defining action and therefore, according to Deleuze, has the linguistic equivalency of a *noun*.

The shot now becomes a center in a decentered universe, from which radiate certain other properties. One is the *action-image*, setting up a relation between the viewer (subject) and shot (object) and implying that the object has a *destination*. A perception-image might frame a piece of fruit, but the action-image could frame it, in a certain context, as *food to be eaten*. The action-image therefore has the linguistic equivalency of a *verb*. The third and final aspect, the *affection-image*, requires the first two and is the expression of a continuous but suspended feeling toward them—the quality of experience attached to the unconsummated movement from the object's definition to its destination. This desire has the linguistic equivalency of an *adjective*. To quote Deleuze:

> But the interval [in the relation between perception-image and action-image] is not merely defined by the specialisation of the two limit-facets, perceptive and active. There is an in-between. Affection is what occupies the interval, what occupies it without filling it in or filling it up. It surges in the centre of indetermination, that is to say in the subject, between a perception which is troubling in certain respects and a hesitant action. It is a coincidence of subject and object, or the way in which the subject perceives itself, or rather experiences itself or feels itself "from the inside" (third material aspect of subjectivity). It relates movement to a "quality" as lived state (adjective). Indeed, it is not sufficient to think that perception—thanks to distance—retains or reflects what interests us by letting pass what is indifferent to us. There is inevitably a part of external movements that we "absorb", that we refract, and which does not transform itself into either objects of perception or acts of the subject; rather they mark the coincidence of the subject and the object in a pure quality. This is the final avatar of the movement-image: *the affection-image*. (1986: 65)

The crucial idea here is that we "refract" in ourselves the relation between what we define and how it might act, or how we might act toward it. This refraction exists in addition to the object and *the possibility* of the act: it is the relation to both. Anthropological knowledge can be considered in just such categories, and the problems of conveying such knowledge can be viewed in relation to just such an analysis of cinematic structure (or proto-language). I may know of an object and I may know objectively of its use or purpose, but I still know little until I know its contemplated quality *in use*. There is a link between this trichotomy and Deleuze's applications of Peirce's concepts of Firstness, Secondness, and Thirdness. In the Marx Brothers films, Harpo represents Oneness (Being), Chico, Twoness (Action), and Groucho, Threeness (Mental relations) (Deleuze 1986: 197–205). Hitchcock is all about Thirdness because the actors, the plots, the "MacGuffins" are mere devices. He is interested in our attitudes toward relations between subjects who may be of little interest in themselves.

One can of course extend this basic triadic form to the construction of meaning at the level of editing, at a metaphorical level, and at the level of the work as a whole. Film both signifies and yet refuses signification. It asserts itself as *figuration*, but to the extent that it implicates filmmaker and viewer, it transcends it. As in novels, or in the segmented narratives of cartoon strips, its gaps are not merely elisions, but part of a world with which filmmaker and viewer are complicit.[10] For Merleau-Ponty, the words of a novel can "refract" the novelist and reader in a similar way. He observes that a novel expresses *tacitly*, citing the example of Julien Sorel's trip to Verrières and his attempt to kill Mme de Renal:

> Stendhal suddenly found an imaginary body for Julien which was more agile than his own body. As if in a second life, he made the trip to Verrières according to a cadence of cold passion which itself decided what was visible and invisible, what was to be said and what was to remain unspoken. The desire to kill is thus not in the words at all. It is between them, in the hollows of space, time, and significa-tion they mark out, as movement at the cinema is between the immobile images which follow one another. The novelist speaks for his reader, and every man to every other, the language of the initiated—initiated into the world and into the universe of possibilities confined in a human body and a human life. What he has to say he supposes known. He takes up his dwelling in a character's behavior and gives the reader only a suggestion of it, its nervous and peremptory trace in the surroundings. If the author is a writer (that is, if he is capable of finding the elisions and caesuras which indicate the behavior), the reader responds to his appeal and joins him at the virtual center of the writing, *even if neither one of them is aware of it.* (1974: 73–74, emphasis in original)

How can the anthropologist grasp the meaning of a ritual that over the years (as Christina Toren puts it) has been "inscribed in [the] very bodies" of the participants? (1993: 464). Anthropological understanding is rarely achieved through unitary meanings. There is never a single code. Film offers anthropol-ogy, alongside the written text, a mixing of embodied, synaesthetic, narrative, and metaphorical strands, corresponding to Barthes's "braid" of significa-tions. In discussing the kava ritual in Fiji, Toren writes: "When I as a for-eigner and anthropologist talk of the meaning of kava ritual, I can grasp that meaning *only* as metaphor. What I cannot do, except through some imagina-tive effort at empathy, is grasp its meaning as an aspect of the complex set of processes by which a Fijian child becomes a Fijian young person, an adult, an old person" (p. 464).

Even here, the anthropologist can understand only *partly* through meta-phor, and indeed only partly in any case. I understand a goatherd's loss of his son *partly* through the killing of livestock (of kids). I understand the meanings of photography *partly* through dressing up, or a missing child, or hands on a garden wall. I understand education among the Boran *partly* through the meaning of "lion" and "elephant." In Rouch's *Jaguar* (1967) I understand labor migration *partly* through a legend of invasion.

Although films construct knowledge of several kinds (structural, experiential, and so on), the acts of constructing and "reading" these can sometimes impede one another. Certain kinds of knowledge may even be mutually exclusive, as Anthony Forge's discussion of Abelam children's and adults' mental worlds suggests (cited in Toren 1993: 465). Thus, to some degree, the descriptive may be incompatible with the explanatory, or the explanatory with the experiential. In anthropology these kinds of knowledge have traditionally been arranged hierarchically, with explanation dependent upon, but ranked higher than description, and description ranked higher than experience. This is in part the legacy of a logocentric tradition. Film alters this hierarchy, favoring experiential understanding over explanation. Whether such domains of knowledge eclipse one another depends partly upon the medium, but also upon the maker's priorities within the work. Differences between eidetic and cognitive categories, for example, can perhaps be conveyed in a film simultaneously, but the differences between an explanatory and an experiential grasp of a social phenomenon may be irreconcilable, at least within current conventions. Contrary to scholarly assumptions, additional contextual information may destroy rather than enhance understanding. A familiar example is the spoken commentary that interposes itself between viewer and subject. The use of film in anthropology thus produces certain disjunctions with accepted views of anthropological discourse. A film is in some respects closer to music, theater, and ritual than to anthropological writing, which stresses distance and cross-referencing. Like ritual, its meaning is both propositional and performative (to use Bloch's terms). This has implications for educational uses of ethnographic film (which tend to ignore film's performative aspect) and for self-reflexivity. However, this issue is not entirely absent from anthropological writing. As Peter Loizos notes:

> Clearly, our understanding of an ethnographic text might be enhanced if we knew more about both the social profiles of the key informants, how they related to each other and to the ethnographer. However, to write in such a way that every statement was keyed to a particular informant, and the dynamics of relations between the main informants were plotted throughout the period of fieldwork, would result in a pre-ethnographic volume, the book you have to read before you read the main text, something like the "key" to *Finnegan's Wake*. (1992: 181)

Ethnographic films have adopted a variety of documentary forms, ranging from didactic to observational to interview-based. At the same time, ethnographic film has played an important part in the development of documentary, an influence that has often gone unrecognized. In considering the future of visual anthropology, we may wonder what aspects of cinema will fit the current interests of anthropology, and what potentialities of cinema may encourage new anthropological interests. Reservations have been expressed about the role of some documentary forms in visual anthropology (Banks 1994; MacDougall 1975). However, documentary has all too often been dismissed as though it were a single hegemonic form. In fact, documentary consists of diverse and evolving styles which may answer to different purposes in anthropology. It was in documentary that many of the issues of representation and self-reflexivity that now concern anthropology were first raised. Like writing, the cinema has a history. To consider cinema culture irrelevant to visual anthropology is like considering literature irrelevant to anthropological writing, at the very time when the writing of anthropology has become a matter of intense interest.

## Thinking the Visual

Current debates about the writing of anthropology are not merely about the place of the author and the subject in the text but also about the place of the reader. Ethnography that leaves no space for the reader assumes the transparency of language and disregards the contingency of reading. But the irony here is that this consideration must be transformed back into the necessity of *reading the author* in the text. Marilyn Strathern summarizes one aspect of this shift:

> For some while now it has become widely accepted that the fieldworker must be written back into the text as also its author and reproduce the conditions of his or her encounter with the other. Reflexive anthropology sees the resultant production as a dialogue between anthropologist and an informant, so called: the observer/observed relationship can no longer be assimilated to that between subject and object. (1987: 264)

But how does this new relationship reflect back upon the reader? How does one read the author's "conditions of his or her encounter with the other"? Is it a matter of providing a description, a key, or a set of clues? And how well is the author placed to provide this? Is the encounter to be understood simply in terms of subject and object, or in some other framework? Elsewhere, Strathern suggests an answer:

> As I understand at least one strand of the new position, the "self" in (self-) reflexivity *is not a person*. It is an artefact—the ethnography. The questions that [James] Clifford and others pose are about the making of the artefact; "voice" is a metaphor not for the individual subject (the ethnographer) but for how what is

spoken sounds and is heard (the ethnography) or how what is made apparent is to be seen. If one attends to the author it is because there is more to the production of artefacts such as ethnographic texts than the illusion of the transparent writer allows. (1989: 565–66)

If it was once an attendance to the author *as person* that was emphasized, that emphasis has now shifted to the very flesh of the work. In the 1960s and 1970s it seemed essential to some ethnographic filmmakers and anthropologists to make films that self-consciously demonstrated the presence of the filmmaker. Many of these films were explicitly about epistemology and included such works as *Chronique d'un été* (1961), *The Wedding Camels* (1977), and *The Ax Fight* (1975). They asked the question: What, in these circumstances, is it possible to know? But these films had already been preceded by films that were implicitly reflexive, including many of Rouch's more personal films, such as *Jaguar* and *La Chasse au lion à l'arc* (1965), in which his presence was always felt.

The major shifts in documentary style and technology that took place at the beginning of the 1960s were themselves expressions of an attempt to resituate the author in relation to the audience. Seen from today's perspective, and from disquiet with the objectifying gaze of observational film style (MacDougall 1975; Nichols 1981; Ruby 1977), it is easy to miss the point that both the observational and participatory approaches were part of the same effort to move documentary away from its earlier anonymity toward a more personal and authored cinema. The aim was to create a documentary cinema embodying the perspectives of actual observers, even if these observers were not seen—in contrast to the disembodied observation of a documentary style based upon the *découpage classique* of Hollywood cinema (as in the Griersonian tradition, for example). This philosophical aim expressed itself in a radical revision of filming and editing techniques. In place of a camera that resembled an omnscient, floating eye which could at any moment be anywhere in a room (with a close-up, an over-the-shoulder shot, a reverse angle), there was to be a camera clearly tied to the person of an individual filmmaker. Instead of an editing style that re-created spaces out of fragments, collapsed time, and simulated the points of view of the subjects, there was to be an editing style favoring sequence-shots and camera movements representing the eye behind the viewfinder.

To many of us making films in this period, it was important to assert—polemically and emblematically—the presence of the filmmaker: to remind audiences that a film was a human product and not a transparent window on reality. It was important to break the taboo of filmic anonymity by including scenes of people reacting to the camera (previously forbidden to documentary) and acknowledging the film as an encounter between the filmmaker and the subject. This aim, however, was not the final objective; it was rather to permit a more contingent and historicized basis of social and cultural description. Furthermore, many films of "direct cinema," while rejecting the shooting and editing styles of Hollywood, were attracted to its narrative strategies (e.g. *Salesman* [1969]), thus creating a paradoxical relationship with the fiction film. This came about partly as a result of the reaction against the insistently didactic and expository structures of earlier documentaries, which derived from journalism, education, and propaganda (as in *The March of Time* films with their "voice of God" narration). Documentary looked for new models and found them in Italian Neorealism. These films showed how it might be possible to make films about actual people that conveyed a sense of their lived experience. But this form demanded a shift in the engagement of the audience from reliance upon spoken commentary to a more independent and active form of involvement. Transferred to ethnographic film (with the use of subtitles) these principles promised a new way of approaching other cultures.

In fact, films following this model were rare: most adopted some expository devices such as interviews, or collage-like constructions inspired by *cinéma vérité* and the genre-mixing of fiction filmmakers such as Godard, Makavejev, and Glauber Rocha. Consciously participatory films (*Waiting for Harry* [1980] and *Celso and Cora* [1983], for example) soon demanded more from themselves and their audiences than the simple recognition of a filmmaking encounter: they evolved into complex interactions between filmmaker and subject. But many films tended to turn self-reflexive references into an empty formula, or what Strathern (citing Paul A. Roth) calls "stylised self-reflection no more guaranteeing authenticity than a pose of detachment" (1989: 565). It was obvious that this sort of emblematic reflexivity had outlived its usefulness.

Reflexivity in fact involves putting representaton into perspective as we *practice* it. A second and more considered view of reflexivity has sometimes conceived of it as contextual *information*. In Ruby's paper of 1975 he characterized it as "an explicit description of the methodology used to collect, to analyze and to organize the data for presentation" (p. 107). He added: "It may not be particularly important *where* the methodology is revealed—within the film itself . . . or in a published article. . . . What is important is the absolute scientific necessity for making methods public" (p. 109). Armed with this information, the viewer would then be able to judge the validity of the film's conclusions.

But what form might this kind of reflexivity take? Perhaps ideally another film showing the film being made; but more realistically it might include information on language competence, length of fieldwork, filming techniques, and so on. It could of course say little about intelligence, perspicacity, originality of thought, or empathy—all this would have to be determined in other ways. In 1980 Ruby stated that "being reflexive means that the producer deliberately, intentionally reveals to his audience the underlying epistemological assumptions which caused him to formulate a set of questions in a particular way, to seek answers to those questions in a particular way, and finally to present his findings in a particular way" (p. 157). But although such a disclosure can certainly be attempted, scientific inquiry tends to move in less clinical ways, and the most fundamental epistemological assumptions of any age are internalized as scientific ideology rather than being fully conscious. Recently, Ruby has widened the agenda of reflexivity, at least for documentary filmmakers: "As the acknowledged author of a film, the documentarian assumes responsibility for whatever meaning exists in the image, and therefore is obligated to discover ways to make people aware of point of view, ideology, author biography, and anything else deemed relevant to an understanding of the film" (1991: 53). This is a tall order, and perhaps an arrogant one, for whatever meaning exists in the image (if meaning can be said to be *in* the image) will vary widely for different viewers. The information required to ensure "nonaberrant" readings would seem to be potentially unlimited.

Such an approach to the problem of interpretation constitutes what might be called an *external reflexivity*. However, the objections to defining reflexivity in this way (as information) are two: (1) that it does not go far enough, and (2) that it attempts to erect reflexivity as a structure exterior to the work. That is to say, it proposes a frame of reference within which we are to assess the work (whether this is given in the work itself or provided separately). This metacommunication becomes the new standard, the new (and real) point of reference for scientific truth, displacing the work itself. Because it frames the frame, so to speak, it is considered to be more accurate, more valid, more scientific. It gives us an interpretation of known bias. This implies an ultimately achievable "correct" interpretation and a way of restoring to representation its scientific objectivity. Thus, in the guise of insisting on the mediated nature of film, it actually maintains the ideology and mechanisms of nineteenth-century positivism intact: object separate from subject, body separate from mind, work separate from reader. In effect, it perpetuates what Strathern has called "the illusion of the transparent writer" by believing that the writer can eventually be *made* transparent.

This sentiment is comprehensible as a response of some anthropologists to the so-called "crisis of representation," but it seems largely defensive of scientific orthodoxy and not to grasp the fundamental insights of recent thinking about textuality. It assumes a privileged level of discourse outside the work. It sets out to cleanse the film of its contingency. It implicitly treats films as good or bad copies of reality rather than interpretive works. The problem with external reflexivity is not that it is useless but that by presenting itself as prior rather than secondary to the work it becomes a kind of philosophical *non sequitur*. Followed to its conclusion, it is undermined by what it fails to take into account: the implication of the author in the work.

It is therefore necessary for visual anthropology to take reflexivity to a further stage—to see it at a deeper and more integral level. The author is no longer to be sought outside the work, for the work must be understood as including the author. Subject and object define one another through the work, and the "author" is in fact in many ways an artifact of the work. As James Clifford observes, "It has become clear that every version of the 'other,' wherever found, is also the construction of a 'self,' and the making of ethnographic texts . . . has always involved a process of 'self-fashioning' (Greenblatt 1980)" (1986: 23–24). The author's relation to the subject therefore cannot be seen in ideal terms independent of the text, nor independent of a reading of the text. Just as the subject is not innocent of the author, neither is the author innocent of the reader.

A concept of "deep" reflexivity requires us to read the position of the author in the very construction of the work, whatever the external explanations may be. One reason for this is that the author's position is neither uniform nor fixed, and expresses itself through a multileveled and constantly evolving relation with the subject. The fieldworker often works in a way that is exploratory and intuitive. This is a dynamic process affecting various aspects of the work unevenly. Indeed, it can be said that for the anthropologist the process of producing a work of anthropology lies very much in progressively *discovering* what this relation is. The difference between observer and observed, self and other, is by no means always clear, because each of us as a social actor shares in a shifting sense of identity with others. The anthropologist is constantly feeling out his or her position, experiencing differences in levels of understanding, as well as the shifts of mood and rapport characteristic of fieldwork.[11]

One of the difficulties involved in placing much confidence in external reflexivity is that the author is poorly placed to define the terms in which the work should be read. The things that matter most are likely to be those in which the author is most deeply implicated. To the perceiving mind, the conditions of its perception are often invisible. Such things are more often embedded than consciously articulated, and if Bourdieu and Passeron are right that explanations usually imply a protective *mis*construing of the situation, a description of methods and assumptions must in principle be viewed with suspicion. To accept the author's description of his or her relationship to the subject is a little like placing a review of police procedures in the hands of the police. If we accept it, we may be less likely to look at it critically ourselves. We need to read it in the work itself. To the extent that a filmmaker is examining a subject from a particular perspective (it is more often ambiguous), the nature of that perspective will only be accurately encoded in the materials of the film. Whatever secondary insights the filmmaker can provide must come after the event in a separate process of reflection.

The "self" in contemporary anthropologists' self-reflexivity derives from their consciousness of inscription. As Strathern observes, the modernist anthropologist explains, while the postmodern anthropologist "leaves that work to the reader" (1987: 266). But far from being an obstacle, this is the characteristic approach of filmmakers. They are involved in an *embodied* analysis of the world that reveals itself in objects, framings, movements, and nuances of detail. It appears in what Fredric Jameson calls the "signatures" of the visible. Its meanings are "written" in a complex and often intuitive interchange with the subject—in form, choice of imagery, and visual style. The film articulates particular qualities of engagement—an intellectual and social engagement, but also a set of organizing emotions. Conversely, it is this engagement with the world that stimulates the eye and mind behind the camera to see in distinctive ways. The presence of the filmmaker may be grasped through very small responses and details—sometimes merely in the static proximity of the camera.

It is the intention that the work be "read" on this level of meaning and subtlety that constitutes its deeper reflexivity. It need not proclaim itself in explicit interventions, nor does the absence of these necessarily imply that the author intends the work to be read as unmediated, objective reality. Ethnographic films no longer require the ritualized reminders that they are constructions. An author's personal reticence may in fact show trust in the audience's recognition of this fact, or be eloquent of a particular spirit of attentiveness to the subject. Reflexivity at this level is also densely textured. It combines intellect and feeling in a way that cannot be translated or summarized in other terms. If many ethnographic films fail to provide such reflexivity, it is in part because doctrines of scientific objectivity have led to an erasure of the filmmaker from the film.

Distrust of the visual—its potential to arouse dangerous feelings, to lead to misunderstandings or reinforce prejudices—has tended to place upon visual anthropologists an impossible burden. Good films contextualize internally; that is, they attempt to create a world in which misreadings are less appropriate. A film that consistently reinforces prejudices has often failed to create a sufficiently complex encounter with its subjects. Certainly films, like other works, must anticipate a range of audiences. But films cannot second-guess all prejudices or eventualities. Nor should they be obliged to jeopardize or compromise their approach to accommodate insensitive viewers. This is not irresponsibility, or art for art's sake, or neglect of the audience; on the contrary, it is a matter of respect for the audience and for the subject. Self-reflexivity, if it takes the form of a cumbersome structure of explanation, may be completely at odds with the narrative or emotional logic of a work. It may act to block precisely those forms of understanding that visual anthropology makes possible.

There is one further factor that has dramatically altered the forms of address of both anthropology and visual anthropology. Perhaps never again can anthropologists use the external self-reflexive mode as they once did, for this self-reflexive "voice" was always implicitly directed toward their anthropological colleagues, invoking a set of very private interests. The world has now changed, and one's first audience is as likely as not to be the subjects themselves. As Strathern observes,

> over the last 20 years, certain apparent dichotomies between writer, audience, and subject have folded in on themselves. If anthropologists write now about 'other peoples,' they are writing for subjects who have become an audience. In describing Melanesian marriage ceremonies, I must bear my Melanesian readers in mind. That in turn makes problematic the previously established distinction between writer and subject: I must know on whose behalf and to what end I write. (1987: 269)

In the eyes of *my* subjects, my film will not be judged by how it makes the obvious points. They will set a much higher standard. I must go beyond what is implicit between us. I shall not be able to speak as the expert, nor shall I feel comfortable about belaboring the elementary things we both already know. My work will be judged by its good faith toward them and its understanding of their perceptions of the world, without pretending to be their view of it. I shall want to *begin* at the point of our common knowledge and speak of the things we both value, if possible with a comprehension that earns their respect. If they disagree with me, or if I go on too long about things that don't interest them, I shall hope they at least acknowledge my right to have those interests. If I am self-reflexive, that self-reflexivity must be about the relationship between us, not a way of speaking behind my hand to some foreign audience. But if I have done my job well, that need may be irrelevant. Those things will already be in the film.

[1995]

## Notes

A version of this paper was first prepared for the 1995 School of American Research advanced seminar "Visual Anthropology at the Crossroads." I am grateful to the seminar participants for their comments and to Leslie Devereaux, Ian Keen, and Gary Kildea for their comments on an earlier draft.

1. From his introduction to *Reinventing Anthropology* (Hymes 1972: 45).
2. From his speech, "The Centenary of Photography," at the Sorbonne on January 7, 1939 (Valéry 1970).
3. See Geertz's discussion of this in *Works and Lives* (1988: 49–72).
4. See, for example, Kenneth Read's *The High Valley* (1966), Jean L. Briggs's *Never in Anger* (1970), and Anna Grimshaw's *Servants of the Buddha* (1992).
5. See, for example, Berry & Sommerlad (n.d.), Hearn & DeVore (1973), and Martinez (1990).

6. From *Rethinking Anthropology* (Leach 1961: 26–27).

7. Films do, of course, contain words in spoken and written form, and film images may even have some quasi-lexical properties when they are used, as in Eisensteinian montage, in highly simplified and symbolic ways. However, even in this case, the lexical properties hardly define or exhaust the effects of the images.

8. See, for example, Lacan (1977), Ekman, Friesen & Ellsworth (1972), Gombrich (1972), and Kertesz (1979).

9. Personal communication, 1995.

10. In this regard, see Gombrich (1960: 330–58) on the strategy of elisions of the early cartoonist Töpffer.

11. See, for example, David Maybury-Lewis's *Akwe-Shavante Society* (1967); and Stanley Brandes's perceptive account of how the fieldworker's position fluctuates (1992).

# CHAPTER THREE

# The Subjective Voice in Ethnographic Film

## The Problem of People

THROUGHOUT THIS century we have seen both anthropologists and critics periodically shift their attention between the competing claims of analytical and experiential knowledge. With written works this has often meant choosing between situating oneself outside the work as an interpreter or inside it as a reader. In anthropology it has meant seeing human cultures either from the viewpoint of the disinterested social scientist or the indigenous social actor. Anthropologists have taken to heart, sometimes concurrently, Malinowski's famous injunction to "grasp the native's point of view, his relation to life, to realize *his* vision of *his* world" (1922: 25) and Lévi-Strauss's dictum, "Anthropology is the science of culture as seen from the outside" (1966: 126).

It is generally acknowledged that these perspectives are interdependent. We are taught that observation should precede analysis, that before one can interpret one must read. But critical theory and anthropology have often run aground on the problem of reconciling the analytical with the experiential. The predicament of the critic has been put succinctly by Bill Nichols, with regard to film criticism, in the paradox: "If I am to analyze this film properly, I must not mistake it for reality; but if I do not mistake it for reality, I cannot analyze it properly" (1981: 250). For the anthropologist the paradox might go, "If I am to understand this socio-cultural system properly, I must not adopt the indigenous view; but if I do not adopt the indigenous view I cannot understand it properly."

In recent decades there has been a growing conviction that analytical and experiential perspectives are neither opposed nor hierarchical—that is, that experience is not just the messy prerequisite for knowledge. Rather, the two are complementary and of comparable importance. Nor should the experiential be viewed merely as uncritical emotion, detached from intellectual experience. Finally, as counterpoised responses to the same historical phenomena, the two perspectives should be capable of reconciliation within a broader framework of knowledge. In the social sciences hermeneutic, narrative, autobiographical, multivocal, and descriptive methods now share the field with schematic analysis of a more traditional kind, and interpreters of written and other texts have attempted to enlarge structural and semiotic approaches with more subjective and socially contingent readings. The same insight that first applied a linguistic analogy to social patterns in terms of *langue* has now seemingly turned its attention to *parole*.

This view appears to transcend alternations of academic fashion, where one tendency often seems to be simply the temporary corrective of another. I think this is because the focus has shifted to the problem of representation itself. In a sense, for the first time since the splintering of philosophy into separate disciplines, there is a current in the direction of a reintegration of knowledge, not by means of grand theory but by borrowings between disciplines and, more broadly, between the arts and the sciences. This process has been described as a blurring of genres (Geertz 1980). I prefer to see it as an effort to heal what are increasingly regarded as ailing genres, flawed by reductionism and ethnocentric thinking. The willingness to borrow, to cut across the grain of human perspectives, has become a way of combating intellectual and moral tunnel-vision. This sometimes creates a kind of vertigo as anthropologists and critics stand on the boundaries of their disciplines. They rightly fear losing their balance, but there is often, as well, a powerful urge to jump.

How to regard the individual and his or her experience has been a perennial and nagging problem in anthropology. At one time anthropologists viewed the experience of individual social actors, like the experience of individual readers of a text, as a suggestive but finally unreliable indicator of collective experience—although in practice the reliance they sometimes placed upon a few informants dangerously compromised this view. Life histories gathered in fieldwork became part of the anthropological data, to be merged together for general conclusions and occasionally drawn upon for vivid examples. These histories were valued for the irreducible proofs they contained, and for the larger proof that a living subject actually underpinned the more abstract concerns of anthropology. Yet there was always an interest in subjective experience for its own sake, an interest that went beyond the mapping of a culture or the legitimation of the discipline. Anthropologists clearly desired, and often tried, to describe the special "feel" of living in another society, the distinctive world view of its inhabitants, a view delimited by language, physical setting, and the horizons of acceptable behavior.

The problem was that such descriptions of the subjective world of individuals also tended toward the composite, and eventually toward the comparison and classification of composites (as in Ruth Benedict's *Patterns of Culture* of 1934) in which the experiences of any actual person were useful only as illustration. In classical ethnographies the descriptions take the form: "Posos believe . . . " or, "If you are a Poso, you. . . ." Anthropological interest in subjective experience was thus channeled into holistic thinking that, crucially, promoted the reified notion of a single ethnographic reality, just as descriptions of social structure did. One odd hallmark of positivist social science has thus been its deep faith in a mystical object—a shared social experience that exists outside history and beyond the individual. In such an anthropology the individuality of the subject is preempted by the anthropologist's own individuality, a consciousness at one remove, to be shared with an individual still further removed, the reader.

Today, by contrast, the experiences of individual social actors are seen increasingly as vantage points within a society which, in the complex dynamics of their engagement, structure particular "readings" of social phenomena. The portrayal of subjective experience becomes a strategy for resituating anthropological understanding within the multidimensional richness of a society. The goal is not simply to present the "indigenous view," nor to invade voyeuristically the consciousness of other individuals, but to see social behavior, and indeed culture, as a continuous process of interpretation and re-invention.

What might be called the "problem of the person" in anthropology echoes a similar concern in documentary film. In Bill Nichols's view, "a central question posed by documentary is what to do with people" (1981: 231)—actual, living people as distinct from the imaginary people of fiction. Elsewhere he poses this question in somewhat different terms, as a question of magnitude. The documentary film gives us images that are indexically linked to people who have lived; however, as in all cinema (like all ethnography) the people themselves are absent. Documentary is thus faced with the problem of "a body too few," the missing body, which must be reconstituted by the film. What relation does this figure bear, Nichols asks, to the historical person? How can the filmmaker hope to create a representation commensurate with the magnitude of what it describes? (Nichols 1986). Or, we might ask, how can any representation approximate the self that every self knows itself to be?

Both documentary and anthropology are faced with this problem, and perhaps also with a false issue. Full access to another consciousness cannot be achieved, and let us hope never will be. But the attempt need not necessarily be viewed as either futile or reprehensible. Such an objective can still be approached and in that approach produce what Dai Vaughan has called an "unconsummated" understanding (Vaughan 1976: 26). Representing the subjectivity of the historical person is a very different matter from attributing subjectivity to a fictional character. Some may choose to leave the evocation of subjectivity to the domain of imaginary art. Alternatively, one may try to incorporate in documentary and anthropology, first, the codes for communicating subjective experience used in everyday life and, second, the narrative systems that resituate the "reader" in circumstances different from his or her own. Documentary representation may finally produce a fiction, but (in Nichols's phrase) it is a fiction unlike any other (1991: xv, 105–98).

Ethnographic film, as a form of documentary, has often been regarded by cinéastes as obscure and by anthropologists, at least until recently, as lacking intellectual substance—at best, a side-line of anthropology, or an area of failed promise (MacDougall 1978; Marcus 1990). Occupying this marginal position, it seems also to have aroused deep suspicions—on the one hand, of extending anthropology's indecent appropriation of the voices of colonized peoples, on the other of making anthropological claims that it, or its practitioners, have no intention of fulfilling. Of the explanations offered for this second view, one of the most common is that ethnographic filmmakers lack the methodological rigor and scientific perspective of anthropologists (Rollwagen 1988; Ruby 1975). But I think more probably ethnographic film provokes such responses because its ambiguous intimacy with its subject sharpens and brings to the fore the anthropological problem of the person, exposing to view a contradiction that anthropological writing can more easily elide: that although the raw unit of anthropological study remains the individual, the individual must be left by the wayside on the road to the general principle. Yet this individual is the troublesome hitch-hiker whom ethnographic filmmakers always seem to pick up and who is sometimes felt to claim altogether too much of their attention.

If this issue can be addressed more fully, I foresee the problems of documentary in dealing with the historical person, and those of anthropology in dealing with the individual social actor, converging to make the ethnographic film a focus of more serious interest and investigation. This in turn may offer a more precise role for film in anthropology and more intellectually productive directions for ethnographic film itself.

## An Interior State

The value of the subjective voice, in anthropology and in the documentary film, is that it can give access to the crossing of different frames of reference in society—to what otherwise is contradictory, ambiguous, and paradoxical. One can plot these intersections objectively, but it is arguable that one can only understand them experientially. As Nichols notes, the social forces that result in contradictions, and that in society may eventually work themselves out historically, can be resolved in a film (and perhaps also in an anthropological text) through narrative strategies that allow us to experience them (1986: 110–11). Building upon Bateson's and Lévi-Strauss's ideas, he has shown how fictional narratives are generated out of double binds (1981: 96–100). In fact, these situations of irreconcilable imperatives, which in life and fiction produce aberrant behavior—like catatonia, or putting your own eyes out—resemble those moments in intellectual life when the crossing of different disciplinary perspectives produces anger and bizarre behavior among righteous academics.

The fiction film creates a multileveled web in which its characters are contained and seen to struggle. The documentary film attempts to contain the historical person through a parallel set of strategies, but importantly also by allowing us to glimpse the ultimate failure of those strategies—by creating, as Nichols puts it, "the subjective experience of excess, the discovery . . . of a magnitude of existence beyond containment" (1981: 111). It thus perversely denies what it offers. This effect is partly produced by the recognized gulf between film images and their profilmic antecedents, but it is also achieved through evocative and ironic tactics that put the historical person in a dimension beyond that attainable by the film. Thus is extended to the spectator an experience not unlike that of the characters of fiction, who suffer the consequences of a paradox even if they do not understand it.

Anthropologists become aware of a similar disjunction when reducing their fieldwork experiences to writing, and they may take lateral action to resolve it by writing outside the discipline (Lévi-Strauss 1974; Turnbull 1973). Recent experimental ethnographies include the formal signalling of experience exceeding containment, but so do even many classical ethnographies. Writing of animal sacrifice among the Nuer, Evans-Pritchard says that it dramatizes a spiritual experience, but "what this experience is the anthropologist cannot for certain say. . . . Though prayer and sacrifice are exterior actions, Nuer religion is ultimately an interior state" (1956).

The ethnographic film, even as it aspires to the portrayal of the subjective, must make a similar disclaimer. The subjective voice is always mediated and fragmentary, however much it appears to be the independent voice of another person. In a strict sense, the only subjectivity in film-viewing is that of the spectator, the only subjective voice that of the filmmaker. Subjectivity is thus both a product of the work and a quality we assign to the work, always subject to revision and "rereading."

In what follows I shall be concerned with the subjective voice as part of the construction of the subject, rather than the voice of the filmmaker. I shall hope to show how certain ethnographic films from a primarily Euro-American practice have attempted to give insight into the lived experiences of people in other cultures and suggest the range of strategies that have been used for situating the viewer in different relations to filmic depiction and discourse. I do not propose here to judge the validity of particular interpretations, and in any case such judgments suggest a simple relation between sign (film) and signified (society) which in fact may be complex. Films intend certain "readings" on the basis of prevailing cultural codes, and within a certain range one can say there are correct readings and misreadings. But it is an error, I think, to apply communications theory too literally to films by looking upon them as messages. A film is not ephemeral like a telephone call but remains to be reused and re-viewed. It is perhaps less like a message than like a cultural artifact such as a table or chair, and like them it retains the grain of the materials from which it was made.

I shall be primarily concerned with specific efforts to portray subjective experience across cultural boundaries, rather than the varied forms of cultural expression found in national cinema styles, minority and alternative filmmaking, and indigenous media production—although clearly, practioners in these areas are increasingly addressing multiple audiences. Finally, I define ethnographic film here, as elsewhere (MacDougall 1981), as a broader cultural category than films made within, and for, the discipline of anthropology. Anthropologists had a hand in some of the films, but most are addressed to a wider public audience, although few have actually come from the mainstream of industrial cinema or television.

## Frames of Reference

The subjective voice in films, as in literature, is often associated with first-person discourse or its double, the central character around whom the action develops. However, subjectivity in films is not simply a matter of identifying a speaker or seer. And although the modes of narration in literature and film sometimes run parallel, there are significant differences. It is not that film lacks a pronominal code, but that the pronouns are often implicit or unstable. A film can involve the subjectivities of its subjects, the viewer, and the institutional or individual filmmaker in compound ways. From a textual point of view, each of these perspectives can become an "I," from which the other two are redefined as "you" or "they," just as kinship terms are dependent upon who is speaking. The perspective can oscillate between two or more focuses, or assimilate both, as when we begin to associate our viewpoint in the film with a first-person speaker who has previously occupied a third-person category. This is the kind of shifting that occurs in Conrad's layering of speakers but that in film occurs in much less clearly marked ways.

Critics such as Nick Browne (1975) have shown that the conventions of filming and editing do not simply direct us to different visual points of view in a film but orchestrate a set of overlapping codes of position, narrative, metaphor, and moral attitude. Subjectivity is therefore not merely a function of visual perspective. We are, in Browne's terms, "spectators-in-the-text." Our "reading" of a film, and our feelings about it, are at every moment the result of how we experience the complex fields this orchestration creates—largely dependent upon who we are and what we bring to the film. This complexity extends to our relation to different modes of cinematic address.

One can get a sense of this in even quite early films in which cinematic rhetoric was still relatively undeveloped. *Living Hawthorn*, made in 1906, addresses the viewer from a variety of stances, and unintentionally provides an example of the transformation of the descriptive into the subjective. The subjective effect is fleeting and depends not upon the filmmakers' narrative agency but upon a form of direct address that was soon to be largely excluded from the cinema.

The film was made in Australia by William Alfred Gibson and Millard Johnson as a quick money-spinner. They would come to a town, film as many people as possible, develop and print the film overnight, and then hire a hall the next day and charge people admission to come and see themselves. *Living Hawthorn* runs only about fifteen minutes but in that time manages to include shots of the streets from a moving vehicle, a range of factory and shop fronts with their workers, a civic ceremony with a marching band, the arrival of the mayor in a motor car, and scenes inside the municipal swimming baths. In doing all this it employs a variety of strategies. Mounting a camera on a moving vehicle was a trick known at the time to produce excitement. Some of the events are clearly directed for the film, as in the appearance of the mayor, or when the workers come filing out of their workplaces carrying the tools and products of their trades. At the civic ceremony the filmmakers are given a privileged vantage point. The final scenes in the municipal pool, on a men's bathing day in an era of strictly segregated bathing, give the film a touch of the sensational and play a parting trick on the townspeople of Hawthorn.

However, a number of street scenes in the film are shot in a more observational style and seem intended to give a sense of ordinary life as it is lived. This aim is often compromised by the tremendous public interest in the presence of the camera. Children jump and dance in front of it, wobble past on bicycles, push each other, and throw their hats in the air. In these brief moments the coolly disengaged stance of the camera—firmly established by this time in urban street photography—is violated. As people look into the lens, the viewer suddenly has the sense of being looked at, and looked at in this case with apparent delight. Forget that this is not so, that the people looking so directly at the camera are not seeing us; there is nevertheless the momentary sensation even today of communion with people over ninety years ago [Figure 6.]

6. The look into the camera. From *Living Hawthorn* (1906).

The glance into the camera evokes one of the primal experiences of daily life—of look returned by look—through which we signal mutual recognition and affirm the shared experience of the moment. It is the look of exchange that says, "At this moment, we see ourselves through one another." The encounter produces a phatic reversal of roles, in which the viewer seems to be regarding himself or herself with the eyes of the other. In a Lacanian sense, the self is reaffirmed and mirrored in these comparatively rare direct glances from the screen. In *Living Hawthorn* they have the effect of situating the audience in a psychological relation to the people on the screen. They also make clear that in films the usual narrative devices for creating identification with people need not always be present.

Subjective identification in ethnographic films occurs in both their narrative and nonnarrative forms. In character-centered films, as in the character-narration of Hollywood, it can result from the imperatives of dramatic structure. This may require little more than a person wanting something, with obstacles placed in the way. Hitchcock tells us that if in a film a person is seen searching somebody's room as the owner comes up the stairs, "the public feels like warning him. 'Be careful, watch out. Someone's coming up the stairs.' . . . Even if the snooper is not a likable character, the audience will still feel anxiety for him" (Truffaut 1967: 51). A weak level of subjectivity could therefore be expected to arise from many comparable situations—from hunting scenes, for example, as Robert Flaherty no doubt realized.

On a closer textual level subjective identification with film characters has often been attributed to manipulation of point-of-view, as it was developed in the "classical" Hollywood cinema. This was achieved largely through the technique of shot/countershot, tying the spectator's point of view to that of a character (Branigan 1984; Dayan 1974; Oudart 1969). But although one may share the visual viewpoint of a character, one may identify more strongly with another, sometimes even with the person who is the object of the first character's gaze (Browne 1975: 33). Nor are we usually asked to see from the literal perspective of a character but rather from a position in fictive space allied to theirs, as if we were looking over their shoulder. This implies that subjective identification too is more a matter of alliance than union: our emotional perspective requires a similar displacement. In ethnographic films this is subject to a further cultural displacement, which in the more successful examples lies somewhere between exoticism on the one hand and an all-embracing humanist leveling on the other.

These conventions have implications for documentary that are largely irrelevant for fiction. Although our access to fictional characters is limited, how much more limited must be our access to the mind and body of an historical person? Further, our relation as spectators to the narrative agency of documentary is more complex than in fiction. Rather than dealing with products of the imagination, we are dealing with real human beings encountering a filmmaker who coexists with them historically. The question of the filmmaker's agency in representing them is thus implicitly pushed into the arena of the film. We are faced with a double task of interpretation. We interpret the perplexing exteriors of social actors in some ways as we interpret people in daily life, but we also perceive them through the narrative apparatus that the filmmaker has erected for us. On this epistemological level, at least, documentary confronts us with more complex forms than we are asked to deal with in fiction.

The different guises of subjectivity result from the different possible ways of combining three cinematic modes that I shall here call *narration* (including actual narrative story-telling, but also description), *address* (which may be direct or indirect), and *perspective* (which may focus on testimony, implication, or exposition). These variants could be said to occupy separate regions of potential within a notional triangle formed by the subject, the viewer, and the filmmaker.

Film technology has had a direct bearing on these choices. In the silent era titles provided the only medium for direct address by the filmmaker and the only medium for actors' dialogue. Titles were used sparingly for a variety of reasons: because of the illiteracy of audiences, because reading too many titles proved wearisome, and because translating them made international versions more difficult to produce. If the technology had existed to superimpose titles rather than intersperse them, silent films might well have evolved differently. As it was, dialogue and direct address were minimized and the emphasis was upon observation and enactment. With the coming of sound this emphasis was reversed. Commentary suddenly became almost continuous in the documentary and spoken dialogue took over the fiction film to such an extent that the art of cinema was widely thought to have perished. One consequence of this history is that the subjective voice, with but few exceptions, was first developed visually, then later in commentary, and later still in synchronous dialogue.

The modes of *perspective* in film are sometimes difficult to disentangle because in narrative they need not conform to literal point of view, and in description they can be confused with the filmmaker's first-person role as the source of the film's narration. Thus perspective is not a function of who is seeing or speaking but rather an indicator of a primary locus of expression. It can be most usefully understood as an emphasis placed variously upon first-person *testimony,* second-person *implication,* and third-person *exposition.* In this sense it is not inherent, but *assigned.* It represents the filmmaker's direction to the viewer to grasp the primary perspective of the narration. Does it lie in someone addressing the camera directly (the "I" of direct address testimony)? Does it lie in the viewer being drawn into the film experientially, through such devices as shot/countershot (the "you" of implication)? Or does it lie in the activities of others studied from a certain distance (the "they" of exposition)? The varieties of perspective can be further delineated by how each communicates the subjective voice:

> *Testimony*, the first-person perspective, approaches subjectivity through the self-expression of the film subjects. It is found in films (or sequences) in which the primary source of experiential information is communicated to us by those who have had the experiences. Although it sometimes occurs in spontaneous dialogue, it is typically the mode of interior monologue, confession, and interview.
>
> *Implication* is the mode that involves the viewer in the processes of lived experience. It is the method of much fictional narrative, and of "classical" Hollywood film editing. It creates identification by allying the viewer to the perspectives of specific social actors, saying in effect, "You also are experiencing this."
>
> *Exposition* is the mode of third-person narration, by a third person displaying and explaining the behavior of other third persons. It gives access to states of mind and feeling by describing them or demonstrating their exterior signs. It is a mode that tends to create empathy rather than close identification—that is, it circumvents the subjective experience of interiority. However, it can situate social actors quite powerfully in a social or narrative sense so that we ask ourselves how we would feel or behave in their place.

## Approaches to Subjectivity

The portrayal of subjectivity in ethnographic film can perhaps be examined best through films that introduced or significantly developed distinctive approaches. Although there is a rough chronology to the examples that follow, it does not necessarily imply direct links between them but more often a common link to larger trends outside ethnographic film in the intellectual and methodological history of documentary. Ethnographic filmmaking has developed no major schools or genres of its own, and a particular approach is sometimes represented by the work of only one or two filmmakers.

Very early in its history the cinema bifurcated in two ways: into narrative and descriptive channels, on the one hand, and into fiction and nonfiction on the other. Narrative did not necessarily have to be fictional, any more than it does today. For example, the earliest narratives included a fiction film of a child stepping on the gardener's hose, then releasing the flow to squirt him in the face (*L'Arroseur arrosé* [1895], or in English, *Watering the Gardener*) and a nonfiction film, *Le Déjeuner de Bébé* (1895). The earliest ethnographic films (and chronophotographs), such as those of Félix-Louis Regnault, A. C. Haddon, and Walter Baldwin Spencer, tended to follow the descriptive and nonfictional modes, recording formalized events such as ritual dances and the techniques of pottery-making and fire-making. There was little room here for expressing subjectivity, and it would generally have been considered beside the point. Yet one often senses a gloomy forbearance on the part of the subjects as they perform what the filmmakers seem to have demanded of them. Scenes such as these were increasingly presented as spontaneous performances, making them a kind of documentary fiction.

After 1910 a few films about non-European societies appeared that suggested a dawning of interest in an indigenous point of view. These were modeled roughly on fiction films, which by now dominated the commercial film industry. The best known today is perhaps Edward S. Curtis's *In the Land of the Head-Hunters* (1914), a love-story filmed among the Kwakiutl of British Columbia. But there was also the missionary film *The Transformed Isle* (1917) filmed in the Solomon Islands between 1907 and 1915, in which narrative sequences of local warfare and European "blackbirding" are staged with considerable panache. At one point the film invites us to adopt the perspective of the islanders, with the title: "Let's go with them and see what they see." Films such as these set the stage for the work of Flaherty and for a long-lasting approach best described as *ethnographic narrative*. These films take various forms, which can be grouped as exterior, interior, and descriptive dramatizations.

### Exterior Dramatization

Among exterior dramatizations Flaherty's *Nanook of the North* (1922) is far and away the most famous. It has been discussed variously for its authenticity, its fakery, its romanticism, and its formal qualities. Flaherty's cinematic approach may have been innocent of many of the narrative devices of point of view that had recently been pioneered by D. W. Griffith, but the film derives considerable subjective effect from its overall framing of a family confronting adversity and its treatment of intimate details of Inuit life. The film is a dramatization in that its structure is composed of scenes that first develop the characters and their antagonist, the arctic environment, and then build through various tests to the climax of a blizzard. To this end, Flaherty carefully staged many sequences with "Nanook" (actually named Allakariallak), based on their shared knowledge of Inuit life.

Flaherty's signal technique was not to enfold the spectator in the actors' visual perspectives but to play upon dramatic tension and curiosity. He involves us in a good deal of waiting for things to happen, just as his subjects wait for things to happen. This third-person observation in long takes, celebrated by André Bazin as an alternative to seamless continuity editing, in fact operates structurally to achieve much the same results as continuity editing. Rather than being unco-opted witnesses of events unfolding in their own time (as for example when Nanook hunts the walrus), we are held as firmly by the dramatic logic of the scene as if we had been invited to identify with Nanook's visual point of view.

Similarly, Flaherty uses a technique of arousing curiosity and then satisfying it—a technique that resembles the shot/countershot pattern of continuity editing. He will, for example, show us an unexplained activity such as cutting a block of ice, only to reveal later that it is to become the window of the igloo. Or, as in his next film, *Moana* (1926), he will show us part of an object, such as a palm tree, before he allows us to identify it in its entirety. By this technique Flaherty implicates us in the process of decoding the film without implicating us in the viewpoint of the subjects themselves. The technique might be thought to distance us from Nanook's world, since Nanook is manifestly always one jump ahead of us in understanding, but the effect is curiously the opposite. As the ice window slides into position, we have a moment of elation at this ingenuity, as though we had thought of it ourselves. We find ourselves placed within the communal resonance of a small but satisfying achievement as though we were present at the event, much as we might join in the satisfaction of changing a tire while actually doing no more than hold the tools. In Flaherty's later work this stance of third-person observation was only occasionally broken, despite the increasing sophistication of the cinematic techniques available to him.

Flaherty's subjective inflections of third-person narration were innovative,

7. Interior dramatization. From *Finis Terrae* (1929).

but in 1922 perhaps the most obvious new departure of *Nanook of the North* (although less obvious today) was its centering of an indigenous person as the hero of a film. *Nanook*, which appeared in the same year as Malinowski's *Argonauts of the Western Pacific*, was not the usual fanciful portrayal of noble savagery. Nanook was neither a fictional super-native, like a James Fenimore Cooper Indian, nor a native prodigy, like Bennelong, to be brought to Europe, dressed fashionably, and admired. By raising an unknown, living person from a so-called primitive society to the status of protagonist, the film confronted cultural stereotypes and suggested the possibility of identification with what was popularly viewed as an alien savage consciousness. Although the image of Nanook soon became a new stereotype, even as Nanook himself was dying of hunger, one can still glimpse in this effort of Robert and Frances Flaherty an early popularization of cultural relativism and an implicit denial of social evolutionary theory.

Since Flaherty, ethnographic filmmakers have developed the various possibilities of exterior dramatization, including further fictionalization, as in Knut Rasmussen's *The Wedding of Palo* (1937); dramatic framing of discrete interactions, as in some of John Marshall's Ju/'hoansi films and his *Three Domestics* (1970); and detailed accounts of the quests of individuals, as in *The Kawelka: Ongka's Big Moka* (1974) and Jean-Pierre Olivier de Sardan's *La Vieille et la pluie* (1974).

### Interior Dramatization

It is interesting to compare Flaherty's work with a film that seems like a precursor of Flaherty's own *Man of Aran* (1934) but in which the dramatization is *primarily* concerned with evoking subjective experience. Today Jean Epstein's *Finis Terrae* (1929) is all but forgotten, but in its time it was highly praised (Abel 1984: 500). Like *Man of Aran* it is a fictionalized documentary, but set on remote islands off Brittany (in the *département* of Finistère) rather than off the Irish coast. Both films use local non-actors and deal with the theme of surviving in a harsh natural environment. But there the differences begin. Epstein's kelp-gatherers are seen as members of a contemporary if remote community rather than as romantic anachronisms, and the film focuses on illness, the dangers of isolation, and the friction of personalities rather than on stoic heroism and idealized social relations. The film is primarily concerned to express the experience of a youth who contracts blood poisoning from a cut on his thumb while working with a companion and two older men on a waterless outer island. This story, by its very plainness and almost casual cruelty, seems meant to make a bourgeois audience aware of people for whom accidents and suffering are not always ameliorated by social institutions or happy endings. [Figure 7.]

Epstein's rough sea is often portrayed in slow motion, and the use of wide angle rather than long lenses gives the landscape an unsettling emptiness rather different from Flaherty's heroic skylines. Throughout the film are shots evocative of human absence and irrational forces, such as a broken dish being gradually washed away by the tide. Early in the film, in the incident in which Ambroise cuts his thumb, a bottle of wine is broken and there is an argument between Ambroise and the other youth, Jean-Marie. This is edited in an abrupt fashion reminiscent of Soviet cinema and certain avant-garde and surrealist films of the period such as Buñuel's *Las Hurdes* (*Land Without Bread* [1932]). Later, again in an avant-garde mode, Epstein creates a dreamlike montage of Ambroise's delirium in which he sees his own oddly extended arm.

Epstein's focus is upon his main characters' subjective experience of their isolation. Flaherty, by contrast, seems to have preferred to evoke the experience of people at a certain remove. This is consistent with the valedictory air that runs through all his films, and in the fishing scene in *Man of Aran,* or the extreme close-ups of faces he introduced in *Moana*, we remain spectators; in his last film, *Louisiana Story* (1948), the subjective experience of the Cajun boy is not so much created through the boy's eyes (except, notably, in the scene of the oil derrick) as through Flaherty's own detailed evocation of the swampland environment.

Throughout Epstein's film, there are many instances of point-of-view editing that contrast with Flaherty's approach, but it is equally in the structures of third-person narration that Epstein, like Flaherty, effectively communicates the subjective experience of being in and of a place, as when Jean-Marie sculls his boat through the fog with Ambroise lying unconscious in the bottom. These scenes work by transference, as we project our own impressions upon the only character in the scene. In this sense *Finis Terrae* seems to prefigure Antonioni's placing of figures in an environment—Monica Vitti on a rocky Mediterranean island thirty years later in *L'Avventura* (1960), or Steve Cochran in the foggy Po Valley of *Il Grido* (1957). Epstein also exploits the textures of objects and faces in close-ups in a way that links sight with the sense of touch, producing the strong synaesthetic effect of feeling the objects as they might be felt by the characters in the film: the roughness of cloth, the coldness of rocks, the scab being scraped from Ambroise's thumb—possibilities similarly exploited in early Soviet and French avant-garde cinema.

With the coming of sound the dominant mode of documentary film became emphatically one of description and explanation. If the earlier confinement of text to screen titles was a barrier, this gave way to a flood of words. The emphasis was on the direct address of spoken commentary, which had its origins in the lecture circuit and the emergent medium of radio. The resulting films bore the stamp of the institutional spokesman, the teacher or, in the case of the strident American *March of Time* series, the voice of God, making assertions about other people with an assurance that left no room for their point of view.

This model continued into the 1950s, when it was transmogrified into television. The ethnographic version tended toward holistic descriptions of small-scale societies (*Mokil* [1950]; *The Land Dyaks of Borneo* [1966]), explications of ritual and technology (*Duminea: A Festival for the Water Spirits* [1966]; *Dani Houses* [1974]) and annotations of anthropologists' research footage, such as that of Gregory Bateson and Margaret Mead (*Childhood Rivalry in Bali and New Guinea* [1952]; *Bathing Babies in Three Cultures* [1954]). In one curious variant there were attempts to subjectivize the subject, seemingly because the films were aimed at children. The result was an endless stream of self-styled "educational" films with titles such as *Indian Boy of the Southwest* (1963) and *The Little Indian Weaver*. Occasionally a child's voice was used in the first person, usually with embarrassing results.

During this period the cost and difficulty of recording synchronous sound, or using post-synchronized dubbing, put the possibility of synchronous dialogue beyond the reach of most ethnographic filmmakers. British social documentary, however, gradually adopted it, so that by 1936 there were studio dialogue scenes in *Night Mail*, and by 1938 a film such as *North Sea* was made up almost entirely of scripted sequences, edited in fictional style, in which working people played themselves. There were also a few notable experiments in the testimonial mode using synchronous interviews: Arthur Elton's *Workers and Jobs* (1935) and the better-known *Housing Problems* (1935), which he codirected with Edgar Anstey. One effect of the Great Depression and World War II seems to have been to turn the attention of European nations inward toward their own subcultures, producing a spurt of documentary dramatizations such as Georges Rouquier's *Farrebique* (1947) about farm life in France and Visconti's *La terra trema* (1948). This was a link backward to silent dramatic documentaries and forward to Italian Neorealism, which was to have important consequences for later observational ethnographic films. It established a model based on event-centered narrative rather than on explanation, and it implied that one could learn about other cultures through a combination of observation, empathy, and induction.

## Descriptive Dramatization

The strategy of *descriptive dramatization* seems to have arisen in the interval between the period of the "illustrated lecture" documentary and the advent of "direct cinema" and *cinéma vérité*, with their capacity to record natural sounds and synchronous dialogue at small cost and with small crews. In the early 1950s John Marshall began making film records of the San peoples of southwestern Africa. In 1956, when this material was archived at the Harvard Film Study Center, plans were made to produce five long films and fifteen or twenty shorter ones. The only long film completed was *The Hunters* (1958). A second, known informally as *Marryings*, was rough-cut but then taken apart and reintegrated into the rushes. *The Hunters* constructs the story of a thirteen-day giraffe hunt out of footage shot on various different occasions, in some cases even using shots of a different person to stand in for one of the main characters. Marshall tells the story on the sound track, producing a hybrid of the traditional lecture film and the dramatized documentary. The camera tends to observe rather than draw the viewer into the scene, but the sound track develops an intimate and subjective, albeit third-person, perspective. This even extends to imputing thoughts to the characters. The film is notable for presenting itself implicitly as a cinematic version of a San hunter's tale, of a sort that might well be repeated and poetically embroidered around a campfire. In this respect, its form and semifictionalized construction, although later dismissed by Marshall as a Western overlay, may not necessarily be greatly at odds with San narrative practice, and the film to some extent parallels Jean Rouch's approach to indigenous story-telling and legend at about the same time (see below).

In 1961 Robert Gardner, who had been involved in the post-production of *The Hunters*, made the film *Dead Birds* (1963) about ritual warfare among the Dani highlanders of New Guinea. *Dead Birds* takes the voice-over dramatization of *The Hunters* a step further. Gardner knew pretty clearly in advance what sort of film he wanted to make, and he proceeded accordingly in his casting and filming. Unlike Marshall's camerawork, much of Gardner's is in the second-person mode of shot/countershot. In keeping with the key metaphor of birds, one scene is even shot from the point of view of an owl. As in fiction films, sound is used to overlap discontinuous action, creating a suturing of time. There is considerable parallel montage, or intercutting of different actions so that they appear to be happening simultaneously, as when the film cuts between men fighting and women getting salt from a brine pool.

Perhaps more significant than these specific narrative devices is the overall construction of the film. Gardner builds a story around certain characters who stand in an implied but only symbolic relationship to one another. Thus, out of the man Weyak and the boy Pua, Gardner creates a father-son archetype with a resonance for Western viewers and a utility for the plot that one suspects would not have borne the same significance for the Dani. In fact, Pua does not appear closely related to Weyak at all, and we are simply told that he "lives in a village close to Weyak's." The introduction of Weyak's wife Lakha completes the familiar circle of a nuclear family. The creation of these characters, their needs and problems, is consistent with the character-centered narration of much Western fiction.

Interestingly, Gardner elects to write most of his spoken text in the present tense, with certain archaic turns of phrase and, toward the end, a tendency toward iambic pentameter. We are introduced to Weyak in the following terms: "Among those who tell why men must die is Weyak." In part, the present tense serves the atmosphere of legend and the mythic metaphor through which Gardner wishes to explain Dani thought. It also imparts a further degree of intimacy, as when Weyak is looking out across the fields in the valley: "The sight never fails to please him, even when his thoughts concern the enemy and what they must be planning." There is an immediacy in such sentences as, "Today Weyak is especially alert." Pua is characterized as a small swineherd, more timid than most, and we are told "Pua waits for manhood," giving him an objective in life to add to the welfare of his pigs.

The film is structured along the classical dramaturgical lines of exposition, conflict, rising action, reversal, climax, and resolution. This is a matter of framing events that occurred during the filming and that Gardner was either able to film or otherwise represent. The killing of the boy Weyakhé occurs unexpectedly, and in fiction the author would have been there, but of course Gardner was not, nor does he film the actual news of the death. What the film gives us instead is a freeze-frame as a man turns his head, with sudden background sounds of weeping; a shot of ducks taking off from the river; shots of empty watchtowers; and a stick floating down the river, which catches in the grass (signifying the stick of a boy swineherd).

The reversal of fortune represented by Weyakhé's death is centered by the film as though it had happened to Pua, and from this point onwards Weyakhé is Pua's surrogate self, just as Weyak is his surrogate father. To seal the relationship we are told, "Pua and Weyakhé were friends, being of similar age and disposition." The point at the river where Weyakhé was killed has been carefully set up earlier in the film as a place where Pua could be in danger, so that when the death occurs, we feel, "It could have been Pua." In the events that follow, an enemy is killed, avenging the death, and the film moves swiftly toward its conclusion as Weyak's group celebrates in the gathering darkness.

I do not propose to discuss here the anthropological validity of Gardner's interpretation of Dani thought and culture. Some anthropologists have criticized it sharply, just as some have criticized the view of gender relations among the Hamar in *Rivers of Sand* (1975) and the portrayal of Hindu society in *Forest of Bliss* (1985). But I will point out several aspects of the film and Gardner's overall interests which I believe are significant steps in the development of ethnographic film. Some of these are related to the attention he pays to subjective experience.

It is fair to say that Gardner is not particularly interested in the subjective experience of the Dani for its own sake, although there are moments in the film of intense personal sympathy. In fact, he has said that his interest in the Dani was secondary to his interest in what their experience might demonstrate about certain issues "of some human urgency" (1972: 34). The subjective view of ritual warfare in *Dead Birds* is therefore meant to make the viewer see warfare from another perspective, on its own premises, by a process of identification with people of a different society. Gardner wrote: "I wondered if a greater understanding of violence in men could be achieved if it was studied in a metaphysical contextcompletely different from our own. I wanted to see the violence of war through altogether different eyes, and I dared hope that new thinking might follow from such an altered perception" (Gardner and Heider 1968: xiii). Writing four years before making the film, Gardner had compared human perception to the distorting eye of cinema. He suggested that film might produce reactions in the viewer affording "some approximation of the feelings of those to whom the experience actually belonged," or failing this, it could at least make people "more deeply aware of the validity of what they witness" (1957: 347–48). This appears on one level to be merely a reaffirmation of the values of cultural relativism. Looked at more closely, it seems to me to be a link with efforts to position anthropological research in relation to seemingly puzzling behavior in such a way as to understand it in the first instance as a dimension of emotional life (Rosaldo 1980), and in the second instance as a function of how another society constructs personal identity.

There are several other points of interest. Gardner's use of a Dani myth represents an effort to incorporate textual material into ethnographic film as an explanation of behavior, and at least it can be said that Gardner's use of the myth is not merely token but comprehensive. Gardner's interpretation of Dani experience through literary conventions is an instance of a filmmaker crossing generic lines in a way in which an anthropologist would usually not; yet in the present climate of experimentation, more than thirty years since Gardner's film, I would not be surprised to see it done convincingly. Works such as Michael Jackson's *Barawa and the Ways Birds Fly in the Sky* (1986) may point the way for at least a few anthropologists. Lastly, Gardner's aim coincides with the aim of many anthropologists to turn the experience of other societies back upon their own as cultural critique.

In contrast to Gardner's rather utilitarian use of characters, a number of approaches in ethnographic film began to develop about the same time that took a much deeper interest in individual personality and its relation to society. It is perhaps significant that these approaches appear in films about societies in which changes are creating stress and ambiguity, and in films at the junctions between different cultures. These approaches can be roughly classed as psychodynamic—in their emphasis upon the conceptual and experiential worlds people inhabit and upon culture as it is reflected and re-created in the mind. Ethnographic films fitting this description have taken varied forms, ranging from psychodrama to cultural reexpression to ethnobiography.

## Psychodrama

In 1953 Jean Rouch began shooting his film *Les Maîtres fous* (1955), which portrayed secret rituals in which members of a Hauka cult in Ghana (then the Gold Coast) were possessed by the spirits of figures in the local British power structure, such as the Governor, a doctor, and a general. The end of the film, where we see the members of the cult in their lowly jobs in Accra, forces a retrospective reading of the earlier material as a kind of psychological safety valve for their frustrations and loss of dignity under colonial rule.

It seems clear that in these events Rouch recognized the revelatory power of role-playing. In his next films he began to develop a form of ethnographic psychodrama. For *Jaguar* (1967), filmed in 1954, he enlisted three young men from the savannah of Niger to make a journey to the cities of the south in search of work and adventure. Their journey in fact followed a well-known labor migration route of the period. In making the film the three were also living out certain ambitions of their own, and Rouch later added a sound track in which they improvised dialogue, narrated the story, and commented on their own performances. The feeling of subjective experience in the film is vivid because it derives from several different sources: the character development on screen, the narrative flow that sweeps the viewer along as a participant, the redoubling of the actual upon the fictional, the spontaneous voices evoking places, encounters, desires, and memories. The film also operates on the level of legend, which Rouch was later to develop in his film *La Chasse au lion à l'arc* (*The Lion Hunters*) (1965).

In *Moi, un noir* (1957), Rouch focuses more closely on fantasy in the lives of young men who are new arrivals to Treichville, a district of Abidjan in Côte d'Ivoire. Fiction and reality mingle as they adopt the movie gangster roles of Eddie Constantine and Edward G. Robinson in the back alleys and bars where they pass their time. But as the film makes clear, fiction is not simply fiction: it becomes reality in the formation of consciousness. And it is a significant feature of this liminal world.

The following year, 1958, Rouch began *La Pyramide humaine* (1961), a film that turned role-playing into a more conscious exercise of the participants, this time secondary-school students in Abidjan. The film is posed as an experiment in race relations, in which the black and white students agree to increase their social interaction while at the same time inventing and acting out an interracial love story. The participants discuss their feelings about the experiment within the film, an approach that Rouch used again and extended in *Chronique d'un été* (1961), set in Paris two years later. [Figure 8.] From this Rouch produced his enigmatic dictum: "When people are being recorded, the reactions that they have are always infinitely more sincere than those they have when they are not being recorded" (Blue 1967: 84).

After *Chronique d'un été* Rouch gave up psychodrama, believing it to be too dangerous to the people involved (Blue 1967). But the method he had explored had opened up an approach in which testimony was transformed into narrative, an externalization of interior space. Rouch's experiments took place in an atmosphere of political change and shifting cultural boundaries. In their effort to bring alive the experience of living through those times, I believe

they prepared the way for Rouch's next efforts, which involved speaking with
his camera in a voice not unlike that of a spirit medium.

### Cultural Reexpression

Rouch's answer to his repudiation of psychodrama seems to have been to
begin using himself rather than others as a primary subject. (In speaking of *La
Chasse au lion à l'arc*, begun at about this same time, he said, "The film . . .
is much less the lion hunt as it actually exists than myself in the face of this
phenomenon" [1971: 135]). In the long series of *Sigui* films begun in 1966
with Germaine Dieterlen, he began recording a complex ritual cycle of the
Dogon that is performed only every sixty years. In the *Sigui* films, and in
*Funerailles à Bongo: Le Vieil Anai* (1972), he joins processions through the
village while filming. One has the sense of being surrounded and of moving
through spaces—not necessarily as a Dogon, but as Rouch possessed by the
Dogon.

*Tourou et Bitti*, made in 1971, directly concerns spirit possession, which
can only occur upon the playing of two ancient drums, "Tourou" and "Bitti."
The film is essentially a single sequence-shot of ten minutes' duration. After-

8. Psychodrama. Angélo and Landry in *Chronique d'un été* (1961).

wards, upon viewing the film, Rouch said he believed the camera acted as a "catalyst" for the trance, and that while filming he himself had gone into what he called "cine-trance" (1981: 28–29), an idea that he was later to describe in the following terms:

> I often compare it to the improvisation of the bullfighter in front of the bull. Here, as there, nothing is known in advance; the smoothness of a *faëna* is just like the harmony of a travelling shot that articulates perfectly with the movements of those being filmed. . . . It is this aspect of fieldwork that marks the uniqueness of the ethnographic filmmaker: instead of elaborating and editing his notes after returning from the field, he must, under penalty of failure, make his synthesis at the exact moment of observation. (1974: 41)

I interpret this notion of cine-trance both literally and metaphorically. There is no doubt that filming can induce a trancelike state in which the camera operator feels a profound communion with surrounding people and events and indeed feels possessed by a spirit emanating from them. In these curious ballets, one moves as though directed by other forces, and the use of the camera feels more than anything like playing a musical instrument. Nevertheless, I believe that what Rouch means to suggest by "cine-trance" is a more complex idea about ethnographic representation. The filmmaker can never duplicate another people's experiences, but, Rouch proposes, by internalizing aspects of their life he or she can reproduce them in the first person through the camera. Cine-trance perhaps represents a form of ethnographic dialogue, or at least one half of such a dialogue, in which the ethnographer celebrates his or her own response to a cultural phenomenon. It seems to me in retrospect that most of Rouch's films have been such a celebration of his own sensibility in encountering another society.

There are a few other films that perhaps fit this description, of which I note specifically Basil Wright's *Song of Ceylon*, made in 1934, and Les Blank's films on music in the American South and Southwest. Wright's film, in particular, reflects an ecstatic experience, an epiphany. It was, Wright said, "the only film I've made that I really loved, and it was in fact a religious experience" (Wright 1971: 53).

## Ethnobiography

Jorge Preloran employs the term "ethnobiography" to describe his films portraying people in the marginalized folk cultures of his native Argentina (Preloran 1987). In its approach ethnobiography shares some of the testimonial qualities of Rouch's work, but it is more closely related to the "life history" genre of ethnography. Preloran would begin by making long journeys into remote parts of Argentina, gathering sound recordings of his subjects' reminiscences and reflections on their lives. He would return later to shoot the film in short fragments with a spring-wind camera, finally drawing upon the sound recordings he had made to construct the film's voice-over soundtrack. He refined the technique in such films as *Imaginero* (1970), *Cochengo Miranda* (1974), and *Zerda's Children* (1978). [Figure 9.]

Preloran's films are based on dialogues with his subjects, and this perhaps strikes us most forcefully in the English versions in which we hear both the original Spanish and Preloran's own voice translating it. However, this dimension is also partly suppressed, since we do not hear Preloran's eliciting questions. It is in fact in the images that Preloran provides both interpretation and contextualization. The dialogue is here reestablished on the level of the intertextual play of the verbal and visual. These films also provide an opportunity, rarely given, for film subjects to express their own assessments of the effects of larger historical forces on their lives, and one senses that the framework that Preloran creates acts as a stimulus for such reflection. The style of filming is in itself unusual, in that it consists of layerings of details that situate the viewer, with a subjective implication, in the immediate environment of the speaker.

Preloran's objective, he has said, is to see a culture through the eyes of one of its members, in order to give a voice to powerless and dispossessed groups in Argentine society (Sherman 1985: 36). Ethnobiography, whatever its aims as advocacy, attempts to create portraits of individuals of other societies in some psychological and historical depth. While it is ostensibly a way of depicting culture from the inside through an insider's perspective, it is framed by an outsider's concerns. In its doubling of subjectivities and its attempt to reconstitute the culturally different historical person it creates a conundrum, the charged space of an encounter. Although related to indigenous media production, it differs from it somewhat as biography differs from autobiography, in its strengths as well as its weaknesses.

Preloran's films are similar in form to a genre of documentary exemplified by Roman Kroiter's *Paul Tomkowicz: Street-Railway Switch Man* (1954) and Richard Chen's *Liu Pi Chia* (1965). In these films the narrator does not speak for the subject but is, or purports to be, the subject speaking. But ethnobiography should be seen as extending beyond this formal strategy and to include other ethnographic films that concern the consciousness of individual social actors. These may use on-camera interviews and span a lifetime, as in *N!ai, The Story of a !Kung Woman* (1980), or attempt to portray a person at a particular juncture in his or her life, as in *The Spirit Possession of Alejandro Mamani* (1975), *Lorang's Way* (1979), *The House-Opening* (1980), and *Sophia's People* (1985).

A final cluster of approaches to subjectivity could be classed as *contextual*. These have produced ethnographic films that somewhat distance the social actors from the viewer and do not evoke the same level of identification as dramatizations and psychodynamic approaches. They permit an insight into

9. Ethnobiography. *Imaginero* (1970).

subjective experience by allowing the viewer to interpret social actors' responses within a specific context, either elaborated by the film or defined by a
particular context of interaction with the filmmaker. These approaches depend
variously upon observation, interview, and interchange.

## Observation

An alternative to the provocation employed in European *cinéma vérité* was
the North American observational approach pioneered by such filmmakers as
Richard Leacock, Robert Drew, and the Maysles brothers in the United States
and by Terence McCartney-Filgate, Michel Brault, and others at the National
Film Board of Canada. The ethnographic use of observational documentary
style was first practiced by John Marshall, who began shooting event-centered
sequences of the life of Ju/'hoansi people in southwestern Africa in the 1950s.
Two other important bodies of work in this style are Timothy Asch's Yanomamö films and the Netsilik Eskimo series begun in 1963 under the direction
of Asen Balikci.

The aim of these films was to record events in long synchronous takes,
without major directorial intervention, so that the scenes, when properly contextualized, would reveal or demonstrate the cultural basis of interpersonal

behavior.[1] They often give access to the emotional life of people through their portrayals of characteristic social interactions, which are allowed to play out as much as possible in real time. The nuances of personality and discourse contained in such scenes, and their potential value for social analysis, can be seen in a film by John Marshall, filmed in 1957–58, called *A Joking Relationship* (1966), in which a young married girl, N!ai (the subject of Marshall's later biographical film), flirts with her great uncle, /Ti!kay. Such small dramas of self-presentation resemble scenes from earlier dramatized documentaries, but they are fundamentally different in their emphasis upon spontaneous events.

In making the Netsilik Eskimo series, the approach of Robert Young, one of the primary cinematographers, was central both to filming interpersonal behavior unobtrusively and structuring it visually. The subjective effect—that is, the access given in this instance to perceived emotions—could be said to result from an "intimate" documentary camera style, which Young had already developed in filming the family scenes in *Cortile Cascino* (1962), made with Michael Roemer in 1961. In one of the Netsilik films about family life, filmed inside a large igloo, the camera establishes one person, a young mother, as the person from whose point of view we tend to experience the scene. It does this not by adopting her visual point of view but by making her the visual and metaphorical center of attention. As in many fiction films, a special relationship is established with a character not by employing the formal devices of character-narration but rather through the structure of the scene itself.

Despite this sensitivity to individuals, the Netsilik films did not provide subtitled translations of spoken dialogue. The first ethnographic films that did—among them *The Feast* (1970), *Nawi* (1970), several of Marshall's early "sequence" films, and *Imbalu: Ritual of Manhood of the Gisu of Uganda* (filmed 1968; released 1988)—began to give access not only to visible expressions of emotion but also to the intellectual life of their subjects, including the feelings and accounts of personal experiences that might be expressed in the course of their conversations. The introduction of subtitled speech was in fact a crucial step in liberating the ethnographic film from the stranglehold of voice-over commentary. [Figure 10.] It also made possible a form of ethnographic narrative cinema that was no longer confined to nonverbal behavior nor dependent upon commentary—films such as *Naim and Jabar* (1974), *The Wedding Camels* (1977), and *Joe Leahy's Neighbours* (1988).

*Interview*

One predictable consequence of subtitling synchronous speech was to increase the use of the interview in ethnographic films. The interview had emerged from journalism to become a key element in public affairs television

That's how it was while we grew up.

10. Subtitled speech. From *To Live with Herds* (1972).

and the documentaries of the 1960s. From an anthropological point of view, the interview was an obvious resource as one of the main information-gathering techniques of fieldwork.

Interviews in films not only convey spoken information but also unspoken information about the contexts in which they occur. They allow the speakers to describe their subjective experiences of past and present events, while simultaneously we interpret the emotions and constraints of the moment. The presence of a person talking on the screen can have a powerful effect upon us because of the resemblance of this situation to many of the situations in which we watch, and identify with, people in daily life. Interviews are perhaps the ideal medium for confession and self-revelation, but also equally for misinformation. In this connection, it is important to see interviews as representing limited perspectives and uneven mixtures of candour and self-justification. A film that demonstrates this is John Marshall's *N!ai*. As N!ai speaks, one has a sense of a performance addressed not only to Marshall, who has known her since childhood, but to others around her with whom she is shown to be in considerable friction. The film is eloquent of the emotional confusion of one individual in an uprooted indigenous society. By contrast, the private and confiding interviews with women in Melissa Llewelyn-Davies's films *The Women's Olamal* (1984) and *Memories and Dreams* (1993) are used to reveal women's attitudes generally toward disputes and gender relations. By including two or more women in the interviews the films allow a degree of consensus to emerge.

Films that include interviews with several people offer a more complex picture of inquiry and validation and sometimes a greater possibility of cross-checking responses. Unlike the results of sociological questionnaires, many judgments about reliability of testimony are left to the viewer. At its best, in such films as *The Eskimos of Pond Inlet* (1977) and *Maragoli* (1976), this approach permits a kind of understanding that can incorporate multiple perspectives and transcend much apparently contradictory evidence. But interviews can also easily be used selectively, without the eliciting questions, and in fragments to support a particular argument, relying on the audience's assumption that the authority of the speakers validates the authority of the entire structure—a criticism legitimately leveled at many of the interview-based political documentaries of the 1970s and 1980s.

Although most interviews are employed to reveal personal attitudes and deliver information, the interviews in Roger Sandall's *Coniston Muster* (1972) are put to a somewhat different purpose. The film is first of all important for its foregrounding of individuals at a time when Australian Aboriginal people were still widely portrayed as anonymous social objects. It does this partly by eliciting stories. The effect upon the viewer is of encountering an individual personality in all its forcefulness. But it is in the story-telling that the viewer also begins to read a distinctive cultural style and perceive another possible conceptual world.

There is a further form of testimony, which lies somewhere between the formal interview and story-telling. This is conversation with the filmmaker, freed from the formality of the question-and-answer format. It can produce a different kind of volunteered information (sometimes even turning questions back upon the filmmaker) and often includes the sort of low-key dialogue that consists of an accretion of comments, disagreements, and speculations. It can veer off to include other people who are nearby and move back and forth between them and the filmmaker, lessening the gap between formal filmmaking and first-person experiences familiar to most viewers. These situations resemble those of participant observation in which much ethnographic knowledge is actually acquired. In this way they are capable of providing a commentary on the contingency and provisional nature of anthropological understanding, absent in films that purport to speak with absolute authority.

### Interchange

In some films the context of interaction with the subjects tilts toward further involvement. The filmmaker intervenes increasingly in their lives or, often without intending to, becomes a major focus of their attention. Sometimes these films provide a catalyst for their actions and a mirror in which to see themselves. Their interchange with the filmmaker lies at the heart of the film, although not necessarily at the heart of all the behavior that the film depicts.

Rouch provoked the action of films like *Jaguar*, but he was not *in* them. But in *Chronique d'un été* he and the codirector Edgar Moran emerge as major characters. Morin's scenes with the young Italian woman, Marilou, have the emotional intensity of psychiatric interviews. In documentary films such as *Home from the Hill* (1985) and *The Things I Cannot Change* (1966) filmmakers have been targeted behind the camera by lonely and talkative subjects, and the latter film, a study of a poor family in Montreal, becomes an extended monologue in which the father hijacks the film to explain his predicament and vent his feelings. Ethnographic films are rarely based on such occurrences, but relationships of dependency and the opening of new horizons resulting from the filmmaking have undoubtedly affected some film subjects deeply, for better or worse. Through ethnographic films, some participants achieve a measure of fulfilment and prestige in their own communities. Frank Gurrmanamana, who successfully organizes the ceremony shown in Kim McKenzie's *Waiting for Harry* (1980), is a clear example. But by contrast, the father in *The Things I Cannot Change* is known to have suffered community ostracism when the film was televised, and James Blue has described how Peter Boru, the boy in *Kenya Boran* (1974), behaved at the end of the filming in 1972: "He said, 'You have shown us a life we can never lead, and I don't want to be reminded of it.' And he walked off and wouldn't say good-bye after that" (1975: 35). In an effort to address such issues, Jorge and Mabel Preloran have made the consequences of filmmaking the focus of their film *Zulay Facing the 21st Century* (1989), about one of their film subjects, Zulay Saravino.

In Gary Kildea's *Celso and Cora* (1983) the interchange between filmmaker and subjects is not merely a feature of the encounter, but is developed to explore their subjective world. One of Kildea's aims is to counter the Western conception of Third World poverty as a stereotyped "condition" that, to an outsider, reduces its members to an abstraction upon whom further injustices can more easily be practiced. He wants to make it clear that although people like Celso and Cora are poor, they do not see themselves as defined primarily by their poverty. During the course of the filming both Celso and Cora talk separately to Kildea as well as including him in their own discussions. When eventually they quarrel and split up, Celso adopts Kildea as his companion and confidant.

Other ethnographic films emphasize such relationships more formally and aim at more specific areas of knowledge. In *Jero on Jero: A Balinese Trance Seance Observed* (1981) Jero, a Balinese spirit medium and healer, watches a film made of her while she was in trance. As she follows her own image on a video monitor she grasps the anthropologist (Linda Connor) by the hand and provides an emotional commentary on her filmed behavior, her ideas about spirit possession, her understanding of the supernatural world, and her reactions to seeing herself in trance.

## The Subjective Camera

There is finally the possibility of a truly subjective camera. The use of a camera by the subject of an ethnographic film occurs briefly in a few films (*My Family and Me* [1986]; *A Wife among Wives* [1981]), but largely as an emblem of a personal exchange with the filmmakers. To my knowledge there are as yet no ethnographic films that integrate long segments of indigenous filming with those by an outside filmmaker, nor collaborations incorporating the different perspectives of several filmmakers. Some indigenous media production has specific ethnographic intentions, but this rarely extends to the conscious use of a "first-person" camera, although an exception is *Intrepid Shadows* (1966) by Al Clah, one of the Navajo participants in the Sol Worth–John Adair experimental Navajo film project. In a special category may be Marc-Henri Piault's *Akazama* (1986), an epistemologically complex film in which Piault uses the camera "in the first person" in some ways like Rouch (and with a continuous voice-over commentary as though spoken or thought at the time of filming) to reveal the problems of filming and interpreting the enthronement of a West African king.

## The Seen and the Unseen

Looking back on this history of efforts to encompass the subjective voice in ethnographic film, one can find few statements of the motives for doing so. There are several recurrent themes—"giving a voice" to others; seeing another culture through individual actors; reproducing indigenous perspectives in the viewer—but these seem insufficient to explain a tendency that has been pursued with such persistence and ingenuity. We are left with a set of questions about the pursuit of the subjective voice. What are its motivations? Is it a means to an end or a fulfilment? What aspects of subjective experience are attainable in film? What place does the subjective voice occupy in filmmakers' conceptions of culture and society? Is the attempt to reveal the subjective an act of communion or merely of invasion?

The search in ethnographic films for analogues of subjective experience seems first of all to have been an effort to apply a corrective to increasingly abstract descriptions of colonized and marginalized peoples. It was seen to be within the powers of film to make the exotic and strange at least comprehensible if not familiar, and this accorded with liberal sentiments from early in the century. The fiction film provided a ready model and ideological framework for this at certain periods, particularly after 1910 with the emergence of new modes of filmic narration (in Griffith's work particularly) and after World War II with the advent of Italian Neorealism.

I consider a second part of the quest related to the perhaps perverse tendency among filmmakers to distrust visual representations and to seek to transcend them. There is an irony in the disjunction that has grown up steadily between anthropologists and filmmakers, in that anthropologists, by and large, have wished film to make increasingly accurate, complete, and verifiable descriptions of what can be seen—that is, of behavior, ritual, and technology—whereas filmmakers have shown a growing interest in precisely those things that cannot be seen. It was never the physical body that was felt to be missing in ethnographic films. The body was constantly and often extravagantly before us in its diversity of faces, statures, costumes, and body decorations. It was all too easy to present such images with their accompanying exoticism. What was missing was not the body but the experience of existing in it.

There is thus in ethnographic filmmaking not only a journey of discovery from the abstract to the personal but from representation to evocation. I mean to suggest here something akin to Stephen Tyler's notion of replacing the scholarly or artistic object by a discourse which, because it evokes, need not represent (1987: 206). In recent years one also sees a movement away from monologue toward—not even polysemic or polyvocal expression—but polythesis: an understanding that comes out of the interplay of voices rather than merely their co presentation. Paul Willemen has noted the curious fact that while the tendency of radical cinema has been to reassert the importance of material and historical structures over the Western tradition of character-narration centered in the individual, the movement of ethnographic film has been precisely the reverse, away from structures toward individual experience.[2] In both cases the purpose can be seen as corrective. The dangers for ethnographic film lie in overcorrection, of exchanging one reductionism for another.

I have outlined three general strategies by which ethnographic films activate the subjective voice. Such distinctions are of course artificial, although they may help to characterize the emphasis of different films. The subjective voice is more often like an aerial image that forms only as a convergence of light-waves. It is usually evoked in the intersection of what I have called testimony, implication, and exposition.

Toward the end of his essay, "Questions of Magnitude," Bill Nichols writes of a necessary but unstable balance in which the person in documentary is held suspended, allowing the film to explore matters "that exceed any one logic or code, that are, among other things, magnitudes in excess of any discursive frame" (1986: 122). Evocation of the person for Nichols, following Fredric Jameson, seems to require a crossing of the trajectories of the historical, narrative, and mythic to overcome the closure of past structures of containment. I have put the problem in somewhat different terms, but I believe the intersecting and contradictory frames of subjectivity lead to a similar conclusion. Testimony is what gives us the subjective voice of the historical person, yet we are implicated in the destiny of others through narrative; and the mythic potential of social actors is heightened through the distancing created by exposition.

The interpenetration of these perspectives may be seen as a metaphor for the interpenetration of cultural perspectives that increasingly characterizes human communities. Firm distinctions between self and other, East and West, North and South become less certain in the contemplation of almost every social arena. These changes have begun to undermine some of the assumptions upon which traditional critiques of power relations have been based, including those about disciplines such as anthropology. The changes now occurring should make clear that some of these critiques exhibit the same kind of reductionism that science itself has often embraced in abstract representations that separate sign from signified, observer from object, analysis from experience. Such a realization may cause us to turn increasingly toward addressing the problems of interpreting multifaceted cultural relations.

The search for the subjective voice in ethnographic film often reflects, perhaps surprisingly, a repudiation of Western ideologies that celebrate the isolated individual consciousness as the only locus of understanding in a hostile but unquestioned (or supposedly "natural") social order. In many of the films I have discussed it is instead the means toward a more complex understanding of a cultural consciousness that consists of discourses between different subjectivities. In this sense it is an effort to construct a way of looking at the world that is intersubjective and, finally, communal.

[1989]

## Notes

This essay was written during a visiting fellowship at the Humanities Research Centre at the Australian National University in 1989, a year the Centre devoted to the theme of film and the humanities. I am grateful to the Humanities Research Centre for their support. It was first published in *Fields of Vision*, edited by Leslie Devereaux and Roger Hillman (Berkeley: University of California Press, 1995), copyright © 1995, The Regents of the University of California, and reprinted by permission.

1. It should be noted, however, that the situations that were filmed in this style were often provoked by the filmmakers—if not directly, as in setting up interviews, then indirectly, through the pressure of the filmmakers' interests and expectations. In the case of the Netsilik Eskimos series, the Netsilik had been explicitly asked to live as they had lived in the period before contact with Europeans, the camera then recording their spontaneous interactions within this somewhat artificial framework.

2. Personal communication, 1989.

# PART TWO

# Beyond Observational Cinema

Truth is not a Holy Grail to be won: it is a shuttle
which moves ceaselessly between the observer and
the observed, between science and reality.
—*Edgar Morin[1]*

THE PAST FEW YEARS have seen a recommitment to the principle of observation in documentary filmmaking. The result has been fresh interest in the
documentary film and a body of work that has separated itself clearly from the
traditions of Grierson and Vertov.[2] Audiences have had restored to them the
sense of wonder at witnessing the spontaneity of life that they felt in the early
days of the cinema, seeing a train rush into the Gare de La Ciotat. This has not
been a response to the perfection of some new illusion, but to a fundamental
change in the relationship that filmmakers have sought to establish between
their subjects and the viewer. The significance of that relationship for the
practice of social science is now felt as a major force in the ethnographic film.
This would seem an appropriate moment to discuss the implications of observational cinema as a mode of human inquiry.

In the past, anthropologists were accustomed to taking their colleagues'
descriptions on faith. It was rare to know more about a remote society than the
few persons who had studied it, and one accepted their analyses largely because one accepted the scholarly tradition that had produced them. Few monographs offered precise methodological information or substantial texts as documentary evidence in support of their claims.

Ethnographic films were rarely more liberal in this regard. The prevailing
style of filming and film editing tended to break a continuum of events into
mere illustrative fragments. On top of this, ethnographic filmmaking was a
haphazard affair. It was never employed systematically or enthusiastically by
the anthropological profession as a whole. *Moana* (1926) was the work of
Robert Flaherty, a geologist and explorer, *Grass* (1925) of adventurers who
later went on to make *King Kong* (1933). Until very recently most ethnographic films were the byproducts of other endeavors: the chronicles of travel-
ers, the works of documentary filmmakers, and the occasional forays into film
of anthropologists whose major commitment was to writing. In most cases
these films announced their own inadequacies. When they did not, neither

were they wholly persuasive. One often wondered what had been concealed or created by the editing, the framing, or the narrator's commentary.

Even classic films such as John Marshall's *The Hunters* (1958) left important areas of doubt. Could one accept that this was how the Ju/'hoansi of the Kalahari conducted long hunts, given the fact that the film was compiled from a series of shorter ones? In Robert Gardner's *Dead Birds* (1963), could one be confident that the thoughts attributed to the subjects were what they might really have been thinking?

In recent years ethnographic filmmakers have looked for solutions to such problems, and new approaches to documentary filming in Western society have provided most of them. By focusing on discrete events rather than abstract concepts or impressions, and by seeking to render faithfully the natural sounds, structure, and duration of events, filmmakers have hoped to provide the viewer with sufficient evidence to judge the film's larger analysis. Films such as Marshall's *An Argument about a Marriage* (1969), Roger Sandall's *Emu Ritual at Ruguri* (1969), and Timothy Asch's *The Feast* (1970) are all early attempts of this kind. They are "observational" in their manner of filming, placing the viewer in the role of an observer, a witness of events. They are essentially revelatory rather than illustrative, for they explore substance before theory. They are, nevertheless, evidence of what the filmmaker finds significant.

To those of us who began making ethnographic films when *cinéma vérité* and American "direct cinema" were revolutionizing documentary filmmaking, this approach to filming other societies seemed all but inevitable. Its promise for social science appeared so obvious that it was difficult to understand the years of unrealized potential. Why, we often wondered, with time running out to document the world's fast-changing cultures, had it not been anthropologists rather than journalists who first conceived of such a use for film and struggled for its perfection?

The observational direction in ethnographic filmmaking had, after all, begun vigorously enough. The very invention of the cinema was in part a response to the desire to observe more precisely the physical movements of human beings and animals, starting with the chronophotography of Eadweard Muybridge (1887) and Étienne-Jules Marey (1883) in the 1870s and 1880s.[3] Scientists such as Félix Louis Regnault and Walter Baldwin Spencer quickly went beyond the popular interests of Lumière, making essentially observational film records of technology and ritual in non-Western societies.[4] Flaherty's work, for all its reflection of his own idealism, was rooted in the careful exploration of other people's lives. It heralded the achievements of such diverse filmmakers as Merian C. Cooper and Ernest Schoedsack among the Bakhtiari of Iran, O. E. Stocker and Norman Tindale in Australia, and Gregory Bateson and Margaret Mead in Bali and New Guinea. From then on, the ethnographic film fell heir to the fragmentation of imagery that had originated in the Soviet cinema and that began to dominate the documentary film with the coming of sound.

It could be said that the notion of the synchronous-sound ethnographic film was born at the moment Walter Baldwin Spencer decided to take both an Edison cylinder recorder and a Warwick camera to Central Australia in 1901. It became a practical possibility in the late 1920s, only to be neglected in documentary films until the 1950s. In 1935 Arthur Elton and Edgar Anstey demonstrated what could have been done more widely by taking sound cameras, bulky as they then were, into the slums of Stepney and documenting the lives of the inhabitants.[5] To say that they were ahead of their time is only to note with regret that they should not have been.

When highly portable synchronous-sound cameras were finally developed around 1960, few ethnographic filmmakers jumped at the chance to use them as though long awaiting the event. Two exceptions were Jean Rouch in France and John Marshall in the United States. Rouch's work was to have a major influence on both fiction and documentary filmmaking in Europe. Marshall had already practiced a makeshift kind of synchronous-sound filming in the 1950s among the Ju/'hoansi. His observational approach foreshadowed the discoveries of the Drew Associates group and the National Film Board of Canada in North America, although the originality of his early work only became evident with the release, long after *The Hunters*, of his shorter films from the Peabody-Harvard-Kalahari expeditions.

Filmmakers who followed an observational approach quickly divided along methodological lines. Unlike the followers of Rouch, those in the English-speaking world were hesitant to interact with their subjects on film, except occasionally to interview them. Their adherence to this principle had an almost religious asceticism, distinct from the speculative approach of Rouch and other European filmmakers.

It is this self-denying tendency of modern observational cinema that I should like to examine. It is the tradition in which I was trained, and it has an obvious affinity to certain classical notions of scientific method. But this very orthodoxy could well make it a dangerously narrow model for ethnographic filmmakers of the future.

Many of us who began applying an observational approach to ethnographic filmmaking found ourselves taking as our model not the documentary film as we had come to know it since Grierson, but the dramatic fiction film, in all its incarnations from Tokyo to Hollywood. This paradox resulted from the fact that of the two, the fiction film was the more observational in attitude. Documentaries of the previous thirty years had celebrated the sensibility of the filmmaker in confronting reality; they had rarely explored the flow of actual events. Although this style had produced such masterpieces as Basil Wright's *Song of Ceylon* (1934) and Willard Van Dyke and Ralph Steiner's *The City*

(1939), it was a style of synthesis, a style that used images to develop an argument or impression.

Each of the discrete images in such documentaries was the bearer of a predetermined meaning. They were often articulated like the images of a poem, juxtaposed against an asynchronous sound track of music or commentary. Indeed, poetry was sometimes integral to the film's conception, as in Pare Lorentz's *The River* (1937), Basil Wright and Harry Watt's *Night Mail* (1936), and Alberto Cavalcanti's *Coalface* (1936).

In contrast to this iconographic approach, the images of the fiction film were largely anecdotal. They were the pieces of evidence from which one deduced a story. The audience was told little. It was presented with a series of contiguous events. It learned by observing.

It seemed that such a relationship between viewer and subject should be possible with materials found in the real world. In our own society this had indeed become the approach of filmmakers such as Richard Leacock and Albert and David Maysles, who were fond of quoting Tolstoy's declaration that the cinema would make the invention of stories unnecessary. For those of us interested in filming outside our own society, the films of the Italian Neorealists, with their emphasis upon the economic and social environment, seemed like mirror-images of the films we hoped could be made from real events in the ongoing lives of other peoples.

The classical voice of the fiction film is the third person: the camera observes the actions of the characters not as a participant but as an invisible presence, capable of assuming a variety of positions. To approximate such an approach in the nonfiction film, filmmakers must find ways of making themselves privy to human events without disturbing them. This is relatively easy when the event attracts more attention than the camera—what Edgar Morin has called "intensive sociality" (de Heusch 1962: 4). It becomes more difficult when a few people are interacting in an informal situation. Yet documentary filmmakers have been so successful in achieving a sense of unobtrusiveness that scenes of the most intimate nature have been recorded without apparent embarrassment or pretense on the part of the subjects. The usual practice is to spend so much time with one's subjects that they lose interest in the camera. They must finally go on with their lives, and they tend to do so in their accustomed ways. This may seem improbable to those who have not witnessed it, yet to filmmakers it is a familiar phenomenon.

I have often been struck in my own work by the readiness of people to accept being filmed, even in societies where one might expect a camera to be particularly threatening. This acceptance is of course aided by de-emphasizing the actual process of filming, in both one's manner and one's technique. While making *To Live with Herds* (1972) among the Jie of Uganda, I used a camera brace that allowed me to keep the camera in the filming position for twelve or more hours a day, over a period of many weeks. I lived looking through the viewfinder. Because the camera ran noiselessly, my subjects soon gave up trying to decide when I was filming and when I was not. As far as they were concerned I was always filming, an assumption that no doubt contributed to their confidence that their lives were being seen fully and fairly. When, at the end of my stay, I took out a still camera, everyone began posing—a clear sign that they recognized this as essentially different from cinema.

I would suggest that at times people can behave more naturally while being filmed than in the presence of other kinds of observers. A person with a camera has an obvious job to do, which is to film. The subjects understand this and leave the filmmaker to it. The filmmaker remains occupied, half-hidden behind the camera, satisfied to be left alone. But as an unencumbered visitor, he or she would have to be entertained, whether as a guest or as a friend. In this, I think, lies both the strength and the weakness of the observational method.

The purpose behind this curiously lonely approach of observational cinema is arguably to film things that would have occurred if one had not been there. It is a desire for the invisibility of the imagination found in literature combined with the aseptic touch of the surgeon's glove—in some cases a legitimation, in the name of art or science, of the voyeur's peephole. It has even been reduced to a formula for anthropology. Walter Goldschmidt defined ethnographic film as "film which endeavors to interpret the behavior of people of one culture to persons of another culture by using shots of people doing precisely what they would have been doing if the camera were not there" (1972: 1).

Invisibility and omniscience. From this desire it is not a great leap to begin viewing the camera as a secret weapon in the pursuit of knowledge. One's self-effacement as a filmmaker begins to efface the limitations of one's own physicality. The filmmaker and the camera are imperceptibly attributed with the power to witness the *totality* of an event. Indeed, they are expected to. Omniscience and omnipotence.

It is an approach that has produced some remarkable films. And for many filmmakers it has in practice a comforting lack of ambiguity. The filmmaker establishes a role that demands no social response from the subjects, and he or she then disappears into the woodwork. Allan King's *Warrendale* (1966) and *A Married Couple* (1969) make the audience witness to scenes of private emotional anguish without reference to the presence of the film crew. In the film *At the Winter Sea-Ice Camp, Part 3* (1968), from the Netsilik Eskimo series, the Inuit subjects seem altogether oblivious of Robert Young's camera, and in Frederick Wiseman's *Essene* (1972), a study of people striving painfully to live communally in a religious order, one sometimes has the curious sense of being the eye of God.

When films like these are functioning at their best, the people in them seem bearers of the immeasurable wealth and effort of human experience. Their lives have a weight that makes the film that caught but a fragment of it seem trivial, and we sit in a kind of awe of our own privileged observation of them. That emotion helps us accept the subjects' disregard of the filmmaker. For them to notice the filmmaker would amount almost to a sacrilege—a shattering of the horizons of their lives, which by all rights should not include someone making a film about them. In the same way, some scholars resist descriptions in which anthropologists are acknowledged as instruments of cultural contact and change.

Audiences are thus accomplices in the filmmaker's voluntary absence from the film—what Richard Leacock called "the pretense of our not being there" (Levin 1971: 204). From a scientific standpoint, the priorities of research also de-emphasize the filmmaker, because to pay attention to the observer is to draw valuable attention away from the subject at hand. Finally, the literature and films we have grown up with have shaped our expectations: Aeneas is unaware of Virgil; the couple on the bed ignores the production crew of twenty standing round. Even in home movies people are often told not to look at the camera.

Filmmakers begin as members of an audience and carry part of that attitude with them. But the act of filming tends to interpose its own barriers between the observer and the observed. For one thing, it is difficult for filmmakers to photograph themselves as an element in the phenomenon they are examining unless, like Jean Rouch and Edgar Morin in *Chronique d'un été* (1961), they becomes "actors" before the camera. More often it is through their voices and the responses of the subjects that we feel their presence.

Perhaps more important, filmmakers exhaust most of their energy making the camera respond to what is before it. This concentration induces a certain passivity from which it is difficult to rouse oneself. Active participation with the subjects suggests an altogether different psychic state. This may partly explain the successes of cinema as a contemplative art.

Among ethnographic filmmakers, another restraint is the special reverence that surrounds the study of isolated groups. The fragility of these societies and the rarity of filming them turns the filmmaker into a recording instrument of history—an obligation which, if accepted or even felt, must necessarily weigh down efforts to pursue more specific lines of inquiry.

This distancing view is often reinforced by an identification with the audience that may cause a filmmaker to mimic, consciously or otherwise, their impotence. As members of an audience we readily accept the illusion of entering into the world of a film. But we do so in complete safety, because our own world is as close as the nearest light switch. We observe the people in the film without being seen, assured that they can make no claims upon us. The corollary of this, however, is our inability to reach through the screen and affect *their* lives. Thus our situation combines a sense of immediacy with an absolute separation. Only when we try to invade the world of the film do we discover the insubstantiality of its illusion of reality.

In their attempt to make us into witnesses, observational filmmakers often think in terms of the image on the screen rather than their own presence in the setting where the events are occurring. They become no more than the eye of the audience, frozen into their passivity, unable to bridge the separation between themselves and their subjects.

Finally, however, it is scientific objectives that have placed the severest strictures on ethnographic film. Inevitably, the extraordinary precision of the camera-eye as a descriptive aid has influenced conceptions of the uses to which film should be put, with the result that for years anthropologists have considered film preeminently a tool for gathering data. And because film deals so overwhelmingly with the specific rather than the abstract, it is often considered incapable of serious intellectual articulation.

Certainly there are enough ethnographic films containing crude or dubious interpretations to explain, if not justify, such a conclusion. Films risking more legitimate, if more difficult, kinds of analysis are often flawed in the attempt. Still others receive no credit because their contribution exists in a form that cannot be assessed in the terms of conventional anthropology. Each of these factors adds weight to a widespread view among anthropologists that attempts to use film as an original medium of anthropology are simply pretexts for self-indulgence. What is more, each attempt that fails can be viewed as one more opportunity lost to add to the fund of "responsible" ethnography.

With data-gathering as the objective, there is of course no real need for the making of films, but merely for the collection of footage upon which a variety of studies can later be based. Indeed, E. Richard Sorenson (1967) suggested that footage might be collected with only this broad objective in view. Yet much bad anthropological writing is a similar gathering and cataloguing of information, deficient in thought or analysis. This is not far from the criticism that Evans-Pritchard levels at Malinowski:

> The theme is no more than a descriptive synthesis of events. It is not a theoretical integration, . . . There is consequently no real standard of relevance, since everything has a time and space relationship in cultural reality to everything else, and from whatever point one starts one spreads oneself over the same ground. (1962: 95)

The same criticism could be made of many existing ethnographic films. If this is a valid criticism—if ethnographic film is to become anything more than a form of anthropological note-taking—then attempts must continue to make it a medium of ideas. There will inevitably be more failures. But it seems probable that the great films of anthropology, as distinct from ethnography, are still to be made.

Curiously, it is the survival of the data within the context of thought, inescapable in the cinema, that is responsible for the impatience of many social scientists with film as a medium for anthropology. The glimpse gained of the original field situation may be so immediate and evocative that it proves tantalizing to those who would like to see more, and infuriating to those whose specific theoretical interests are not being served. Thus an ecological determinist may well dismiss as shallow a film in which the study of social relationships takes precedence over ecology.

Films prove to be poor encyclopedias because of their emphasis upon specific and delimited events viewed from finite perspectives. Yet surprisingly, it is often the supposed potency of film to record everything that has led to its disparagement. At first glance, film seems to offer an escape from the inadequacies of human perception and a factual check on the capriciousness of human interpretation. The precision of the photographic image leads to an uncritical faith in the camera's power to capture, not the images of events, but the events themselves—as Ruskin once said of some photographs of Venice, "as if a magician had reduced reality to be carried away into an enchanted land" (1887). So persuasive is this belief in the magic of photography that it is assumed by scholars who in the rest of their research would challenge far more circumspect assumptions. When disillusionment comes, it is therefore profound.

The magical fallacy of the camera parallels the fallacy of omniscient observation. It may result from a tendency in viewing films to define what has been photographed by what one is seeing. The film image impresses us with its completeness, partly because of its precise rendering of detail, but even more because it represents a continuum of reality that extends beyond the edges of the frame and which therefore, paradoxically, seems not to be excluded. A few images create a world. We ignore the images that could have been, but weren't. In most cases we have no conception of what they might have been.

It is possible that the sense of completeness created by a film also lies in the richness of ambiguity of the photographic image. Images begin to become signs of the objects they represent; yet unlike words or even pictographs, they share in the physical identity of the objects, having been produced as a kind of photochemical imprint of them. The image thus continually asserts the presence of the concrete world within the framework of a communicative system that imposes meaning.

The viewfinder of the camera, one might say, has a function opposite to that of the gunsight that a soldier levels at an enemy. The latter frames an image for annihilation; the former frames an image for preservation, thereby annihilating the surrounding multitude of images that could have been formed at that precise point in time and space. The image becomes a piece of evidence, like a potsherd. It also becomes, through the denial of all other possible images, a reflection of thought. In that double nature is the magic that can so easily dazzle us.

Observational cinema is based upon a process of selection. The filmmaker is limited to that which occurs naturally and spontaneously in front of the camera. The richness of human behavior and the propensity of people to talk about their affairs, past and present, are what allow this method of inquiry to succeed.

It is nevertheless a method that is quite foreign to the usual practice of anthropology or, for that matter, most other disciplines. (Two exceptions are history and astronomy, which time and distance require to function in the same way.) Most anthropological fieldwork involves, in addition to observation, an active search for information among informants. In the laboratory sciences, knowledge comes primarily from events that the scientist provokes. Thus observational filmmakers find themselves cut off from many of the channels that normally characterize human inquiry. They are dependent for their understanding (or for the understanding of the audience) upon the unprovoked ways in which their subjects manifest the patterns of their lives while they are being filmed. They are denied access to anything their subjects know but take for granted, anything latent in their culture that events do not bring to the surface.

The same methodological asceticism that causes filmmakers to exclude themselves from the world of their subjects also excludes the subjects from the world of the film. Here the implications are ethical as well as practical. By asking nothing of the subjects beyond permission to film them, the filmmaker adopts an inherently secretive position. There is no need for further explanation, no need to communicate with the subjects on the basis of the thinking that organizes the work. There is, in fact, some reason for the filmmaker not to do so for fear it may influence their behavior. In this insularity, the filmmaker withholds the very openness that is being asked of the subjects in order to film them.

In refusing to give the film subjects access to the film, filmmakers are also refusing them access to themselves, for this is clearly their most important activity when they are among them. In denying a part of their own humanity, they deny a part of their subjects'. If not in their own personal demeanor, then in the significance of their working method, they inevitably reaffirm the colonial origins of anthropology. It was once the European who decided what was worth knowing about "primitive" peoples and what they in turn should be taught. The shadow of that attitude falls across the observational film, giving it a distinctively Western parochialism. The traditions of science and narrative art combine in this instance to dehumanize the study of humanity. It is a form in which the observer and the observed exist in separate worlds, and it produces films that are monologues.

What is finally disappointing in the ideal of filming "as if the camera were not there" is not that observation in itself is unimportant, but that as a governing approach it remains far less interesting than exploring the situation that actually exists. The camera *is* there, and it is held by a representative of one culture encountering another. Beside such an extraordinary event, the search for isolation and invisibility seems a curiously irrelevant ambition. No ethnographic film is merely a record of another society; it is always a record of the meeting between a filmmaker and that society. If ethnographic films are to break through the limitations inherent in their present idealism, they must propose to deal with that encounter. Until now they have rarely acknowledged that an encounter has taken place.

The main achievement of observational cinema was that it has once again taught the camera how to watch. Its failings lie precisely in the attitude of watching—the reticence and analytical inertia it induces in filmmakers, some of whom feel themselves agents of a universal truth, others of whom comment only slyly or by indirection from behind their material. In either case, the relationship between the observer, the observed, and the viewer has a kind of numbness.

Beyond observational cinema lies the possibility of a *participatory cinema*, bearing witness to the "event" of the film and making strengths of what most films are at pains to conceal. Here the filmmaker acknowledges his or her entry upon the world of the subjects and yet asks them to imprint directly upon the film aspects of their own culture. This should not imply a relaxation of purposefulness, nor should it cause filmmakers to abandon the perspective that an outsider can bring to another culture. But by revealing their role, filmmakers enhance the value of the material as evidence. By entering actively into the world of their subjects, they can provoke a greater flow of information about them. By giving them access to the film, they make possible the corrections, additions, and illuminations that only the subjects' response to the material can elicit. Through such an exchange a film can begin to reflect the ways in which its subjects perceive the world.

This is a process that goes back to Flaherty. Nanook participated in creating the film about himself, "constantly thinking up new hunting scenes for the film" (Flaherty 1950: 15). During the filming of *Moana* (1926), Flaherty projected his rushes each evening, building upon the suggestions that came from his subjects. Despite some notable exceptions, few filmmakers today are willing or able to invite such insights.

To the degree that the elements of one culture are not describable in terms of another, the ethnographic filmmaker must devise ways of bringing the viewer into the social experience of the film subjects. This is partly an act of analysis, partly what Redfield called "the art of social science." But it can also be a process of collaboration—the filmmaker combining the skills and sensibilities of the subjects with his or her own. This requires that, whatever their differences, they at least have in common a sense that a film is worth making.

Rouch and Morin's *Chronique d'un été*, about a diverse group of young Parisians, explores their lives within the context of their interest in the film itself. Despite the anonymity of the actual camera operators,[6] there is no pact made with the audience to ignore the role of the film's directors. On the contrary, it is the making of the film that binds them and their subjects together.

*Chronique d'un été* is an elaborate experiment that was very much a product of the intellectual and filmmaking climate of the 1960s. Yet it is remarkable how few of the ideas of this extraordinary film managed to penetrate the thinking of ethnographic filmmakers in the years after it was made. The approach proved too alien to an effort preoccupied with the needs of teaching or the urgency of preserving general records of imperiled societies.

It is, of course, the value of such records that is open to question. They may be unable to answer future anthropological questions except in the most superficial manner. An exhaustive analysis of a social phenomenon usually requires that the data be collected with the full extent of that phenomenon in mind. It is clear from the body of Rouch's work that he views broad salvage anthropology, based upon no defined perspective, as more hazardous to the future understanding of past societies (and therefore to a theoretical understanding of culture) than a study in which the investigator is passionately and intellectually engaged. If it is acutely perceived, he seems to say, the part may more truthfully represent the whole than the survey, which succeeds only in capturing its most superficial aspects. This is at odds with the view of Lévi-Strauss that anthropology is more like astronomy, seeing human societies from afar and only discerning their brightest constellations.

In Rouch's approach, anthropology must therefore proceed by digging from within rather than observing from without, which all too easily gives an illusory sense of comprehension. Digging necessarily disturbs the successive strata through which one passes to reach one's goal. But there is a significant difference between this human archaeology and its material counterpart: culture is pervasive and expresses itself in all the acts of human beings, whether they are responding to familiar or extraordinary stimuli. The values of a society lie as much in its dreams as in the reality it has built. Often it is only by introducing new stimuli that the investigator can peel back the layers of a culture and reveal its fundamental assumptions.

In *Kenya Boran* (1974), which James Blue and I filmed in 1972, part of what is revealed resulted from just such a process. Without the participation of our subjects, certain aspects of their situation would have remained unexpressed. Once, during a typical men's conversation over tea, we asked a man, Guyo Ali, to raise the subject of the government's advocacy of birth control. The result was an explosion of disagreement from Iya Duba, the most conservative old man present. In his reply he set forth his view of the logic of having many children in a pastoral society, followed by an impasssioned defense of cattle and cattle herding, which he was unlikely to have delivered without some such strong provocation. It was in fact the clearest expression of Boran economic values that we encountered during our stay.

Involvement with one's subjects can become a kind of pose—the fleeting recognition of the film crew that gives a sense of candor but reveals little else. For a film to gain meaning from the breakdown of old narrative conventions, that recognition must develop into a genuine conversation.

Sometimes one hears only half of the conversation. The oldest examples go back to those ruminative testimonies of lonely people, of which Roman Kroiter's *Paul Tomkowicz: Street-Railway Switch Man* (1954) is perhaps the archetype and Jorge Preloran's *Imaginero* (1970) the most compelling document. Sometimes it becomes a performance—the compulsive talking of a subject stimulated by the camera, as in Shirley Clarke's *Portrait of Jason* (1967), or Tanya Ballantyne's *The Things I Cannot Change* (1966). The out-of-work father in the latter film cannot resist the offer to control the image of himself presented to the world. Yet he bears out Rouch's dictum: whatever he tries to be, he is only more himself.

Sometimes role-playing provides the necessary stimulus. In Rouch's *Jaguar* (filmed in 1954, completed 1967) his young protagonists respond to the invitation to act out an adventure for which they have long been eager. They use the pretext of the story to reveal a private image of themselves, just as Marceline in *Chronique d'un été* uses the pretext of a film role to speak of her painful return from a concentration camp.

This is a kind of participation, but it remains one in which the film manipulates its subjects. A further step will be films in which participation occurs in the very conception and recognizes common goals. That possibility remains all but unexplored—filmmakers putting themselves at the disposal of the subjects and, with them, inventing the film.

The promise of a useful relationship between film and anthropology is still crippled by timidity on both sides. Its fulfillment will require an enlarging of the acceptable forms of both film and anthropology. Anthropology must admit forms of understanding that replace those of the written word. Film must create forms of expression reflecting anthropological thought. Films, rather than speculation, will finally demonstrate whether these possibilities are real. Ethnographic filmmakers can begin by abandoning their preconceptions about what is good cinema. It is enough to conjecture that a film need not be an aesthetic or scientific performance: it can become the arena of an inquiry.

[1973]

# Epilogue[7]

The observational and participatory approaches of the mid-1970s can now be seen more clearly as part of a larger stylistic change that was then reshaping ethnographic filmmaking. They followed a series of earlier changes that had introduced narrative, didactic, and poetic approaches into ethnographic film, and they were to be followed by films emphasizing self-reflexivity, intertextuality, and other elements of the postmodern idiom. Each initiative has survived in some form, and together they constitute a continually widening stylistic repertoire for ethnographic film.

The borderline between observational and participatory cinema now appears more blurred. In the 1970s it was *tendencies* that concerned many of us. In stressing the differences we perhaps minimized the more significant departure that both approaches marked from earlier styles of documentary. Both, by acknowledging that a film was the product of human agency (a filmmaker holding a camera) and not an anonymous and "definitive" institutional statement about a subject, attempted to put the audience in a better position to interpret the material presented to it.

Although many observational filmmakers may have wished to film "as if the camera were not there," none of the best of them believed they were producing complete, unmediated documents, nor did many of them ever hold that observational film could be ideologically transparent, as some critics have assumed.[8] Indeed, the prevailing spirit of observational cinema was contrary to such a view, and its claims were correspondingly modest. Interviews of the period show that the filmmakers cautioned time and again against taking their work as omniscient or politically neutral.[9] In retrospect, their work now appears manifestly personal in its choice of subject matter and its emphasis on the perspective of the individual filmmaker. The observational method always implied the contingency and provisional status of its findings, and it was perhaps more the fault of audiences and critics that they failed to read observational films for what they were.

Since then anthropology has also changed, and the more naïve hopes expressed for "objective" film records are heard more rarely. Similarly, the early strident calls for ethnographic film to become more scientific—or else to acknowledge itself to be art or entertainment  have been tempered by the reali zation that many previously unquestioned assumptions about scientific truth are now widely questioned. It is more generally accepted that the positivist notion of a single ethnographic reality, only waiting for anthropology to describe it, was always an artificial construction.

Partly as a consequence, the kind of anthropological knowledge based on schematic description has lost some of its former authority, while anthropological description based on experiential perspectives has regained some ground. The result is to endow the descriptive and evocative potential of film with new interest, and to suggest that knowledge of the kind conveyed by film may have renewed anthropological validity. Indeed, some recent anthropological writing is conceived in the modalities of the cinema.[10] This shift in emphasis perhaps offers new openings for film in anthropology. Ethnographic film is less often admonished to follow conventional scientific models in order to be of anthropological value. It is acknowledged to have its own legitimate

methods. By following these it may more effectively fill some of the epistemological gaps in anthropological writing, and indeed permit new perspectives to emerge in anthropology.

In the foregoing essay I sketched a possible future for participatory cinema
as one of collaboration and joint authorship between filmmakers and their
subjects. Today I am more inclined to see this as leading to a confusion of
perspectives and a restraint on each party declaring its true interests. I would
prefer in its place a principle of multiple authorship leading to a form of *intertextual* cinema. Through such an approach ethnographic film may be in a
better position to address conflicting views of reality, in a world in which
observers and observed are less clearly separated and in which reciprocal observation and exchange increasingly matter.

[1992]

## Notes

This essay was written for the International Conference on Visual Anthropology held
in Chicago in 1973 as part of the IXth International Congress of Anthropological and
Ethnological Sciences. It first appeared in *Principles of Visual Anthropology*, edited by
Paul Hockings (The Hague: Mouton, 1975).

1. From his preface to *The Cinema and Social Science* by Luc de Heusch (1962: 5).

2. Many consider Vertov the father of observational cinema, and to the extent that
he was committed to exploring the existing world with the "kino-eye" there can be no
doubt of his influence. But Vertov's films reflected the prevailing Soviet preoccupation
with fragmentation and synthesis, taking their temporal and spatial structures more
from the perceptual psychology of the observer than from structures of the events
being filmed. This was not a cinema of duration, in the sense that André Bazin attributed it to Flaherty.

3. Muybridge first attempted to photograph horses in motion in 1872 but only
achieved success in 1877, using a system of threads stretched across the track, which
were attached to the shutter releases of a bank of cameras. In 1883 he was invited by
the University of Pennsylvania to conduct a program photographing human beings and
animals in motion, for which he developed much more sophisticated techniques. A
book of photographs of horses was published by Leland Stanford in 1882, and Muybridge's sixteen-volume publication of animal photographs appeared in 1887. Thomas
Eakins, the American painter, became interested in Muybridge's work at least as early
as 1879 and later made his own chronophotographs of human beings in motion. In
Germany, Ottmar Anschütz was conducting similar experiments in chronophotography
of people and animals in 1885. In France, Étienne-Jules Marey adapted a device of the
astronomer Pierre Janssen to make consecutive photographs of birds in flight on a
single rotating photographic plate, publishing the results in 1883. Formerly the chief
assistant of Marey, Georges Demeny bridged chronophotography and cinema by showing motion pictures of diverse scenes in a 60mm gauge in 1895, the same year as the
Lumière brothers' celebrated "Salon Indien" screening.

4. Regnault began by filming Wolof pottery-making techniques at the Paris Exposition Ethnographique de l'Afrique Occidentale in 1895, but his chief interests were in physiology and styles of body movement. Baldwin Spencer was encouraged to film Aranda dances and ceremonies in Central Australia in 1901 by Alfred Cort Haddon, who had used a Lumière camera to record fire-making techniques and dances during the Cambridge Expedition to the Torres Strait in 1898. The Viennese physical anthropologist Rudolf Pöch filmed in New Guinea in 1904, and in Southwest Africa in 1907 he made the earliest ethnographic film for which the accompanying sound has been successfully synchronized.

5. *Housing Problems* (1935), made for the British Commercial Gas Association.

6. Roger Morillère, Raoul Coutard, Jean-Jacques Tarbès, and Michel Brault.

7. This epilogue was written almost twenty years later, for the second edition of *Principles of Visual Anthropology* (Hockings 1975), in which the article originally appeared.

8. See, for example, Cavadini and Strachan (1981) and MacBean (1983).

9. For a closer look at this, see interviews with many of these filmmakers in Levin (1971), Rosenthal (1971), Rosenthal (1980), and Sutherland (1978).

10. See, for example, Michael Taussig's *Shamanism, Colonialism and the Wild Man: A Study in Terror and Healing* (1987).

# CHAPTER FIVE

# Complicities of Style

I WILL BEGIN WITH what may turn out to be one of the stranger footnotes in the history of visual anthropology. A number of years ago a researcher in psychology was devising an experiment to measure castration anxiety among American men (Schwartz 1955). In order to trigger the anxiety he hit upon the tactic of putting his experimental subjects in a theater and subjecting them to screenings of film footage of Aboriginal subincision operations in Central Australia. We may find this disturbing for several reasons, not least of all because we are unused to seeing culture shock being dealt out quite so cavalierly. It tends to alarm whatever remains of our sense of cultural relativity.

But in retrospect the researcher's methods may have a crude irony for us. For quite some time, and again in a recent study (Martinez 1990), we have seen mounting evidence that many films designed *not* to shock, but to bridge cultural differences, have quite the opposite effect when shown to at least some audiences. Most anthropological and ethnographic films are not made exclusively for anthropologists, and if one of the underlying metaphors of the anthropological endeavor is to cure the disease of cultural intolerance, then it is clear that for some recipients the medicine may be wrong or too strong. We are finally beginning to take more seriously how audiences interact with films to produce meanings. But that is only one of the issues. We need to pay equal attention to the prior issue of how the implicit discursive forms of filmic representation overlap and interact with the cultures they seek to portray.

It is a commonplace that when Flaherty went to Samoa and the Aran Islands he failed to find the dramatic conflict of *Nanook of the North* (1922) and had to invent it. Granted that he may have invented much of the drama of *Nanook* as well, this is the kind of obvious, large-scale observation that may keep one from going on to ask related questions, such as why some societies (the Inuit, for example) are so heavily represented in ethnographic film as compared to anthropological writing; why some societies are represented largely by films on ritual and material culture; and to what extent ethnographic films are influenced by their search for (or creation of) strong central characters. In this regard one thinks immediately of the "stars" of the ethnographic cinema, among them Nanook, Damouré, N!ai, and Ongka.

The relation between knowledge and aesthetics is always tricky, and that between anthropology and film especially so, in part because the legitimacy for anthropology of a kind of knowledge expressed in images has yet to be fully addressed. Defining the world in writing may appear better understood, but that is often because this older method assumes a literary and linguistic tradition in common with a cultural one. When the subject is another culture, a different and less well explored set of problems arises.

Gilbert Lewis, in a paper called "The Look of Magic," has described how in *The Golden Bough* Frazer's accounts of unfamiliar cultural practices give them an oddness bordering on the surreal, making them more likely to be ascribed to magical beliefs than to everyday rationality. Indeed, he suggests that anthropological writing may make the ordinary strange simply because it *is* writing, unable to contextualize certain details sufficiently to prevent them from emerging in a lurid isolation. Pictures can help to solve this particular problem but they will inevitably introduce problems of their own. For each form of representation, Lewis says, "the conventions may need to be modified for new and unfamiliar subjects" (Lewis 1985: 416).

## Film Style vs. Cultural Style

One of the difficulties in developing a coherent discipline of visual anthropology has been pinning down basic principles from a filmmaking practice that is both slender in output and that undergoes a major technological and stylistic shift every few decades. These shifts occur because ethnographic film is not simply an alternative technology for anthropology but has its own history as part of a larger cinema culture. Compared to the rate of chopping and changing in ethnographic filmmaking, the methods of anthropology sometimes appear to have remained in a steady state.

For all that, the fickleness of ethnographic film method is in many ways illusory. Despite certain injections of anthropological ideas, its origins lie in the essentially European invention of documentary cinema, which embodies in its stylistic conventions still earlier European inventions and assumptions about behavior and discourse. Compared to the stylistic diversity of human cultures, and even considering the variations in documentary film style, this makes it quite consistent and specific in its cultural outlook. If new subjects require new conventions, it can be said that ethnographic film has often failed to find them. This stylistic narrowness has led to an unevenness in how films represent the social reality of other societies, rather like the troughs and ridges that a particular wave system creates by reinforcement and cancellation as it passes over other wave systems beneath it. Such an imbalance may also mean that as documentary film conventions are diffused into an international film language, particularly by television, they are likely to have a differential effect on the self-expression and survival of local cultures.

I would suggest that the dominant conventions of ethnographic film make some societies appear accessible, rational, and attractive to the viewer, but applied to a society with a very different cultural style they may prove quite inadequate and inarticulate. They may indeed make the society look strange, and in terms even stronger than Gilbert Lewis describes. And no amount of external explanation or contextualisation may make much difference.

This is not simply a matter of the cultural gap between filmmaker and subject or subject and audience. The cultural incompatibility is more deeply embedded in the representational system itself, including its technology, and without radical changes, the result will be much the same whether it is used by a First, Third or Fourth World filmmaker, most of whom share a global film culture.

Film has a psychological plausibility that tends to naturalize many of these conventions into invisibility. Filmmakers may be aware that alternative approaches to filmmaking are possible—Sol Worth, John Adair, Eric Michaels, and Vincent Canelli have been at pains to show this—and yet not be fully aware how their own filmmaking practice channels their efforts in certain directions and frustrates them in others. This not only affects the success or failure of individual films but may predispose filmmakers (and need I add, television companies) to make films in certain kinds of societies rather than others, or if they have less choice in the matter, to focus on a particular selection of cultural features, such as ceremonial events and technology. These can take on an exaggerated importance simply because they appear more "filmable," just as language and kinship have perhaps figured more prominently in anthropology because they are more easily written down.

The problem is often declared by an absence, or by an awkward or bizarre stopgap solution. Many films give evidence of the bafflement that has confronted their makers—films that suddenly resort to romantic imagery, narration, or a 1940s Hollywood montage when they are unable to follow a subject where it might otherwise lead them. Other films betray a hollowness behind the devices they employ. People are followed almost by reflex, doing things as though those things had a cumulative significance, but the significance never materializes. The camera zooms in on a face which reveals precisely nothing. Worse than just showing nothing, these false emphases contribute to an image of a world that is mute and off balance.

Such strangeness is the overriding quality to me of a considerable number of films on Australian Aboriginal society, including some films of my own and some made by Aboriginal filmmakers themselves. They give off a characteristic cultural tone, like a tuning fork, but it is like a sound heard at a great distance, or the spectral signature of a star. Sometimes the filmmaker's unfamiliarity or lack of sympathy with Aboriginal society can be blamed, but often it seems to have more to do with complexities in the subject and styles of cultural expression unmatched by a comparable cinematic style.

William Stanner, probably the most perceptive and politically engaged anthropologist writing about Aboriginal society in the 1950s, linked the problem to Aboriginal frames of reference. "[The] fundamental cast [of Aboriginal

11. Turkana oratorical style. From *The Wedding Camels* (1977).

thought]," he wrote, "seems to me to be analogical and *a fortiori* metaphorical. . . . I am suggesting that the association of European and aboriginal has been a struggle of partial blindness, often darkened to sightlessness on our part by the continuity of the aborigines' implicit tradition" (1958: 108–9). That sightlessness, he might have added, extends as well to the implicit presuppositions of our own habits of description and depiction.

If such difficulties cripple some ethnographic films, it is also true to say, without belittling the filmmakers, that other films have benefited from cultures that seem positively to lend themselves to the codes of Western filmmaking. Peter Loizos has praised the special cogency of the interviews in Melissa Llewelyn-Davies's film *The Women's Olamal* (1984) and has noted how, without intruding on events, the film observes the unities of time, place, and person of classical Greek tragedy (1993: 133). We get just the information we need to interpret the events, and these explanations come from the Maasai themselves, either in direct address to the camera or in observed interactions. The drama is Aristotelean and the Maasai are found to be superb explicators of events in their own lives and social system. Other filmmakers, including myself, have found a similar openness and eloquence in the cultural style of East African pastoralists, at a time when the aim was to get away from *ex cathedra* explanations and rely instead upon the self-revelation and social interactions of the people portrayed. [Figure 11.]

That aim reflected a Western realist tradition dependent upon a certain literalness of words and deeds and a focus upon events that crystallized deeper social issues. But for this to work requires that the social actors conduct themselves in the world in somewhat the same terms. It requires a society in which there is a positive value placed upon explicitness of speech, the expression of personal emotion and opinion, and the public resolution of conflict—although not necessarily to the extent of public adversarial debate, as in *The Women's Olamal*.

But I think these assumptions penetrate to another level as well. Even when ethnographic films do not follow models of classical dramaturgy—and most in fact do not—they make use of certain formal conventions of camerawork and editing that derive from it. Thus even a film guided by an anthropological commentary and concerned with economics or politics will do so in visual terms that reflect Euro-American expectations of causality, chronology, and interpersonal behavior.

## The Look of Documentary

If ethnographic writing assumes that we can be told, even if we cannot always experience, ethnographic films, even when they include explanatory commentary, assume that we will learn something experientially from the images, and in some sense make them our own. Films attempt to create a trajectory of understanding, beginning with images that make certain claims upon us. These claims are typically produced through acts of disclosure that create a sense of obligation in the viewer toward the viewed, and this can be compared to a form of submission or display of vulnerabiliity in which the subject invites our protection or interest. That is why the term "exposition" must be taken not only in the sense of setting out the subject and its context but in the literal sense of self-exposure. From the privileged knowledge that results, the audience embarks upon a problem or a journey.

The repertoire of shooting and editing techniques in both fiction and nonfiction films is employed in the first instance to gain the viewer's complicity, by disarming and penetrating the subject from every angle. It is a repertoire of exaggeration, overstepping the bounds of normal vision. There are wide-angle shots and close-ups for expansion or intimacy; montage and continuity editing to condense and intensify significant actions; and sequence-shots to direct an unwavering gaze at nuances of behavior. In documentary, various kinds of direct and indirect address have been added to these expository techniques, perhaps in recognition of the fact that although self-disclosure can be written into a script, special conditions such as the interview must be created to extract it in real life.

Some conventions seem related to implicit expectations about behavioral style, such as the assumption that characters will assert their personalities and desires visually, in ways that can be registered in close-ups of the face. The reaction shot, the over-the-shoulder shot, and the point-of-view shot all show a preoccupation with expressive behavior and response, designed to convey information about inner states and invite identification. These techniques reflect the Western interest in developing an ideology and psychology of the individual, usually in preparation for some test. As cinema relies more and more upon easily recognizable "types" (and this seems a trend in international action movies), it rejoins other theatrical traditions and is capable of wider shots, just as the masks and costumes of Kabuki theatre and Greek tragedy, and of certain sports, permit a huge stage and viewing at great distances. A further implication of the close-up—as it is used in interviews with experts, and especially in the case of television "talking heads"—is the assumption of a hierarchical and specialized society in which certain persons have the authority to define social realities and speak for others.

Interiority and the character-narration of Western cinema are encoded not only in the close-up but also in devices such as the shot/counter-shot, or reverse angle, designed to construct an imaginary geography in which the characters can move and which can become the temporary home of the viewer, or what Nick Browne (1975) has called the "spectator-in-the-text."

Other kinds of structures, such as sequence construction, point to cultural assumptions that perhaps have more general implications. For example, it seems to me that the condensation of time characteristic of classical Hollywood continuity editing, and the similar reduction of physical processes to a series of key steps in much documentary editing, point to an essentialist rather than an elaborative view of knowledge, which may have repercussions in how films represent the discourse and activities of other societies. It may well be that what is important to members of those societies lies between the shots, or in the unbroken continuity of part of the action, even if the whole process is never shown. The linearity of such editing may also go against the grain of a way of thinking that is fundamentally multidirectional in recognizing the different manifestations of objects and events. Western conceptions of causality are also implicated in such structures, as well as in the emphasis upon strict chronology in reporting events, which we can see in the predeliction for characters making formal entrances and exits from the frame, and in elapsed-time markers such as the fade and dissolve.

An exception, but a significant exception to this temporal linearity, is the convention of parallel action cutting, in which the film alternates between two actions so that they appear to be happening simultaneously. On the microlevel this kind of editing results in the simple cutaway, whose overriding purpose is commonly to bridge a temporal gap. But when it is used on a larger scale, parallel cutting tends to imply a convergence of the two lines and an eventual collision. This can be taken as the visual analogue of the conflict structure around which so much of Western filmmaking revolves.

For Western filmmakers, conflict is an almost essential discursive principle—if not in an obvious form, then in the form of issues or problems requiring resolution. It is like the carrier frequency of all other matters. Conflict structure in ethnographic films tends to mean filming events in which conflict—real or potential—brings cultural imperatives to the fore. An initiate passes a test and reconfirms a hierarchy. An episode of childhood rivalry explains how personalities are formed. Whether or not Ongka's *moka* ever comes off, or Harry ever turns up, events have occurred that reveal the principles by which people live. At a deeper level, such events reveal the unresolved paradoxes within a society that generate conflicting messages about the management of authority, allegience, and desire.

The strategies of ethnographic filming often involve seeking out significant rents in the social fabric, such as N!ai's sense of rejection and alienation in !Kung society. There is an echo in this process of the propensity of observational cinema to lie in wait for the moments in life when people let their social masks slip and literally "give themselves away." The emphasis may be upon traditional sources of tension, or contradictions between "correct" and actual behavior, or even upon a person who is so specialized or marginal in the society as to provide a revealing perspective on it. These approaches may sometimes make more sense to the anthropologist/filmmaker than to the people being filmed, but in many societies conflicts are perfectly legitimate topics of attention and often focus issues for people. They may even be seen in some sense as therapeutic eruptions which provide opportunities to readjust the social landscape.

But the reliance upon conflict structure also presupposes a society in which people traditionally get embroiled in contradictory sets of obligations and in which some benefit is seen in living through the consequences. In another society this might be deemed sheer foolishness. My experience of Aboriginal society leads me to think that it systematically resists approaches based on conflict structure and most of the expository conventions of cinema. This is partly due to a style of discourse which, as Stanner noted, is highly allusive and, when not formal, often laconic and multi-pronged. Speech here does not provide an open channel to personal feeling and opinion, nor does the close-up of a face. Personal reticence is deemed a virtue, and language is only one of the surfaces of the complex spiral of art, reference, and ritual that I have increasingly come to think of as a "heraldic" culture. [Figure 12.]

Thus, from a filmmaker's perspective it would perhaps be hard to find a greater contrast to the outspoken and skeptical pragmatism of East African pastoralists than the style of Aboriginal social interaction. Conflict is carefully contained behind the scenes, and should it break out of formal control is considered far from therapeutic and highly dangerous. Contentious issues are systematically avoided or dealt with in parables. This is not to say that Aboriginal people are not personally ambitious or contentious, but the public weal resides in the constant reinforcement and repair of personal relationships.

12. A "heraldic" culture. Photograph made during the filming of *Good-bye Old Man*, 1975.

It could also be said that the form of Aboriginal self-expression is more typically one of inscription than explanation. A film consistent with Aboriginal culture would tend to be enumerative rather than comparative and might typically consist of a demonstration of rights to land, knowledge, or other cultural property. For Aboriginal people, *showing* is in and of itself a sufficient act and can constitute a transmission of rights. Thus a film in these terms need not explain anything or develop any argument or analysis; rather, by simply existing it has the potential to be a powerful political or cultural assertion.

## The Voices of Ethnography

To be helpful, recognition of the interactions of different cultural styles must be seen in relation to the larger purposes of ethnographic representation. Ethnographic film is different from indigenous or national film production in that it seeks to interpret one society for another. Its starting point is therefore the encounter of two cultures, or as some would put it, two "texts" of life; and what it produces is a further, rather special cultural document. Increasingly, though, ethnographic films cease to be one society's private notes or diaries about others. They reach multiple audiences and I think must now be made with this in mind. They will certainly be seen and used by the societies they portray. One conclusion, therefore, is that they should become more precise—and perhaps more modest—about what they claim to be. (There is a corresponding obligation on viewers to read these limits more accurately.) Another is that they should begin looking in two directions instead of one.

This is really a question of how ethnographic film conceives and frames its subjects. Since 1898 ethnographic filmmaking has undergone a series of revolutions, introducing narrative, observational, and participatory approaches. With each, a set of assumptions about the positioning of the filmmaker and the audience has crumbled. Now it is the single identity of each of these that is under review. If we are in the midst of a new revolution, as I believe we are, it is one that is interested in multiple voices and that consists in a shift toward an *intertextual* cinema.

I think we are already seeing the changes in a new emphasis on authorship and specified cultural perspectives. Films are less often posed as omniscient or definitive descriptions, but equally, filmmakers are less likely to claim a spurious oneness with their subjects. Societies are no longer portrayed as monolithic, or unpenetrated by external and historical forces. But this is only the beginning of changes that could affect both the conventions and larger structures of ethnographic filmmaking.

The focus on authorship has two important consequences: first, in clarifying the provenance of films, and second in making the search for new directions in film strategy more understandable and acceptable to audiences. (A film with declared interests can more easily afford to be unusual.) Other modifications of film conventions will come from cultural borrowing or from explicit responses to conflicts in cultural style. I think we will increasingly regard ethnographic films as meeting places of primary and secondary levels of representation, one cultural discourse seen through, or inscribed upon another. In place of the usual centered and linear models may come more films employing repetition, associative editing, and nonnarrative structures. The de-centering of subject matter could result in films that look at the unexamined or peripheral aspects of what were previously taken to be the significant events.

The other implication of these shifts, and probably the more important one, is the recognition that ethnographic films for multiple audiences must confront contending versions of reality. Further, they must acknowledge historical experiences which overshadow any text and which inevitably escape from it. I think we shall therefore see films that become repositories of multiple authorship, confrontation, and exchange. We shall see more ethnographic films that re-deploy existing texts and incorporate parallel interpretations. We shall see more films that begin from separate directions and converge upon a common subject.

In recent years ethnographic films have become less insular in opening themselves to the voices of their subjects. Increasingly, too, ethnographic films concern themselves with the crossing and mingling of different cultural traditions. This need not, in my view, lead to an indiscriminate cultural relativity, of mirrors within mirrors and unending nesting boxes, nor does it imply an abandonment of anthropological analysis. It may instead help us to recast the problem of Self and Other more productively as a set of reciprocal relations in which film, when all is said and done, plays only a very small part.

[1990]

## Note

This essay was written as a keynote address for the Royal Anthropological Institute's IInd International Festival of Ethnographic Film, held at the University of Manchester in September, 1990. It was first published in *Film As Ethnography*, edited by Peter Ian Crawford and David Turton (Manchester: Manchester University Press, 1992).

# CHAPTER SIX

# Whose Story Is It?

ABOUT TWENTY YEARS ago anthropologists and ethnographic filmmakers began to feel uneasy about the unchallenged dominance of the author's voice in ethnographic descriptions. Both began to open their work more fully to the voices of their subjects. The intervening years have seen a tendency toward dialogic and polyphonic construction in ethnography. More recently some observers have argued that the voices in these works remain as subjugated as before, always appropriated in some discreditable way to what are, in the end, the ethnographer's projects. This has engendered a new round of self-criticism, sometimes resulting in fundamental doubts about the possibility of cultural description, sometimes in a paralyzing and, at times, proselytizing sense of guilt. Those who keep writing anthropology or making films today do so with a greater awareness of the politics and ethics of representation. But this awareness can also lead to a decidedly condescending and moralistic strain of ethnocentrism. In our preoccupation with the part others play in our concerns we may be less likely to pay attention to the part we play in theirs.

Films are objects, and like many objects they may have multiple identities. An axe-head to you may be merely a paperweight to me. Films that are inwardly dialogic, juxtaposing the voices of author and subject, may also be outwardly so, by appearing as something quite different to each of them. I have a photographic postcard from the 1930s that shows a Maasai man with a spear in one hand, a herdsman's stick in the other, and a Nestlé's condensed milk tin stuck through the lobe of one ear. This photograph and its connotations can be "read" on a variety of levels, from that of the original joke (a "savage," making a mistake about a familiar object) to a reminder of the impact of Nestlé's infant formulas on the Third World. But what I see in it at this moment is the appropriation of one society's product to another's use. [Figure 13.]

Such an image is paradoxical and surreal, like Max Ernst's zoomorphic landscapes, or a funerary jar used as an umbrella stand.[1] Its humor lies in its incongruity, in the simultaneous perception of two different frames of reference, in boundaries crossed. Certain ethnographic films present a similar paradox of two separate cultural meanings embodied in one image, like the well-known visual pun of the duck which is also a rabbit. [Figure 14.] Indeed, such films can be said to exist as two quite separate cultural objects, each appropriating certain features of the other.

Anthropology, in its traversing of cultural realities, is always on the verge

13. Photographic postcard of Maasai man, Kenya, 1930s.

of the surreal, but it endeavors to neutralize what Malinowski called the "co-efficient of weirdness" through the rationale of cultural translation (Clifford 1988: 151). The lesson of surrealism, however, is that the experience of para-

14. The duck which is also a rabbit.

dox is in itself significant and must be grasped to generate new perceptions. Thus, if these films have special value, anthropologically or more broadly, it is that they enable us somehow to confront the intersecting of the worlds they describe.

The properties of these worlds sometimes exert contradictory and disturbing gravitational forces on the ethnographic materials that anthropologists and filmmakers create. Photographs and films, perhaps more than written descriptions, seem liable to distortion in this way, because of the continuity they share with the physical and sensory life of their referents. Such ties to another existence, at once subversive and at odds with the intentions of the maker, and yet also frequently in collusion with them, can become the strength or the demise of many an ethnographic film. What I shall now describe must, for fieldworkers, be a fairly common but perhaps underdescribed phenomenon: that of feeling one's work disintegrating and being pulled back and reclaimed by the lives that generated it.

In October 1978, Judith MacDougall and I shot material for a film at an Aboriginal outstation in northern Australia, where a small group of people were attempting to resettle their traditional clan land. Their plans hinged on a few old cattle yards left over from missionary days, which they hoped to turn into an economic base by mustering the wild cattle that roamed the surrounding bush.

It is important to realize how precarious the survival of such small Aboriginal groups was, both culturally and economically. In the settlement these people had left, fifty kilometers to the north, the 800 inhabitants spoke seven different Aboriginal languages. Some clans consisted of only a handful of people, and their future as autonomous groups depended upon the strength and ambitions of a few active family members.

Living at the outstation were about thirty people, many of them young and inexperienced at cattle work. They were led by an old Aboriginal man who

15. Ian Pootchemunka in the cattle yard at Ti-Tree outstation. From *Three Horsemen* (1982).

had been a drover and stockman all his life. He was no longer physically strong, and what was clear from fairly early on was that most of the work of the station was in fact being done by his nephew's son, a thirteen-year-old boy named Ian Pootchemunka. Ian worked hard, set an example for others, and saw himself as eventually taking over from the old man. As in much of Aboriginal life, the group's prospects seemed here to depend crucially upon the strength and survival of one person.

Our filming, rather like this account of it, began by concentrating on the old man and ended on the boy. But not long after we finished filming, we heard that the boy had died of an illness. At this stage my perception of the material shifted quite radically. In some unaccountable way I felt that the film footage was now bound up with the boy and belonged to him, not in some proprietory way, but existentially. It seemed like a physical piece of his life, his hopes and his death, and inseparable too from the community to which he belonged. Although this changed perspective was occasioned by his death, I believe it was always an inherently available one. When we heard of his death we felt that the film, as a film, had also died. We only returned to it some time later when the boy's parents asked us to complete it in his memory (*Three Horseman* [1982]). [Figure 15.]

The point of recounting this is to ask: whose story was it? Was the film our story or his? By what means can we distinguish the structures we believe are in our films from the structures that are discerned in them, often without our knowing, by their subjects? And is a film in any sense the same object for those who made it, for whom it may have the status of discourse, and for those who in passing have left their physical traces upon it? The question of "whose story?" thus has both an ontological and moral dimension.

Some films construct new narratives out of other peoples' lives, as Flaherty's often did.[2] One could say that John Marshall's *The Hunters* (1958) does this in its creation of the story of a long hunt out of several shorter hunting expeditions. Many other films, including some of Marshall's such as *An Argument about a Marriage* (1969), *A Joking Relationship* (1966), and *The Meat Fight* (1973), take their structures more directly from the events they record. They become stories from the filmmaker's perspective by their framing of these events, although the participants would perhaps neither frame them that way nor recognize them as stories in their own narrative tradition.

Still other films attempt to accommodate indigenous narrative forms, either by mimicking them in their own structures (*The Hunters* is, arguably, conceived as a San hunting tale) or by utilizing the narratives of indigenous speakers. Roger Sandall's *Coniston Muster* (1972) is built around a group of stories told by Aboriginal stockmen, and more recent ethnographic films regularly incorporate interview material and stories addressed to the filmmaker and the camera.

But the inclusion of indigenous narrative often raises the question of whether the film is making indigenous statements or merely absorbing a device into its own narrative strategies. Inevitably a method that purports to disperse some of its authority to its subjects is also capable of using this to reinforce its own. This has long been a critical issue in interview-based documentaries. As Bill Nichols has noted, in many of these films "a gap remains between the voice of a social actor recruited *to* the film and the voice *of* the film" (1983: 23).

Sometimes this problem is avoided by clearly marking the use of indigenous narrative as a stylistic device, inviting us to read it in a complex way as the author's perception of another narrative mode. Rouch's film *La Chasse au lion à l'arc* (1965) begins with a Gao storyteller's epic tale of lion hunting, setting the stage for Rouch's own epic treatment of the hunt for a lion called "The American." In a similar way, Robert Gardner borrows the Dani fable of a snake and a bird at the beginning of *Dead Birds* (1963) to lend mythic resonance to his own story of ritual warfare, and to offer a paradigm for it.[3]

In another Rouch film, *Jaguar* (1967), this overlapping of voices is more complex. To make the film, Rouch invited three young men to enact the sort of adventure that was common for just such young men to undertake in the 1950s. This is their story, and yet through the strange circumstances of filmmaking here they are, *playing* their story. They also recount it on the sound track in a mixture of improvised dialogue, jokes, and reminiscence. As in *La Chasse au lion*, we feel we are witnessing the genesis of an epic tale, which will be elaborated over the years to eager youths in the village. And this aspect of the film soon becomes recognizable as the distinctive voice of Rouch, for whom the story is not just of a single African journey but a celebration of the collective experience of a generation of young Africans. Anecdote is here transformed into legend. By the end of the film it is this second narrative voice that is dominant. The story is now Rouch's and its subjects have become mythic figures. "These young men," he tells us on the sound track, "are heroes of the modern world."

Anthropology in recent years has been questioning its earlier aspirations toward scientific positivism and many of the conceptual categories through which it has described life in other societies. Recent ethnographies acknowledge in their own design what anthropologists have posited for years—that people experience the world through different conceptual frameworks. The limitations of the ethnographer's voice are not necessarily offset by the inclusion of indigenous quotations. The language of the classical ethnographies has been found inadequate for reaching broader understandings of certain aspects of culture, particularly in societies with substantially different notions of the self, which previous invocations of the "native point of view" tended to take as unproblematic.

Recognition of this inadequacy has led to approaches oscillating between critical introspection on the one hand and a search for new formal and multivocal strategies on the other. Anthropologists are now more conscious that they too are telling stories. But curiously, although ethnographic filmmaking has followed a parallel course, it does not seem to have done so notably under the inspiration of anthropology. The challenging of authorial certainties, of received stylistic conventions, the introduction of self-reflexivity, the moves toward subtitling indigenous speech (allowing the inclusion of indigenous texts) all appear to have emerged from ethical and epistemological questions that documentary filmmakers began asking themselves thirty years ago. It is probably true to say that ethnographic filmmakers became sensitive to some of these textual implications independently of ethnographic writers.

If anthropologists once resisted the idea that they were telling stories, they have now certainly made up for it. Modern ethnographies are often extremely complex stories of other lives, or stories of anthropological encounters in the field. They may be manifold constructions, juxtaposing indigenous texts with anthropological reflections and analysis.[4] By using the words of their informants, anthropologists (and ethnographic filmmakers) bring into their work the narrative forms and cultural assumptions embedded in speech. Wherever "quotation" occurs, an indigenous narrative model is possible.

For all that, there are persisting doubts about this form of representation. If ethnographies now incorporate other voices, what textual independence do these voices actually have? In one sense, all texts used in this way are subordinated to the text of the author. This may be more true of written ethnography than film, in which more unencoded information can be said to "leak" from the images, but in both cases the author makes certain decisions about what texts to include or exclude.

It can be argued that it is only through the author's agency that we are allowed to hear other voices, by a process of "transmission." But the question of how other voices can be transmitted is really preempted by another question: how the materials out of which a work is made act themselves to define and control its meaning. If a film is a reflection of an encounter between filmmaker and subject, it must be seen to some degree as produced by the subject. It is a rare book or film that emerges at the end of the process as the author preconceived it. The shape of the text may be said to take on characteristics of the subject by virtue of "exposure" to it, like a photographic plate.

This, of course, is the specific aim of certain films. Observational filmmaking was founded on the assumption that things happen in the world which are worth watching, and that their own distinctive spacial and temporal configurations are part of what is worth watching about them. Observational films are frequently analytical, but they also make a point of being open to categories of meaning that might transcend the filmmaker's analysis. This stance of humility before the world can of course be self-deceiving and self-serving, but it also implicitly acknowledges that the subject's story is often more important than the filmmaker's. This can be seen as a necessary first step toward a more participatory cinema.

Sometimes there is no question whose story dominates. The scenes of youth culture in Karel Reisz and Tony Richardson's *Momma Don't Allow* (1956), for example, exceed any simple aesthetic or sociological "framing." As in this case, the most explicitly observational films are usually fragments, or fragmentary. This is true of many of Timothy Asch's Yanomamö films. It is also true of most of John Marshall's African films, as well as his series of films on the Pittsburgh police, which have titles like *Three Domestics* (1970), *Henry Is Drunk* (1972) and *You Wasn't Loitering* (1973). Longer observational films are more often patterned on the narratives of realist fiction—for example, the Maysles brothers' *Salesman* (1969), Gary Kildea's *Celso and Cora* (1983), and Bob Connolly and Robin Anderson's *Joe Leahy's Neighbours* (1988).[5]

Short observational films often come about accidentally, since the observational method typically involves filming things without knowing how they will turn out. An instance of this is a film we made in Uganda, which began with a group of Jie men making leather straps and spear covers. A conversation started up in the casual way these things do, and then evolved into a heated discussion and argument about the behavior of motor cars and their drivers. The resulting film (*Under the Men's Tree* [1974]) is really no more than this fragment, surrounded by a few other sequences of talk and cattle herding. Its primary logic is the logic of the conversation.[6] This basic structure is sometimes blurred, and framed by other material, but it remains the dominant one.

Other films "belong" to their subjects in a different sense. I mean here particularly films that revolve around a single person. Often they are planned in this way, but occasionally someone emerges unexpectedly from the background and lays claim to them, as happened in Tanya Ballantyne's film *The Things I Cannot Change* (1966) and in *Three Horsemen*, as described above.

One is always aware of this possibility in a negative sense when making films. There are people in any group who will be drawn to the film or the filmmakers, just as there are people who will volunteer to be an anthropologist's informants. Sometimes it is simply because they are intelligent and inquiring of mind. Sometimes they are marginal people, attracted to the outsider from a sense of their own awkward status, or in search of fulfillment. Many view themselves as brokers, experts or intermediaries. They can pose a challenge to the filmmaker's carefully guarded sense of control, for they are inclined to put themselves at the center of any enterprise. One can resist them or be drawn to the complexities in them. The opposite case can also occur. When we were filming in northern Kenya in 1973–74, we heard about Lorang, one of the most senior men in the area, but initially he wanted to have nothing to do with us. We gradually got to know him, became friends, and ended up making an entire film about him (*Lorang's Way* [1979]).

There are many instances in documentary cinema of the physical and spiritual being of a person seeming to overflow the film that set out to contain it. The film "transmits" the person's presence, but it is as though the film is then consumed by it. Bob Dylan looks out from the film *Don't Look Back* (1966) as if to say, "This isn't much, and I will do what I like with it."

But the presence may not be so canny or assertive. Sometimes there is a gradual shift in the orientation of a film toward a particular narrative voice. In a series of films we made about Sunny Bancroft, an Aboriginal stockman in rural New South Wales, it was only while making the third film (*Sunny and the Dark Horse* [1986]) that we recognized the links between his personal style and the broader Australian tradition of narrative poetry and tall tales, as found in the works of Banjo Patterson and Henry Lawson.[7] I think this was a case, more common than one perhaps supposes, of a local culture slowly gaining an influence over the filmmakers and the film. There are many variations on this theme, one of which is evident in Rouch's films made under what he calls "cine-trance," such as *Tourou et Bitti* (1971).

Some films aim at just such an overflowing. The filmmaker Jorge Preloran has created a sub-genre of ethnobiographical films centered around extensive sound-recordings of his subjects recounting their lives. It began with Hermogenes Cayo, a religious painter and wood carver from the high plateau of

Argentina. The fullness of a single life is the overriding quality of this film, *Imaginero* (1970), and other films such as *Cochengo Miranda* (1974) and *Zerda's Children* (1978). To Preloran the film is, in certain essentials, the work of the subject himself—his voice, his words, the images of him, and the images he himself has made. Preloran has created the film, but then (to quote Preloran),

> one day the film is completed. . . . And suddenly the film is not mine any-more. . . . It has a life of its own; suddenly Hermogenes is there in direct commu-nication with the audience, and you are left out in the cold. (Sherman 1985: 37)

I need not defend Preloran here on charges of naïveté. He is as aware as any-one of how a filmmaker analyzes, selects, and finally constructs. His point is, I think, a more sophisticated one which goes beyond the assumption that film-makers, or any other makers of cultural artifacts, exert total control over their work. Just as we see that the maker is the locus of a set of cultural and histori-cal forces, so too we must see the film in the same light, and acknowledge the maker as but one aspect of its coming into being. Here I side with Roland Barthes in holding that a film or a photograph is both coded and analogical, and that it can never be wholly the maker's fabrication.

I turn now to a rather different way in which films are impressed and, in-deed, possessed by their subjects: when they become bound into a relationship with the subject as part of a larger set of cultural meanings. Some films are of little interest or immediate consequence to those who appear in them. They belong to a discourse to which they are largely indifferent. That famous re-mark of Sam Yazzie, the Navajo elder, to John Adair and Sol Worth—"Will making movies do the sheep good?"—is not some sage comment on the pre-tentions of academics but a statement of different cultural priorities.

Clearly, films matter to their subjects when they have practical or symbolic implications for them. Films are shaped as much by the structures into which they are placed as by their avowed form and intention. The making of some films is thus part of a social process larger than the film itself. This can be said of many films in the abstract—commercial fiction films are part of a social process too—but I am concerned here with films that are explicitly structured by what their subjects expect of them.

The Aranda of Central Australia can have expected little from the films of Walter Baldwin Spencer when he made them in 1901, nor can the Dani have expected much from Robert Gardner's sixty years later, especially as in Gard-ner's view "one essential advantage lay in the fact that the Dugum Dani did not know what a camera was" (1969: 30). One might look for more precise expectations among people more knowledgeable about the media, except that many apparently sophisticated people are merely flattered or intimidated when a camera is turned in their direction. Americans and Europeans are all too ready to put themselves unquestioningly in the hands of "media professionals." Perhaps, then, one should look to films of advocacy for such an influence—except that many of these are made on behalf of people who are never consulted. I know of no easy way of identifying such films, except to say that they tend to be films in which the makers were to some degree under the direction of the subjects. One might include here the more improvisational passages in Flaherty or Rouch, where scenes were constructed *for* the film. But I should like to look at another group of films in which rituals or ritualized relationships impose a signifying structure.

Australian ethnographic filmmaking has been concerned with Aboriginal ritual performance from the very beginning and there is a large body of work devoted to it. It includes an important series of films made by Roger Sandall with the anthropologist Nicolas Peterson in the 1960s and another group of films made by Ian Dunlop with the anthropologist Howard Morphy more recently. In both cases it is fair to say (and they have said it themselves) that often neither filmmaker nor anthropologist had a very clear idea of what was going on until after the fact.

Sandall's work tends to emphasize the spacial relationships and choreography of the rituals. Dunlop's gives more attention to the role of ritual leaders and translates more of the conversations and song texts. But at the time of filming, both filmmakers had to follow the course of events and take advice as best they could. The organizers of the rituals, for their own prestige, had an interest in conducting them properly under the eye of the camera, and they also had an interest in how the films would be used. The most secret rituals could be shown only to the legitimate owners or certain permitted outsiders. In more public rituals, certain meanings—of song texts, for example—could not be disclosed because they belonged to a particular clan or smaller kin group. In these films the actual words may be recorded and translated literally, but their significance often may not be evident to outsiders. The filmmaker is always under instruction, and many of the film's meanings remain known only to the film's subjects.

This sense of ownership is strongly articulated at the end of Kim McKenzie's film, *Waiting for Harry* (1980), when the ritual's organizer, Frank Gurrmanamana, tells the assembled participants:

> This film is mine. . . . Now men everywhere will see my sacred emblems, just as, in many places, I have seen theirs. So. The emblems I hold so dear are now on a film, so the film is also dear to me.

These films serve political and ritual purposes. Even if it is not always evident to the outside viewer, they are part of a continuing process of cultural reinforcement and contestation. They have themselves become emblems.

I shall attempt to describe, from the perspective I gained while making it,

16. Angus Namponan and his children near Cape Keerweer, northern Queensland.
From *Familiar Places* (1980).

the cultural and political circumstances of one such film, *Familiar Places*
(1980), shot in Australia in 1977. It does not concern ritual as such, but ritual
is never far in the background. What may be of interest is the way in which it
enters into a complex network of relationships intersecting what film theorists
like to call the "profilmic event."

    The film was made near Cape Keerweer on the coast of the Gulf of Carpen-
taria in northern Queensland. It was made at a time of considerable pressure
on Aboriginal communities by mining interests and State government authori-
ties. The film records part of a journey made by a group of Aboriginal people
and a young anthropologist to map sites in traditional clan country. This is a
complex landscape of salt pans and estuaries, filled with places of significance, both secular and sacred. It is an area of increase centers (where
specific creatures may be encouraged to multiply), secret wells, cremation
grounds, and sites where totemic ancestors are said to have carved out the
inlets and sandhills. Different parts of the land belonged to different clans, but
when we made the film few people had visited it for thirty or forty years.
Almost everyone lived at the old mission settlement of Aurukun 100 kilometers to the north. The young people had never been here, and for older people,
returning meant reorienting themselves to a terrain they had perhaps last seen
when they were themselves young.

The film concerns a dozen or so people but focuses primarily on an old man, Jack Spear Karntin, a younger couple (Angus and Chrissie Namponan, who are bringing their children to see their traditional land), and the anthropologist, Peter Sutton. On the sound track Sutton provides a rough chronology of the journey and outlines his views on the significance of the mapping process.

Looking at this casually, Western viewers might suppose they were in familiar narrative territory. Sutton appears to be in charge of the story as well as the expedition. Old Jack Spear appears to be making nostalgic visits to places of his youth. The couple, the Namponans, appear to be caught between two worlds and somewhat uncertain of their own culture. The children look like any children enjoying a holiday. [Figure 16.]

A different perception of these relationships, and of the film as a whole, first requires recognizing that although Sutton is the voice "in the film" he is not necessarily the voice "of the film"—indeed he is only one of a set of players in a complex cultural drama. We attempted in the film to reveal certain aspects of this drama and Sutton's role in it. In one scene Angus Namponan puts pressure on Sutton to map his country rather than other people's, because time is running out before the Australian "wet" sets in. This is one of the points at which the political significance of the mapping, and Sutton's involvement as an agent of Aboriginal interests, is evident. People speak to one another in the film, but they are also speaking for other audiences, and they are aware of the film itself as a channel of communication.

When we came to analyze this situation we could point to more than a dozen separate "voices" or directions of discourse represented in the film. For example, although Aboriginal people may be speaking to Sutton, they are also addressing one another, and through the film other audiences, both Aboriginal and non-Aboriginal.[8] However, such an analysis focuses on speaking and telling, and in an important sense this misses the point, for films are also about *showing*. For Aboriginal people this may be culturally of far greater consequence than it is for others. If we ask, "Whose story is it?" in Aboriginal terms, we may have to enlarge considerably our conception of what is *narrative*.

Aboriginal people in this part of Australia commonly speak of "story places" when referring to totemic sites, for these are places that were discovered and left for future generations when the spirit ancestors moved over the land. Such events can of course be recounted as "stories," but more importantly they form points in a larger narrative of travel through the country. The concept of totem, as an emblem of clan identity, is thus intimately bound up with the idea of story or narrative. A spoken reference, or the showing of a totemic object, conjures up both one's clan identity and the narrative associated with it. Thus, as Peter Sutton noted himself soon after the filming, a film can be conceived of by Aboriginal people as one more medium of reference, for ritually *showing* and thus giving recognition to objects and places. In

17. Chrissie Namponan introduces one of her children to the spirits. From *Familiar Places* (1980).

doing so it takes on all the accompanying connotations of "story" and narrative. If this happens, the film itself becomes a new story and object of totemic significance. It is not perceived merely as the filmmaker's story; it becomes, in effect, Aboriginal cultural property (Sutton 1978: 1).

When the Namponan children are being introduced to their country for the first time, the showing is not only to familiarize them with it. It is an act of investiture, a formal endorsement of their rights to the country. The showing, and their seeing, stand in place of what we might consider a formal statement or delineation of rights. Showing here constitutes a kind of charter. It demonstrates the crucial importance of the visual in Aboriginal law and culture. [Figure 17.]

As we were filming we became aware that the perception that Aboriginal people had of the mapping, as a recognition (or "*registration*") of their clan territories, extended to the film itself. There are many expressions of this in the film, as when Jack Spear formally addresses the camera and sound recorder; but simply by the act of participating in the film people are appropriating it for an Aboriginal purpose. Sutton has written that "when filming is 'permitted,' it is a mistake to see this permission as a passive acquiescence out of mere politeness, cooperativeness or desire for money. In a great many cases, film is being actively *used*" (Sutton 1978: 6). Moreover, it may be essential that the filming be done by an outsider, who fulfils the traditional role of *pant*, or disinterested adjudicator, since a local person would clearly be placed in an equivocal position if asked to witness another person's claims (Sutton 1978: 3–4).

Here it becomes possible to say that the film is no longer outside the situation it describes, nor has it merely been expanded through self-reflexivity or acknowledgment of its fuller meanings. It is inside someone else's story. If one seeks to define its shape at this level of interpretation, one may say that the film not only reflects Aboriginal narrative by moving physically over the country, but has become formally part of an implicit Aboriginal narrative of ritual display.

Whenever cultural forces within a subject act upon the structure of a film in the ways I have described—through the patterning of an event, a personal narrative, appropriation to a local function, or in some other way—the film can be read as a compound work, representing a crossing of cultural perspectives. Sometimes the process goes no further. We are familiar with films in which we "see through" the assumptions of the maker to those of the subjects, and are aware of their mutual illegibility.

Whether a film is capable of generating more complex statements seems to depend upon the filmmaker's ability to make the film more than merely a report on a cultural encounter and, instead, embody it. Rouch, for example, comes upon his subjects in the act of self-discovery, in the borderlands between cultures or in the liminal zones of ritual and possession. He sees liberation in the crossing of boundaries, which finds its metaphor in the scene in *Jaguar* where Lam, Illo, and Damouré slip behind the police post to enter the unknown land of the Gold Coast. Rouch is a kind of cultural gun-runner. A different filmmaker (a Kim McKenzie or Marc-Henri Piault, for example) might make films that express the constant testing and reinvention of culture, or that (in the case of Jorge Preloran) represent the emergence in his subjects of an historical consciousness. But this kind of film can only exist when filmmakers regard their work as more than a transmission of prior knowledge. They need to approach filming instead as a way of creating the circumstances in which new knowledge can take us by surprise.

[1991]

## Notes

This paper was first presented on May 23, 1991 at the NAFA (Nordic Anthropological Film Association) Conference in Oslo. It is reprinted by permission of the American Anthropological Association from *Visual Anthropology Review* 7 (2) (fall 1991): 2–10. I am grateful to several of the NAFA participants for their comments, and I am particularly indebted to Peter Sutton (1978) and Fred Myers (1988) for their earlier discussions of *Familiar Places*.

1. Buñuel's *Las Hurdes* [*Land Without Bread*] (1932) is provocatively surrealist in a similar way in its presentation of European squalor and misery in the guise of a travelogue, accompanied by the "high art" of European classical music, in this case the Brahms Fourth Symphony.

2. However, in making *Nanook of the North* (1922), Flaherty's relationship with the Inuit seems to have permitted a more open approach. A number of scenes were first suggested by Nanook and then acted by him.

3. Similarly, I use the recounting of the myth of Purrukuparli at the beginning of *Good-bye Old Man* (1977) as a way of linking the events surrounding the *pukumani* ritual to Tiwi ideas of death.

4. See, for example, Walter Goldschmidt's *Kambuya's Cattle* (1969), Paul Rabinow's *Reflections on Fieldwork in Morocco* (1977), and Peter Loizos's *The Heart Grown Bitter* (1981). The latter is structurally very innovative and brings to mind A.J.A. Symons's seminal biography of Frederick Rolfe, *The Quest for Corvo* (1934).

5. An exception is the work of Frederick Wiseman. His films on American public institutions, such as *Hospital* (1969) and *Welfare* (1975), follow a theme-and-variations structure in which the fragments are subsumed by discourses on regimentation and the fallibility of all such institutions.

6. In certain contexts the film perhaps has ironic implications, but these remain implicit. The response of some American and European students to the film has been: "Here are a remote people talking about their world. But no, we are mistaken, they are also talking about ours."

7. The two earlier films made with Sunny Bancroft are *Collum Calling Canberra* (1984) and *Stockman's Strategy* (1984). A fourth, shorter film was also made, called *A Transfer of Power* (1986).

8. These variously directed discourses may be described as follows. To begin with:
    1. Sutton is speaking to his imagined audience.
    2. The filmmaker is also speaking to an imagined audience.
    3. The Aborigines are speaking to one another.
    4. The Aborigines are speaking to Sutton.
    5. Sutton is speaking to the Aborigines.
    6. Occasionally the Aborigines speak to the filmmaker.
    7. Occasionally, too, the filmmaker speaks to the Aborigines.
    8. One might also guess that during the filming, the filmmaker spoke to the Aborigines through Sutton, which in fact was the case.

But here things become more complicated, because:
    9. The Aborigines are speaking to an imagined audience *through* the film.
    10. The Aborigines are speaking to one another through the film.
    11. The Aborigines are speaking to Sutton through the film.
    12. The Aborigines are speaking to an imagined audience through Sutton.

And finally:
    13. The filmmaker is speaking to the Aborigines through the film.
    14. The filmmaker is speaking to Sutton through the film.
    15. Sutton is speaking to the filmmaker, through the film; and
    16. Sutton is speaking to the Aborigines, through the film.

# CHAPTER SEVEN

# Subtitling Ethnographic Films

THE APPEARANCE IN THE 1970s of the first subtitled ethnographic films produced an effect upon viewers not unlike that of seeing the first subtitled feature films in the years after World War II. Before that, almost all ethnographic films had been constructed around a voice-over commentary which spoke about the people concerned but rarely allowed them to speak themselves. If their voices were heard at all, what they said was either ignored (suggesting it was not really worth understanding) or was translated by another voice that covered their own words and, in a sense, spoke *for* them. Now, as ethnographic films adopted subtitles, the people in them began to achieve some of the immediacy, individuality, and complexity of people in fiction films. Conveying their speech in subtitles in effect accorded them the status of people who appeared in feature films from France, Italy, or Japan and suggested they had an equal right to be heard. It paid attention to their intellectual life—indeed, often acknowledged for the first time that they had an intellectual life—and provided a new pathway to their thoughts and feelings. In documentary films, the speech of people in even remote, small-scale societies now began to be treated much as it was in "direct cinema" documentaries about Europeans and Americans, which for the past decade had increasingly emphasized conversations and interviews. Subtitles propelled ethnographic films into a new phase. Audiences no longer listened to spoken information *about* people in these films but began to watch and listen to them more directly.

Although a number of ethnographic filmmakers of the 1950s and 1960s were concerned with the speech of their subjects, almost none of them had attempted to use subtitles. Jean Rouch chose to work primarily in French, the colonial *lingua franca* of the West African states where he made most of his films. Although he increasingly used synchronous sound (indeed was one of the pioneers of it), films such as *Moi, un noir* (1957), *La Pyramide humaine* (1961), and *La Chasse au lion à l'arc* (1965) either used commentaries in French (spoken by Rouch or his subjects) or dialogue in French, rather than subtitled African languages. Rouch continued to reject subtitles for many years, considering them an intrusion upon the images, and perhaps also upon the poetic power of commentary. Robert Gardner also opted for voice-over commentary when producing *Dead Birds* (1963), making little attempt to record Dani dialogue while shooting with an unblimped Arriflex camera. A few lines are dubbed in, but for the most part Gardner himself gives us the words and thoughts of his subjects, as John Marshall had done before him in *The Hunters* (1958). Gardner's interests lay elsewhere than in conversation, as his subsequent films show. In the mid-1960s Asen Balikci and Quentin Brown decided against subtitling the dialogue in the Netsilik Eskimo series, preferring separate printed texts and an unencumbered screen in films intended for use in schools. Jorge Preloran, in his film *Imaginero* (1970), gave a spoken translation of the words of his protagonist, Hermogenes Cayo, but treated this in a spontaneous, almost antiphonal way, taking care not to cover up the original speech. Although Roger Sandall used synchronous sound in making his films of Australian indigenous rituals in the mid-1960s, he argued that if he had used subtitles they would have amounted to little more than "semantic noise," because the shots captured only unrelated fragments of speech, while the ritual songs were too esoteric and repetitive to be comprehensible to outsiders (1969: 18–19).

At some point during 1961 Timothy Asch and John Marshall began editing *A Joking Relationship* (1966), a conversation between N!ai and her great-uncle /Ti!kay filmed by Marshall among the Ju/'hoansi in the Kalahari in 1957–58. It was one of a series of single-event films, including *A Group of Women* (1969) and *Men Bathing* (1972), that they were to make for teaching purposes out of Marshall's extensive footage, after scrapping a much longer film called *Marryings* modeled more closely on *The Hunters*. Unlike such films as *A Curing Ceremony* (1969) and *N/um Tchai* (1974), *A Joking Relationship* was essentially a verbal encounter that cried out for translation. The idea of subtitling it was so obvious that it seems to have come to Asch and Marshall simultaneously. Subtitled European films had been shown increasingly widely in America since World War II, stimulated by the growth of American tourism abroad and, according to Asch, by the return of soldiers from Europe who wanted to see films in their original languages (1991: 128). One day Asch went to see Godard's *À Bout de souffle* (1960) at the Brattle Theatre near Harvard University, and he remembers the moment of revelation when he thought of subtitling the Ju/'hoansi films. But when he mentioned the idea to Marshall, he found that Marshall had thought of it too.[1]

Marshall's "sequence films" received only limited circulation for several years. Few were released before 1970, and not all of the remainder were subtitled. But by 1968, when Asch filmed *The Feast* (1970) and I shot *Imbalu* (directed by Richard Hawkins, released 1989), both films focused on speech and were meant to be subtitled. By then it would not have occurred to me *not* to film with this in mind, and it was central to my approach when I filmed *Nawi* (1970), *To Live with Herds* (1972), and *Under the Men's Tree* (1974) with Judith MacDougall later in 1968.[2] After completing *The Feast*, Asch and his associate Napoleon Chagnon returned to Venezuela to produce a major series of "sequence films" on the Yanomamö, many incorporating subtitles as a matter of course.

Subtitles soon became part of the language of ethnographic films. In many ways they were a more fundamental element in them than in fiction films, which tended to be made in the filmmakers' own languages, with subtitles figuring primarily as an afterthought for foreign audiences. It is true that some European coproductions envisaged multiple national audiences, but they dealt with this by post-synchronizing the dialogue in several languages. When feature films were made, little if any consideration was given to the effect subtitles might have upon visual content, much less to using subtitles actively as a means of emphasis. Very often films were subtitled on the basis of a post-production script alone, with the duration of each title derived from a formula. But when subtitles were used in ethnographic films, their effect upon the audience had to be taken into account from the very beginning. Subtitling became one of the creative ingredients of the filmmaking process.

The difficulties of translating speech in ethnographic films contributed to this more integrated approach to subtitling. Often the translations available were rough or ambiguous, having been made not by the filmmakers but by native speakers whose grasp of the filmmakers' language was limited, or by anthropologists who were still in the process of learning the local language. Sometimes the dialogue was translated during the editing, as the filmmakers looked at a rough-cut on an editing machine; or the film was edited by referring to earlier transcriptions and translations of the field tapes. In either case, the subtitling called for considerable imaginative interpretation and condensation. The result was often the product of a chain of translations, starting with a complete but rough literal translation of the rushes, proceeding to a more idiomatic version of the scenes to be used, and ending with several steps of adapting this to the actual screen time available and the cadences of the original speech. Longer utterances had to be broken down into a series of separate titles. The final step involved spotting the beginning and end-frames of each title, usually directly on the workprint. At this point fine adjustments of meaning and tempo were made, in an effort to restore some of the allusiveness and spontaneity lost in the process of condensation.[3]

## Subtitling As Interpretation

The specific constraints of subtitling might be regarded as the unfortunate but unavoidable consequences of this method. Alternatively, they can be seen as an integral part of the analytical and interpretive process that all filmmaking involves. Subtitling is certainly open to error and abuse, for it has the potential to make people say what the filmmaker wants them to say. But subtitling is also one of the many ways of making connections within an abundance of fragmentary and often multivalent film material. Films always present a reconstruction of the material shot or otherwise acquired for them, shaped both by the ideas and the particular aesthetic sensibility underlying the film. In this context there is no absolute standard of accuracy in translation, and one's priorities may vary considerably when (for example) making an archival record or a film for a wider audience. Completeness and literalness of translation may not be the primary objectives, for the filmmaker may be seeking to express personal and cultural meanings at a deeper level.

Documentary film material is generally complex and ambiguous, and since conversations in life are less orderly and economical than in fiction, they tend to offer more choices than fiction films about what to subtitle and how to subtitle it. In fiction, dialogue is usually coherent, and lines of dialogue rarely overlap. In documentary, this is rarely the case. Often several people speak at once, and several topics are discussed intermittently. When scenes are included to make particular points or announce significant themes, the way in which the subtitles are written can make the difference between thematic clarity and confusion. How a line is phrased often points a scene in a particular direction. In scenes with a great deal of dialogue, the subtitles nearly always make a selection from what is actually said. Certain topics can then be given precedence over others, reinforcing a similar process that has occurred in the shooting. Implied meanings, or meanings only understandable in a larger context, can be made more explicit, and garbled statements can be streamlined. If topics overlap or are pursued discontinuously, there will be a tendency for the filmmaker to tie together the threads of meaning and omit the interrruptions.

Subtitling is one of the final acts in making a film. Before it occurs, the subject matter has been chosen out of a myriad of choices, the filming has followed its many diverse twists and turns of planning and chance, the camera has framed certain images and not others, and at least the larger pieces of the film have been hacked out of the rushes. The writing and placing of subtitles involves considerable polishing and fine-tuning, but unlike the *ex post facto* subtitling of a feature film, this remains part of the creative process, influencing the pacing and rhythm of the film as well as its intellectual and emotional content. Subtitling is also specific to the language in which the film is made. If a film is to be re-subtitled in another language, even the mildest of filmmakers can become quite menacing if the producer suggests this is merely a technical process.

In writing subtitles, the filmmaker has a variety of ways of shading their meaning according to his or her broader knowledge of the scenes and the people in them, just as in life we unconsciously make adjustments for the meanings of what people say according to what we know about them. The same words, in the same tone of voice, can express a compliment or an insult, a statement or a question. Earlier scenes in the film may help us know what is meant, but the film in fact provides a very limited context. The filmmaker may therefore consciously or unconsciously "recontextualize" some of the resulting ambiguities when writing the subtitles, introducing nuances that otherwise would exist in the scene only in a latent form.

All documentary films construct "characters" out of the images of the historical persons who appear in them. From the few minutes of screen time taken out of a person's life, the audience is asked to build up its own more comprehensive imaginative portrait. What is seen expands to fill the void of what is not seen, creating a figure of more limited and sometimes more exaggerated proportions than the person known and filmed on a day-to-day basis by the filmmaker. The filmmaker may choose to emphasize certain aspects of character or, through a different selection of materials, attempt to create a more rounded portrait, but there is always the risk that people in ethnographic films will be reduced simply to their social roles. The way in which subtitles are written can help to offset this by stressing personal identity and individuality. In many cases the most obvious literal translation is the best one, but not always. How a person responds verbally to situations is an indication of his or her inner life and underlying attitudes toward others. Sometimes the filmmaker knows enough about the speaker to be able to find translations that are less literal but better express a state of mind or define a continuing relationship.[4]

This sort of shaping is evident in such early subtitled films as Marshall's *An Argument about a Marriage* (1969). Here the dialogue translations, while not resorting to slang, manage to convey the colloquial speech and distinctive personalities of the speakers.

/Ti!kay [to group]: He's too deficient to keep the wife he has. *[To /Qui]* You're insane! Crazy! I shouldn't even listen to a lecher. Did you ask your father-in-law? Your wife? Even when you wear pants among these naked simpletons you're still nothing.

N!ai: I'll have no part of these wretched, jealous people. I'm sick of it; let's get our firewood.[5]

As well as contributing to the distinctive voices of the characters, subtitles also direct the audience to particular strands of meaning within a scene and to larger themes in the film as a whole. A line of dialogue that is heard at a distance, or in passing, and which might otherwise go unnoticed can, by being subtitled, be given greater thematic prominence in the film. In this way, subtitles act on the verbal level somewhat as the camera and editing act on a visual and structural level to single out subjects and frame human relationships. This way of giving emphasis also plays a part in deciding which lines of dialogue to subtitle when there are several overlapping ones to choose from.

Subtitles frequently force a compromise between length and nuance. Different languages require different lengths of time in which to express similar ideas. In the process of translation, filmmakers must therefore sometimes sacrifice subtlety to fit a given length of time available on the screen. Translators of poetry face similar dilemmas, constrained as they are by meter and rhythm. Much of the skill in writing subtitles lies in reconciling such conflicting objectives. In shortening a line of dialogue to fit a particular interval, the filmmaker may have to choose an idiom which, although less appropriate, still preserves the suggestion of a secondary meaning, since this may be preferable to losing that meaning altogether.

A departure from close, literal translation may be necessary to compensate for the loss of adjacent material. Thus, a subtitle may include a shade of meaning not contained in the original line but carried over from an earlier part of the dialogue, where the idea has had to be dropped for lack of space. This is perhaps the most common kind of "poetic license" adopted in subtitling. Another, as I have mentioned, is to inflect the dialogue with meanings borrowed from a wider knowledge of the situation and therefore not available to most viewers. Since this possibility is open-ended, filmmakers generally approach it with restraint and with respect for the evidential value of the film. But making such choices underlines the fact that every film chooses among various possible views of its subject rather than providing a comprehensive or disinterested account.

## The Connotations of Words

Earlier in *An Argument about a Marriage*, Kxao /Gaisi says: "If it weren't for the Marshalls, /Ti!kay wouldn't have wives of his own." /Ti!kay responds: "Screw the Marshalls!" (Reichlin and Marshall 1974: 3). This is an interesting reflexive moment, and it nicely expresses /Ti!kay's effort to disassociate himself from the Marshalls in order to strengthen his arguing position, but here the language of the subtitles also shifts from liveliness into slang. One can see the problem—how to translate /Ti!kay's remark. It isn't really a question of propriety, although "Fuck the Marshalls!" might have seemed a little excessive at the time this film was edited. The problem is the parochialism of language. "Screw" has a long history in English slang, but it now feels somewhat dated. It is also perhaps more an Americanism today than an expression commonly used by English speakers around the world. It exemplifies the problem of how to write subtitles that will last.[6]

As this case demonstrates, words in films tend to be culturally specific in ways that many other elements—styles of photography, for example—are not; or at the very least, it shows that with words we are highly sensitive to cultural incongruity. Many of us have seen foreign gangster films in which the characters unaccountably start saying "gonna" and "dame" in the subtitles. There is some sort of twisted logic operating when translators think that suggesting an equivalent social milieu in their own society takes precedence over far greater cultural differences. Inevitably, the national and regional connotations of slang will override almost all other cross-cultural parallels. It is as absurd for Jean Gabin to speak Brooklyn slang as it is for him to speak Cockney. Faced with the probability that there will be a considerable cultural distance between audience and subject, the maker of ethnographic films must find a form of English (or another language) which will express that distance without idealizing or trivializing it.[7] Although no forms of speech are culturally neutral, some lie in a middle region between cold formality and an abundance of regional associations. Like music, language dates quickly, and it is therefore advantageous to choose words that will transcend changes in idiom. The most successful subtitles give an impression of transparency: of conveying meaning and emotion without ever suggesting to us an inappropriate time or place.

Many people today seem to prefer subtitles to voice-over translations in documentary films. One reason is not hard to find: the use of synchronous sound presupposes that one will hear what is said, unlike earlier forms of documentary in which the images emphasized elements other than speech. If voice-over translations prevent us from hearing the inflections of the original voices, we may well resent them. Setting aside that objection, why should we still prefer a more abstract and differently encoded form of translation (written subtitles) to the much closer analogue of a spoken one? The answer here may lie in the degree of abstraction, since we may prefer the relative indeterminacy of the written word to the stronger regional connotations of actual speech, when those connotations must almost invariably be wrong.

In certain countries such as the U.S.A. and Germany, where television executives have decided that viewers dislike reading subtitles (or where they declare that subtitles detract from the image), attempts are often made to restore certain cultural qualities to voice-over translations, both as a way of making them seem more authentic and sidestepping the unwanted local associations of an American or German (or other) voice. Informalities of speech are introduced, including slang, and people speak English with foreign accents, as though to suggest that this is how the original speakers would speak English if they could. If the object were simply to mask the cultural specificity of the translating voice, almost any foreign accent would do—but producers generally look for a plausible voice. One Kenyan woman, Musindo Mwinyipembe, was so gifted at doing this sort of work that her voice was used in several films made in different parts of Africa. If the audience is completely unfamiliar with the society shown, the producers face a problem. Under those circumstances, what sort of foreign accent is appropriate? Perhaps the only answer lies in greater abstraction, in a "foreign" accent that no one could possibly recognize, with no associations but foreignness.[8]

There are of course several alternative strategies. One is to make the translating voice clearly unrelated to the original speaker—a woman for a man, an adult for a child, and so on—but few producers have the courage to allow this. Another solution, in films with many voices, is for one speaker to translate them all, or for the translating voice to be obviously that of the filmmaker, as in Jorge Preloran's English-language versions of his films.[9] But as we have seen, the use of subtitles does not entirely circumvent problems of this sort. Written words also carry manifold cultural meanings, and written translations are far from indeterminate. The wrong words can be as off-putting as the wrong voice.

## Duration and Placement

The precursors of subtitles were the dialogue intertitles of silent films. Like other intertitles, these were necessarily used sparingly, and a great deal of effort went into making them as efficient as possible. Their graphic potential was also sometimes exploited by using special typefaces and decorations.[10] Other experiments with intertitles included the dramatic changes in size and timing used in many Soviet films, culminating in Victor Turin's *Turksib* (1929). But after the arrival of the sound film, subtitles translating dialogue were usually calculated to a formula, supposedly based upon the average reading speed of the audience.[11] It was only when subtitles became an important part of the filmmaking process that the experiments of the silent era were revived.

In writing and placing subtitles, the filmmaker may attempt to reinforce the tempo and mood of a conversation, or allow certain ideas to take on an added emphasis by holding a particular subtitle a little longer on the screen. The final subtitle of a scene will sometimes be treated in this way as a form of punctuation, or to foreshadow the content of the ensuing scene.[12] Through prolongation, subtitles can underpin certain aspects of the editing, smoothing transitions and heightening juxtapositions. Subtitles can also be shortened to create a stacatto effect to increase tension, or lengthened to cover an awkward camera move. Backgrounds that are visually busy, or that shift due to camera movement, may require that subtitles be held longer on the screen than those against stationary or simple backgrounds.

Subtitles have a cadence and rhythm of their own, independent of the rhythm of the spoken dialogue. This can be used in counterpoint to or in reinforcement of the recorded sounds of speech, but the greatest sense of comprehension is normally afforded when each subtitle is synchronized to begin at the start of (or a frame or two after) its corresponding line of dialogue, and is proportionately of the same length.[13] The audience may well become doubtful if a long speech is translated simply as "Yes." Filmmakers usually try to link each subtitle to a specific utterance, but this may not always be possible if the dialogue is very fast or long sentences have to be broken down into a series of titles. In these cases, where the titles are "out of phase," it has been my experience that the rhythm of the subtitles is dominant over the rhythm of the speech, and it is therefore often more important to maintain the rhythm of the subtitles than to try to match them exactly to the original utterances. On other occasions, filmmakers may find themselves obliged to create a false synchrony, placing a subtitle over a line of dialogue to which it does not belong (it usually belongs to the adjoining one). Although most audiences will be misled, one assumes that native speakers will not, but as they are unlikely to be reading the subtitles anyway, it is often the filmmaker who feels the most discomfort at this procedure.

At the end of *To Live with Herds* there is an exchange of formal greetings on the sound track that is so rapid that there was no way the subtitles could keep up with them. I could think of only two ways of dealing with this—either to slow down the exchange by spacing out the greetings with segments of "atmosphere" track, or letting the subtitles begin with the exchange but run on long after it had finished. It seemed abhorrent to tamper with the greetings, so I chose the second alternative, but this resulted in a certain ambiguity. Although many viewers interpret the scene "correctly" (that is, as a translation that takes longer in the form of titles than the spoken words), it has a different meaning for others. Some assume that a piece of the sound track is missing and that the greetings are actually meant to be heard throughout the subtitles. Others see the absence of sound as a transcendental effect, lifting the feelings expressed in the greetings to a higher plane. One viewer has even told me that the scene represents my wish, conveyed in a silent greeting back to the Jie, that they may always "live with herds." This has some truth. But choices of this kind are rarely made for one reason alone and, as every filmmaker knows, it is not unusual for films to find some of their meaning and power through circumstances such as this.

## The Limitations of Subtitles

In recent years the subtitling of ethnographic films has not only become commonplace but the norm in many countries. Even ethnographic films made for television are now routinely subtitled in Britain, France, and Australia, and this practice is gradually spreading.[14] Because subtitling has coincided with a number of other changes in documentary cinema, it is not altogether possible to assess its impact, in part because the use of subtitles has generally accompanied the use of synchronous sound. It is, for example, difficult to know the extent to which the increased use of interviews in ethnographic films results from the possibility of subtitling them or from a more general trend toward an interview-based documentary form. Nevertheless, we can at least suggest some of the ways in which subtitles have affected responses to ethnographic films and changed their content.

One of the most obvious effects of subtitling is to convert the raw recorded speech on a sound track into a written text. This text is determined by the translator and filmmaker, and to a large extent it banishes alternative readings and establishes itself as definitive. It is very difficult to suggest in a subtitle that the speaker might have meant something else. The process distils out of a range of implicit or possible meanings certain explicit ones. Subtitles thus have a narrowing influence, for they are like a stamp of possession on a film, projecting a particular interpretation. Although the people in the film are speaking to each other, subtitles are one of the ways in which the filmmaker speaks to us.

Subtitles also have an accentuating effect. When people in films speak about the fundamental concerns in their lives, they often do so in an off-hand manner that reflects the continuity of those understandings in their lives. Subtitles tend to isolate and heighten this material, which would otherwise merge with its background. In this way they act to extract and crystallize the central issues of a film, making its thematic architecture stand out in sharper relief. The randomness and indeterminacy of everyday speech is transformed into a more formal text, projecting a greater air of intentionality and coherence. Even the act of putting spoken words into writing gives them added weight and literary qualities. What was once transitory and open-ended is now made permanent and part of a larger design, more recognizably a "cultural" product. As a film progresses, what is thus dignified by subtitles sets up particular resonances with what we have already seen and sensitizes us to particular aspects of the scenes that we are about to see.

The experience of reading subtitles is very different from listening to recorded speech. Subtitles appear on the screen as a succession of discrete units, or quanta. Each phrase is packaged, as it were, and delivered to us whole. This is very different from responding to a continuous flow of conversation, in which the meanings unfold irregularly in the process of formation. Subtitles also have the effect of "doubling" the spoken words, much as one instrument in an orchestra doubles another of a different timbre. This tends to make the words more pithy and prophetic. The regular spacing of the titles can also create a certain passiveness in us as viewers, due partly to the effect of their rhythm, partly to the fact that they are fed to us piecemeal, never requiring us to work out the sense from the more agglomerated mass of the dialogue itself. We become both word-dependent and word-oriented, so that if a scene appears in which there are no subtitles, we feel at a loss. Any speech left unsubtitled seems like a mistake, or we feel cheated by the filmmaker.

Subtitles are also limiting in another way. It is often said that the time it takes to read them prevents us from watching the images properly. The extent of this problem may be exaggerated, for quick readers tend to grasp the entire frame, image and subtitle, as one whole. For them the reading of text becomes integrated with watching the facial expressions and movements of the speakers. However, there is no doubt that there is some loss of freedom to make a more casual inspection of the image, for subtitles impose their own impera-tive: it is very difficult *not* to read them when they are on the screen.

Perhaps the most serious limitation is that subtitled dialogue tends to make us conceive of films more in terms of what they *say* than in what they *show*. This can pose a problem if the filmmaker wishes to emphasize nonverbal ele-ments in the film, particularly in scenes of conversation. I faced this problem toward the end of *Tempus de Baristas*, in a scene between two of the main protagonists, Pietro and Miminu. To me their manner toward each other was far more important than what they actually said, and I took the chance that by this time the viewers would care enough about them, and understand them well enough, to respond to them substantially on a nonverbal level. Although the narrative is partly advanced through their discussion of the future, much of the importance of the scene, I believe, lies in what we can see of how far they have come in their emotional life and view of themselves. A number of shots in the scene were therefore included almost entirely on the basis of these qual-ities.

One unexpected consequence of subtitled speech may ultimately be its po-tential to reduce the expressive and analytical range of ethnographic films. The comparative ease of using subtitles today, and their wide acceptance, may encourage filmmakers to focus excessively upon dialogue and interviews, to the neglect of other forms of (nonverbal) social practice and personal experi-ence. In the case of interviews, this could result not only in an inordinate emphasis upon speech, but upon speech and speaking situations of a very specialized kind. A related danger is that expressive uses of sound could be eroded, if sound-recording increasingly means only recording people talking. To a certain extent this has already happened. With technical advances in the automatic recording of synchronous sound, particularly by video cameras, sound has become linked to the spoken word in an almost exclusive way. Effects such as these were hardly the aim of those who, thirty years ago, saw synchronous sound and the use of subtitles as ways of widening the range of ethnographic filmmaking.

Although a number of these effects are of a technical and formal nature, they may have wider social and political implications for ethnographic film. Subtitles may induce in viewers a false sense of cultural affinity, since they so unobtrusively and efficiently overcome the difficulties of translation. They may reinforce the impression that it is possible to know others without ef-fort—that the whole world is inherently knowable and accessible.[15] Subtitles, therefore, while they may create a fuller sense of the humanity of strangers, may also contribute to our complacency about them, perhaps sustaining a be-lief in the ability of our society to turn everything found in the world to our use. This suggestion of control is perhaps one of the risks one inevitably runs in any effort to express one's understanding of others, but divorced from the difficulty of gaining such an understanding it may lack a necessary corrective. Films that now so easily convey what other people say would do well to remind us that there are also more obdurate, private, and unknowable dimensions of their lives.

[1995]

## Notes

This essay was first published in a considerably different version in *Visual Anthropology Review* 11 (1): 83–90, Spring, 1995.

1. According to Asch (in personal discussion, April 1993), it was seeing the raw footage for *N/um Tchai* that suggested editing the Ju/'hoansi material into a series of "sequence films." He remembered *A Joking Relationship* as being the first of these to be edited, and about the same time shooting the subtitles for the film *A Group of Women* "off the wall in a printing frame."

2. In April 1968 both Hawkins and I had seen examples of Marshall's subtitled films at the Colloquium on Ethnographic Film held at the University of California at Los Angeles.

3. Increasingly, much of this work is performed on computer screens, using a video copy with time code to spot the in- and out-frames. The subtitles can be typed in directly and the effect of their placement assessed immediately.

4. In *Tempus de Baristas,* which I made in 1992–93, there is a scene in which Pietro becomes angry with his father, Franchiscu, after Franchiscu has given him orders in a rather hectoring tone. The tension soon passes, and in talking about the future, Franchiscu says, "You'll be starting a new life, then?" Pietro replies, "Certainly." He uses the Italian word, "*Certo*." This could have been subtitled in several ways: "Of course," "Certainly," or simply, "Yes." Although "Certainly" at first seems literally correct, "Of course" is perhaps a closer translation, in its self-assurance and brevity. "Certainly," by contrast, is softer and more measured in English. (For that softness, Italians and Sards might use "*Naturalmente*.") In the end, though, I decided on "Certainly." "Of course" struck me as too abrupt and suggested an aggressiveness between son and father which I didn't think accurately reflected their relationship. "Certainly," although softer in sound than "*Certo*," carried an edge of irony which expressed Pietro's good will and moderated, without entirely extinguishing, the slight tone of arrogance I sensed in his reply.

5. From the transcription in *An Argument about a Marriage: The Study Guide* (Reichlin and Marshall 1974: 4).

6. "Never mind the Marshalls!" or "Forget the Marshalls!" might have avoided this problem, but it is always easy to be wise after the event. Besides, Asch and Marshall may have wanted to preserve the element of rudeness.

7. Flaherty was guilty of both, and Merian C. Cooper and Ernest B. Schoedsack, in their last pseudo-documentary epic *Chang* (1927), included such lines as: "The very last grain of rice is husked, O very small daughter!" (Barnouw 1974: 50).

8. An oddity which exemplifies this confusion is the commentary in the BBC film *Two Girls Go Hunting* (1991), which although written in the first person from the point

of view of the European filmmakers is, illogically, spoken with an African accent—and not even, one suspects, an accent of Ethiopia, where the film was made.

9. See *Imaginero* (1970), referred to earlier, as well as *Cochengo Miranda* (1974) and *Zerda's Children* (1978).

10. In *The Film Till Now*, Paul Rotha complained of "white scrawly lettering jumping about on an imitation leather background" (1930: 299).

11. The formula used by Dai Vaughan, who subtitled many feature films in the 1960s, was first to allow 16 frames "for the eye to register the presence of a title. If it is a two-line title, allow a further 8 frames for the eye to travel to the start of the second line. Then allow one letter (or space, or punctuation mark) per frame of film." The original dialogue was to be split into measured sections corresponding to the subtitles before it was translated, and the translations then made to fit the allotted spaces. These and other guidelines, attributed to Mai Harris, are summarized in an unpublished document which Vaughan prepared for the students of the National Film and Television School of Great Britain. Vaughan is also the distinguished editor of many documentary and ethnographic films, for which the subtitling was approached in quite a different way.

12. See, for example, Pietro's lines in *Tempus de Baristas*: "Anyway, waiting on people or serving at a bar . . . I haven't the patience for it." These are given both added thematic weight and value as punctuation at the end of a scene by being left on the screen longer.

13. An odd psychological effect was produced by a copy of one of my films in which, through a laboratory error, the subtitles were consistently printed ten frames early. Viewers were surprised by the curious sense of knowing what people were going to say before they said it—almost of knowing what they were thinking.

14. Brian Moser fought and won the battle for subtitles with the management of Granada Television in Great Britain in the mid-1970s with the series *Disappearing World*. See Henley (1985). La Sept/ARTE regularly show subtitled ethnographic films on French-German television. SBS Television, the multicultural television network, pioneered the use of subtitles in Australia, and the ABC (Australian Broadcasting Corporation) now regularly shows fiction and documentary films with subtitles. Indonesian television shows a high proportion of its overseas programs, including game shows and soap operas, with Indonesian subtitles.

15. These comments could be said to apply equally to dubbed-in dialogue; however, the very clumsiness of dubbing often draws attention to itself, creating more awareness of the technical process and cultural disjunctions involved than subtitling does.

# CHAPTER EIGHT

# Ethnographic Film: Failure and Promise

ETHNOGRAPHIC FILMS CANNOT be said to constitute a genre, nor is ethnographic filmmaking a discipline with unified origins and an established methodology. Since the first conference on ethnographic film was held at the Musée de l'Homme in 1948, the term has served a largely emblematic function, giving a semblance of unity to extremely diverse efforts in the cinema and social sciences. A canon of ethnographic films has gradually emerged, and in recent decades a movement has grown up nourished by foundation grants, further international conferences, theoretical publications, and training programs.

Faced with defining ethnographic film, some writers have concluded that one can only say some films are more ethnographic than others, or that films become ethnographic by virtue of their use.[1] Since all films are cultural artifacts, many can tell us as much about the societies that produced them as about those they purport to describe. Films can thus serve as a source of data for social science in the manner of myths, rock paintings, and government papers. From World War II onwards, fiction films as well as documentaries have been studied sporadically for their ethnographic content.[2]

In practice, most discussions of ethnographic film set aside films useful to anthropologists as naïve cultural documents and narrow the field to those made with some discernible intention of recording and revealing cultural patterns. Some writers, including Jean Rouch (1975) and Luc de Heusch (1962), have refused to pursue further distinctions, arguing that to do so is to inhibit the cross-fertilization of varied approaches. Others have marked out taxonomic, functional, or stylistic categories within ethnographic film.[3] André Leroi-Gourhan (1948), for example, divided the field into research films, general audience films of some ethnographic interest, and films of purely exotic intentions. Asch, Marshall, and Spier (1973) created the terms Objective Recording, Scripted Filming, and Reportage to identify broad subcategories. Very often, however, the most complex and influential works function on several levels and defy such strict classification.

One distinction that remains useful in discussions of the field is that between *ethnographic footage* and *ethnographic films*. Films are structured works made for presentation to an audience. They make manifest within themselves the analysis that justifies such a presentation. Films are analogous in this sense to an anthropologist's public writings and to other creative or scholarly productions. Footage, on the other hand, is the raw material that comes out of a camera, and no such expectations attach to it. It can perhaps best be compared to an anthropologist's field notes and may be used for a variety of purposes, including the making of films.

The work of Félix-Louis Regnault stands as the type and earliest example of ethnographic film footage. In 1895, the same year the Lumière brothers held the world's first public film screenings, Regnault filmed the pottery-making techniques of a Wolof woman at the Exposition Ethnographique de l'Afrique Occidentale in Paris. Ethnographic film is thus as old as the cinema, which itself arose out of the research apparatus invented by Eadweard Muybridge and Étienne-Jules Marey to photograph human and animal locomotion. Regnault published a scientific paper based on his film record, which clearly differentiated his aims from those of the Lumière brothers, for whom film was primarily a commercial novelty (1931). He regarded the camera as a laboratory instrument that could fix transient human events for further analysis, and he went so far as to predict that ethnography would only attain the precision of a science through the use of such instruments (Rouch 1975: 437). The celluloid strip with its chemical emulsion was to be the fixing medium of anthropology.

Commercial film directors such as Georges Méliès and Edwin S. Porter soon turned the Lumières' cinema of visual bonbons into a narrative medium. In 1914 Edward Curtis produced a story film played by Kwakiutl actors in authentically reconstructed Kwakiutl surroundings,[4] and in 1922 Robert Flaherty released *Nanook of the North*. Flaherty's work resembled Curtis's in its attempt to reconstruct a traditional culture, but in other respects it was fundamentally different. Flaherty did not emphasize the dramatic conventions that had by this time reached such sophistication in fictional films. His sophistication was of a more conceptual kind. In place of a smoothly running story line is a procession of loosely linked observations, reflecting his fascination with technology and his joy in the revelation of personality through spontaneous behavior. The film becomes a construct of texts about Inuit life and character, centered around themes of cultural dignity and ingenuity. In contrast to Curtis's film, *Nanook* is manifestly an exploration of the society itself.

The work of Regnault and Flaherty defines alternative tendencies in ethnographic film that have persisted to the present day. For those working in the tradition of Regnault, the camera has been regarded primarily as an instrument for gathering cultural data. The process of analyzing the data has remained largely external to the footage itself. For Flaherty and his followers, film has provided a means not only of recording human behavior but also of leading the viewer through its intricacies according to some system of communicative logic.

## Ethnographic Footage

The gathering of ethnographic footage has taken two major forms: *research footage,* made to serve specific scientific inquiries, and *record footage,* made to provide general documents for archiving and future research. A more recent phenomenon is the production of ethnographic footage for teaching purposes.

Research footage permits the study and measurement of behavior that cannot be approached adequately through direct observation. The most obvious beneficiaries of this resource are the disciplines that have grown up around the cultural patterning and communicative aspects of body movement. These include proxemics, pioneered by Edward T. Hall, Ray Birdwhistell's kinesics, the choreometrics of Alan Lomax and his associates, studies of facial expression by Ekman, Eibl-Eibesfeldt and others, and Adam Kendon's studies of sign language and gesture.

The successful use of research footage often requires painstaking frame-by-frame analysis. In some studies where the emphasis is on the internal dynamics of behavior, film can provide data in the form of case studies; in others where it is on repetitive patterns, film can provide extensive data for close analysis and cross-cultural comparison. The controls necessary in the case-study method usually encourage researchers to produce their own footage. In some cross-cultural studies researchers have been able to make do with footage drawn from other sources. In this way a secondary kind of research footage comes into existence through its specialized use.

One of the most extensive projects to exploit the possibilities of research footage was the Choreometrics Project, which treated dance as a formal manifestation of the movement styles that permeate other cultural activities. To provide a world sample of dance forms the project drew upon a wide assortment of materials found in documentary, fiction, and archival film. It thus opened to study a particular form of human cultural expression as a coherent, modulated system, making use of information that in most cases went unrecognized at the time it was recorded.

Regnault's early work focused on African movement styles, and for many years the use of research footage was limited to studies of physiology, ritual, and the technological aspects of culture. The breakthrough to new uses came in 1936–38 with Gregory Bateson's and Margaret Mcad's famous study of Balinese character formation (1942), which demonstrated the potential of film for analyzing interpersonal relationships. Still and motion picture cameras were used to gather data on social interaction in general and parent-child interaction in particular. As the project progressed, filming was directed toward documentation of increasingly specific behavioral situations. Some of the possibilities suggested by the Bali project have been pursued in laboratory settings, such as in the interpretation of family therapy interviews.

Other researchers have continued to apply film to field situations. A study by E. Richard Sorenson and Carleton Gajdusek compiled a research footage collection to investigate child growth and development and the clinical manifestations of *kuru,* a degenerative neurological disease of the eastern New Guinea highlands. Sorenson (1976) later used research filming to test hypotheses about personality development derived from an examination of footage shot among the Fore, one of the original groups studied for *kuru.*

The term *record footage* applies to material made for more broadly descriptive purposes than material produced as research footage. To anthropologists, and to others conscious of the mutability of cultures, photographic records appear to offer a means of preserving some irreducible embodiment of societies that will vanish or undergo radical change. A film record is not the thing it records, but as a direct photochemical imprint it shares in its reality in a way that written descriptions cannot. As Susan Sontag (1977: 154) has observed, Bardolators would prefer, if it were possible, a barely legible photograph of Shakespeare to a detailed portrait of him by Holbein the Younger. Much record footage has been devoted to compiling inventories of culture, and film records always hold out the possibility that, like lumps of charcoal collected years ago, they may reveal things we never expected.

The making of record footage goes back to 1898, when A. C. Haddon included a Lumière camera in the scientific kit of the Cambridge Anthropological Expedition to the Torres Strait. Like Regnault, Haddon had great hopes for film as an aid to anthropology, but primarily as a medium for general ethnographic documentation. Despite his influence, record filming was not widely adopted as a standard fieldwork activity. Most anthropologists who continued to shoot film did so in much the same spirit as they took still photographs—occasionally, and often almost as a respite from what they considered their legitimate work.

The value of film records as a resource for anthropology was more widely acknowledged with the acceleration of social change that accompanied World War II. In the postwar years a number of projects revived Haddon's concern for systematic anthropological filming. During the Peabody-Harvard-Kalahari expeditions of 1950–59 and subsequent projects, John Marshall and his associates shot close to 2 million feet of 16mm color film on Ju/'hoansi families in the Nyae Nyae region of the Kalahari, producing what remains the most comprehensive visual ethnography of any small-scale human society. During the same period, the *Encyclopaedia Cinematographica* was established at the Institut für den Wissenschaftlichen Film at Göttingen. One of its aims was to acquire and preserve film records of carefully chosen "thematic units" of human behavior. At the University of California, Samuel Barrett directed a program to film the food-gathering techniques of Native Americans, and in Australia in the mid-1960s Roger Sandall, working with the anthropologist Nicolas Peterson, embarked on a project to film Aboriginal ritual for the Australian Institute of Aboriginal Studies. Another project, primarily devoted to recording Aboriginal material culture in the Western Desert, was carried out in the same period by Ian Dunlop of the Australian Commonwealth Film Unit with the anthropologist Robert Tonkinson; and with Maurice Godelier, Dunlop later produced *Towards Baruya Manhood* (1972) and *Baruya Muka Archival* (1991), detailed records of initiation in the New Guinea highlands.

Out of some of these projects came films as well as record footage, the result of processes of selection and interpretation that became increasingly necessary during filming in order to represent complex events. It is perhaps ironic that these films are better known than the extensive footage the projects were designed to gather.

Education and television, rather than research, have been the financial mainsprings of most ethnographic film activities in recent years. These sources have made possible projects whose significance for visual anthropology goes well beyond their immediate uses. Generous foundation funding for curriculum development in North America led to the filming of the Netsilik Eskimo series, directed by Asen Balikci in 1963–68 as part of the elementary-school program *Man: A Course of Study*. This was the first of several projects designed to immerse students in another culture and provide them with the materials for deriving principles of social behavior. The resulting footage was a revelation to anthropologists and ethnographic filmmakers for its intimate and uninterrupted camera takes of interpersonal relations. Similarly, the *Disappearing World* programs for Granada Television in Great Britian have been widely used in teaching and have produced footage—such as that by Leslie Woodhead and David Turton about the Mursi—that is also of potential value for research purposes.

When the Netsilik films first appeared, very little of John Marshall's Ju/ 'hoansi footage of the 1950s had been seen except for his film *The Hunters* (1958). Few people were aware that in recording intimate events he had in many ways anticipated the achievements of the Netsilik project.[5] Marshall now began to edit some of this material into segments for teaching anthropology, drawing upon his extended sequences of structured social interaction. Timothy Asch, who worked with Marshall in editing the Ju/'hoansi material, wished to apply the pedagogical ideas they had developed together to the initial filming process, and with Napoleon Chagnon he subsequently produced over fifty film sequences on the Yanomamö of southern Venezuela. Marshall went on to produce an analogous project on the Pittsburgh police—ostensibly for legal and law enforcement studies, but also, as he put it, as an ethnography of the police. These projects at the very least gave the collection of visual records an immediate utility. They also shifted the emphasis of record-making from an impersonal cataloging of cultural features toward a representation of culture perceived through individual lives.

Of the other film material shot over the years by anthropologists in the field, little is available either for research or teaching. Where it has all gone, no one knows: much of it, certainly, into attics, trunks, and dustbins, and a smaller proportion into film archives, such as those of the Smithsonian Institution and the Australian Institute of Aboriginal and Torres Strait Islander Studies. Only a few fragments of Haddon's Torres Strait footage have survived to the present day, and Baldwin Spencer's footage of 1901 and 1912 from Central and Northern Australia lay forgotten in its original containers at the National Museum of Victoria until it was rediscovered by Ian Dunlop in the 1960s.[6] Even properly archived ethnographic film material remains largely unknown and unused by anthropologists, in part as a result of its dispersal in different countries and the lack of comprehensive catalogues and study facilities.

Increased archival activities and research projects using film have raised questions about methods of collecting and documenting record footage. Much footage has been found to be useless for research because of the ways in which some filmmaking conventions have fragmented temporal and spatial relationships, or because the footage has not been properly documented. Some cross-cultural studies are frustrated because no one has filmed certain cultural features in adequate detail. The situation is reminiscent of the problems faced by anthropology in the nineteenth century before basic field methods were brought into common use by successive revisions of *Notes and Queries on Anthropology* and the example of Malinowski and Rivers (Urry 1972). The guidelines developed in the 1950s by Gotthard Wolf at the Institut für den Wissenschaftlichen Film took a step toward establishing scientific standards for the selection and recording of behavioral items, but at the risk of being excessively reductionist about culture. Later work at the IWF has shown a more flexible approach.

In the 1970s Sorenson and Jablonko (1975) proposed a general model for gathering visual records. Although they acknowledged that it was impossible to predict what data might finally prove significant, they suggested a tripartite strategy of sampling techniques based upon intuitive, planned, and semirandomized responses to social phenomena. Such a model presupposes that different forms of sampling can offset one another's deficiencies, but it cannot overcome any major cultural bias that may dominate all three forms of sampling in an individual observer. A more formidable difficulty with any global system of ethnographic documentation is its obligation to cover a broad spectrum of cultural features. Out of the endless possibilities that present themselves to an observer, to say nothing of those that may be uncovered through particular research interests, only a small proportion can be filmed. The camera can never be everywhere at once, and multiple cameras become hopelessly intrusive.

The problem immediately becomes apparent when one tries to film the full ramifications of even one small social event. Sampling techniques tend to discourage filming the complexities of social experience as they might appear to the participants, and this can leave a significant gap in our understanding. The danger lies not so much in the limitations of such methods as in the seductive belief that they can record all that really matters about human societies. As in anthropology itself, ethnographic filming must balance attempts at comprehensive documentation with intimate explorations of particular phenomena.

## Ethnographic Films

Ethnographic filmmaking owes as much to cinema's rapidly evolving forms as written anthropology does to styles of literary and scientific discourse that have developed over several centuries. The cinema inherited dramatic and literary conventions, and almost from the start the narrative efficiency of words (at first in the form of titles) vied with that of photographic images. The storyteller's voice, in the form of spoken commentary, still retains a hold on many documentary films and most television journalism, but in dramatic films it has largely dropped away, leaving language to the dialogue of fictional characters. This difference in the employment of language has produced one film tradition in which images illustrate a verbal argument and another in which the images (in the sound film including spoken dialogue) must carry the burden of revealing a coherent line of development. Ethnographic films span both traditions and can thus be seen as either illustrative or revelatory in approach, the first form obviously bearing the closer resemblance to expository forms of anthropological writing.

Illustrative ethnographic films make use of images either as data to be elucidated by means of a spoken commentary or as visual support for verbal statements. The form has often lent itself to misuse, since a plausible narration script can often impart authority to the most fragmentary images. That possibility has encouraged the gathering of attractive but disconnected material and the creation of "films" out of material that does little to substantiate the assertions of the commentary. At its worst it produces the illustrated lectures familiar in travelogues and classroom films. It is at its best in providing an analysis of behavioral patterns, or in making general surveys of individual societies, or in films on ritual or other formalized events, such as Gary Kildea's and Jerry Leach's *Trobriand Cricket* (1976).

In illustrative films, verbal analysis provides what James Blue once called the film's "transport mechanism"—that which gives it its sense of forward movement. Revelatory films, on the other hand, require the viewer to make a continuous interpretation of both the visual and verbal material articulated by the filmmaker. Voice-over narration does not necessarily relegate images to an illustrative role provided the voice is an integral part of the subject matter.

Thus Jorge Preloran's *Imaginero* (1970) gives us the spoken autobiography of its protagonist, Hermogenes Cayo, and Basil Wright's *Song of Ceylon* (1934) utilizes the commentary of the seventeenth-century traveler Robert Knox as a "found" object.

Revelatory films very often follow the chronological structures perceived in events. A classic example on a large scale is Merian C. Cooper's and Ernest Schoedsack's film of 1925, *Grass*, which traces a Bakhtiari migration of thousands of people to their highland pastures. William Geddes's *Miao Year* (1968) is organized around the annual agricultural cycle. Melissa Llewelyn-Davies's *The Women's Olamal: The Social Organisation of a Maasai Fertility Ceremony* (1984) follows the course of a dispute between Maasai women and men, leading to the performing of a fertility ceremony. Usually the events are more circumscribed, however: a ritual (*Larwari and Walkara* [1977], *A Celebration of Origins* [1992]), a ritualized event (*The Feast* [1970], *The Wedding Camels* [1977]), or a small episode of social interaction (*Debe's Tantrum* [1972]).

Sometimes a chronological narrative provides the transport mechanism that links discontinuous material (Flaherty's *Moana* [1926], Bob Connolly and Robin Anderson's *Joe Leahy's Neighbours* [1988], Joanna Head and Jean Lydall's *Our Way of Loving* [1994], Gary Kildea's *Valencia Diary* [1992]) In Robert Gardner's *Dead Birds* (1963) the attack and counterattack of cyclical raiding is presented through the experiences of two of the people affected by it.

Social processes that occur over long periods of time, or other aspects of culture that do not yield to narrative exploration, may require more conceptual film structures. *Nanook of the North* (1922) is an early attempt in this direction. Gardner's *Forest of Bliss* (1985) examines themes of death and regeneration in the Indian holy city of Benares through a complex interweaving of cultural symbols and daily activities. In *Kenya Boran* (1974) James Blue and I attempted to reveal processes of social change through sets of interactions among people at different points in the social and historical matrix. *Sophia's People* (1985) examines the condition of exile through a family's bakery, which focuses both their energies and sense of loss. *The Path* (1973), which deals with an event (the Japanese tea ceremony) that would ordinarily invite conventional narrative treatment, instead presents it through evocative techniques designed to convey its meaning for the participants.

In the 1960s, lightweight synchronous sound cameras and film stocks of increased sensitivity opened up a new dimension of private, informal behavior to patient and unobtrusive filmmakers such as Richard Leacock and Michel Brault. The Netsilik Eskimo series first dramatized the possibilities of this approach for ethnographic film, making apparent the curious veil that earlier films had drawn across the observation of people in their daily lives.

Observational filming, using synchronous sound, emphasized the spontaneous dialogue of the film subjects rather than a commentary spoken by the filmmaker or anthropologist—or more often still, an anonymous reportorial voice. Before being employed in ethnographic films, such conversations had already become a major element in documentary films made in Europe and North America (*Primary* [1960], *Chronique d'un été* [1961], *Pour la suite du monde* [1963]), but in the Netsilik films viewers began to listen to a language they could not understand. It became obvious that in these films the audience lacked direct access to information and to an expression of intellectual and emotional life that they took for granted in films about their own society. Subtitles translating indigenous dialogue made their appearance in John Marshall's *A Joking Relationship* in 1966, but his other subtitled Ju/'hoansi films were only released some time later, beginning in 1969. Two other subtitled films, Asch's *The Feast* and my film *Nawi*, were both shot in 1968 and released in 1970.[7] Since then the filming and editing of many ethnographic films has been largely determined by the dialogue of the subjects. Subtitling cannot convey all the nuances of speech apparent to a native speaker, but it seems the most efficient and least objectionable method of bringing literate audiences into the verbal world of other peoples. It was adopted in the *Disappearing World* television series in 1974, largely through the persistent efforts of the series producer, Brian Moser.

Speech, of course, reflects personality as well as culture. Synchronous sound has helped to reveal the range and diversity of personality types that exist within cultural norms. In Asch's films on Dedeheiwä we gain an insight into the personal world of a Yanomamö shaman. In *Rivers of Sand* (1975), *Lorang's Way* (1979), and *The Spirit Possession of Alejandro Mamani* (1975) we meet people unreconciled to what others in their society accept, sharpening by contrast the cultural elements under examination. As Flaherty realized, to show individuals coping with problems is one way of affirming their dignity and the rationality of their choices. Some assessments of the effects of ethnographic films upon students suggest that access to the intellectual life of individuals in other societies may be an essential step in recognizing their humanity.[8]

At first the intimacy afforded by lightweight camera equipment created euphoria among filmmakers, who saw in it a means of extending an inquiry into the real world that had previously been possible only in the realm of fiction. But observational filming also prepared the way for undermining the conception of cinema as disembodied observation. It became increasingly clear that the illusion of authorial invisibility could lead to a false interpretation of the behavior on the screen. Some filmmakers came to believe that their films should not only be revelatory, but also self-revelatory, containing evidence of the encounter that had produced them.

One can see the shift taking place in *Lonely Boy* (1962), a film made by the National Film Board of Canada. An interview scene that would ordinarily be condensed through conventional editing (in which the owner of the Copacabana orders his waiters around and chats with the film crew) is included in the film intact. It is perhaps there partly for its novelty, but it has the larger effect of turning the film upon itself and raising questions about how films deal with reality. It has become more difficult to think of ethnographic films as definitive representations of events, independent of the processes that produced them, and ethnographic filmmmakers have begun to look upon their work as more tentative forays into cultural complexity, in which individual films become parts of a continuing inquiry. Such thinking has led to some films being made as "texts" to be explored, rather than as statements of anthropological conclusions. It has also meant that larger bodies of material, like the Asch-Chagnon Yanomamö corpus, can now be read as metafilms whose content can be endlessly rearranged to yield new insights.

The most important aspect of the observational approach is that it represents an effort to pierce through the individualistic reconstructions of reality that once characterized documentary film style in order to bring audiences closer to events as independent witnesses. Through the use of unbroken camera takes that replace the synthesis and condensation of film editing, filmmakers seek to respect the temporal and spatial integrity of events. Even so, filming does not become a simple, objective process. The camera, through its positioning and framing, continues to see selectively, and the burden of interpretation falls with a new immediacy upon the filmmaker at the time of filming. Observation of informal, nonrecurring events precludes shooting scenes from a variety of angles or shooting them more than once. The manipulation of the camera thus comes to reflect a particular sensibility and process of thought. In responding to the flow of interpersonal behavior, the filmmaker irrevocably defines and shapes the meaning of relationships that will be perceived by the audience. That process requires the same depth of understanding that informs all good anthropology.

## Film and Written Anthropology

Ethnographic film has always produced a fascination that seems disproportionate to taking the measure of human societies. Photographic images capture a wealth of detail that an observer can only begin to describe, and make possible a way of physically possessing external reality, not merely possessing knowledge about it. At first anthropologists acquired images much as they acquired objects for museums: records of technology, of dances, and of physiognomy and musculature. O. E. Stocker went so far as to film his subjects copulating for the camera.

In 1900, after his return from the Torres Strait, Haddon wrote to his friend

Walter Baldwin Spencer, enthusiastically describing the motion picture camera as "an indispensible piece of anthropological apparatus." Perhaps few anthropologists would make so sweeping a claim today, but the sentiment typifies the hopes that have periodically been held out for ethnographic film.

Edgar Morin, writing in 1962, reaffirmed the suitability of film for recording what he termed intensive, ceremonial, and technical sociality, but added:

> There is the rest, the most difficult, the most moving, the most secret: wherever human feelings are involved, wherever the individual is directly concerned, wherever there are inter-personal relationships of authority, subordination, comradeship, love, hate—in other words, everything connected with the *emotive fabric of human existence*. There lies the great *terra incognita* of the sociological or ethnological cinema. (1962: 4)

Jean Rouch had begun to explore some of these possibilities in his West African films of the 1950s. In *Les Maîtres fous* (1955) the "emotive fabric" of an urban cult ritual is shown to be inextricably linked to the daily experience of the participants as colonial subjects. Gardner's *Dead Birds* (1963), filmed in 1961, attempted even more explicitly to identify the relationships between human psychological needs and cultural forms. These films did not, however, establish a theoretical framework or methodology for ethnographic filmmaking as a discipline. Both Rouch and Gardner worked in a personal and often intuitive manner—a circumstance which failed to provide an academically acceptable path for anthropologists to follow. Nor were the films themselves easily assimilated as contributions to anthropological knowledge. They were often admired by anthropologists for their insights, but they were almost equally often dismissed in the same breath as works of "art" rather than science.

Neither Rouch nor Gardner have sought to defend the contributions made by their films in conventional anthropological terms, but both have expressed a belief in the power of film to communicate across cultural frontiers. To Rouch this power is elusive, and his references to it are elliptical:

> There are a few rare moments when the filmgoer suddenly understands an unknown language without the help of sub-titles, when he participates in strange ceremonies, when he finds himself walking in towns or across terrain that he has never seen before but that he recognizes perfectly. (1975: 89)

Rouch's efforts have gone into extending these moments from brief episodes to entire films, cultivating a gift which, as he has remarked, sometimes comes to "masters, fools, and children" (1975: 90). In 1957 Gardner explained his own intended approach as a form of mimesis:

> If it was possible . . . to render a realistic account in film of some seemingly remote experience, then these capacities [of sharing experience] might reasonably be expected to produce reactions in those who saw it which, in meaningful-

ness, had some approximation to the feelings of those to whom the experience actually belonged. (1957: 347)

The value of at least one form of ethnographic film was thus seen to lie in a communication of indigenous perspectives which might illuminate more formally derived knowledge. Such films sought to evoke the interior world of people who had previously been shown only as objects of research.

By the mid-1960s ethnographic film seemed to its partisans to offer anthropology a scientific technology and an opening toward avenues of research that might serve as a corrective to narrow scholasticism. The expectation arose that anthropology might evolve from a discipline of words into one embracing the perceptions of a visual medium, and that film would finally attain the importance in the mainstream of anthropology that the early pioneers had predicted for it.

No such revolution has yet taken place. Ethnographic filmmaking has not become a significant occupation of anthropologists themselves, nor have films affected the broader conceptualization of anthropology. Considering only the record-making potential of ethnographic film, Margaret Mead called its history a "wretched picture of lost opportunities," blaming her discipline for "our gross and dreadful negligence" (1975: 4–6).

In retrospect, the disappointment of hopes for a rapprochement between film and anthropology seems only a further episode in a chronic complaint. Toward the end of his career, Regnault (1931) deplored the indifference to scientific uses of film that followed his early efforts. The example set by Bateson and Mead, while it stimulated widespread interest, produced no surge of comparable projects. De Brigard (1975) and Mead (1975) have examined possible reasons for the reluctance of anthropologists to employ film. Some of these are practical: filmmaking is too costly, too intrusive, and too difficult. Others are historical: film techniques in the early years were inappropriate to the shifting concerns of anthropology, nor could they assist anthropologists in salvage ethnography conducted through interviews with informants. Mead viewed most of these explanations as rationalizations. She blamed anthropologists for their conservatism, arguing that they selfishly sacrificed a research tool of immense potential to maintain an orthodoxy of words in which they felt secure and competent.

The tenor of this argument is not that anthropologists were behaving rationally, but that they were too timid, too lazy, and too self-indulgent to seize upon the benefits of film. But it is perhaps these very benefits that require further examination. In its attributes as a medium, and in the models it offers for communication, what possible use can film be to anthropologists? In a review of an ethnographic film written in 1977 an anthropologist remarks:

The analysis of ethnography requires the probing of a complex of minute particularities in a search for demonstrable connections; it is always tentative and de-

mands detachment, openness and uncertainty. The bossy one-eyedness and distorting beauty of film, on the other hand, seeks to simplify, disarm, and impose.
(Baxter 1977: 7)

The description of anthropological method may be idealized here and the
view of film unduly harsh, for we know that films often render the specific at
the expense of the general; but in his impatience the reviewer correctly identifies the difficulty that anthropologists have in reconciling the observations of
film and its forms of discourse to those they customarily employ. The same
reviewer writes:

> I confess to a feeling of unease about any film which aspires to be more than a
> simple record or an animated teaching aid, because there is a basic incompatibil-
> ity between the purposes of anthropology and the aims of film. Each seeks quite
> different aspects of truth and utilizes quite different means of stitching scraps of
> culture together creatively. (1977: 7)

This may be a polite way of excusing the deficiencies of many films, but it
also expresses an inclination among anthropologists to locate the aspirations
of ethnographic film in familiar territory. If anthropologists have consistently
rejected film as an analytical medium, and if they have themselves often relegated it to subordinate record-making and didactic roles, the reason may not
be merely conservative reluctance to employ a new technology but a shrewd
judgment that the technology entails a shift in perspective which raises major
problems for scientific conceptualization. The incompatibility need not necessarily be one of attitudes, for both anthropologists and filmmakers can respect
the particularities of culture and accept reversals of their preconceptions.
Rather, it lies in a discontinuity of modes of description and discourse.

The discontinuity arises first on the descriptive level. There is a profound
difference between viewing photochemically produced images of objects and
reading the signs of written language that represent them. The sign (the word)
is at once undifferentiated compared to the image, which remains specific and
continually asserts complexities that defy simple interpretation. Film images
thus pose a challenge to the processes of language that classify objects and
behavioral acts.

There are other important differences of context and articulation. In anthropological writing, information is conveyed serially. Each item appears in isolation, already stripped, as it were, for anthropological action. There is little
possibility of transmitting simultaneously a cluster of associated items. The
effect of simultaneity ("the milking pot rests on the knee"; "the woman sings
while the child plays") is a product of creative reconstruction. In ordering
descriptive items, the writer draws upon a comprehensive mental image which
is already organized conceptually. The choices made, however unintentionally, establish an emphasis ("the child plays while the woman sings") which is

of a different order from that imparted by the selective techniques of cinematography. While it may be possible for an anthropologist to cite data that conflicts with a particular analysis—to try to leave space for alternative interpretations—a radically different interpretation may require data that lies completely outside the scope of the original description.

Description in these terms is really a misnomer when applied to film. Films present images for our inspection, and the information contained in them is described only in the sense that a circle is described by a pair of compasses. The filmmaker marks out the boundaries within which the objects of analysis can be found. These objects preserve their individuality and remain embedded in a context which presents itself as a continuum to the viewer.

Film is not of course without codes of signification, but its discourse is perhaps best described as a reflection of shifting attention rather than the direct representation of thought that in everyday life we associate with language. Even the most selective tool of cinematography, the close-up, leaves the object connected to the world around it, which extends beyond the edges of the frame. It may contain as much information as a wider shot, only in a narrower field. Film editing creates meaning by implying relationships between the contents of shots, as does the movement of the camera from one field to another; but with both techniques the connotations of the material for the viewer may override its denotative meaning or the significance being attached to it by the filmmaker. Film images do not constitute a lexicon of the kind available to the anthropological writer, nor can they be organized with the same grammatical assurance.

As filmmaking tends toward longer unbroken camera takes (sequence shots), filmmakers find themselves dealing with passages of material in which different objects of signification increasingly vie for attention. A shift in the relationship between two people may be masked for the viewer by more intensive activities occurring within the shot. This kind of perceptual noise is overcome in fiction films through scripting that excludes distracting material. But the context of actual social intercourse is rarely so simple. The distraction may itself be of concern to the film, placing further demands upon its structural rhetoric.

Anthropologists have sensed these and kindred difficulties which make film so different from words in conveying information and ideas. In anthropological writing, concrete details are held in suspension at the crucial moment to permit abstract expression; in film they are omnipresent. At the same time, film becomes attractive to anthropologists for its contextualization and rendering of data through means other than linguistic signs. This creates ambivalent attitudes toward ethnographic films which aspire to present a theoretical analysis by revelatory means, since that requires a manipulation of the data itself. It may also account for the fact that ethnographic films are more readily accepted by anthropologists when they keep data and analysis clearly separated in visual and verbal domains. But such a separation cannot finally allow ethnographic film to make its most distinctive contribution to the understanding of humanity. It is, after all, the articulated witnessing of human behavior that film can provide but that written anthropology cannot. With that as an objective, the invention of new forms that balance the intellectual and informational potential of film becomes an urgent necessity for ethnographic filmmakers.

## The Film-As-Text

The future development of ethnographic film is open to a number of strategies. Ruby considers that the conventions of documentary film are altogether inappropriate to the practice of visual anthropology and has noted that "anthropologists do not regard ethnography in the visual mode with the same or analogous scientific expectations with which they regard written anthropology" (1975: 104). He has argued that ethnographic films must become more scientific, describing culture from clearly defined anthropological perspectives. Ethnographic filmmakers must become more conscientious in revealing their methods and "employ a distinctive lexicon—an anthropological argot" (p. 107). In contrast to conceptions of ethnographic film that would settle for less, such a view asserts the primacy of film as a communicative system and holds out the hope of a visual anthropology as rigorous as the written anthropology that preceded it.

Ruby is certainly right in stating that films embody theoretical and ideological assumptions in their organization, and that filmmakers should not only become conscious of that coding but make the forms of their work consonant with their analyses. But his proposal presupposes a rough semiotic equivalency between written anthropology and potential visual codes that would make a similar kind of discourse possible. It raises the question of whether a visual medium can express scientific statements about culture at all comparable to those that can be stated in words. If it cannot, the understandings communicated by film may always be radically different from those of anthropology and equally unacceptable to anthropologists.

Christian Metz (1974) and Peter Wollen (1972) have held that in film, image-symbols can take on the characteristics of linguistic signs, but other studies in the semiology of the cinema suggest that film is neither lexical nor grammatical in a linguistic sense and that its communicative structures are constantly reinvented.[9] If this is the case, the documentary conventions that Ruby refers to as inappropriate models for ethnographic filmmaking probably exist only as a backdrop for more complex, extragrammatical processes. The very structural flexibility of film may make scientific communication and the creation of a conventionalized anthropological visual argot doubtful possibilities.

Even if it were possible to devise codes that would allow film to approach the forms of written anthropology, one must ask whether such an approach would open up the most productive path for ethnographic film. Not only does film have capacities for revelation that differ from those of language, but it provides an opportunity for interrogating the concept of scientific communication, which assumes that language is an instrument for transmitting messages that progressively delineate the external world. From fairly early on a few films have implicitly challenged that assumption, and such thinking has begun to transform the modern ethnographic film, leading to what may be called the ethnographic *film-as-text*.[10]

Peter Wollen has recognized a parallel development in the cinema as a whole, arguing that film was a latecomer among the arts in repudiating the ideology of traditional aesthetics. While literature and painting were exploring their own communicative systems and assuming new forms that questioned the mediating role of the artist, film was still in the age of the nickelodeon. Only more recently, in the work of such filmmakers as Godard, Makavejev, and Glauber Rocha have filmmakers attempted to create objects that exist as "texts" to be plumbed by the viewer. These films refute the notion that ideas about reality become suitable replacements for it. In place of the monologues of previous films they offer areas of inquiry. According to Wollen,

> the text is thus no longer a transparent medium; it is a material object which provides the conditions for the production of meaning, within constraints which it sets itself. It is open rather than closed; multiple rather than single; productive rather than exhaustive. Although it is produced by an individual, the author, it does not simply represent or express the author's ideas, but exists in its own right. (1972: 163)

If Wollen's examination had included ethnographic films, he would have found this approach adopted well before Godard in the work of Flaherty and Rouch. The underlying insight of the film-as-text is that a film lies in conceptual space somewhere within a triangle formed by the subject, filmmaker, and audience and represents an encounter of all three. *Nanook* has a methodological and structural complexity which permits it to transcend Flaherty's particular brand of romanticism. More than any of his later films, it represents a collaborative effort between the filmmaker and his subjects to devise a rich and open-ended cultural document. In Rouch's *Moi, un noir* (1957) and *Jaguar* (1967) the subjects play roles that arise out of their own experience and become a part of it. These films make available to the audience an interior world that interacts with the surface reality that the filmmaker documents with the camera. In *Jaguar* a third element is added: the commentary of the subjects upon viewing the film, which allows the film to incorporate the self-reflexive responses of those who appear in it.

*Chronique d'un été* (1961) was probably Rouch's most important contribution to the methodology of the film-as-text, as an inquiry into how filmmaking represents but also influences the experience of its subjects. What *Chronique* achieved at one blow was the destruction of conventions that in traditional films sustain the filmmaker's authority and bolster myths about the perfection of knowledge. Such conventions guard against access by either the subjects or the audience to a film's sources and creation. In written anthropology they can perhaps be compared to the suppression of field notes in favor of neatly compiled data or, finally, a dissertation which appears as a product of pure thought, uncomplicated by struggle and praxis.

The film-as-text stimulates thought through a juxtaposition of elements, each of which bears a relationship to the intellectual framework of the inquiry. These elements may reveal information on how materials were gathered, provide alternative perspectives by the film's subjects, or present the evidence out of which the film proceeds. This produces a kind of filmic montage, but montage in which the contributing passages retain an internal life and are not reduced, as in the montage of Eisenstein, to the level of iconic signs. The result is a form of filmmaking in which observational cinema (or the cinema of duration advocated by André Bazin and other realist critics) can coexist with the generation of meaning through the collision of dissimilar materials.

A significant number of ethnographic films display elements of this approach. In the use of sound alone, spoken narrative that would once have represented the filmmaker's viewpoint has been replaced by the film subjects' commentary, as in Preloran's *Imaginero* (1970), Eric Crystal's film on Toraja ritual, *Ma'Bugi* (1971), and Judith MacDougall's *The House-Opening* (1980). In Roger Sandall's *Coniston Muster* (1972), Rouch's technique of using the film to elicit comments from his subjects is combined with a further juxtaposition of filmed remarks by the subjects and observations of their activities. In *The Mursi* (1974) a tripartite sound track contains the synchronous dialogue of the subjects (translated on the screen in subtitles), the filmmaker's remarks on the relationship between the filming process and the situation as he found it, and an interpretive commentary by the anthropologist, David Turton.

The juxtaposition of scenes has been developed more fully in the documentary tradition than in ethnographic films, although *Song of Ceylon*, made in the 1930s, employs it extensively (between image and image, and image and sound) and spans both categories. In Pierre Perrault's and Michel Brault's films of the 1960s about Québecois society (*Pour la suite du monde* [1963], *Un Pays sans bon sens* [1969]), fragments of conversation and action are composed into complex cultural statements, and in one instance (*Le Règne du jour* [1966]) parallel editing is used to provide a comparison of French and French-Canadian culture. In Mark McCarty's and Paul Hockings's film *The Village* (1969) the technique is used to compare old and new features of Irish peasant society. In *To Live with Herds* (1972) it relates processes of nation-building to their effects upon Jie pastoralists, and in *Photo Wallahs* (1991) it presents contrasting approaches to photography in a specific cultural setting.

Timothy Asch's *The Ax Fight* (1975), a film simultaneously about Yano-mamö social conflict and anthropological method, uses five segments to provide separate perspectives on an event and its ethnographic interpretation. We see first the unedited roll of film shot during the fight. This is followed over black screen by the sound recorded after the film ran out, including Asch's and Chagnon's conversation about what has just happened (not only are they in doubt but jump to the wrong conclusions). In two further segments, interpretations of the fight are given through a close reexamination of the original footage and the use of commentary over a kinship diagram. The film closes with a conventionally edited version of the fight in which shots are sometimes used out of chronology to give a sense of continuity. Although the film only shows how a small portion of the information given us was actually gathered, it dramatically underscores the precariousness of anthropological understanding during fieldwork.

Unlike *The Ax Fight*, the film *Kenya Boran* (1974) relies primarily upon scenes of informal conversation to reveal larger social patterns. The film consists of a geometrical structure built upon the encounters of four persons: a traditional herdsman, a friend who is a minor government functionary, and their two sons, one of whom has received schooling and the other who hasn't. The behavior of each in relation to each of the others provides a separate axis upon which the audience can plot the values and constraints governing their differing lives. Through the convergence of these axes, a composite image is presented of the choices that irrevocably separate people during periods of rapid social change.

Probably none of these films makes a scientific statement in purely filmic terms, but most raise anthropological questions that further examination of their contents can help to answer. They draw upon anthropological thought, but also upon the quite different means by which filmmaking can articulate the experience of the viewer.

The cinema, of which ethnographic film is a part, has become increasingly concerned with problems of evidence and methodology; and in films that eschew a scientific label—such as Roger Graef's documentary television projects in Great Britain, Frederick Wiseman's films on American institutions, and Bob Connolly and Robin Anderson's New Guinea films—one can often find more thorough and original examinations of social phenomena than in those that assume the label of anthropology. Ethnographic filmmaking can now hardly return to the impressionism of the solitary artist, but it seems equally unlikely that it can abandon its intellectual roots in the cinema and veer toward a specialized scientific language. Film can never replace the written word in anthropology, but anthropologists are made conscious by their field experience of the limitations which words impose upon their discipline. We are beginning to discover how film can fill some of the blind spots.

[1978]

## Notes

This essay was first published in *Annual Review of Anthropology* 7 (1978): 405–25, ©
1978 by Annual Reviews Inc. and reprinted with permission. It has been revised to
include additional references to more recent films.

1. For the first perspective, see Emilie de Brigard's "The History of Ethnographic
Film" (1975), and Karl Heider's *Ethnographic Film* (1976); for the second, Sol
Worth's "Toward the Development of a Semiotic of Ethnographic Film" (1972).

2. The best-known example is Ruth Benedict's *The Chrysanthemum and the Sword*
(1946), a study of Japanese culture "at a distance." But see also Bateson (1943), Heider
(1991), Kracauer (1947), and Weakland (1975).

3. For example, see Griaule (1957) and Sorenson (1967). I also distinguish among
several different film types in "Beyond Observational Cinema," which is included in
this volume.

4. Originally entitled *In the Land of the Head-Hunters*, Curtis's film was restored
and reissued in 1973 as *In the Land of the War Canoes* with a sound track of Kwakiutl
dialogue and music prepared by Bill Holm, George I. Quimby, and David Gerth.

5. A significant difference between the two projects, however, was that the intimate
events of the Netsilik project took place within a reconstruction of Inuit life of an
earlier period, whereas Marshall's filming of the Ju/'hoansi, although it sometimes
excluded modern influences, was an attempt to record life as at was generally lived at
the time.

6. For a first-hand description of the rediscovery of this material, see Dunlop (1983:
11–12).

7. Another ethnographic film, *Imbalu: Ritual of Manhood of the Gisu of Uganda*,
directed by Richard Hawkins and filmed by me in 1968, was also intended to be subtitled, but it was not released until 1989. John Marshall has written that although he
filmed without fully synchronous sound among the Ju/'hoansi in 1957–58, he nevertheless planned to lay in roughly matching sound to "convey what people were really
saying in subtitles" (1993: 41).

8. For studies of the reception of ethnographic films, see Berry and Sommerlad
(n.d.), Hearn and DeVore (1973), and Martinez (1990).

9. For an overview of some of these theories see articles by Pasolini, Eco, Abram-
son, and Nichols in Bill Nichols's *Movies and Methods* (1976). See also David
Bordwell's discussion in *Narration in the Fiction Film* of the role of *énonciation* in
filmic discourse, as defined by Émile Benveniste (1985: 21–26).

10. The concept of a film as a "text," which in the 1970s made possible new ways of
exploring the construction of films, was also conceptually limiting in that it suggested
that films were composed of "meanings" to be "read" rather than images to be perceived in more complex ways. Characteristic of this semiotic approach was Metz's
focus on the denotative systems of fiction films, largely ignoring documentary films
and the connotative aspects of film images. However, in his later writings on psychoanalysis and cinema he significantly revised this approach, giving more attention to the
relation of the spectator to the film.

# PART THREE

# CHAPTER NINE

# Unprivileged Camera Style

FILMMAKING CAN BE A protracted process, with long delays between shooting a film and editing it. Hence filmmakers are apt to make their discoveries at the worst possible time: when the film isn't yet finished, but when it's too late to go back and shoot it differently. Discoveries of this kind may explain why so many films seem like uneasy compromises or reworkings of "found" material.

In 1968, after Judith MacDougall and I had finished shooting *To Live with Herds* (1972) in Uganda, we made a discovery that was hardly novel but that suggested some of the ideas I shall mention here. We had been filming in Jie compounds, which were surrounded by heavy stockades of interwoven sticks. One entered by crouching and passing through a low doorway. Inside, the area was like a roofless room, with a clean-swept earthen floor. Having managed to enter with our filming equipment we usually settled gratefully in one place. This we found also suited our filming. It generally provided an adequate field of view and was acceptable to the Jie, who also spent much of their time in fixed positions around their compounds. [Figure 18.]

18. In a Jie compound, Uganda, 1968. From *To Live with Herds* (1972).

As we became more experienced, we began looking for the optimum position in which to place ourselves. This was the point from which we would have an unimpeded view of most social activities. We often remained there, but sometimes we shifted to a second camera position, either because the center of social interaction had shifted or for the quite different reason that we knew a second camera angle would be useful when the time came to edit the film.

Often, for example, a conversation viewed from only one position was unsatisfactory because certain persons were seen at the expense of others, whose backs were to us. It was also difficult to record the steps of a process like millet beer-making from one position, when each step seemed to require its own particular angle. Finally, when little seemed to be happening and the camera ground on and on, we knew that later we would be able to cut to a shot from another angle without awkwardness or a sense of disjunction. At least that was what we thought.

These notions persisted through the synchronizing and viewing of our rushes. We were pleased with the material and were confident we could use the best of it in a film. It was only when we started editing that we began to have doubts. These would start when we had used a long take of a conversation, had cut to a shot from a second camera position, and had then returned to the first angle again. For some reason it wasn't working, despite the fact that this pattern of intercutting dialogue was the mainstay of most of the films we had seen in our lives.

Reluctantly, we abandoned this approach. For many sequences we ended up discarding all of the footage from either one position or the other, although both contained valuable material.

At first, when we asked ourselves what had happened, we blamed the framing of our shots. Later we began to see that this wasn't the real problem. The problem lay in a contradiction in premises: denying to the audience on the one hand what we had been offering it on the other.

What we were trying to give was a sense of being present in a Jie compound, a situation in which few of our viewers would ever find themselves. There were several reasons for this—to counteract prevalent representations of "exotic" people, to express the realities of fieldwork, to record informal aspects of culture, to allow individuals rather than types to emerge—and a number of things made it possible: our subjects' acknowledgment of our presence, our long and static camera takes, and the very low energy-level of much that we filmed. We were not singling out dramatic subjects for attention so much as opening the film up to a kind of anti-subject-matter: apparently inconsequential events that were more like what one would witness in ordinary experience than choose as film subjects.

By intercutting shots from two or more camera positions we found we were taking away that immediacy by invoking a style of fictional filmmaking incompatible with the idea of real people sitting in a compound filming other real people. We were aware that the conventions of fiction had considerably influenced documentary films, but we had underestimated their significance and the extent to which we and other filmmakers had been taught to accept them as appropriate.

The term *privileged camera angle* was often used in discussions of Hollywood films to describe a camera position that could not be occupied in everyday life—a shot from a fireplace, looking through the flames, or a shot through a mirror or wall, or perhaps a distorted or surrealistic effect, such as a shot from the lap of a fat man looking up his nostrils. Such shots were common in thrillers and psychological dramas of the 1940s and reached back to German Expressionism. But privileged camera angles are really the common coinage of fiction films and only become noticeable when they strain the audience's credulity. Pressed a little further they become jokes, like the opening of *The Tin Drum* (1979) in which we and little Oskar look down his mother's birth canal toward a world he regards with horror.

Most shots in fiction films are privileged because there is no acknowledged observer, and in any case one cannot imagine an unknown person being given such access to other people's lives. These films posit an invisible observer with special powers that merge the consciousness of the author and audience. The viewpoint is rarely that of a character. Frame enlargements from fiction films make it evident that most point-of-view shots are in fact only analogues of the viewpoint of a character. The eyes of the actors rarely look directly into the camera as they would if it were substituted for one of their interlocutors. Because of this, documentary films can adopt the shooting style of fiction without the contradiction that the camera has actually "become" a nonfictional person.

The editing of fiction films also takes liberties, but with time and space rather than with conventions of privacy. It is understood that within dramatic sequences no time need elapse at a cut, and this power is confirmed by the continuity of the sound track. Thus the eye of the observer shifts instantaneously to new positions without the necessity of traveling between them. Television directors now switch from one camera to another, but the effect of instantaneous switching is a conceptual, not a technological creation. Although multiple cameras have been used since the early days of the cinema, the same effect is usually achieved by a series of separate camera set-ups. The idea is older than films, which simply matched images to an invention of fiction.

Fiction films are experiences of magical observation, defying ordinary physical limits and forms of accountability. If they have often been called dreamlike, it is because they give us a sense of untrammelled will.

When people began taking snapshots just before the turn of the century they would say, "Look at the camera." Later, responding to a new impulse, they began to say, "Don't look at the camera. Go on with what you were doing." They wanted photographs of life, but as though photography had not occurred. In producing this effect they were led irrevocably into fiction.

Something similar happened in film. The directness of many of the "primitive" films made between 1895 and 1920 resulted from an acknowledgment of the act of filming. They were often about the specific historical moment when a cinematographer came to town. Later such scenes disappeared from the cinema, banished by a professionalism that viewed any internal evidence of filmmaking as an aesthetic error. "As you know," Basil Wright once said, "in the old documentary days, as soon as someone looked at the camera, you threw that shot out because the illusion of reality had been lost" (1971: 41). Documentary films were supposed to be distillations of truth, transcending the human agencies that produced them. Making them was a matter of high seriousness and careful composition. Except when events were even more dramatic than filmmaking itself, as in theaters of war, life stopped when the cameras appeared. It had to be started up artificially when the cameras rolled, and so another component of fiction was added: people became actors impersonating themselves.

Ved Mehta has described how television perpetuates a form of fictionalized documentary—the intimate portrait—by relentlessly molding its subjects to its needs. The film was *Chachaji, My Poor Relation: A Memoir by Ved Mehta* (1978) about his second cousin Bahali Ram, a film for which Mehta was hired as the "writer."

> "Tell Daddy Chopra to push open the screen door and summon Chacha and give him an errand," Bill says. "Tell Chacha to keep on turning the pages of the ledger until he's called."
>
> I tell Chopra and Chachaji what to do, and Bill shouts "Board!"
>
> Chopra pushes open the screen door, as instructed, and calls out, "Lalaji, come inside. Bring ledger."
>
> Before Chopra can finish his lines, Bill yells "Cut!" Chachaji spoiled the shot by jumping up at the sound of Chopra opening the door, instead of waiting for Chopra to call him.
>
> And so the morning goes, until we think we finally have enough good material to make a sequence of Chachaji being sent on an errand. (1980: 63–64)

Implicit in a camera style is a theory of knowledge. British documentary films of the 1930s and 1940s were concerned with essences, and the camera was only one of several tools for conveying what one already knew about life. Colin Young has observed that there was an Art Director on Grierson's *Drifters* (1929); and in *Night Mail* (1936) there was no contradiction seen in the use of studio techniques to get the shots of letter-sorting en route to Edinburgh. A railway carriage was put up on blocks, lit, and rocked rhythmically by stagehands.

One view is that the aims of documentary were ahead of its means, and it wasn't prepared to wait. Synchronous sound-recording outside the studio was an adventure, attempted in only a few documentary films like *Housing Problems* (1935). Documentaries had a hard time competing with direct experience or, more importantly one suspects, with the concentrated energy of story films. Authenticity became a matter of effect, as is made clear in *The Technique of Film Editing*, first published in 1953 and "written and compiled by Karel Reisz with the guidance of [a] Committee appointed by the British Film Academy":

> [The] need to obtain apt, incisive "raw stuff" before editing begins is demonstrated most forcefully in the production of the simplest form of documentary—the reportage film. . . . The facts alone are of interest and the director's task is to present them as authentically as possible.
>
> At first sight nothing would appear to be simpler than to present an exciting event in an exciting way. Actually, as we shall see, to achieve a convincing impression of an actually observed scene, a most elaborate editing process may have to be brought into operation. (Reisz and Millar 1968: 125–26)

If one were to look for a turning point in the domination of documentary films by fiction, one would have to find the point at which filmmakers ceased merely to exploit the persuasive powers of film and began to examine their ideological implications. Dziga Vertov was one of the first to do so, but one would have to wait until almost the 1960s to find very many others. The revolution of the British "Free Cinema" movement and of "direct cinema" and *cinéma vérité* were directed against two kinds of privilege: the privilege inherent in an aesthetic that resulted in the living people of films being subordinated to an anonymous creator, and the privilege of studios, television companies, equipment manufacturers, and exhibitors to institutionalize the styles and intellectual assumptions of filmmaking. The light-weight sound cameras of Richard Leacock, Michel Brault, and Albert Maysles were the first that could be used as personal instruments, after years in which sound was either added to images in the cutting room or resulted from the use of huge cameras requiring teams of technicians. After the first flights of fancy—that cameras which could go anywhere could also record everything—filmmakers began facing the implications of film as a personal form of record-making. It would reflect more directly the interests and circumstances of the observer, and it would be unable to claim the definitive authority of films of the past. It would resituate the audience in relation to the subject, and this meant resituating the filmmaker in relation to the audience.

The result was the notion of an *unprivileged camera style:* a style based on the assumption that the appearance of a film should be an artifact of the social and physical encounter between the filmmaker and the subject. To achieve this, some filmmakers began to relinquish the formal privileges that sustained the Olympian omniscience of story-tellers. Others saw it primarily as a matter of principle: that it was unethical to present the lives of real people through the devices by which imaginary characters were created. Living human beings were not merely the raw material for stories or the illustration of concepts. They had their own existence in defiance of any documentary film that might be made about them, and this demanded that they be treated for what they were.

Of course, this fervor had its own ideological blindness. "Direct" cinema shifted different powers into the hands of individual filmmakers, who could be equally ruthless in other ways towards their subjects and audiences. There was also much room for self-deception: for believing that the meaning of events was self-evident in images of them, or that filming something made it interesting, or that people were no longer influenced by being filmed, or that filmmaking was a mystical or philanthropic activity in which creative ambition played no part.

Ethnographic film constituted a special case of documentary. Cinematic conventions attracted particular attention both as an expression of culture (the Worth-Adair Navajo experiments, for example[1]) and because of the debate over how film could serve as evidence for anthropology, stimulated by Jean Rouch, Colin Young, Jay Ruby, and others. The debate soon shifted to how film could become a medium of anthropological inquiry. But awareness of the stylistic revolution occurring in documentary film made its way only slowly into ethnographic films, even though two of the leading innovators in documentary, Jean Rouch and John Marshall, were ethnographers. Most films were cast in a lecture form that asserted the authority of the commentator, not the footage. Others, ranging from "educational" films involving anthropologists to television travelogues, continued to direct their actors rather than observe them and employed the shooting and editing techniques of fiction.

Two films about hunters are characteristic, made more than fifty years after Flaherty's famous walrus-hunting scene, which André Bazin celebrated as an alternative to staging and montage. In *Cree Hunters of Mistassini* (1974) and *Pygmies of the Rainforest* (1977) the hunters are seen in shots just before the kill with their weapons aimed in the general direction of the camera. Thus either we must accept that the hunters allowed the film crew to get between themselves and their prey or that these shots were made at another time, probably after the hunt was over.


In the 1950s John Marshall, equipped at first with only a spring-wind camera and non-synchronous recorder, began filming passages of personal interaction among the Ju/'hoansi of the Kalahari. He filmed as though their voices would be heard and his lengthy shots would be seen intact—a curious approach at a time when documentary films were mosaics of shots. Most cinematographers knew that even if they filmed continuous events their shots would be cut up and the fragments edited into a new synthesis. The original temporal and spatial relationships would be lost. In these circumstances, almost everyone shot to get the fragments, not the continuity. But Marshall was young and had been sent out to do a job of ethnographic documentation, not to make documentary films. As so often happens at the beginnings of things, he thought he was doing something quite ordinary, although what he was attempting foreshadowed the wave of the future. His sequence-shots, with the sound laboriously "scissor-synced" to the picture, can now be seen as early examples of an effort to put the viewer into a relationship with the subject more like the filmmaker's own.

Sequence-shots restore to the audience something of the continuity of perception of an individual observer. They are also probably the key feature of a camera style that seeks to sever itself from the imagery of fiction and tie itself to the specific historical act of filming. Other aspects of this style can be called "unprivileged" only in contrast to styles that gain immunity by not subjecting themselves to the risks and consequences of that act, for clearly anyone with a camera enjoys certain privileges as an observer. Unprivileged camera style is a negative notion, a corrective. It is an assertion of the obvious: that filmmakers are human, fallible, rooted in physical space and society, governed by chance, limited in perception—and that films must be understood this way. The renunciation of stylistic privilege is not a recipe for enlightenment but a point of reference for communication. It attempts to narrow the distance between the person who makes a film and the person who views it. There is no longer a compulsion to occupy an advantageous camera position at any cost; a "bad" shot which nevertheless contains useful information, and which would once have been removed as "unprofessional," is now preserved.

A film by Gary Kildea, *Celso and Cora* (1983), incorporates many of the shifts I have been discussing. It concerns the lives of Cora and Celso, street-vendors in Manila. Kildea began working entirely alone, a "one-man-band" of camera, microphone, and tape recorder. He felt this approach was necessary to protect the obligations he had assumed toward the family, but later he found it too difficult and completed the filming with an assistant from the Philippines. He edited the film himself, and he refused many aspects of conventional film editing. The illusion of continuous time, except within shots, is avoided—one might say, purposefully destroyed— by the interpolation of short lengths of leader, like the blackouts or intertitles that once separated shots in silent films and which reappeared (for reasons similar to Kildea's) in a few ethnographic and fictional films of the 1960s and 1970s.[2] This approach also frees Kildea from the necessity of conventional editing transitions between shots. Thus

19. *Celso and Cora* (1983).

Kildea draws our attention to the fact that the film is composed of fragments taken out of the lives of his subjects. One suspects such an approach would be anathema to most television programmers.

At one point Kildea shot footage from the driver's window of one of the trains that regularly pushes through Kahilom, the quarter in which the family lived. In the end he felt unable to use any of this material because it was too alien to their experience, a view of their quarter that they would never see.

Kildea is clearly a privileged observer—a white, middle-class filmmaker in one of the innumerable microcosms of the Third World—but his camera style reaches out to the subjects and to us in the audience in an attempt to make our analysis of what he is doing less problematical. The film is composed of long sequence-shots. In one shot made early on in the filming, Celso and Cora are looking at new lodgings they hope to occupy. After examining the room in some detail Celso asks when the filming is going to start. Upon discovering that the camera has been running all the time, he returns to his examination of the room apparently unconcerned. The shot provides a crosscheck on his reactions, and although it is not a definitive one it helps to delineate the relationship Kildea has established with his subjects. [Figure 19.]

Later in the film a shot occurs which tells us more about this relationship and also about Kildea's attitude towards the audience. Cora and Celso have had an argument and have separated. On top of this, Celso has been told he can no longer sell cigarettes in front of the Tower Hotel, where he had been scraping enough money to get by. He has been up all night with his small daughter, Maricel, at a new selling point down the street. It is now dawn and he has come to the foreshore of Manila Bay with Maricel to give her, as he puts it, "some sun and sea breeze." He is preoccupied with his problems but starts telling Kildea about the strangers nearby. One woman, he says, looking past the camera, is probably trying to cure her baby's cough with the sea air. One guesses that Kildea is intent at this moment on watching Celso, but the camera comes slowly around and looks at what Celso has described before once again returning to him. Considering the difficulties of the shot it is very skilful, but the woman is far away and the view of her cursory. Many film-makers would have stayed with Celso and got a shot of the woman later to use as an insert. Kildea prefers to show us his problem: the image of Celso lost, the demands of the moment observed.

Not all the things we might wish to know about other people are recognizable or even permissible subjects of inquiry to them. Often matters that touch them the most deeply and that are most revealing of their concerns are the most closely guarded. The mysteriousness of filmmaking once gave filmmakers special access to the lives of their subjects, particularly in cultures where films were little understood. The spread of communications is now putting an end to that privilege. People are becoming increasingly aware of the risks and potential benefits of films about them, and filmmakers must pay special attention to the hazards of exposing their subjects to official reprisals or the ostracism of their neighbors.

This can force filmmakers in one of two directions: either to abandon entire areas of human relations or develop new approaches with their subjects that allow sensitive topics to be explored. For films to be properly interpreted, the nature of these new "contracts" must be understood by the audience. Increasingly, filmmakers are bringing their relationships with the subjects into the foreground of their films. These encounters can develop into informal exchanges quite different from interviews. As the filmmaker is drawn further into the subject area of the film, the audience is drawn into the position the filmmaker originally occupied.

The process can be as much a feature of overall film structure as of camera style. Rouch's and Morin's *Chronique d'un été* (1961) was posed explicitly as an experiment in documentary filmmaking, with Rouch and Morin taking center stage. Other films such as Chris Marker's "letters" to his audiences, Mike Rubbo's *Waiting for Fidel* (1974), and James Blue's *A Few Notes on Our Food Problem* (1968) in their various ways turn the filmmaker into an identifiable intermediary with the audience, grappling with a subject. When we made *To Live with Herds* we were content to include sequences in which our presence was occasionally acknowledged. By the time we made *The Wedding Camels* (filmed 1973–74, released 1977), we were attempting quite consciously to show through film what it is like to be an observer in the midst of

20. Arwoto's compound, during the filming of *The Wedding Camels*, 1974.

a complex event, trying to make sense of it. [Figure 20.] The film takes its structure from the inquiry. It is clear that we miss a good deal. Much of the rest is filtered through the testimony of participants, whose own vested interests must be taken into account. Any knowledge of the event is finally provisional, and in this sense the film is about what one can and cannot know.

[1982]

## Notes

This essay was first published in the Royal Anthropologial Institute newsletter *R.A.I.N.* 50: 8–10 June, 1982.

   1. For an account of this, see Sol Worth and John Adair's *Through Navajo Eyes*.

   2. See, for example, Godard's *Vivre sa vie* (1962), Timothy Asch's *The Ax Fight* (1975), and my film *To Live with Herds* (1972).

# CHAPTER TEN

# When Less Is Less

THERE IS A HIDDEN problem in documentary film—the problem of the long camera take and what to do with it. With the exception of interview material, most of the shots in contemporary documentary films and television programs are only a few seconds long. This is in marked contrast to fiction films and television dramas in which whole scenes are sometimes played out in a single shot. Documentary thus finds itself in the curious company of television commercials and music videos in seeking to maintain audience interest through the dynamics and variety of quick cutting. The long take has become the *terra incognita* of the modern documentary film, a blank space in a practice that devotes itself almost entirely to other properties of the shot. And this is contrary to its heritage, for documentary was born in the pleasures of watching such ordinary events as leaves shimmering on a tree or a train arriving at a station.

Not long ago I spent eight months filming in the streets of a small town in northern India. The finished film (*Photo Wallahs* [1991]) is intentionally one of counterpoints and disjunctions and not at all a smoothly flowing narrative. Yet while I was filming, something odd occurred which I still don't fully understand. I began to shoot a kind of "shadow" film along side the main film. This notional film—notional because it remains unmade—consists of long camera takes which quite clearly could never have been used in the main film. My justification for shooting these long takes was that we could at least extract and use pieces of them. But in the back of my mind they actually constituted an alternative film, a counter-film to the one we were making. They formed a necessary antidote, a way of holding on to qualities that are so often lost when a film is structured for its likely audiences. I remember thinking at the time: "Is it possible to go back to zero, to film as if the cinema has just been invented? What would it be like to work like Louis Lumière when he first set up his camera on the street?"

Some of these long takes last five or six minutes (200 feet of 16mm film); none are shorter than a minute or two. To watch these shots one must suspend one's usual movie-going and television-watching expectations. But these expectations serve as a frame of reference for what I want to discuss here.

Like a spark or a stab of lightning, a film shot discharges most of its meaning at once, within the first few microseconds of appearing on the screen. It is all there, its connotations and denotations alike. If we close our eyes after that first instant, the meaning survives. The mind arrests it like the shutter of a camera. What follows in our response may be very different—a sudden adherence to something happening within the shot, or a kind of coasting perusal. Or so it can be if the shot continues. But most shots are not allowed to. In filmmaking few shots are used in their entirety. Most are shot long and cut short.

Christopher Pinney has argued that still photographs are more indeterminate than films, offering the viewer more because they dictate meanings less. Social scientists in particular, he suggests, are afraid of still photographs and prefer film because "still images contain *too many meanings* whereas the desirability of film lies precisely in its ability to constrain meaning through narrative chains of signification. . . . They close off plural readings in the temporal flow of succession and destruction" (1992: 27). The temporal and sequential structure of film thus "provides a fortification against undesirable and 'unwarranted' readings" (p. 28).

But applying this argument to film itself produces a curious reversal of Pinney's observations. Short camera takes resemble still photographs in their fixing of a single image, but by their very brevity they disallow the kind of perusal of the image over time permitted by photographs and by longer takes. Longer takes, which create sequential chains and the narrative cloistering of meanings, also undermine these very meanings by leaving the viewer more time to ignore or challenge them. It can thus be said that the long take comes eventually to resemble the still photograph more closely than the short take, at least in these "lexical" properties.

Just as shots may be short or long, so there are short films, long films, and occasionally very long films which are rarely seen. While no one would argue that how one reads entire films is analogous to how one reads individual shots, there is perhaps a connection between the visual context within which a shot is framed and the footage from which a finished film is extracted. Dai Vaughan writes of an ideal cinema, never perhaps to be achieved because tending towards an impossible conflation, "something which would attain to a narrative significance whilst remaining random" (1986: 162). The films that have come closest for him have been certain documentary films for television shot in *cinéma vérité* or long-take style: "Not the rushes, yet not the fine cuts and most certainly not the transmitted versions with their cellophane wrap of commentary and captions and studio presentation, but the films as they stood when their narrative structures had just begun to emerge with the patient chipping away of the surrounding substance, yet were still perceptibly of its density and of its mass" (p. 163).

I want to examine this problem of the ideal and the actual, the object within grasp yet somehow lost, and draw a broad analogy between the way in which shots are reduced in length in films and the way in which an entire body of footage shot for a film is reduced to produce the finished film. On the way I hope to question some of the assumptions that underlie these practices.

## Disquiet in Documentary

Long takes were not always the exception. In the early days of the cinema, when all films consisted of a single shot, they were the norm. Louis Lumière's first films ran for up to a full minute uncut—the length of a roll of film at the time. Some of Georges Demeny's shots (filmed in the 60mm gauge as early as 1895) ran to forty seconds. That is very long by today's standards, even in fiction films (Salt 1974), although a few directors (Jancsó, Jarmusch) have created distinctive styles around very long takes. In television documentary the average length of a shot is closer to five seconds, excepting interviews and "talking head" presentations. These shots tend to be cut automatically at the point where it is assumed audience attention drops, or where there is any suggestion of a pause in narrative flow.

The great enemy of documentary (and oddly, rather a taboo topic of discussion among filmmakers themselves) is the "dead spot" in which nothing seems to be happening. Film producers are terrified of such moments, for they are terrified of audience impatience.[1] I suspect that the taboo status of this topic goes back to an inherent contradiction in documentary principles. In the early days of *cinéma vérité* and "direct cinema" the prevailing ideology had it that dead spots weren't supposed to exist. Ordinary life was deemed to be worthy of everyone's attention. But documentary filmmakers still contrived to avoid dramaturgical dead spots, cutting around them or focusing on exciting events and famous people. Documentary, whatever its ideology, still took its shape from fiction or journalism. It had to defend its interest in the ordinary by making sure that the ordinary played well. There was a tacit understanding that you didn't talk publicly about this. Who cared to admit that documentary actually concealed the lacunæ characteristic of ordinary life and chose only the best bits, just like the fiction filmmakers?

What constitutes a "long take" is obviously an artificial and somewhat arbitrary concept, formed in relation to an average notion of shot length and affected by content and position as well as by duration. Long takes are perhaps better defined by their structural qualities than by their length. Does the shot, for example, form an entire sequence in the film, or is it merely part of a more extended, edited sequence? In this analysis, the term "long take" refers more to a method of film construction than to actual length. Brian Henderson (1971: 9) has pointed out that although Murnau uses a long take style, his shots are actually quite short. In his films the viewer's attention tends to be focused more upon developments within shots than upon linkages between them.

It is also evident that shots of long duration are not necessarily more revealing than if they had been shorter—for example, shots of repetitive activities or shots containing limited information which is rapidly grasped by the viewer. It is no use comparing generically different materials. Duration is perhaps the least important criterion in comparing a static, practically empty frame and a frame crowded with activity. And yet . . . and yet, as I shall argue later, absolute duration does finally matter. It is not wholly subjective and has its own measure of influence upon our reading of shots.

## The Viewing of Images

It seems almost self-evident that how long we look at an image affects what we see in it and how we interpret it. Even if there were no other evidence of this, it has been shown that the eye successively scans an image in a series of fixations. If the time for doing this is cut short, the eye is able to fix on fewer points and the mind creates a less extensive version of what David Marr has called the "primal sketch" (Rosenfeld 1984). In talking about viewing film images it is useful to place the process in the context of viewing practices generally. How does film-viewing differ from viewing other kinds of images, such as still photographs?

Sometimes the length of time we devote to a still photograph is determined for us, as when a train we are on flashes by a billboard with a photograph on it. The frequency with which we view photographs is also often beyond our control: it is the aim of advertisers to expose us to the same pictures as often as possible, although many photographs, such as those in newspapers, we see only once, and then usually briefly. Others, such as family snapshots, may be seen again and again—and we may choose to study them for quite long periods.

When we watch films in a theater we exchange the role of private consumer of images for that of public participant at a spectacle. Our choices become more limited. Not only are the still photographs of the film regulated to 24 or 25 per second, but the length of time we have to view each shot is precisely dictated. We thus surrender an important part of our control over the image, although not all of it. There is still the possibility of searching the shot and interpreting it to some degree independently—for example, by looking for "peripheral detail" (Cardinal 1986). How we interpret it depends upon who we are and what assumptions we bring to it. This is a fertile process, the images of the film interacting with the characteristics of personality, culture, and society that define us. This means that shots may carry quite different connotations even for people of very similar background, and larger differences of gender, class, race, and education will produce even greater variations. Despite this, there are some habits of film-viewing that will hold broadly true for audiences with a shared set of cultural expectations. If the following description is in any way recognizable, it is because it applies to a quite specific set of filmmaking and film-viewing conventions.

## Responding to the Shot

For Western, middle-class viewers (at least), the initial response to a shot is determined both by its content and placement in the context of the film and by various plastic and compositional elements of the shot itself. The audience, from its grasp of the context, quickly identifies the intended center of signification of the shot. In a typical character-centered film, for example, imagine that a person whom we have already seen walks down a street and encounters a stranger. Our attention attaches to this person, is then transferred to the stranger, and then perhaps shifts back again to the familiar character. We take in certain background details, but we identify the primary meaning of the shot as residing in what happens to the major character. This primary meaning—perhaps corresponding to what Eisenstein termed the "dominant"—need not be a person, or even a specific visual object. For example, a slow pan over a city may simply signify "a sunny morning in San Francisco" (as in Hitchcock's *Vertigo* [1958]).

Dramatic films thus extend to us a challenge that is a little like a game. We are invited to participate in creating the meaning of each shot by recognizing its narrative or expository center. The length of the shot is gauged so that we must carry this out fairly quickly, leaving little time for other considerations. This contrast between a centered meaning and other coded and uncoded information in the shot may be thought of as a figure-ground relationship. What is identified as figure, and what as ground, is a result of placement and, as Nick Browne has shown for sequences of shots, may also shift and depend upon duration. Previously noted details may be brought forward retrospectively by a new context. Centered meanings may be forgotten in a process Browne calls "fading" (1975: 34–35).

However, there is a certain threshold of narrative or expository efficiency beyond which the motivated meaning of the shot is exhausted. If the shot unexpectedly remains on the screen without further developments, we may feel impatience or annoyance, during which we perhaps look away or withdraw our attention. If the shot continues still longer we may move to a third stage of what might be called "digressive search," when we begin to bring a very different and more idiosyncratic kind of interpretive process to bear upon the shot. In films like Andy Warhol's *Sleep* (1963) and *Blow-Job* (1964) our expectations are deliberately confounded and we are provoked into supplying the images with meaning. Audiences, however, are generally asked to stretch the rules only so far. And when they are asked to do so they are usually offered compensations.

How we respond is shaped not only by our conventional expectations but by the rules that the film itself establishes. In Stanley Kubrick's *2001: A Space Odyssey* (1968), for instance, shots early in the film are purposely lengthened considerably beyond the norms of Hollywood editing. The result is that when the climaxes come we accept that they develop at an almost dreamlike pace.

The viewing of film shots may also be affected by neurophysiological processes that are still not well understood. There may be a point at which the recognition of any sign becomes subject to a certain cognitive loss or slippage. For example, after a period of time our attention may automatically shift from a particular visual figure or thematic focus to "ground" or background material. This may be related to the directional switching that occurs when we study the diagram of a cube, or the experience of figure-ground switching familiar from such examples in Gestalt psychology as seeing a picture alternately as a vase or two symmetrical faces. It may have to do with the different functions of the two hemispheres of the brain, or with the way in which different cells in the visual cortex respond to highly specific shapes in the environment (Gardner 1985: 273). It is possible that digressive search is triggered by such processes, so that a search for alternative configurations and meanings follows the "saturation" of an initial act of recognition.[2]

Such a schematic description of how we read film images cannot, of course, pretend to deal with the many convolutions of pattern recognition or the kinds of layered responses that may be part of reading the denotative and connotative content of complex images.


## From Rushes to Films

Few documentary filmmakers would deny that their films are highly selective and expressive of a particular culture and ideology. At the same time, when filmmakers measure their films against their experience of the world they often find them lacking. What has been referred to as a "crisis of representation" in a broad spectrum of human studies has resulted from just such a sense of discrepancy between experience and the existing paradigms for representing it (Marcus and Fischer 1986). The present intellectual climate may encourage filmmakers to pursue this sense of discrepancy a little further.

It is true that documentary filmmakers have periodically questioned the inherited assumptions of their calling. This has happened notably around the years 1935, 1960, and 1975. Ethnographic filmmakers, in their brushes with other arts and rhetorics, have perhaps been particularly inclined to do so. But even they have seemed unwilling to confront perhaps the most deeply seated

assumption of all: that films are necessarily superior to the raw materials shot
for them.

Despite this, it is not uncommon to hear filmmakers say: "The real film was
in the rushes." I have an instance of this from Roger Graef, the maker of many
documentary films for British television. In an interview with Alan Rosenthal
he says,

> In one film we shot 100,000 16mm feet. That's fifty hours. . . . These *vérité* films
> are usually best in the rushes. All fifty hours tend to be interesting. It's like a
> long-running serial. Strangers wandering through our viewing rooms tend to sit
> there and come back, and back, and back because they want to know what's
> going to happen next. It's got that kind of excitement to it. There *is* a problem in
> structuring them. The films tend to be next best at something like six or eight
> hours. . . . And then there's a terrible problem because all of the subplots, all the
> nuances, all the things that aren't going to survive, but do feed the sense of real-
> ity, all have to be cut. (Rosenthal 1980: 179)

There is in descriptions like this, and in the experience of many filmmakers, a
pervasive sense of loss that is not about a quantitative difference but a qualitative one. It is as though once a film has been pruned to achieve what it actually
sets out to achieve—a coherent narrative or analysis—certain qualities perceived in the rushes have been edited out of it. This contradicts the accepted
notion of creative economy that "less is more," and that "the work is greater
than the sum of its parts." The feeling seems to be that the work has clearly
become less than the sum of its parts. It is not merely a reduced semblance of
the longer work but has been reduced in other important ways in achieving its
final statements.

This is not to revert to the naïve view that film footage is some kind of
unmediated evidence that contains the "truth" about external reality. If that
were so there would be little point going beyond the rushes themselves. It
would deny that editing does in fact introduce its own higher order of truth
and understanding. Rather, the sense of loss seems to identify positive values
perceived in the rushes and intended by the filmmaker at the time of filming
but unachieved in the completed film. It is as though the very reasons for
making films are somehow contradicted by the making of them. The processes of editing a film from the rushes involve both reducing the length overall and cutting most shots to shorter lengths. Both these processes progressively center particular meanings. Sometimes filmmakers appear to recognize
this when they try to preserve some of the qualities of the rushes in their films,
or reintroduce those qualities through other means.

Much of what is lost from the rushes is a sense of the historical contingency
of the images—the actual conditions under which films (and meaning) are
produced. Film rushes are as much a chronicle of a film's production as they
are of its supposed subject. The excitement Graef describes—of wondering

what will happen next—is really the excitement of sensing that in the rushes *anything* can happen next. While finished films suggest a generalized present tense, rushes seem to unfold in the even more immediate present of a camera running. What editing removes are the stigmata of this historical moment. The shots that remain have been domesticated. They are neither tangential nor contradictory nor incontinent nor otherwise incapable of being marshalled to the film's purpose.

What does one lose then, from the rushes? One loses, I think, qualities of spaciousness, context, and historicity, and these can be described in four different ways.

## Qualities Sacrificed to the Film

First, one loses *excess meaning*—meaning in excess of what the film expresses and requires. This is not merely what remains unexplored in the subject that can still be found in the rushes, but all material that escapes from what might be called the "economy of signification" of the film.

Second, there is a loss of *interpretive space*—a closing off of the legitimate areas in which the viewer is invited to supply meaning. The film dictates a certain standard of relevancy. As it moves toward its final form, the background around the centered subject is gradually whittled away. This controls the viewer's relationship to the footage in two ways: first, the background is made to appear incidental and subservient to what the film designates as a sufficient reality. Second, the background itself is physically thinned out by cutting, thus further reducing the opportunities for "irrelevant" intervention. Although different films provide different kinds of interpretive space for the viewer, this space often merely allows the audience to endorse the filmmaker's meaning rather than participate more actively in creating it. Viewers of rushes, by contrast, constantly interject their own interpretations.

Third, there is a loss of the *sense of encounter*. As the film becomes a polished, professional work, its connections with the historical act of filming, which were so evident in the rushes, gradually disappear. This is especially true of television documentaries, which typically begin with a title sequence whose purpose is to characterize the program as a fully packaged (and therefore predigested) institutional product.

Fourth, there is a loss of *internal contextualization*. In editing a film to its final length there is an inevitable loss of material that would otherwise clarify and extend the meaning of the material that is retained.

Throughout the editing process there is a constant tension between maintaining the forward impetus of the film and providing enough contextual information so that the central narrative or argument continues to make sense. As the film becomes shorter, the analysis becomes cruder. Filmmakers continually sacrifice footage which they know would permit a more complex understanding of the subject but which, for reasons of length, the film cannot afford. To solve this problem, such gaps and elisions are often roughly patched over with spoken commentary.

## The World Within the Shot

Films and shots are complex structures, each evoking a larger world. Just as there are levels of contextual material within the footage shot for a film, so there are levels of contextualization within the shot itself. Loss of context can occur in discarding footage, but it can also occur when individual shots are made shorter.

Filmmakers are aware of this. Sometimes they include an occasional long take simply to reinject into their film some of the qualities perceived in the rushes. But for a few filmmakers the long take becomes a way of redefining the terms in which the film addresses its audience. Such an approach does not necessarily imply a realist aesthetic of the kind championed by André Bazin and many of the Italian Neorealists. Brian Henderson (1971: 10–11) notes this in the case of Ophuls, whose long takes can be highly choreographed, and in the case of Godard. He describes a long take in Godard's *La Chinoise* (1967) that tracks past the shacks of Algerian workers in Nanterre to a modern university complex.

> Eisenstein [he writes] would have cut from a shot of the one to a shot of the other, making the juxtaposition for the viewer, obliterating time and space relations to make a clearcut social relation. Godard observes the time and space relations and lets the viewer make the social relation.... He does this by virtue of the long take's continuity of dramatic space and time, which this usage reveals as itself a form of argumentation or demonstration; the shot has its own internal relations, its own logic. This instance of the shot seems Bazinian but, far from fidelity to the real, Godard rips this bit of footage from its grounding in the real and puts it down in the midst of a highly abstract film essay. (1970: 5)

In this shot Godard uses a long take to create what Walter Benjamin called a "dialectical image"—an internal contextualization of a specific kind, in which one foreground element is qualified by another. But long takes permit contextualization of several kinds. They reveal relationships that link foreground with background, they reemphasize the objective presence of disparate physical objects in the shot, and they provide the "stage" for the enactment of human behavior that reveals individual identity.

*Foreground/Background Relationships:* A simple instance of linking between foreground and background within a shot is the way in which a moving camera defines the geography of a space. The perception of spatial relations is always a problem in the cinema because of the monocular vision of the camera, but by shifting the perspective, camera movement allows us to make sense of these relations. This movement must of necessity occur over time. A similar kind of spatial linking is produced by the quite different movement of people or objects *within* the frame. Thus the long take may be crucial to defining the geographical context within which a character exists or an action takes place. It is also obviously important in delineating actual matters of time, such as how long it takes a person to perform a particular task—something that is normally masked by the condensation of edited sequences.

Long takes can also reveal the relations between simultaneous actions and coexisting objects in one setting. These may be complex social interactions or (as in the Godard example) connections between people and their surrounding social and economic environment. The objective conditions and historical processes that shape people's lives may often be more effectively demonstrated by appearing in the same frame than by being shown in the juxtapositions of editing, provided we are given a sufficient intellectual framework for interpreting them. This interpretation may require a conscious *reapplication of detail* from the margins of the film to its center.

*The Persistence of the Physical:* As I have mentioned, we sometimes subject an image to a process of digressive search. We inspect details that escape the film's inscriptions of meaning, resisting what Roger Cardinal calls the "fixation on congruity" (1986: 118). Such details can play a role in film that goes beyond either the pleasure of discovery or a merely supportive "authenticity."

Realist documentaries have tended to rely on background detail to legitimate their choice of what is significant in the foreground, just as historical dramas provide set dressing of the proper period to make us accept their version of history. The long take, however, can serve another, related purpose: to assert the independence and autonomy of a physical, "background" world and the constantly shifting relations, or lack of them, between material and social being. Presented in this way, physical objects reassert their stubborn and oblivious existence—what Barthes would call their "obtuse" presence. They may even appear as surreal, not because they invoke the irrational or the unconscious, but because they force upon us recognition and confrontation with the unnamed and the unremarked.

*The Dimensions of Personhood:* Finally, the long take can make possible a contextualizing behavior which may be essential to recognizing individual human identity. Over time, details about other human beings accumulate for us which eventually coalesce into distinct personalities. There is perhaps a parallel here with John Berger's (1980) distinction between the private photograph, produced and consumed in a context of familiarity, and the public photograph, torn out of its context and presented to strangers. The challenge for the photographer, says Berger, is to restore context to the public photograph.

In daily life it is our observation of people over time that causes us to transform undifferentiated strangers (or human types) into known individuals. Film shots, unlike still photographs, can provide the necessary time frame in which sequences of behavior can unfold, allowing us to distinguish what Gombrich calls the "likeness" from the "mask." Likenesses emerge as continuities in the midst of variations. According to Gombrich, "[T]he film shot can never fail as signally as the snapshot can, for even if it catches a person blinking or sneezing the sequence explains the resulting grimace which the corresponding snapshot may leave uninterpretable" (1972: 17).

In documentary, the long take can help redress the decontextualization of the fragmentary public image, or in Berger's terms, restore the context of the private. Such recontextualization can be seen clearly in ethnographic films, which for much of their history have defined people of non-Western cultures by their roles or occupations, as anonymous actors in exotic social mechanisms. They were almost always mask, never likeness. Longer camera takes with synchronous sound and subtitled dialogue provided a means of refiguring the relationship between the person on the screen and the viewer. More effective than narrative or other humanizing strategies, it was these uninterrupted passages of behavior which, despite cultural differences, gave the necessary clues to discovering the person within the indigenous social actor.

## Long-Take Prospects

The long take has been associated with the very earliest motion pictures and with two recent periods in the history of documentary. In the *cinéma vérité* and "direct cinema" films of the 1960s it was used to record extended events and conversations. In the political and biographical films of the 1970s and 1980s it was used largely to record interviews. These latter films were strongly influenced by television journalism, which produced its own special use of the long take in building programs around eminent "talking heads." The long take proved equally serviceable in discovering them in European cathedrals, on Andean railway journeys, or amidst the flora and fauna of African jungles.

In each of these cases the long take has been used for quite specific and, arguably, quite narrow purposes. Even so, some of these uses have been equivocal or self-contradictory. In the period of *cinéma vérité* and "direct cinema" an important model for documentary was Italian Neorealist cinema—films such as *La terra trema* (1948) and *Umberto D* (1952), which themselves borrowed ideas from earlier styles of documentary. But the attempt to reproduce in documentaries the literary qualities of fiction (as in *Salesman* [1969]) tended to confine the use of the long take to largely narrative, quasi-fictive functions. Paradoxically, many of the other potentialities of the long take—for articulating space and time, relating people to their environment, exploring human personality—were being more adventurously investigated in fiction, in the work of directors like Godard, Antonioni, Resnais, and Rossellini. In the second period, of interview-based documentaries, the long take seems to have been devoted almost entirely to creating an oral narrative and establishing the authority of the interviewees.

There have of course been alternative tendencies and exceptions to this pattern. Leacock's *Queen of Apollo* (1970), Rouch's *Tourou et Bitti* (1971), Wiseman's *Hospital* (1969) and Kildea's *Celso and Cora* (1983) all use long takes in distinctive and sometimes idiosyncratic ways. Experimental (and "underground") films have provided other kinds of explorations. One should include here, along with the films of Andy Warhol, the work of Michael Snow, Stan Brakhage, and Trinh T. Minh-ha. In other recent documentaries, filmmakers such as Amos Gitaï and Claude Lanzmann have used the long take to subvert traditional constructions of foreground and background. However, for most filmmakers there remain serious obstacles to developing these possibilities. Film length is one of them. Films must either conform to conventional lengths, using fewer shots, or develop into much longer films. But who will watch longer films, especially if they wilfully include the dreaded "dead spots" of ordinary life as legitimate content?

Segmentation suggests one possible strategy. There have been a number of experimental documentary series for television, such as Craig Gilbert's *An American Family* (1972), Roger Graef's *Police* (1982) and Melissa Llewelyn-Davies's *Diary of a Maasai Village* (1985), but so far these have tended to reproduce in documentary the interlocking story structures of drama series or have been composed of essentially self-contained episodes. In neither case has segmentation led to a noticeable expansion of conventional film time to allow for longer takes.

Ultimately the problem of film length is related to the larger problem of how to articulate longer shots to produce meanings. Without commentary, conventional documentary editing usually finds long takes intractable unless they are tracing a clear narrative line, as in Graef's films. Using longer takes gives fewer opportunities to signify by means of the cuts between them. Longer takes are also likely to be complex entities, creating problems of intellectual focus. They characteristically contain ambiguities, interruptions, and competing centers of attention. The content is mingled in ways that make it difficult for the filmmaker to isolate "signal" from "noise." In scripted fiction, "noise" is generally present only when it is put there on purpose to create verisimilitude, but documentary footage is rarely so tidy. Voice-over commentary has traditionally provided one means of superimposing meanings upon such material, but always at the cost of distancing it and reducing the viewer's engagement with its physical immediacy.

These obstacles are of course only obstacles in the context of a specific set of filmmaking conventions and viewing practices. The real test is whether long takes can find a place in quite new communicative structures. New technologies and shifts in popular culture at least open up certain possibilities for this to happen.

First, viewers' expectations of films are likely to change as some filmmaking practices that are now marginal enter the mainstream. This could alter the ways in which people actually "read" long camera takes. At the moment the tendency in commercials and music video seems toward ever shorter takes, but this could contribute to a greater tolerance for associative, nonnarrative editing and eventually for more films patterned on structures other than conventional stories or arguments. Films may emerge that require greater retrospective reconstruction in the mind. Against this must be weighed the way in which the formats of television journalism seem actually to have narrowed the structural repertoire of documentary.

Second, unexplored opportunities exist for combining words with images, perhaps especially with long takes. One could cite the use of multiple voices on the sound track, voices used in less regular patterns, voices addressing us in new registers. There is no equivalent in documentary, so far as I know, to the whispered commentary that accompanies live golf telecasts. Words may also be deployed more effectively in titles and intertitles, as they once were in Soviet silent films and have been occasionally since in such films as *Japan— The Village of Furuyashiki* (1982) by Shinsuke Ogawa. The history of documentary contains other experiments worth examining and pressing further, such as the use of spoken verse in the documentaries of the 1930s. One might expect certain parallel developments to evolve from the emergence of rap videos.

Third, one can imagine more complex layerings of sound and image. As precedents one can point to Godard's "middle period" films (*British Sounds* [1969]), Clément Perron's *Day after Day* (1962), and several of Amos Gitai's documentary films (*House* [1980] and *Ananas* [1983]). Sounds can make us reinterpret what is nominally background and, on some occasions, reconstitute it as thematic foreground.

A fourth strategy open to documentary is to make a much more consciously analytical use of the camera. Reframing with the camera resembles a form of montage which selects, connects, and juxtaposes different images, but in "real time." In fiction films it is possible for such an approach to be scripted, as in Hitchcock's experimental *Rope* (1948). In observational documentary the situation is very different, requiring on the filmmaker's part an ability to impose a process of thought on the camera's movements while filming unpredictable material. So far few filmmakers have adopted such a demanding interpretive stance while filming or have developed the skills to accomplish it.

But camera movement within a shot allows for certain kinds of irony that are not possible with shorter takes. In Claude Lanzmann's *Shoah* (1985) the long take makes particular reference to the fact that however long one pans over landscapes where atrocities took place, one still sees only landscapes. In effect, one looks in vain for the signified in the signifier. In a number of Godard's films (*Week-end* [1967]; *British Sounds* [1969]) long tracking shots, instead of following characters, as is usual in fiction films, track past them, fixing them not in relation to the film but in relation to their physical and social setting.

Lastly, it is worth noting that new technologies may have a profound effect upon viewing practices, and eventually upon film form. We have yet to absorb the full implications of television. Video, an even more recent phenomenon, combines the privacy of television viewing with much greater control over the selection of viewing material. This could make possible longer works, organized in chapters or clusters of related films. Video also makes it easier to recast old films in new forms, or produce new commentaries on them. As for interactive video and emerging multimedia forms, these may, by giving the viewer even greater control over the investigation of material, generate much more exploratory viewing practices and eventually stimulate the new filmmaking practices that would allow for them.

Neither filmmaking nor documentary will be revolutionized by the long take alone, nor should it be claimed that the long take is in any sense the special province of documentary. But the question of what to do with the qualities that are found in long takes, and yet not found in the films derived from them, is perhaps the quintessential problem of documentary. It brings us closer to the paradox of reduction that lies at the heart of all representation, but which has different implications in fiction than it does in documentary. For within every documentary is a kind of cavity, the negative imprint of the missing persons and events which are *not* there. In struggling with this material, the documentary filmmaker is struggling not only with signs but with the shadows of the living and the dead. If photography does not steal the soul it steals something very like it, something deeply enough felt to generate the fraught ethical debates that uniquely surround the making of documentary films and photographs. These debates more commonly concern what is shown than what is left out. But for the filmmaker the problem is truly one of disposing of the human remains.

[1992]

## Notes

This is an expanded version of a paper that I presented as a Visiting Fellow at the Humanities Research Centre in Canberra in 1989. © 1992 by The Regents of the University of California, and reprinted by permission, from *Film Quarterly* 46 (2) (winter 1992): 36–46. I am indebted to E. Richard Sorenson and Allison Jablonko for the term "digressive search," which I use in rather a different sense from theirs; and to Roger Cardinal for the stimulation provided by his essay, "Pausing Over Peripheral Detail" (1986).

1. Raoul Ruiz, ignoring the taboo, jokes about this in his film about documentary, *De Grands événements et des gens ordinaires* [Of Great Events and Ordinary People] (1979). As the camera pans slowly along a wall after an interview, a voice remarks: "The narrator should say something in this pause."

2. One can get an idea of this by recalling a game that many of us played as children. When we repeated a familiar word over and over again—a word like "hippopotamus"—sign and referent begin to separate until the sign became an unrecognizable phonetic pattern. It then became subject to the mispronunciations that occur with tongue-twisters. A kind of verbal searching led to a play on alternative stress patterns (hippopo*ta*mus), picking out new signs previously hidden in the word—*hip* and *pot*, for example. Part of the pleasure of such a game for children, of course, is precisely this subversion of the linguistic codes of adults.

# CHAPTER ELEVEN

# Film Teaching and the State of Documentary

FILM HISTORY IS NEVER simple, and the history of documentary is especially tangled. Documentary speaks with different voices, both historically and in the present. Each of its historical developments has survived in some form to the present day, so that we live in a veritable thicket of documentary film styles.[1]

One might think filmmakers would be in the best position to predict what will happen in documentary, but often they are not. In the early 1970s I was primarily concerned with problems in observational filmmaking, assuming that the main alternative to this kind of documentary (and in a sense, its provoker) would continue to be the narrated, didactic film dating back to *The March of Time* and more indirectly, the Griersonian tradition. As it turned out, I was wrong. In North America at least, what was emerging into dominance was a form of documentary based on extended interviews and the use of archival footage—a form that was originally pioneered by Emile de Antonio and that gradually took hold in independent cinema in such films as *The Life and Times of Rosie the Riveter* (1980), *Harlan County, U.S.A.* (1976), *The Trials of Alger Hiss* (1980), *With Babies and Banners* (1976), *On Company Business* (1980), *The Atomic Cafe* (1982), and television series such as *The World at War* (1974–75) and *Vietnam: A Television History* (1983).

For me the urgent public issue in documentary at that time shifted from what new directions observational filmmaking should take to whether the documentary record of our own period would end up being primarily a collection of interviews about previous periods. (The focus of my discussions with other filmmakers, however, remained very much what it had been, although perhaps somewhat disrupted by this development.)

When I came to Australia in 1975 it was evident that here too the same historical processes were taking place. Australian documentary filmmakers were beginning to produce their own collages of interviews, archival footage and music, such as *Home on the Range* (1981), *Dirt Cheap* (1980), *Frontline* (1983), *Public Enemy Number One* (1986), *Lousy Little Sixpence* (1982), *For Love or Money* (1983), *Red Matildas* (1985), *Allies* (1983), and so on. A few years before, one of the most exciting developments in Australian documentary had been the Australian Broadcasting Commission's innovative television series, *Chequer-board*, which had begun exploring the lives of people as they lived them. But changes in the emphasis of the series and its eventual demise indicated that it had only occupied a brief bridging position between the new-found possibilities of *cinéma vérité* and the closing in of the interview format.

For me the commitment to documentary has always been a commitment to the possibilities of discovery and testimony—that is, to the proposition that ways can be found to document experiences actually happening to people that have never before been given public expression. The documentary filmmaker's art is to find those experiences and analyze them in such a way as to make them accessible to an audience, and in doing so to propose some theory about their significance. To have made a film that succeeds in doing even a part of that is to add to our common experience.

That definition may indicate where I situate myself in documentary and what direction I would take in training documentary filmmakers. For me, documentary style has always been linked to needs, and conversely, new needs are what generate the impetus for changes in style. If one cannot get at something through conventional means, the conditions are ripe for the emergence of a solution along unconventional lines.

An instance of this is the filming of spontaneous conversation, which called out for a new technology and a camera style based on mobility and synchronous sound. The solutions, and even the problem, weren't always immediately apparent, so these changes came in stages. In *Night Mail* (1936), "documentary" dialogue was shot as in fiction films—the spontaneity was acted out. For *Thursday's Children* (1953), Lindsay Anderson and Guy Brenton filmed synchronous speech but had to do so with a camera mounted on a tripod in a glass box. In *The Days before Christmas* (1958), shot in part by Michel Brault, the camera was now out of the box but still mostly on a tripod, with the exception of one extraordinary mobile shot. Meanwhile Rouch had lost his tripod in Africa and, never feeling happier, didn't bother to get another. The lines were converging. *Jaguar* (filmed 1954, released 1967) was shot hand-held with a spring-wind camera, and the comments and dialogue of the protagonists were dubbed in later. Gradually the steps were taken, by different people in different places, toward the shooting style of *Chronique d'un été* (1961).

The principle of needs eliciting styles applies as much to new concepts of film as to new subject matter. The jump cut began to be used not to change the content of interviews but to acknowledge that something had been left out, and to dispense with the need for cutaways or changes of camera angle, as did the pieces of blank leader separating all the shots of Gary Kildea's *Celso and Cora* (1983). When filmmakers renounced narration, it was not to withhold something but to open up other possibilities. The absence of the narrator was like a phantom image on the retina, making us suddenly aware of what narration had displaced. Style in fact can be viewed as a set of signals about how to interpret what would otherwise be (in Adam Kendon's phrase) "mere film."

Moribund documentary tends to be produced when one already knows how to approach a subject even before encountering it. A classic example in Australia was the long-running documentary television series, *A Big Country*, which produced over 350 films. The subjects were often promising, but they were all too often cossetted by an air of solemn admiration for plucky rural people and subordinated to a bland house style of awkward reenactments and introspective voice-over by the protagonists. Here a safe "house style" prevented real access to the subjects, or perhaps the reverse: a conventionalized attitude toward the subjects had tended to rigidify the style.

Documentary thrives, on the contrary, on risk, and on new and difficult subjects, forcing it to attempt things it has never done before. This is why the history of documentary is often made at its intersections with other disciplines. Ethnographic film, for example, is sometimes considered a peripheral area of documentary, but if one looks closely, it becomes apparent how important grappling with other cultures has been to its evolution, from *Nanook of the North* (1922) and *Song of Ceylon* (1934) to the work of such filmmakers as Joris Ivens, Chris Marker, Jean Rouch, Robert Gardner, John Marshall, Michael Rubbo, and Gary Kildea. Marshall's sequence-shot approach, developed with non-synchronous sound in the Kalahari in the 1950s, was an early flowering of "direct cinema" techniques that came into their own in the 1960s. This early work in Africa underpinned Marshall's work with Frederick Wiseman on *Titicut Follies* (1967) and later his own Pittsburgh Police series.

When James Blue and I began teaching filmmaking at Rice University in 1970, we based our program on the proposition that film was a contemporary medium that could be learned and used by other than professional filmmakers, just as writing, which had once been the preserve of monks and scribes, had passed into general use. There was some question at the time whether film would simply attract the failures from other disciplines. In fact, we found the reverse to be true. It was the brightest students and the most accomplished researchers who were interested. Film seemed to have a special attraction for students of anthropology and architecture, and in some departments it was even felt that we (or perhaps film) were seducing their best students away from them.

We made another discovery at that time which supports the notion that documentary evolves through its adaptations to new problems. We had wondered whether these students, who came to us not as film students but from other disciplines, would take longer to learn film techniques than those in film schools, and whether they would tend initially to produce didactic, uncinematic films. At this time Blue and I (and our two visiting colleagues, Colin Young and Roberto Rossellini) were asking them to make quite radical experiments with film in exercises that were related—but not obviously so—to their main film projects. What we found was that because they had no preconceived image of themselves as film artists, they took a rather matter-of-fact approach to their subjects. But although they began by objectifying and distancing themselves from their subjects, as the process of filmmaking progressed they were soon drawn into a much more direct and intimate relation to them. The resulting films were in fact personal in a way that few of the students would have predicted at the beginning. They were also extraordinarily accomplished and revealed a degree of creative invention that was quite unusual for first films. The corresponding films of film school students tended to be self-absorbed and derivative. These films looked outwards to a subject larger than the filmmaker and, in the process of translating difficult concepts and the experiences of real people, were led into quite original paths of expression.

Again, because these were not film students, they were often quite unaware that they had done anything remarkable. Their films tended to move easily between different modes of filmic discourse and showed a marked lack of regard for generic boundaries.

What can we conclude from this? Not that it is preferable to keep students ignorant of film history (we were simultaneously exposing them to the widest possible range of documentary and fiction films), but that it is important to find students who have something to say—or perhaps more important, will find a subject demanding attention—and then, not teach them techniques of film expression but have them invent the techniques the subjects require. Stravinsky once said (in Leacock's film, I think),[2] "I don't compose music, I invent music." Students should be encouraged to re-invent the cinema.

One of the most profound problems we face as filmmakers and teachers is how to counter the contracting diversity of documentary film forms that often seems to be a response to the influence of television. With rare exceptions, television in most countries tends to institutionalize a few forms of documentary, narrowing both the available public film culture and the marketplace for new films.

If the education of documentary filmmakers is restricted to a set of formulas seen on television, they are likely, consciously or unconsciously, to tailor their own work accordingly. The circle will then be complete: an impoverished film culture will produce fewer and fewer alternatives for television to emulate. To counteract this, it is essential for film schools to expose their students to the full range and breadth of documentary, but this means having those films at their disposal and finding the time for students to look at them. It also means creating an environment in which students will want to look at them, and this depends very much upon the genuine passions of film teachers.

Even in Australia, where there is a fairly lively documentary tradition, the regressive impact upon documentary of a conservative television establishment is evident. Styles derived from public affairs broadcasting and journalism predominate: narrated films centered around an on-screen presenter, wholly narrated films, and interview-based films. Films that can be pre-scripted are vastly preferred by producers and funding organizations—even organizations established in order to stimulate the exploration of society or creative development in the arts. Film length is very often arbitrarily standarized at a television hour, regardless of the demands of the subject—even if the film has little hope of being sold to television. Film subjects are chosen with an eye to their journalistic interest or political timeliness. The sentiments expressed are predictably those that champion underdogs, expose injustice, and side with ideologically respectable causes.

Increasingly, film festivals, with judges drawn from television or television-oriented production, reward these standards. Even writers on film tend to lose their discrimination in an environment that confuses television journalism with documentary. Thus a film on political repression in Chile that almost everyone agreed was workmanlike but undistinguished received documentary awards and much attention in the film press because, as many of the reviewers said, although it was unimportant as a film, its subject was important.

When journalism and documentary are confused in this way the idea of what is important can get curiously skewed. New subjects that are deemed socially relevant draw filmmakers irresistibly—and often (although not always) opportunistically. The range of permissible documentary subjects becomes narrowed to social and political issues or topics of sensational or exotic fascination, and people become unable to envisage other kinds of documentary explorations.

A film such as Gary Kildea's *Celso and Cora*, which is the product of strong social and political commitments but explores its subject with some subtlety, tends to be upstaged by shallower films that wear their politics more prominently and are more explicitly designed to feed on public indignation. Mark Rance's *Death and the Singing Telegram* (1983), which explores death within a tension-ridden family network, received little recognition for its extraordinary social penetration and creative courage, perhaps because its subject was considered too mundane.

Thus a form of self-censorship prevails which discourages documentary that looks closely at the fabric of everyday experience, and few filmmakers have the inclination or courage to approach subjects that are not sufficiently newsworthy to guarantee automatic public interest. Fewer still are willing to explore unfamiliar documentary forms, or forms that don't employ the quick short bursts of stimulation characteristic of journalism.

There are no easy solutions to this kind of regression, but film schools can work to produce documentary filmmakers who are not simply groomed to fit the existing marketplace. Filmmakers should have some concept of the direction they would like documentary to go in their country, they should be willing to take risks, and at least some of them should be prepared to become producers as well as directors. This can lay the groundwork for a television practice which, as in Britain, has sometimes led the way in documentary innovation.

I believe further opportunities for documentary will only be reopened when documentary filmmakers readdress themselves to the potential for *discovery* in films—which many current forms of television journalism systematically repress. Curiously, this is not a process that has ever lapsed in fiction. There, we as an audience are prepared to participate in the interpretation of evidence put before us. But in most television documentary we have been persuaded to relinquish that role, and in exchange for seeing we have settled for being told.

We have even settled for having the experience of discovery lived vicariously for us by surrogates—the breathless and genuine excitement of a David Attenborough in the natural world, or the intellectual and emotional investment of a Kenneth Clark, Carl Sagan, or John Berger in art, science, and human destiny. How one wishes, rather, that our television heroes were what Edgar Morin called "filmmaker-divers" who plunge into real-life situations without prefabricated scripts, and with whom we could discover the world.

Finally, I believe documentary must take stock of how it represents our own era—what I conceive of as "bearing witness." How well have we rendered our own experience of having lived, to say nothing of our perception of the experiences of others? This is not only a matter of the historical record. As world culture becomes more uniform, we and our descendants are in danger of losing much of the knowledge that diverse cultures have gained during their histories. And we are in danger of losing the perspective that comes from understanding that lives can be lived within quite different conceptual horizons from our own.

I have mentioned my reservations about a documentary practice centered on interviews about the past and archival footage. It is unquestionably worthwhile to try to regain and reassess the past, particularly if this bears on current issues, as many of the best films of this documentary genre do. But I fear that if that is primarily what documentary does, we shall have turned our backs on the present and, in the process, leave poorer records of our own time. It may be useful to consider what aspects of our great-grandparents' lives we would wish had been filmed if there had been modern cameras a hundred years ago. By applying that lesson to today we can give some direction to how the cameras of documentary should fill the gaps left after the cameras of fiction and journalism have gone their way.

[1986]

## Notes

This essay was written in response to a "provocation paper" by Colin Young for the Centre International de Liaison des Ecoles de Cinéma et de Télévision in their year devoted to the theme "Training for Documentary." It was first published in *CILECT Review* 2 (1) (November 1986): 105–10. Young began his paper with the following two propositions: "*Documentary* and *fiction* are not the same thing (although they over-lap and have much in common)"; and "*Documentary* and film or television *journalism* are not the same thing (although they both are aspects of non-fiction)" (1986: 115).

1. Bill Nichols has outlined some of these styles and their interrelations in an article called "The Voice of Documentary" (1983).

2. *A Stravinsky Portrait* (1966).

# CHAPTER TWELVE

# Films of Memory

## The Mind's Eye

FILMS HAVE A disconcerting resemblance to memory. They register images with lens and emulsion in a process better understood but often no less astonishing than the physiological processes of eye and brain. Sometimes film seems even more astonishing than memory, an intimation of memory perfected. Two of the journalists present at the Lumière brothers' "Salon Indien" screening of 1895 wrote that motion pictures bestowed a kind of immortality upon their subjects (Jeanne 1965: 10–12). But for many of the first viewers of films, what struck the imagination even more forcefully than the images of living people (who were regarded in the same light as performers) was the participation of the inanimate world in recording its own traces—the evocative minutae of experience which the mind could only roughly register. It was such ephemeral images as the steam from a locomotive, the brick dust from a demolished wall, and the shimmering of leaves that seemed the real miracles of filmic representation (Sadoul 1962: 24; Vaughan 1981).

And yet memory offers film its ultimate problem: how to represent the mind's landscape, whose images and sequential logic are always hidden from view. In the nineteenth century C. S. Sherrington described a sixth sense which he called "proprioception," that consciousness of our own body which confirms our physical identity (Sacks 1984: 46; 1985: 42). We might well consider memory our seventh sense, that awareness of an antecedent existence upon which our intellectual identity and sense of self precariously rests.

Memory is often apparently incoherent, and a strange mixture of the sensory and the verbal. It offers us the past in flashes and fragments, and in what seems a hodge-podge of mental "media." We seem to glimpse images, hear sounds, use unspoken words and reexperience such physical sensations as pressure and movement. It is in this multidimensionality that memory perhaps finds its closest counterpart in the varied and intersecting representational systems of film. But given this complexity, and equally the aura of insubstantiality and dreaming that frequently surrounds memory, we may ask whether in trying to represent memory in film we do something significantly different from other kinds of visual and textual representation. We create signs for things seen only in the mind's eye. Are these nevertheless signs like any other?

## The Translation of Memory

Films that focus on memory do not of course record memory itself, but its referents, its secondary representations (in speech, for example) and its correlatives. In films, objects survive from the past, people reminisce, and certain objects evoke or resemble those of memory. We end by filming something far removed from memory as it is experienced, but instead a mixture of dubious testimony, flawed evidence, and invention. Films of memory could thus be said to represent only the external signs of remembering.

How then are these signs to be read? For the filmmaker, how audiences read them is largely a matter of trial and guesswork, since the minds of viewers are as closed to direct inspection as those of the people filmed. Nor do films, once made, communicate an unequivocal message. They produce different ''readings'' in different viewers, and as time passes are open to continual rereading. If memory itself is selective and ideological, films of memory redouble this and add further codes of cultural convention.

Physical objects might be thought to be least subject to such vagaries, providing films with a kind of independent baseline for memory. This indeed is the rationale of many museums. But objects that survive from the past are not the same objects that they were in the past, and they can thus stand for the memory of themselves only obliquely. Unlike an object seen in a photograph, which bears a parallel relation to other objects around it in a specific past context, the patina of age on an old object tends to exaggerate its status as a sign. This sign is often confused with authenticity. But the least authentic thing about museum reconstructions of the past is that the authentic objects displayed in them are too old. At the time represented, many of them would have been new. Thus, whether displayed in museums or filmed in the recent past, the actual objects of memory are unreliable as expressions of memory. They can only be touchstones for its retrieval or construction.

Despite this, many films equate memory with surviving objects, including photographic images of the past. With the original sources of memory forever beyond reach, filmmakers are tempted to use the surviving photographic record *as if this were memory itself.* Thus documentary films and television programs persistently link interviews with photographs and newsreels, which are presented quite illegitimately as the memories of the speakers.

Such images nevertheless play an important part in our own memories, influencing how we think about the past. They take their place in our culture as physical artifacts, not mere media ''messages.'' Many public figures whom we see on television are as substantial to us as the images of people we see in daily life. And as Frank Tillman (1987) has argued, exposure to photographic images has altered the way recent generations imagine the world. We have always been able to think visually, but until photography we were unable to think photographically. As for most recent historical events, we remember not the events themselves (we were not present at them) but the films and photographs we have seen of them. But these may create a commonality of experience more powerful and consistent as social memory than the experiences of many of the actual participants. As Edmund Carpenter has commented, modern media, and particularly television, extend the images of our dream world (1976: 58).

These public images can serve society at large in the way that family photographs serve smaller communities—as emblems of significant events and transitions, constructing a concept of the past but also providing ways of overcoming it. They may assist in what Yannick Geffroy (using Freud's term *Trauerarbeit*) describes as the "work of mourning" the lost past (1990: 396ff). They do so through repetition and reduction, for representation usually entails both of these. Television news (like its predecessor, the newsreel) rings changes on an essentially unchanging catalogue of disasters, political meetings, sports events, and wars, and it is this limited set of themes, with minor variations, that reassures us that the world goes on as before. But the process is not without emotional cost: like all mourning, viewing the recent past, particularly its horrors, includes a measure of guilty relief at our own survival.

In films of memory, however, there is a frequent collapsing of memory and its sources. The distinction between photographic records and photography's place in people's minds is rarely made. Thus, among the variety of signs that films employ for the objects of memory, photographs and archival footage tend to be used the least critically and most misleadingly.

## The Signs of Memory

Films of memory draw upon a distinctive repertoire of signs. Perhaps most common, and what might be termed *signs of survival*, are images of objects that have a physical link with the remembered past. These memorabilia serve half as symbols of experiences, half as physical proof that they occurred, and like Kane's "Rosebud" they often turn up amidst a clutter of other, less familiar objects. They are "astonishing" and precious not so much for their visual resemblance to remembered objects as for the fact that they are perceived, like Proust's handful of dried lime blossoms, as the "very same" objects.

These objects are remnants of a larger whole, sometimes declaring their connection to it only by the damage they have sustained: a tree whose broken branches tell of a storm, or a bullet-riddled helmet, or the wrinkles on the face of a person being interviewed. Old photographs and films belong to this group of signs not only as historical objects which bear the marks of handling, foxing, and projection, but also (though more loosely) through the direct indexical link which their imagery—their photochemical "marking"—bears to past events.

If objects do not survive to be filmed, films of memory often resort to *signs of replacement*—similar objects and sounds and, at the farthest extent, reconstructions and reenactments, such as those of docudramas. If pressed lime blossoms are unavailable, new lime blossoms will do. In this way, a train rumbling through a modern railway yard becomes a 1940s train to London or Auschwitz. Journeys and the retracing of steps are especially favored by films of memory because revisiting places—like viewing photographs—produces emotions of both retrieval and loss.

At one remove from replacements in kind are replacements in form: what we might call *signs of resemblance*. These offer a looser, iconic link with their objects, filling in the missing pattern of the past by analogy—not, as it were, by striking the missing note, but by supplying its harmonic. They make possible major shifts of magnitude: a day's work or a short trip can now speak of a life's journey. This principle can be seen in Roman Kroiter's films *Paul Tomkowicz: Street-Railway Switch Man* (1953) and *Stravinsky* (1965), which "frame" life histories in a man's last day's work and an Atlantic crossing, and Renata and Hannes Lintrop's *Cogito, Ergo Sum* (1989), in which an elderly Estonian's daily physical struggle becomes a metaphor for his long resistance to Soviet rule. Resemblance, on any of several metaphorical levels, allows a broad range of associative imagery to be brought into play. A cut to an eagle or seagull, for example, is rarely simply an evocative touch. In films, birds singled out for attention seem inevitably to carry an extra burden of aspiration, loneliness, hope, or despair.

Among signs of resemblance, music is the analogue *par excellence* for emotion, and not surprisingly films of memory are choked with it. In these films music serves doubly for emotions imputed to the subject and meant to be aroused in the viewer. In addition, music is used by films of memory for its historical associations. Because musical styles "date" and are culturally specific they make ideal aural icons. A piece of music can almost always be found to fit a particular historical and social milieu. In the past, ethnographic films seemed invariably to use gratuitous (although culturally accurate) indigenous music for this single validating purpose. In mainstream documentary films, accordions, Charleston orchestras, and honky-tonk pianos become the equivalent clichéd accompaniments for archival footage of villages, nightclubs, and working-class neighborhoods.

The conventions of film music persist despite their naïveté and the audacity with which they are used to manipulate audiences. Even in Ken Burns's carefully wrought American television series, *The Civil War* (1990), period music is marshalled throughout as though better to authenticate photographs and quotations from the period. Although the music in the series has been de-

fended as adding textual complexity, it has also been criticized for condition-
ing the audience to view history with a simplistic melancholia (Henderson
1991). By contrast, the British series, *The Great Depression* (1981), sometimes uses only the sound of a projector over compilations of archival footage.
This device may be equally artificial, since even silent films were originally
accompanied by music, but at least it has the merit of drawing attention to the
contingent physical qualities of the film materials rather than cloaking them in
an aura of fateful grandeur.

Although music is generally employed to "double" a specific historical
setting, it can sometimes be cast against type, as Humphrey Jennings demonstrated in *Listen to Britain* (1942) when he juxtaposed Dame Myra Hess playing Mozart at a wartime London concert with the effects of Hitler's bombing.
A more common alternative is to seek out music that is culturally and historically as neutral as possible, representing (it is hoped) nothing so much as pure
emotion. Music may function in this fashion if it is new or has lost its original
connotations through re-use. Electronic music is often chosen because it is
cheap and anonymous, while Andean flutes and pan pipes have been used so
typically to evoke memory that they are now part of an international style,
stripped of other cultural meanings.

## The Sense of Absence

The signs we have considered so far are those most often found in conventional films of historical reminiscence. They bolster the illusion of a recovera-
ble past. They have coalesced to produce a cinematic subgenre whose ritual
ingredients are aging faces (usually of interviewees), fetish-objects from the
past, old photographs, archival footage, and music. This formula is used with
equal impartiality in everything from brief television items to twelve-part series and documentary features. It is a subgenre which purports to tell us our
"true," unwritten history through the testimony of both ordinary people and
famous eye-witnesses. It has a tendency to be elegiac, as though remembering
were in itself a virtue. The age of a speaker is an important index of authority:
the increasing reverence with which historical events are viewed as they re-
cede into the past is transferred to those who remember them. Few films of
this genre ask children what they remember about last week or last year, and
few admit that the old may be forgetful or devious. Indeed, reminiscence is
seen as a burgeoning richness which, if only it could be gathered up quickly
enough, could tell us everything worth knowing about the past. Although such
an approach acknowledges that memory is cultural, it tends to surround its
own interviewees with a spurious neutrality (Nichols 1983).

A few films of memory employ one further class of signs, which we may
call *signs of absence*. These provide a way of confronting the problems of

forgetting and willful distortion, as well as the larger abyss between experience and memory. Although films of memory often claim legitimacy as a way of salvaging first-person experience, they rarely address slippage in the memories of their informants. At the very least, signs of absence place memory in the context of forgetting, and define the past by its irreducible distance from the present.

Signs of absence often make ironic use of objects and testimony, positioning the audience uncomfortably by asking them to make judgments and comparisons, to search for and interject meanings. Here the sign for a lost object becomes not its surrogate but what has displaced it. These signs define memory by its true opposite, an embodied absence. An empty factory thus represents a fully operating one. A market square teems not with peasants and bullocks but with youths on motorbikes. In another variation, first-person testimony is challenged (and reversed) by its positioning in a film—Nixon's air of ingenuousness, for example, in *The Trials of Alger Hiss* (1980). Or it may be offset by the internal evidence of a shot, as in the presence of an overseer with interviewed workers in Amos Gitaï's film *Ananas* (1983), or signs of duress in televised statements by hostages and prisoners of war.

Some films go further still. Beyond the carefully counterpoised "now" and "then" of Resnais's *Nuit et brouillard* (1956) or the verbal and visual evidence of Erwin Leiser's *Mein Kampf* (1960), Claude Lanzmann's *Shoah* (1985) not only asks us to query first-person testimony but to look at empty roads and fields where atrocities took place and search them for what happened there. We look in vain for the signified in the sign. In this constant reiteration of absence we are brought to the threshold of one kind of knowledge about history. In the failure of the sign we acknowledge a history beyond representation.

## The Representations of the Mind

If memory forms an aspect of thought, it is possible to regard films of memory as efforts to approximate the processes by which the mind represents experience to itself. These films harness the memories of the film subjects, the filmmakers and, more indirectly, the film viewers. In a discussion of photographic imagery, Victor Burgin (1982: 194–98) has referred to Mardi J. Horowitz's classification of thought into "image," "lexical," and "enactive" categories (1970: 69–82). Horowitz based his tripartite structure on Jerome S. Bruner's "three systems for processing information and constructing inner models of the external world"—what Bruner (1964) called the "iconic," "symbolic," and "enactive." Both systems resemble, whether directly or indirectly, the sign classifications developed by C. S. Peirce and Roman Jakobson, and seem elaborations on them. Although these modalities of mental representation are usually intermingled in actual thought, they correspond very well to the strategies by which films render memory in images, words, and physical movement. Indeed, we may not fully understand how films use these elements, and ultimately how they affect us, until we have a better understanding of the processes of mind.

By "image" Horowitz means not only visual imagery, but the ability to recall sensory experience generally. It is possible to remember a specific smell or sound, or even "hear" in silence an entire Mozart symphony. Thus, although in films we are limited to sounds and visual images (forays into Odorama and Smellavision notwithstanding), Horowitz's concept of "image" is best understood as *sensory thought*.

The visual imagery of the mind appears to be both more complex and less systematic than the visual imagery of cinema. We might compare two of its operations to those of the voluntary and involuntary muscles of the body. Some images come to us unbidden, the material of dreams and daydreams. They are specific and sharply defined: a face, perhaps never consciously noted before, has the living detail of a face actually seen, or viewed on a movie screen. But images recalled through conscious effort are more often indistinct and elusive. It is a common experience to find the faces of loved ones the most difficult to recall. The more actively one pursues them the more effectively they sidestep the mind's gaze, as though long familiarity had rendered them too complex and heterogeneous for a single image to suffice. Films condense such multidimensional thinking into concrete imagery, stripping the representation of memory of much of its breadth and ambiguity.

The counterpart of Horowitz's "lexical" thought is amply represented in films, although usually in a more studied form (such as commentary) than in the scribbled demotic of daily experience. Actual thought more typically consists of broken fragments of language and a sense of meanings hovering between the verbal and preverbal. Among the few films that attempt to duplicate this is Clément Perron's *Day after Day* (1962), which departs from conventional film writing to give us muttered pieces of nursery rhymes and sudden announcements ("The departure has been delayed indefinitely") as the accompaniment to monotonous piece-work in a paper mill. There is also something rather like it in the headlong rush of notions and placenames in Auden's poetry for the film *Night Mail* (1936).

In representing sensory and lexical thought, films might be thought to have encompassed the essential elements of memory, for images, sounds, and words tend to dominate our conceptions of our own consciousness. This assumption appears to be endorsed by many current social and political documentaries, which reduce these two categories to a simple format of archival footage (the sensory) and interviews (the lexical). It seems taken for granted that this not only represents memory adequately but also, quintessentially, history.

However, Horowitz's third mode of thought, the "enactive," is neither image nor word, but gesture—experience recalled, one might say, in the muscles. We imagine an action through the feel of it—for example, the sense of moving a hand in a familiar motion, such as stirring coffee. One might call this the kinaesthetic dimension of thought, familiar to ourselves but only observable in others when it is translated into actual physical movement, just as lexical thought is only observable when translated into speech. That the images of words on a page are translated into an enactive version of sound production is perhaps well demonstrated by Edmund Carpenter's observation that throat surgery patients are forbidden to read because "there is a natural tendency for a reader to evoke absent sounds, and the throat muscles work silently as the reader scans the page" (1980: 74).

Enactive memory finds its primary filmic counterpart in images of physical behavior, especially behavior of an habitual kind. Of the three categories, the enactive is perhaps the mode of memory closest to the indexical sign, for its form is that of an imprint or direct extension of previous experience. It is evident in certain gestures—when, for example, artisans are at work and the memory of their craft seems to reside "in their hands." Such gestures can express not only the memory of an habitual activity but an attitude toward it, as when a cook breaks eggs with a flourish that combines both pride and expertise.

Enactive memory may take precedence over visual or lexical memory. In a French television report a man descends a stairway in a building in which he was imprisoned in total darkness for over a month. Although he can tell us in words the exact number of steps (there are thirty-one) and we can see the steps ourselves, it is in fact the movement of his feet that tells us most convincingly that he knows when he has reached the bottom.

We may postulate that of all the modalities of thought, the enactive is most closely associated with emotion: that, for example, the memory of shame or triumph is largely an enactive, physiological response, although linked to a visual memory of the situation in which it arose. The dynamics of film editing may constitute, after the portrayal of "habitual" gesture, a second level on which films reproduce the qualities of enactive thought, although precisely how this operates deserves further investigation. Eisenstein characterized the effects of montage as "psycho-physiological" phenomena, and described how in the film *The General Line* (also known as *Old and New* [1929]) a series of increasingly short shots of farmers mowing with scythes caused members of the audience to rock from side to side (1957: 80). At their junctions, film shots produce kinaesthetic responses in the viewer; and much film editing may represent a translation of movement and gesture from enactive thought into a succession of juxtaposed images. Editing also creates imaginary geographies—cinematic landscapes of the mind in which we as spectators walk and take our bearings. It is one of the objectives of films of memory to create such spaces, as analogues of the spatial dimensions of memory. Other aspects of enactive memory may be represented in films through the synaesthetic effects of movement, light, color, and texture.

Horowitz's three modes of mental representation can thus help us to identify correspondences between the processes of memory and filmic representation. To these should perhaps be added a fourth category—that of *narrative* thought. More than simply a property of the other modes, narrative has, it seems to me, good reason to be considered a further primary constituent of thought. Time, which provides the continuum on which memory is registered, here underpins the arrangement of the sensory, lexical, and enactive into sequences. Narrative governs the disposal of objects and actions in time, without which most memory, and even language, would be impossible. Although a certain part of thought is apparently incoherent (even if, perhaps, the product of a deeper logic) there is little we can think of without assigning it a narrative history or potential. We think within a set of narrative paradigms in which objects have origins and futures, and in which even simple actions are constructed out of a succession of lesser ones. This hierarchy of mental structures is reflected in the syntagmatic structures of many popular cultural products, from folktales to films.

## Film and Thought

It is often asserted that the conditions of film-viewing induce a dreamlike state in which the self is stripped of its defenses. Films seem like dreams because we watch them helplessly, deprived of our volition. However, another explanation for this effect may be that films create a synthesis of varied modes of representation that closely mimic the modes of mental representation. Although films are visual, they are also aural, verbal, narrative, and enactive. They slide through different cognitive registers in a way that we find strikingly familiar, so that even people who have never seen films before quickly find them comprehensible, despite culturally specific codes of narration and editing. One may speculate that although experiments in artificial intelligence are widely based on linguistic and mathematical models, film may well offer a more convincing simulation of mind and memory than either of them.

The connections between cognition and film underlie many of the conventions of the cinema (as in the "psychological" editing of Fritz Lang or Alfred Hitchcock) but without, it seems, often being explicitly acknowledged as such. The reluctance to identify narrativity closely with actual processes of thought produces an ambiguity in the point of view of many films, as though films could somehow *think themselves* without reference to an identifiable consciousness. Films of memory, particularly documentaries, often seem uneasy about their own narrativity. Fiction films seem less troubled. Some, like

Resnais's *Hiroshima, mon amour* (1959) and Fellini's *8 ½* (1963), clearly seek to reproduce certain processes of thought through visual imagery and interior monologue. Others do so more obliquely, through strategies of identification with third-person characters, who recite or reenact their memories, as in *Citizen Kane* (1941) or—extraordinarily, since the narrator is supposed to be dead—*Sunset Boulevard* (1950).

Nonfiction films of memory more often seek to stand outside the narratives provided by their human subjects. Instead, they situate these stories in a structure which at times relies on them for narrative impetus but otherwise seeks to create its own narrative about an historical period or political issue. There is a general presumption of interest on the part of the audience, but precisely why they should be interested (or why the filmmakers are) is often never made clear.

There is a certain amount of journalist hubris in such a position. Frequently the presence of testimony itself is taken as its own sufficient justification. This approach dominates film portraits of famous people, such as *Nehru* (1963), in which an interview was virtually forced upon Nehru, and Jon Else's study of Robert Oppenheimer, *The Day after Trinity* (1980), in which the film's authority and that of its subject seem curiously undifferentiated. Memory is *used*, but the fundamental link between constructing the past through reminiscence and constructing the audience's present experience through film is never made. We may thus conclude that many films of memory are uncertain about their own discursive status: in making the assumption that their subjects' reminiscences are worth knowing they somehow dispose of having to define, or speak from, their own particular interests. There is thus a certain emptiness at the heart of such authorship, a fundamental lack of conviction. It may well be that the common tendency to adopt a celebratory stance toward memory is a symptom, and a masking, of that uncertainty.

Processes of thought and memory are generally approached more directly in autobiographical documentaries, which constitute a rapidly growing subgenre of filmmaking. From the early work of Jonas Mekas and Stan Brakhage to later films such as Chris Marker's *Sans Soleil* (1982), these films show a concern for the workings of memory and the problem of how film can represent it. However self-absorbed and self-serving they may be, they are explicit about their uses of the past. Reminiscence is rarely treated as omniscient or transparent, and when photographs are used, as in such films as Corinne Cantrill's *In This Life's Body* (1984) and Antti Peippo's *Sijainen* (1989), they are presented as fragmentary documents, to be interrogated and filled with meaning.

These filmmakers are often dubious about the translation of memory, just as anthropologists have become more cautious about the idea of cultural translation. They confront in the most personal way the "crime" of representation, the gap between signs and their objects. Most makers of films of memory

21.  A family photograph from Antti Peippo's *Sijainen* (1989).

confront the same problem, but often (it appears) in a different spirit. If they regret the sparseness of detail or the inarticulateness of filmed first-person testimony, their response is not to indicate the significance of this gap but to try to improve upon it. The unattainable richness trapped inside their subjects' memories is supplanted by the addition of much illustrative material. The viewer is drawn into a collusion in which the varied signs of memory are brought into play. These are not the abstract and regenerative symbols of literature, but images from the physical world. In fiction films (Robert Bresson's, for example) such representation is sometimes saved from the literalness of its images by a kind of minimalism, an exclusion of the too-explicit. In documentary the closest equivalent of this is perhaps the use of the single, mute object saved from childhood, or the perfectly enigmatic photograph, like that which Antti Peippo shows us of his apparently happy family in *Sijainen*. [Figure 21.] But at this point we must ask whether films of memory are really engaged in representing memory at all. They may instead have moved outside the more verifiable significations of other documentary films and into a domain of evocation. Here film could be said to leave representation behind and to confront the viewer once again with the primary stimuli of physical experience.

## Film, Ritual, and Social Memory

Social memory in small communities is a matter of consensus, a version of the past accepted by various groups for reasons of convenience and solidarity. The particularities of social life prevent any one person from sharing precisely the same perspective or experience as others. Social memory is thus "social" in an active sense: negotiated, provisional, and indicative of relationships. But increasingly, access to common experiences and sources of information in modern society tends to create a monolexical culture, condensing useful fictions like social memory into realities. When momentous events occur it is quite common the next day for people hardly to speak of them, for by then they are already public icons and "news" to no one. This instantaneous production of social memory creates public perceptions which are widespread and seemingly unassailable, but also, because of their very rigidity, brittle and subject to sudden reversals. As the Iraq-Iran and Iraq-Kuwait wars have shown, the victims of today easily become the villains of tomorrow.

The images of film and television combine the durability of artifacts with the force of oral tradition. They are concrete reports from the physical world. In a preliterate society these reports are conveyed by art, ritual, and word of mouth (much of it ephemeral) and become a constantly revised "tradition." With the advent of writing, printing, photography, and electronics they become fixed, even petrified points of reference. As Walter Benjamin (1968) observed, they also take on more explicitly political functions. Yet as film and television endlessly recapitulate past events they also regain some of the functions of ritual. Certain images of the past keep recurring and, like famous still photographs (the napalmed Vietnamese girl; the Andean flute-player in *The Family of Man*) lose their historicity (their status as photography) and become cultural symbols.

Marc-Henri Piault (1989) has noted that the controllers of ritual use it to inculcate an orthodox "tradition" that reinforces their own power, but in the process of constructing such a tradition, ritual simultaneously makes possible its transformation by creating a stage for the confrontation of conflicting interests. One might suppose that "fixed" media representations, which share with ritual the power of authority and repetition without offering such a stage, might avoid such a challenge. Indeed this seems to be widely assumed by their "controllers." From early in this century governments have seen film and other mechanically reproduced images as a secure means of inculcating patriotism and historical orthodoxy. In 1917 General Ludendorff wrote to the Imperial Ministry of War praising the superiority of photography and film as "a means of information and persuasion," an action which eventually led to the founding of the giant UFA studio (Furhammar and Isaksson 1971: 111–12). And in his well-known statement of 1922, Lenin told his Education Commisar, Lunacharsky, "Of all the arts, for us the cinema is the most important" (Leyda 1960: 161).

This trust in photographic iconography is in some measure confirmed by the way in which modern conceptions of the October Revolution are still defined and contained by Eisenstein's images of it. It is quite common for compilation documentaries dealing with the period to mix indiscriminately newsreel footage with scenes from the film *October* (1928). [Figure 22.] Such uses of fictional footage have occurred often, perhaps most notably in the American wartime film series *Why We Fight*. The logical extension of using film to

22. From Eisenstein's *October* (1928).

construct history is to tailor history to its filmic representation, as was done in 1934 in Nuremberg for Leni Riefenstahl's *Triumph des Willens* (1935), perhaps the world's first great "media event" and the outgrowth of such propaganda exercises as the manipulation of the Reichstag fire and the mythologizing of the Hitler Youth hero, Herbert Norkus (notably, through the film *Hitlerjunge Quex* [1933]). But in doing so the creators of an orthodoxy also created a tool for its destruction. Here film images, despite their apparent permanence and consecrated meaning, have proven as open to challenge as earlier forms of ritualized persuasion.

In 1942, after viewing *Triumph des Willens*, Frank Capra (soon to be the producer of the *Why We Fight* series) decided to "use the enemy's own films to expose their enslaving ends" (1985: 332). He realized that by altering the context in which the footage appeared its meaning could be reversed. He thus began exploiting the "stage" that the original producers had created. Since then scenes from Riefenstahl's film have been endlessly repeated, but they have in effect become part of a transfigured view of German history, imbued with quite different ritual significance.

Thus, like ritual, the focal narratives of history provide a medium for political contestation and change. Social memory, although it may be powerfully shaped by film and television, is clearly as vulnerable to revision as the traditions of earlier times. In a description that interestingly parallels Piault's, Edward Bruner and Phyllis Gorfain assert that such narratives

> and similar cultural texts . . . are frequently national stories and rarely remain monologic. They do serve to integrate society, encapsulate ideology, and create social order; indeed, the story may become a metaphor for the state, and poetic means may be used for political purposes. But because these narratives are replete with ambiguity and paradox, an inherent versatility in interpretation arises that allows for conflicting readings and dissident, challenging voices. (1984: 56)

Yet a residue of a clearly *physical* nature remains in film images which is not available in verbal narratives, and its importance should not be underestimated. Film images may be reinterpreted in a variety of new contexts, but the inalterable record of appearance and place contained in them may ultimately prove to have a more profound effect upon our "memory" of history than the interpretations we attach to them.

[1992]

## Note

This essay was written in response to the Vth "Regards sur les sociétés Europééenes" seminar, held in Budapest, July 8–15, 1990, devoted to "Memory." It was first published in *Visual Anthropology Review* 8 (1) (spring 1992): 29–37, and simultaneously in French in *Journal des anthropologues* 47–48 (spring 1992): 67–86.

# CHAPTER THIRTEEN

# Transcultural Cinema

The transcultural: transcending the limitations
of cultures.
The transcultural: crossing the boundaries of
cultures.[1]

FROM THE BEGINNING, the most remarkable and remarked upon property of photography has been its registration of particular detail. It was in this that it triumphed over painting and drawing, producing daguerretype portraits in which every hair was in place, early mug shots for police records, surveys of the surface of the moon, and documents of remote and exotic peoples. When the cinema was born some sixty years later, it was still this capacity to capture the inexhaustible detail of the visible that people found most astonishing.

Less remarked upon, but underlying the specificity of photography, was a second, equally important property. The registration of unique detail depended upon its opposite: the capacity of photography to render the commonplace features of the world in immediately recognizable forms. Without this, almost all photographs would have been confusing or unintelligible. In still pictures, as in films, the strangeness of even the most exotic subject was counterbalanced by a sense of familiarity. Whereas written accounts had always strained to carve out precise descriptions from a general repertoire of words, photography introduced a mode of description in which the particular appeared to ride effortlessly on the back of the general.

This attribute of photography produced a complication in the emerging human sciences, which were then devoting increasing attention to identifying the differences between one society and another. It is a complication they have yet fully to come to terms with. Photographs and films, by reiterating the familiar and recognizable, constantly transcend and reframe their own specificity. Throughout the history of ethnographic film, this underlining of the visible continuities of human life has challenged and, in a sense, opposed anthropology's prevailing conceptions of culture and cultural difference. Ethnographic films have been widely understood as transcultural, in the familiar sense of crossing cultural boundaries—indeed the very term implies an awareness and mediation of the unfamiliar—but they are also transcultural in another sense: that of defying such boundaries. They remind us that cultural difference is at best a fragile concept, often undone by perceptions that create sudden affinities between ourselves and others apparently so different from us.

## Representation and Difference

Pictures and words address us at both a general and a particular level, but they
do so in different ways. This difference has important implications for ethnographic representation, for it gives films and writing contrasting, and in some
cases contradictory qualities. Writing is general in its use of widely applicable
signs (the system of words) and its capacity for abstract expression, whereas
pictures are general in their representation of the physical continuities of the
world. Although both are capable of making other societies seem very different from one's own, each also counteracts this potential in its own way. It has
been said that writing makes the unseen person or custom more strange by
isolating it from its surroundings, thereby giving free rein to the reader's
imagination. At the same time, written descriptions inevitably strip even the
strangest objects of some of their detail, rendering them in a more generic and
culturally assimilable form. A tree in writing remains a member of a category
of trees; a person is first and foremost the idea of a person, somewhat like
ourselves, rather than an assemblage of alien features.[2]

Written descriptions express what can be grasped in their own languages,
and are thus effectively blind (or inhospitable) to things outside them. As
Stephen Tyler observes, this implies "a process of double occultation, for the
ethnographic text can represent the other as difference only inasmuch as it
makes itself occult, and can only reveal itself inasmuch as it makes the other
occult" (1987: 102). In presenting the particular, ethnographic writing elides
or limits many sensory details that might shock or repel us if we were to
confront them directly. In contrast to this, pictures are staggeringly particular
and indiscriminate in detail, but they constantly reiterate the general forms in
which the particular is contained. These forms include the commonalities of
being human that are taken as given and are therefore usually left out of written ethnographic descriptions—in part because the writers' interests lie elsewhere, but also in the interests of economy. Consider having to write, every
time you mentioned a person, that he or she walked on two legs, had a head,
a face, two arms, and so on. Yet every visual image of a person explicitly and
redundantly shows this.[3]

The special attributes of representation ultimately matter—in the most obvious and yet often in the most unremarked ways. Pictures and writing produce two quite different accounts of human existence, however much filmmakers and writers strive to describe the same things. Writing contrives to
evoke the ordinary features and substructure of an entire scene by implication,
and then concentrates its attention on a few notable details. This can result in
the details taking on a disproportionate importance and, in their isolation, a
heightened presence, or strangeness.[4] By comparison, the account produced
by films is at once more and less strange than that of writing. What is noted

and what is left unnoted form a continuous co-presentation, even when details are singled out for attention. Thus, on the one hand, pictures draw our attention to the visible differences between human groups, emphasizing particularities of body type, dress, personal adornment, and habitation. These are the exotic and often attractive features of other societies presented by television, travel brochures, and popular magazines (see Lutz and Collins 1993). Popular literature also pays particular attention to distinctive local products and technologies, and to ceremonies in which beliefs are symbolized in elaborate practices and ritual objects. On the other hand, films and photographs also convey features of human appearance and sociality of a much less diverse and more widely recognizable kind. This forms the other pole of travel literature, stereotypically expressed in pictures of smiling faces and scenes of daily work, as well as in familiar (and often familial) relations of affection, cooperation, and exchange. Travel literature thus manages to combine exoticism with a comforting reassertion of the familiar.

Of these two poles of travel literature, anthropology has, at least in this century, tended to reinforce the first. The strangeness of the ethnographic detail has been accompanied by a search for alterity, for it is around the pole of human diversity that anthropology has defined itself as a discipline. Anthropologists might dispute this on the grounds that anthropology has in fact countered the exoticism of travel literature by demonstrating the rationality of other societies, the ordinariness of their practices to themselves, and in general by promoting a public ethic of cultural relativism. Indeed, many would argue that cross-cultural continuities are always acknowledged in anthropology as the baseline and underpinning of cultural diversity. Furthermore, a significant part of anthropology is concerned with finding general structures of human organization, behavior, and thought. However, cultural difference rather than continuity is inscribed at the very deepest levels of anthropological inquiry. As Nicholas Thomas has observed, "there is great scope for slippage from the appropriate recognition of difference . . . to an idea that other people *must* be different" (1991: 309). Arguably, the practice of *writing* anthropology has played a significant part in this orientation.

Ethnographic writers not only choose not to record many of the cross-cultural continuities that images make manifest, but cannot, for these appear as the ground upon which the figures of anthropology are drawn. Other continuities (of biology, psychology) are often skipped over as belonging more to nature than to culture. Writing contributes to this tendency by favoring certain kinds of descriptions over others. The visible settings and physical interchanges of life are difficult to describe, even for novelists. In anthropology, writers therefore tend to favor the categorization rather than the detailed description of their observations. In this way, the visible and physical often slip through the net of anthropological writing and become attenuated, if not invisible.

As anthropology has changed over this century, visual representation has become less a challenge to it than an irritant. The enthusiasm with which early anthropologists greeted the cinematograph was replaced by frustration with its technical difficulty and an aversion to its links with popular entertainment. Images of people, however much they might reveal about material culture, added little to the understanding of their conceptual worlds or the inner workings of their societies. Also implicit in this aversion to images was not that they revealed nothing but that they tended to reveal the wrong things. Anthropology was concerned with cultural differentiation, whereas images revealed a world of more modulated and overlapping identities. An interest in things visual thus had the potential to readjust the perspectives of anthropology, but only at the cost of creating a countercurrent of the sort W.J.T. Mitchell has called "a moment of turbulence at the inner and outer borders" of a discipline (1995: 542). Visual anthropology has contributed to such a countercurrent. It is already influencing the way in which anthropologists regard cultural boundaries in the modern world, including that most persistent one, between "us" and "them."

## The Person as Phenomenon

When structuralist and post-structuralist critics discuss films or written works, there is a tendency to reduce both to that neutered status: a text. Words lose their sting, their passion, their fascination. Films are just another "discourse." When anthropologists review ethnographic films, they treat them as visual variants of anthropological writing, which although constructed in a different medium are subject to the same sorts of "readings." This view assumes a common ground (and a common outcome) of all ethnographic inquiry, essentially unaffected by the different ways of going about it. Attention then falls on formal, philosophical, and sometimes political issues. How are films structured, compared to written ethnographies? What methodologies do they employ? Whose interests do they serve? Films may even be looked upon as offering new models for ethnographic writing, as in their self-reflexivity or use of montage (see Marcus 1990). Yet in almost none of these discussions is the single, truly radical difference between writing and film ever mentioned—how vastly different the two are *as objects*, and in what they contain.

Here the critics are not being evasive. It is simply very difficult for such a realization to arise in the abstract, once the distinction between writing and film has been reduced to an irrelevancy and it has been shown that one can perform the same critical operations on each. The seeming obviousness of the distinction between verbal and visual "texts" has the power to block, subsume, or make appear insignificant other considerations of difference. Nor does looking at films or photographs necessarily remove these blinders, for we are habituated to regarding visual images as information—or, more precisely, as *demonstrations of themselves*. Armed with the understanding that images are always "about" something, we can look upon almost any image with impunity. The response (or lack of it) described by international relief agencies as "compassion fatigue" is really one of classification: images of starving mothers and children are immediately reclassified by their viewers as examples of the *problem* of famine.

Treating images as just another form of discourse leads to a related disregard for their historical contingency. A photograph ceases to show us a particular someone or something: rather, it announces a topic or makes a point. Eventually this is reflected in what images get made. As Roland Barthes notes of most photographs intended to shock, "we are in each case dispossessed of our judgment: someone has shuddered for us, reflected for us, judged for us; the photographer has left us nothing—except a simple right of intellectual acquiescence" (1979: 71). Dai Vaughan notes that British television executives have come to regard documentary film in a similar way. In their instructions to directors, "they seem to be saying that what is required is an 'impression' of a 'type' of event rather than the record of an actual one" (1985: 707).

Perhaps more worrying is the reluctance of many writers to acknowledge the unique expressive register in which visual images address us. A picture, like a paragraph, may be an object on a page, but we study the two very differently. A photograph always contains more than its meanings, and less. Two portraits may qualify as pictures of my father, but neither has the meaning of "father." This has important consequences even on an informational level. A film or a photograph may tell us a great deal about how someone looks but not his or her name—yet this is one of the most easily accomplished tasks of a written description. The difference between a film and a written text is ultimately far greater than that between a photograph and an x-ray, or a scientific book and a poem, or even a familiar form of biology and one we might find on some distant planet. It is of another order, more nearly like the difference between Magritte's pipe and his picture of it, or my hand as I hold it before me and as I see it in memory.

Such disjunctions of perception and thinking affect how we distinguish human groups from one another and from ourselves. If writing directs our attention to certain aspects of human life and visual images to others, the ways in which we demarcate cultural difference are called into question, and even the notion of cultural difference itself. On what basis, or in what particulars, do we define human groups as culturally "other" (to use that overworked term)? Do not some people in any group have more in common with their neighbors, who speak a different language, than with their own kinspeople? Rather than a single quality, is otherness not a tally of variables, more alert to some differences than to others? If so, what judgments do these categories carry with them?

This whole question might be put in terms of which parts of the human spectrum our different representations most strongly register. If, for example, we were to equate physical appearance and social organization with different kinds of electromagnetic waves, and armed some scholars with radios and others with cameras, what would each "see"? The analogy is crude because representational systems are not measuring devices, but they are nevertheless biased toward certain kinds of content and have a profound influence over the

23.  A leopard-skin chief, from E. E. Evans-Pritchard's *The Nuer*. (Plate XXIV.)

choices of their users. In discussing the contradictions implicit in anthropological categories, Richard Shweder cites Nelson Goodman's response to the idea of making a "faithful" picture of anything. "This simple-minded injunction baffles me; for the object before me is a man, a swarm of atoms, a complex of cells, a fiddler, a friend, a fool and much more" (Goodman 1968; Shweder 1984a). We see here, of course, only the human perspective: a dog's sensory mapping of the world would be very different again. Despite such difficulties, anthropologists have generally assumed that pictures would support and extend their findings. But is it not more likely that, in constructing a different object, pictures will contradict them?

How are we to describe the difference between the words "A leopard-skin chief," the caption for a photograph in Evans-Pritchard's *The Nuer*, and the photograph that accompanies it, attributed to F. D. Corfield?[5] [Figure 23.] Or the caption "Youth (Eastern Gaajok) fastening giraffe-hair necklace on friend" and its photograph?[6] [Figure 24.] Each could be the seed of a larger work: the caption might grow into a book, the photograph into a film. The caption presents us with the written code for something one might say, an

24. Youth (Eastern Gaajok) fastening giraffe-hair necklace on friend, from E. E. Evans-Pritchard's *The Nuer*. (Plate I.)

ostensive (or demonstrative) definition of the sort: "This is a Nuer youth." The photograph, some might assert, is but a different sort of code for a similar statement—instead of a few printed letters, a few printed shades of gray. According to this view, the photograph (although an iconic representation) is just as much a social and cultural construction as the written statement. It does, after all, present us with an image that, compared to the norms of human vision, is reduced, flattened, in black and white, a product of lens design and Albertian perspective, framed by aesthetic conventions (e.g. "the portrait"), by power relations ("appropriation," "colonialism," "surveillance," "the male gaze"), ideology (Western science, liberal humanism), and so on.

But to catalogue what photography shares with writing in this way is also to mask the important differences between them. At perhaps the simplest level, the written caption presents us with a category of person (to which is affixed the category "Nuer"), whereas the photograph presents us first and foremost with the phenomenon of a man. In both photographs the man is smiling broadly at someone or something outside the frame of the picture, suggesting his own experience at that moment. There is nothing to say this is a Nuer man, unless we are able to recognize the distinctive signs of Nuer facial scarification (*gar*) or can piece together less specific cultural information such as the beadwork, the hair style, the bracelets, the leopard skin, the type of spear, and so on. A less detailed photograph, such as Plate XVII ("Boy collecting dung-fuel [Lou]"), might be from almost anywhere in sub-Saharan Africa, yet it is no less particular in designating this one boy out of all history. [Figure 25.] The boy himself has his back to us and makes a statement closer to just "boy" or "African boy." The photograph does not say Nuer to me, much less Lou. There is no clothing or scarification to be seen. The roof-thatching in the background provides the only real clue. Why does Evans-Pritchard include such a photograph? Plate XIII provides a similarly unrevealing photograph of a naked girl in a millet garden. Here I might be able to guess that she is not a Turkana or a Jie girl, for her physiognomy is wrong, her lack of clothes is unlikely; but as I get farther from my area of knowledge, such judgments become less certain. She might be an Acholi or Teso or Dinka girl. For whom, and in what contexts, do these categories matter?

For most people such questions pale beside the presence in the photograph of the person: this one person, now facing us from some remote time and place. We might say, in fact, that the content of a photograph is overwhelmingly physical and psychological before it is cultural. It therefore transcends "culture" in a way that most written ethnographic descriptions do not—both by subordinating cultural differences to other, more visible contents (including other kinds of differences, such as physical ones) and by underscoring commonalities that cut across cultural boundaries. In contrast to ethnographic writing, this transculturality is a dominant feature of ethnographic films and photographs.[7]

It may be argued that we often tend to *see* transculturally as well, and if this is so it is probably for reasons very much like those I have outlined for photographs, for there are no *inherently* transcultural properties in images as images. There are, rather, conventions in the making of images (in the ubiquitous close-up, and in "framing" itself), in our learned responses to viewing

25. Boy collecting dung-fuel (Lou), from E. E. Evans-Pritchard's *The Nuer*. (Plate XVII.)

them, and in the circumstantial differences between everyday seeing and looking at previously made images, which tend to concentrate the transcultural
effects of photographs and films. These have to do not only with the particular
conditions that surround the two kinds of seeing, but with the physical differences between photographic processes and the physiology of human vision.[8]

## The Invisible in Anthropology

Cultural evidence is clearly not absent in visual depictions, nor is the evocation of physical presence absent in written ethnography; however, the very
different properties of these representations offer us one before the other. Yet
even when we have discovered the other properties, we have discovered
something ontologically different. The Nuer youth inscribed in Evans-
Pritchard's ethnography is "Everyyouth," the youth who undergoes *gar* and
goes on raids and marries. To be sure, I can read a wealth of feeling and
observation in such sentences as: "When a Nuer mentions an ox his habitual
moroseness leaves him and he speaks with enthusiasm, throwing up his arms
to show you how its horns are trained" (1940: 38). But this Nuer youth, the
work of Evans-Pritchard's writing and my imagination, is hardly the one I see
in Plate I.

I am suggesting that in photographs and films, cultural particularities may
be only the modulations and oddities that we see worked on the mantle of
human existence. Here, the weight anthropology attaches to cultural difference, and to specific cultural meanings (e.g. bell-oxen among the Nuer), is
perhaps not lost, but it is overridden by our responses to an individual's expression of "moroseness" or "enthusiasm," or such acts as throwing up his
arms—even if the responses and the actions themselves are culturally condi-
tioned. What, then, does the ethnographic object—the person—amount to in
our lopsided representations? In photographs and films is it merely a naïve
first glimpse of someone recognizably human, and in writing a collection of
cultural principles? To what extent can each form offset its limitations to
show the reality of lived experience *and* the underlying principles of a way of
life? But these may be the wrong questions. Given that each medium has distinctive properties, should we not ask instead: what does each still allow us
profitably to "misunderstand"—to understand against the grain? What gaps
does each provoke us to fill in? Different genres of writing and image-making
come equipped with their expected modes of interpretation, the paths to their
intended meaning. Academic books and articles expect a logic of reflection
and judgment to be applied to them, films a logic of recognition and extrapo-
lation. Can we benefit from breaking these rules? What cultural reifications
and distinctions should we treat with suspicion in ethnographic writing; what
evidence of cultural distinctiveness should we search for beneath the transcul-

tural surfaces of film? When, too, should we set aside the practices of Western rationalism and open ourselves to the patterns of resemblance we think we see? If we have to some extent allowed ourselves to be colonized by words, does film not provide a glimpse of what Ashis Nandy, in another context, has called an "alternative social knowledge"?[9]

Anthropology's gradual transferral of "culture" to the cognitive and symbolic domains may now justify renewed attention to the world of appearances. For anthropologists, transcultural resemblances have generally been false friends: one person's nod may be another's shake of the head. This has reinforced the invisible dimensions of culture, strengthening definitions such as Clifford Geertz's that culture is "an historically transmitted pattern of meanings embodied in symbols, a system of inherited conceptions expressed in symbolic form by means of which men communicate, perpetuate, and develop their knowledge about and attitudes towards life" (1973a: 89). Except when they include powerful visual symbols (in films of ritual, for example), visual images have increasingly been regarded as incidental to anthropology. The visible has largely disappeared as a signifier of culture, except perhaps in the popular imagination and in certain older anthropological traditions emphasizing folklore and crafts. Yet for much of the nineteenth century culture was conceived largely in terms of appearance: race, dress, personal adornment, ceremonial forms, architecture, technology, and material goods. Early ethnology exhaustively drew and photographed visible objects. Visual symbols were associated more with material culture than with the inner life. Myths and other oral texts were collected almost as artifacts, paralleling the scientific collecting and cataloguing of animal, plant, and mineral specimens. Yet despite its passion for the minutiae of cultural phenomena, nineteenth-century anthropology was in one respect far more transcultural in its perspective than the anthropology that succeeded it. Evolutionary theory effectively linked people together by allotting them places in the same human hierarchy. However oddly they behaved, it was assumed they did so from ignorance and superstition. That they might live in significantly different mental worlds was a much bigger step to take.

As we know, that step was taken largely through the study of languages; and if the interest in myths, proverbs, and terminologies was a form of collecting, it was also the Trojan horse of linguistics. With language studies, anthropological conceptions of culture gradually shifted from the external to the internal, from visible artifacts and behavior to invisible knowledge and cognition. Photographs and silent films were dumb when it came to language, and almost equally useless for studying other symbolic systems such as kinship and ritual. They were even less helpful in documenting values and beliefs. Except for Bateson and Mead's work in Bali, with its highly psychoanalytic orientation, almost no attempts were made by ethnographic filmmakers until the 1950s to film culture as an internal state, even though experimental and fictional films had been exploring subjective experience since the silent era. The change only occurred when it became possible to make ethnographic sound films, and eventually to film people speaking in synchronous sound. Even then it was some years before the words came from the anthropological subjects rather than the filmmakers.

Anthropologists have thus had both conceptual and practical reasons for their disenchantment with the visual. If we look further, we can also find strategic ones. As anthropology abandoned evolutionary theory it began to celebrate the individual fieldworker, whose mission was to add another piece to the tapestry of human diversity. One looked for the uniqueness and inner consistency of human groups, or for principles underlying the institutions of larger culture areas (such as the economics of bridewealth among African pastoralists, the reciprocity of the *kula*), a leaning most clearly expressed in the hermeticism of British functionalist ethnography. Here the organic perfection of a society seemed to be the very justification for its existence. This sense of singularity of form and ethos became an aesthetic and even moral test of cultural authenticity in the work of Ruth Benedict and many others. Gupta and Ferguson (1992) have argued that the spatial dispersion of peoples furthered such holism by making geographical isolation an implicit sign of cultural distinctiveness. This reinforced the popular conception of unknown peoples as ineluctably alien. We might add to this that written accounts of people who could, at best, be seen in a few hazy photographs, or approached through surreal displays of museum artifacts, added representational distance to geographical distance. Nor could an anthropologist's prestige be hurt by discovering something previously unknown and returning from afar to write about it.

The disciplinary investment in discrete fields of study, and in the celebration of cultural difference, has also reinforced tendencies to view human behavior and consciousness as culturally constructed. The idea of culture as the *sine qua non* of being human is reified to such an extent that, at least among North American anthropologists, human groups have until recently been commonly referred to as "cultures." Writing lends itself to cultural explanations, in that it allows the writer to represent a society from within, based on the participatory experiences of fieldwork. Visual representation, on the other hand, which as it were presents the inner cultural world from without, stresses social agency and the more widely recognizable patterns of social interaction. I refer here to expressions of pleasure or displeasure, the ways in which people move and "inhabit" their environments, their uses of space, common skills in making things, and many of the recurring interactions of childhood and parenthood.

Much recent anthropological interest has focused on personal identity, body praxis, and the role of the senses and emotions in social life. Whether these are seen as "cultural," on the one hand, or biological, psychological, or social on the other, depends both upon one's theoretical interests and what part of the phenomenon one is examining. Sexual identity has both a sexual and gendered dimension. Life stages may be defined variously but are also dependent upon physical age. Anger is a cultural category but also a psycho- logical and physiological response. How one regards these matters may be significantly influenced by one's medium of expression. Visual representa- tions easily express external, behavioral features of emotion, and visual clues to identity, that written descriptions express only with some difficulty. Thus, images of people on a street may reveal continuities across subcultural bound- aries (of dress, gesture, association) that are missed or masked in written ac- counts, where people's own definitions of cultural categories figure more prominently.

Although both writing and films register some transcultural elements, they register different ones. Writing more often emphasizes basic structures, such as those of kinship or exchange, films common gestures and experiences. A smile, even if it conceals discomfiture or anger, still expresses something fun- damental in human relations: the desire to appear sociable, to maintain con- tact. (This applies in a general sense even to a "smile of dismissal" as one is shown to the door.) Writing about the emotions, unless it places them in spe- cific narrative contexts, tends to turn them into disconnected cultural catego- ries. The tendency in anthropological writing to interpret emotion in cultural constructionist terms has thus been criticized for failing to place emotion in a broader context of thought, embodiment, and social agency (Lyon 1995; Lyon and Barbalet 1994; Wikan 1991: 292).

This differential emphasis has important consequences for ethnographic representation more generally. Images and written texts not only tell us things differently, they tell us different things. Although the cultural shaping of iden- tity and emotion may not be so well communicated in ethnographic film as in writing, their role in social interaction may be more clearly expressed, and this may be equally necessary for an anthropological understanding. For example, understanding the form of the initiation ritual in the film *Imbalu* (1989), about circumcision among the Gisu of Uganda, requires that it be seen as a cultural creation. To understand its efficacy requires an understanding of the fear that accompanies initiation, which is created in specific social relations. Similarly, films and written works communicate contrasting aspects of the exercise of power, whether at the level of the family or the state. The methods for exerting power may be culturally various, but many of the effects (suffering, oppres- sion, famine) are not.

A significant feature of filmic representation, approached in only a few "first-person" ethnographies,[10] is a sense of the unique personal identity of social actors. This offers the possibility of comparisons across wide cultural gulfs through resemblances of personality and social behavior. In this way, films replicate some of the experiences of fieldwork. It is not uncommon for anthropologists, after a long period in the field, to observe that someone looks or talks or relates to others exactly like a remembered friend or teacher, even though the two belong to quite different societies and speak different languages.[11] This has implications for what features of personality we consider culturally specific or typical of certain societies, and how we assess the sense of self and autonomy of individuals. From one perspective, the concept of the individual may seem an absolute necessity of human interaction, but from another it has been seen to vary widely, even to the extent of being declared virtually absent in some societies (see Dumont 1970; Geertz 1973b; Geertz 1975).

In their more vivid portrayal of the individual, films thus bring a different perspective to questions of the links between culture and personality. Many of the postulates of broad cultural integration worked out by proponents of the culture and personality school in the 1940s and 1950s have lost their credibility (Shweder 1991), but anthropological writing still generalizes about social actors and promulgates ideas of cultural uniformity. Clearly films may at times veer toward generalizing personality, but they may also reveal more complexities of individual manner and behavior than even anthropological "thick" descriptions of public events, such as Icelandic ram exhibitions or Balinese cockfights.[12] Films revive many of the perennial questions of anthropology. How closely bound by cultural norms and social contexts are individual social actors, and with what frequency do they challenge them? Does any person actually embody a "culture"? How available are different cultural models in a society?[13] Some individuals may successfully combine conflicting strands of "normative" thinking coexistent in their community. Others may appear to act inconsistently, following different codes in different circumstances. Still others may appear to act completely on their own, inspired (as is increasingly possible) by some distantly observed model, or on the basis of some private understanding. But we are dealing here with multiple variables. How often are words and images themselves the authors of such perceptions?

Similar questions could be asked in other domains (how work or time is portrayed, for example), underscoring the contrasts between visual and written works, between depiction and description. In many respects images provide ways of perceiving humanity that are not only transcultural but pre-anthropological: images in which culture is perceived as the background rather than the figure of human relationships. Films in unfamiliar languages, in which much is incomprehensible, nevertheless communicate the objective existence of people in other environments, the affective tonalities of many of their relationships, and the logic of many of their activities. Here "culture" appears not as the defining feature of life (indeed, in pictures the *concept* of culture cannot appear at all) but rather as a set of inflections of the recognizable world. For anthropologists, film thus recalls the everyday encounters of fieldwork out of which anthropological knowledge is distilled. In some ways it reinstates their "other" knowledge: the detailed moments that stand out more strikingly than any subsequent conclusions. Here human beings exist first in their bodies and in certain characteristic predispositions towards the world. If they are aware of their "culture" it is often to exhibit a certain irony toward it—as though they were assured of an ambiguity that every society vouchsafes its members.

## The Challenge of Images

If images show us individuals as unique in consciousness and body—each person distinguishable from all others—they are less capable of showing us the rules of the social and cultural institutions by which they live. Just as speech is accompanied by vocalizations and gestures that are culturally more widespread (or more specific) than the codes of the language being spoken, so photographs and films reveal colloquial aspects of human life superimposed upon more rigid systems of organization. Pictures could thus be said to be like the specific utterances of language, but carrying many of their more generalized meanings.

Nevertheless, images may reveal other systems, no less formalized, that are obscured by the logocentric categories of writing. For example, we may be able to see that two people are digging holes in the ground but not see that they are digging for different reasons. This could be regarded as a self-evident limitation of visual representation—its insensitivity to the cognitive world—but it may equally well be regarded as another sensitivity, giving access to a different range of phenomena (e.g., *how* people dig). If ethnographic film presents us with an apparently less culturally specific view of humanity than ethnographic writing, it also alerts us to a different distribution of specific human characteristics. These concern ways of appearing, making, and doing rather than of naming, conceptualizing, and believing. Although anthropologists have always been interested in such matters, they have increasingly tended to treat them as the visible expressions of an underlying order. The visible has thus been thought to signify a system of secondary rather than primary characteristics. Whatever resemblances they reveal between others and ourselves, these only conceal a deeper reality that sets "them" apart from "us." However, it is possible to turn this relationship on its head, to take the visible as primary, an alternative starting point.

A visual perspective contests many of the classical indicators of boundaries between cultural groups. It also contests the *concept* of boundaries, placing more emphasis upon gradual modulations between groups and upon patterns of borrowing and exchange that written accounts often dismiss as atypical, or simply ignore.[14] Films and photographs are more likely to include telltale indicators of these contacts, however much they try to present a society as isolated and homogeneous. Furthermore, by giving equal weight to elements that social scientists may consider biological, psychological, or otherwise "outside" culture, images call into question the relative importance of "cultural" factors against other forces in human relations. For these reasons, visual anthropology almost inevitably creates challenges to written texts. It not only opens up the transcultural as an issue for anthropology, but is counter-cultural (in the anthropological sense) by drawing attention to the significance of the non-"cultural."[15]

Ethnographic films may lend unexpected support to the call by some anthropologists to "write against culture," as Lila Abu-Lughod (1991) has put it. There have been recent moves to reject or at least reconfigure the "culture concept," an effort that in fact reaches back to the reservations about culture voiced by Lowie and Sapir in the 1920s and 1930s. The current debate includes interventions by such writers as Edward Said, James Clifford, and Arjun Appadurai. Until recently, ethnography has encouraged what Gupta and Ferguson have called "the fiction of cultures as discrete, object-like phenomena occupying discrete spaces" (1992: 7). But culture, as Appadurai puts it, is increasingly "fractal." Culture as a concept also has a complex and contentious history, and is itself easily essentialized, just as the "culture concept" may be accused of essentializing much about human societies. And there is always the possibility that the alternative concepts proposed, such as "discourse" (out of Foucault) or "habitus" (out of Bourdieu), will take on similar functions and implications to those they now question.[16] However, the recent criticisms of the culture concept are persuasive, pointing up a wide range of distortions and limitations: the tendencies it encourages in its users to treat abstractions as realities, to view humanity as made up of discrete and bounded entities, to imply a uniformity and coherence that societies do not have, to deny social groups a place in time and history, and (a criticism made by Said and Appadurai in particular) to perpetuate colonial distinctions between Western intellectuals and all non-Western "others." To offset this, Abu-Lughod proposes abandoning the term "culture" and adopting new strategies in ethnographic writing, focusing upon contending discourses instead of monolithic "cultures," examining the interconnections rather than the separations between groups and individuals (of identity, power, positioning), and writing "ethnographies of the particular." These suggestions have much in common with what ethnographic films have, if not always, at least notably done. To the extent that films have prefigured many of the shifts these writers advocate, they may already have created a certain unease among more conservative scholars. It is perhaps symptomatic of anthropology's wariness of the visual that it rarely makes reference to ethnographic films as part of the anthropological literature on any given subject, or in fact to films at all. As an instance of this, in the same volume in which Abu-Lughod's essay appears, films go unmentioned in the References section, although in the text Appadurai devotes more than two pages to Mira Nair's film *India Cabaret* (1985), calling it a "brilliant model" for ethnography (1991: 205–8).

The critique of discrete "cultures" points to the origins of the concept in colonial history and its continuing ideological ramifications. Talal Asad (1986) sees global interconnections systematically misrepresented in Western descriptions, and ethnographic representation distorted by the power of "strong" languages over weaker ones. Anthropological concepts, through their popularization and effects upon policy-making, ultimately influence how people interpret their own desires, potentialities, and social identities, especially in modern contexts of mobility and competing public discourses. Visual images, in their transcultural properties, may have a particular capacity to represent continuities across apparently radically dissimilar global settings— what Appadurai describes as "ethnoscapes" and likens to landscapes in visual art: landscapes in which the "warp" of putatively stable and discrete communities "is everywhere shot through with the woof of human motion, as more persons and groups deal with the realities of having to move or the fantasies of wanting to move" (1991: 192).

Visual representation, it is worth noting, has intercultural as well as transcultural implications. Images, by standing outside the system of "cultures" and nation-states, create new links based on points of recognition among otherwise separated social groups. Visually based media—including film, photography, television, and video—have already significantly undermined stereotypical perceptions of national identity, often in the face of nationalist interests.[17] A transcultural perspective accommodates cultural shift, movement, and interchange, which more adequately fits the experience of many Westerners as well as populations often identified as indigenous, migrant, or diasporic. Ethnographic film and video, which were once seen as reinforcing established cultural boundaries, are increasingly seen as part of a wider spectrum of cultural representations, much of which is devoted to the very problematics and contradictions of maintaining discrete, indigenous cultures (Ginsburg 1994; Nichols 1994b).

At a more basic level, visual media produce intercultural documents simply in their co-inscription of filmmakers and their subjects in the same work (assuming they do not come from identical backgrounds). The filmmaker's acts of looking are encoded in the film in much the same way as the subject's physical presence. This is fundamentally different from a written work, which is a textual reflection upon prior experience. Ethnographic films almost always contain some trace of this crossing of minds and bodies, whether they mean to or not. By situating the filmmaker explicitly within a social space, interacting with others, such earlier works as Rouch's *Bataille sur le grand fleuve* (1951) or *Tourou et Bitti* (1971) and more recent ones such as Lisbet

Holtedahl's *Is What They Learn Worth What They Forget?* (1996) and Eliane de Latour's *Contes et comptes de la cour* (1993) express the subjectivity and immediacy of these intercultural encounters.

The transculturality of film not only has intercultural but *interdisciplinary* implications. It tends to restore some of the connections between anthropology and sociology broken in the 1950s in the splitting off of ideation and symbol from social agency and material production (Brightman 1995: 512). It reconnects "culture" to the historical and physical world of social actors. This includes a renewal of interest in the consciousness of particular individuals, rather than merely in emic perspectives in a more general sense. In linking anthropology to the psychology of the individual, as advocated long ago by Sapir (1949b), images reveal aspects of what he referred to as "the more intimate structure of culture" (1949a: 594).

The audio-visual and synaesthetic aspects of film also lend support (and may have contributed to) recent anthropological interest in sensory experience. This has strengthened anthropology's links to such fields as ethnomusicology and medicine, and in general to the somatization of social and cultural experience.[18] Although it would be mistaken to deny the possibility of access to sensory experience in anthropological writing, visual anthropology opens more directly onto the sensorium than written texts and creates psychological and somatic forms of intersubjectivity between viewer and social actor. In films, we achieve identification with others through a synchrony with their bodies made possible in large part by vision, a phenomenon discussed in some detail by Merleau-Ponty (1964) and by film theorists such as Vivian Sobchack (1992). Film also has the potential to create more interchange between anthropology and visual aesthetics, once set apart as the "anthropology of art" (and earlier, "primitive art"). Here film and photography present a more integrated view of the aesthetic experiences of daily life, broadening the definition of "visual anthropology" to include the anthropology of the visual, as advocated by Worth, Pinney, and others (Banks and Morphy 1997; Pinney 1995; Worth 1981b).

The interdisciplinary potential of visual anthropology is further extended through its performative aspects—for films, at least, are a form of performance. Through films we are exposed to the illocutionary dimension of ritual, but also importantly to that of everyday social interaction and self-presentation, perhaps moving the anthropological concept of culture somewhat closer to what Bourdieu means by *habitus*. Ethnographic films can re-create the specific dramatic contexts within which cultural and social forces are ultimately played out, making literature (and what Victor Turner calls "social dramas") more relevant to anthropology. Film may also provide a more accessible ground than words for what Renato Rosaldo (1986) calls "novelistic narrative" in ethnography, and for incorporating the suspense and responses of listeners that he considers crucial to oral narratives. Ethnographic narratives also engage with political and moral beliefs by implicating their readers and view-ers in particular emotional responses. Rouch's *Jaguar* (1967) evokes the amoral freedom of the fabulous traveler, sojourner, and invader, whereas (as Elizabeth Mermin [1997] notes cogently) the moral ambiguity of the protago-nist in *Joe Leahy's Neighbours* (1988) seems to create disturbed responses in viewers that can rebound upon the filmmakers a tendency to "blame the mes-senger."[19]

Sound in films links visual anthropology more closely to linguistics and sociolinguistics. Instead of presenting transcriptions of speech, film is able to reproduce almost the full visual and auditory range of verbal expression. This includes gestures and facial expression, but perhaps even more importantly, the voice. Voices are more completely embodied in a film than faces, for the voice *belongs* to the body. Visual images of people, by contrast, result only from a reflection of light from their bodies. In a corporeal sense, then, these images are passive and secondary, whereas a voice emanates actively from within the body itself: it is a product *of* the body. As Roland Barthes observed, it comes from the *muzzle*, which in an animal is the entire complex of nose, jaws, and mouth (1975: 66–67).[20] The physical qualities of speech are, how-ever, always implicit in films, and although they contribute substantially to the understanding of other people (often, as mentioned above, in transcultural ways) they tend otherwise to go unregarded. Nevertheless, speech inevitably brings anthropology closer to the physical and historical moment through its emphasis upon specific contexts, almost always "shot through" with Appadu-rai's evidence of motion, exchange, and globalization. It is more difficult for films than texts to ignore what they deem extraneous, when the extraneous fact is embedded in their object of study.

The interdisciplinary links of visual anthropology verge on what W.J.T. Mitchell calls an " 'interdiscipline,' a site of convergence and conversation across disciplinary lines." In creating resistance to conventional textual dis-courses, images weaken the boundaries between adjacent disciplines. They describe a world in which the physical, social, and aesthetic are intimately intertwined, and in which the performative aspects of social interaction are present, as well as its underlying structures. Images may even be said to con-tribute to a form of *indiscipline* in practices such as anthropology, "a moment of breakage or rupture, when the continuity is broken and the practice comes into question . . . the moment of chaos or wonder when a discipline, a way of doing things, compulsively performs a revelation of its own inadequacy" (Mitchell 1995: 440–41).

This disturbance in anthropology is felt in two dissimilar ways: first, by a seeming indefiniteness as it shades off into other areas (aesthetics, psychol-ogy, history), confusing the discipline at its boundaries; and second, by an all too definite relevance to its central concerns. Images threaten to expose an-thropology to a limitless extension, suggesting an imprecision in what it is all about, exacerbating a process already under way in a proliferation of sub-fields. A further extension is threatened into adjoining areas of mass culture, where anthropology catches a glimpse of its common roots with travel writing and literature. These transgressions are by turns inviting and dangerous. Rationally, they can be seen as parts of the continuum that anthropology shares with other human activities, but in their indeterminacy they create uncertainty about anthropology's focus and direction.

Despite this, images do in fact underline what anthropology is all about. They evoke the life experience of social actors, and also the experiences of fieldwork that always remain prior to anthropological description. Visual representation recalls the kind of learning that Michael Polanyi has called "tacit knowing"—the things we know (the "physiognomies" of a subject) that are "more than we can tell" (1966: 4). They attest to the irreducibility of such knowledge, but also to the processes by which it is gained: an intersubjectivity denied to anthropology in its later, recollective phases. These matters are fundamental to the discipline, yet are infrequently discussed. Images bring them vividly, and sometimes awkwardly, to the surface.

Visual images have a way of undermining writing. They threaten verbal descriptions with redundancy, and often make scholarly conclusions look threadbare. They suggest parallels and resonances that defy easy categorization. To the fieldworker they carry a wealth of associations—personal, historical, political—that their written counterparts strip away. This "excess" may indeed be superfluous for analytical purposes, but its presence is also missed. The visual in fact stands in a relation of "semiotic otherness" to writing (Mitchell 1995: 543), offering up the anthropological in an unassimilable form. For the writer struggling with words, images may seem all too easy, yet they also achieve an enviable closure. To borrow Mitchell's mixed metaphor, the visual is a "'black hole' at the heart of verbal culture" (1995: 543). It is a gravitational force that sucks in, but never exhausts, all that is irreducible to discourse.

## Film and Cultural Translation

Written words are comparatively recent products of speech, and writers are still said to "speak" to us. But in what sense, except metaphorically, can we say that pictures speak? In our preoccupation with sign systems and texts, we tend to lose sight of films as objects and actions. A written sentence may have some approximation to speaking, but before a film is anything resembling the transcription of a speech act, it is a performance of *looking*. How does looking, even in the delimited and controlled manner that it occurs in cinema, conform to the practices we know as anthropology? Is the experience of viewing a film really comparable to reading a text?[21]

Thomas J. Csordas (1993b), citing Paul Ricoeur (and perhaps thinking of

Geertz) has argued that just as anthropologists have come to interpret "cultures" as having properties similar to texts, so they should also understand them as having the properties of embodied experience. The senses and agency of the body should be taken as seriously as thought and symbolization, healing forever the old Cartesian rift between them. Anthropologists should extend their practices of analysis and cultural translation into the realm of bodily experience. So far, the thrust of Csordas's argument is salutary, but at this point it runs headlong into the problem of whether embodied experience can be treated as a text, or is amenable to cultural translation. It may be evoked in writing, but is this in any sense comparable to translating a "culture" that is already conceived in largely symbolic terms? If embodied experience can be turned into text, what sort of text? How is an "anthropology of experience" to be articulated? Are what Csordas calls "somatic modes of attention" communicable in words?

Films and related visual media suggest some other ways of achieving this, and Csordas (although he doesn't mention film) is explicit that vision is not "a disembodied, beam-like 'gaze'" (1993b: 138) but a form of active bodily engagement with the world—a position consonant with recent phenomenological film theory. Nevertheless, it remains problematic to equate the experiential qualities of films with written texts, as though a process of *translating* experience were going on. Rather, it would perhaps be more accurate to say that a film registers or traces the process of looking itself, not as a line drawn between the subject and object of viewing, but as an artifact in which the two are inseparably fused. What appears in the film is not so much a translation of vision as a form of visual quotation, or visual communion. This engages the viewer in a second act of looking, closely bound up with the actions of the filmmaker.

Faced with the task of communicating the physical embodiment as well as the symbolic content of culture, the idea of anthropology as a translation of culture becomes harder to sustain and appears increasingly inadequate. Talal Asad has pointed out that the metaphor of cultural translation was not always a feature of British social anthropology. This was not because there was no interest in language. Malinowski, in common with many early anthropologists, collected masses of linguistic material, but "he never thought of his work in terms of the translation of cultures" (Asad 1986: 141–42). Indeed, one suspects the guiding metaphor would more likely have come from British playing fields: the need to learn the rules of the game. Asad observes that in order for anthropologists to regard other cultures as translatable, they had first to conceive of them as *texts*. This involved transforming one's fieldwork experience into a structure of indigenous thought. Asad quotes Lienhardt's definition of cultural translation as one of "describing to others how members of a remote tribe think . . . of making the coherence primitive thought has in the languages it really lives in, as clear as possible in our own" (Lienhardt 1954: 97). This however assumes that culture is essentially linguistic, from which a form of thought can be distilled and translated. Even if one accepts this principle, cultures are, as Asad has observed, in considerable danger of mistranslation and appropriation by more dominant "languages" (1986: 158). To this can be added the objection that the idea of translation itself always carries an implication of difference and thus *creates* difference. In translation, even the familiar acquires something of the foreign.

I would argue that the objects images record, and certainly many aspects of social experience, are not finally translatable. If ethnographic films convey the nonlinguistic features of culture, they do so not through a process of translation but by a process of physical engagement. In a sense ethnographic films do not "mean" anything, but neither do they mean "anything." They situate us in relation to objects, deploying what is suggestive and expressive in the world. They are analytical through their choice of what to present to us. They convey the dynamics of social relationships, creating explanations through narrative sequences and other filmic structures. They produce simulacra, rather than translations. Without actually mentioning film, Asad notes that in certain circumstances a *performance* of another culture might be preferable to "the representational discourse of ethnography," but that anthropologists are not really interested in this. The anthropological audience is waiting "to read *about* another mode of life and to manipulate the text it reads according to established rules, not to learn *to live* a new mode of life" (1986: 159). In a similar vein, Dipesh Chakrabarty observes that Western intellectuals are uncomfortable dealing with many aspects of non-Western life *except* by "anthropologizing" them, because the master-code of Western thought (Marxist thought included) is a secular, historicist discourse (1993: 423). There are, in any case, many aspects of culture that anthropologists are not normally asked to report upon and that they therefore consign to the privacy of the fieldwork experience. They thus position themselves as intermediaries between the field and the audience. What they express to others is what they have expressed anthropologically to themselves. In a sense films, as a form of what Asad calls "transformed instances of the original," threaten this mediation by bypassing accustomed textual practices. Films thus convey many of the things anthropologists are unlikely or unable to speak about.

Ethnographic films finally produce quite different responses in us than texts that we read, and out of which we construct our own mental pictures. They are by no means unmediated—they are mediated in choice, perspective, and arrangement of their material. But as close correlatives of our physical interaction with the world through vision, touch, and our other senses, images assert the autonomy and, in a sense, inviolability of other people's experiences, which cannot always be assumed to be open to the power of language. In this sense, regarding a film as a text involves some of the same problems as regarding a culture as a text.

## Seeing and "Seeing"

Most critiques of anthropological theory have taken place within a certain metaphorical unanimity, and it is generally critiques from elsewhere (from feminism, Marxism, queer theory, film theory, subaltern studies) that have introduced a different set of conceptual images. By this I mean that anthropology, for all its modernity and even postmodernity, has continued to rely heavily upon metaphors of understanding that would be perfectly recognizable to scholars of the eighteenth and nineteenth centuries. Anthropologists have seen themselves traveling along a road to knowledge, avoiding pitfalls here and there and discovering new paths, now diverging from the highways of grand theory and now rejoining them, but confident that some wider panorama awaits them ahead. The calls for experimental ethnography, for paradigmatic shifts and interdisciplinary borrowing, often have more the quality of readjustments to new terrain than any change of destination. Alternatively, one might refer to anthropology's semantic journey—what Reddy (1993) calls the "conduit metaphor"—in which we all participate and in which knowledge is assured by how well we understand our (and others') transmissions of meaning. But clearly anthropology's master concept, for all its distancing of itself from images, and in common with many other disciplines, has been the metaphor of vision—*understanding is seeing*—and it is partly because of this that film has come to occupy a position in anthropology of catalytic potential.

Most previous challenges to ethnographic description have come from a common grounding in writing. The problems they have raised have been dealt with largely as obstacles to be overcome or gaps to be bridged or filled in. Nicholas Thomas describes this as part of the discipline's commonsense epistemology of quantity. "Defects are absences that can be rectified through the addition of further information, and more can be known about a particular topic by adding other ways of perceiving it. 'Bias' is thus associated with a lack that can be rectified or balanced out by the addition of further perspectives" (1991: 308). However, when the metaphor of understanding-as-seeing collides with seeing as an embodiment of knowledge, one can expect the discipline to experience a more fundamental intellectual disturbance—what could perhaps be compared to a fugue or synaptic short-circuit. This is what I believe happens when anthropology encounters ethnographic film.

The metaphor of vision is to be found everywhere in anthropological writing, and indeed most other writing. Anthropological language, when it encounters vision in film, is thus already deeply impregnated with vision as a symbolic form. The pervasiveness of such metaphorical thinking has been demonstrated by Lakoff and Johnson (1980), and its implications for scientific thought have been examined further by others (Holland and Quinn 1987;

Reddy 1993; Salmond 1982). Analyzing the language of scientific texts, Anne Salmond discusses several prominent metaphors, including "understanding is seeing," "knowledge is a landscape," "intellectual activity is a journey," "facts are natural objects," "the mind is a container," and "intellectual activity is work." Anthropological thinking and expression rely on all of these, but "understanding is seeing" with its associated metaphors is perhaps the most widespread. One could go further. Such notions as emic and etic, or experience-near and experience-distant, derive from an image of seeing in which understanding is a function of both viewing position and an inside/outside, or surface/depth construct. "Exposing problems" or "casting more light" upon anthropological subjects joins the metaphor of understanding-as-seeing with visual metaphors of lightness/darkness and covering/uncovering. "Going to the heart" of a problem joins visual metaphors of surface/depth with bodily metaphors of feeling, centeredness, and authenticity. Even though we may not be consciously aware of using such figures of thought, Salmond makes the point that to ignore them, or attempt to escape from them, is to misunderstand the relation of expression to our experience of the world. At the same time, because metaphors permeate expression, their use means that ultimately "the absolute verification of descriptions is not feasible" (1982: 65).

In films, anthropologists come up against a disjunction between the guided "vision" of anthropological writing and the more ambiguous vision of photographic images, which is perhaps closer to the fertile social ambiguity of speech. Despite the many visual metaphors underlying anthropology, images do not lend themselves easily to anthropological expression and interpretation, either through the filmmaker's vision encoded in them or in the subsequent processes of viewing them. This is not to say they cannot contribute to anthropological understanding, but rather to stress that they cannot do so without a change of expectations. The reasons lie in the properties of images themselves and in the ways in which they are articulated.

Here I would refer to what Ivo Strecker (1997) has called "the turbulence of images" in ethnographic discourse.[22] Visual images have complex connotative potential for the viewer, but more to the point, images of people in social situations (and in particular, film images with sound) convey a complex expressive world in which words, appearances, and actions occupy a continuous social and cultural field. Strecker (1988) has demonstrated eloquently how the symbolic world, which is not fixed but a fertile seedbed of possibilities, extends from verbal expression into the physical behavior of everyday life and then further into formal ritual. In such a web of understandings and maneuverings, there is both a constant interpenetration of the verbal and gestural domains and a more linear movement from thought to speech and action. Building on the concepts of Erving Goffman, Dan Sperber, and Paul Grice, and the "politeness theory" of Penelope Brown and Stephen Levinson, Strecker sees interpersonal relations as settings of "conversational implicature" in which people enact cooperative dramas, or bend them to exert various forms of influence over one another. The point here is that metaphor is not only a feature of cognition and language but extends into visible social practice. This can be seen in the use of metaphorical gestures (McNeill and Levy 1982), in the "interaction rituals" of everday life (Goffman 1967), and in the enactment of "social dramas" (Turner 1981). Film conveys this complex in its interrelations, tying together the world of image, word, and action—resembling what Stephen Tyler (1978: 63) calls an "interactionist view of thought" that combines its verbal (acoustic), visual, and kinaesthetic dimensions.

It is these elements that give film its fluidity and productive ambiguity, but it is also these that make it a difficult medium to integrate with the particular metaphorical and logocentric world of anthropological expression. As Tyler puts it, citing Paivio, "Visual and kinesthetic imagery, because it is open to the external world, is not always constrained by the world of words and the sequential order of verbalization. It is more flexible, rapid, and creative than verbal thought. . . . When we speak of the creative use of language, certainly more is involved than the production of novel sentences" (Paivio 1971: 435; Tyler 1978: 64). Film presents a kind of overload to writing's constraints of professional meaning, even though many kinds of writing engage the reader in forms of "implicature" of their own. This could explain why many anthropologists are attracted to film, but also their caution toward it. They are attracted to its evocation—of a person, a society, a set of meanings—that exceeds its formal denotation. The ambiguities it presents require a creative response, which is to say that like much of social practice it operates through purposeful omissions and invitations. But anthropology, also a social practice, recognizes the intrusion of a different practice and asserts its right of exclusion. Thus films are rarely accepted as components of doctoral dissertations, on the grounds that there is no way of assessing them. To anthropology, ethnographic films appear to flout what Grice has called the maxims of "cooperative" conversation. If shots bear an indexical (and synecdochic) relation to their subjects, films might be said to be more like giant metaphors (in Sperber's terms, productively "defective representations") in relation to anthropology's task of writing about culture.

In these terms, the transculturality of images can be seen as one of the primary violations of anthropological discourse. The cultural ambiguity of images offends particularly against the discursive rule of clarity (Grice 1975: 46). Although language is culturally specific in the arbitrariness of its signs, most images of objects in the visible world are iconically or indexically expressive of a wide range of potential meanings and functions. Visible objects take on symbolic and metaphorical potency through their uses, and it is the different contextualizations of these uses that produce varied understandings. For many of us, an image of a pair of sandals might suggest walking, but for the Turkana of Kenya (or the Hamar, or the Mursi) who use sandals in divination as well as for walking, the image might equally suggest the future, or some more specific preoccupation, such as the coming of the rains.

A similar flexibility can be seen operating in gesture, which is by turns deictic, iconic, and metaphorical. There are different ways of pointing (with the finger, the lips, the chin) but pointing is in itself a form of visual or ostensive definition that can be read cross-culturally. Verbal metaphors may vary from one "culture" to another (see, for example, Salmond [1982] on Maori metaphors of knowledge), but these are not necessarily congruent with the geographical distribution of gestural metaphors. An upward cupping of the hands, simulating a pair of scales, to express "choosing is weighing" (McNeill and Levy 1982: 289–91) is recognized in many mercantile societies, but people in these societies do not necessarily use the same image to *speak* of choosing. Similarly, images of body parts, or certain uses of the body in posture and position, may variously relate to physical sensations, such as heaviness or lightness (e.g. in the downcast look of shame or sadness), or refer to the heart or stomach as the site of feeling, or become metaphors for status (head or foot, high or low, etc.). The point here is not to specify particular modes of expression but to suggest the ways in which films and other visual images give access to the expressiveness of social practice. Much of the transculturality of cinema derives from these physical imbrications and from broader patterns of human agency connected to power and deference. Brown and Levinson, for example, deriving their concept of "face" partly from Goffman's studies of face-to-face behavior, argue that although what constitutes the maintenance of face may vary from one culture to another, "the mutual knowledge of members' public self-image or face, and the social necessity to orient oneself to it in interaction, are universal" (cited in Brown and Levinson 1978; Strecker 1988).

If the images of films often defy the "culture concept," the transculturality of cinema should not finally be taken as a new key to human universals, but rather as a *provocation*. It should lead toward a more wide-ranging argument about the implications of visual recognition in both ethnography and human history. The shock of transculturality makes clear that cultural differences between groups do not always indicate internal cultural homogeneity. Transculturality is also an artifact of regional histories, movements, and communication. The "turbulence" of images may be seen as analogous to the turbulence of modern societies themselves, in their mobility and in the discontinuous global forces that affect different parts of them unequally. It is important to see how others perceive the world transculturally, finding in distant places things they recognize, or reject, or wish to make their own. Debates about ethnographic film can then take their place within a broader disciplinary framework sensitive to transcultural processes of material and cultural interchange. Such a framework should eventually include a recognition of each group's role, and the interconnectedness of its history with that of others.

## An Anthropology of Consciousness?

The value of visual anthropology lies in its distinctiveness from ethnographic writing, including the transcultural properties of visual images. It lies in creating new conceptions of ethnography, rather than adapting vision to written forms. This is what W.J.T. Mitchell means in a broader sense when he writes: "The grafting of a received idea of culture (from cultural studies or from anywhere else) onto a received idea of 'the visual' (from art history, cinema studies, or anywhere else) will produce only another set of received ideas" (1995: 543). Early conceptions of visual anthropology stressed the importance of photography as a loyal handmaiden to the discipline, producing measurements, mnemonics, and substitutes for first-hand observation. Visual anthropology then moved toward holistic descriptions and didactic functions (see Heider 1976). There has since been a growing interest in addressing the experiential aspects of culture and the consciousness of specific social actors. This conception, with its Western bias toward the individual, sees people in all societies as operating within what Victor Turner called "structures of experience," incorporating possibilities of evasion, challenge, redefinition, and (importantly) ignorance. With a nod to Sapir, Turner observes that "culture . . . is *never given* to each individual but, rather, 'gropingly discovered,' and, I would add, some parts of it quite late in life. We never cease to learn our *own* culture, let alone other cultures" (1981: 140). Perhaps not unexpectedly, ethnographic films that treat individuals as experiencing subjects tend to situate them in specific social scenarios and follow the narrative steps that Turner identifies as the transcultural constants of social dramas: "breach, crisis, redress, and *either* reintegration or recognition of schism" (p. 145).[23]

This is not to suggest that visual anthropology need necessarily employ narrative forms, but that these forms make possible a view of social actors responding creatively to a set of open-ended cultural possibilities, rather than being bound by a rigid framework of cultural constraints. In emphasizing the individual, visual anthropologists may be more likely to depart from the idea of culture as a set of discrete structures and approach it instead as a series of variations on a theme: a convergence of the personal, historical, and material at a particular time and place. In the past, this approach has more often been applied within large culture areas such as the Mediterranean or Latin America, where societies share certain underlying histories and characteristics but inflect them differently. Perhaps in the perspectives of visual anthropology, individuals will be seen more often to "refract" such a culture than to typify it. "Culture" as a category may shrink, taking a more modest place beside social, economic, historical, and psychological factors.

In the past, visual anthropology has emphasized visual documentation and utilized a limited range of narrative and didactic models. What will the visual anthropology of the future look like? More precisely, what aspects of visuality itself are likely to influence visual anthropology the most? What I have called the transcultural properties of film and video, although they could lead to synoptic studies framed by universalist theories, seem more likely instead to create a visual anthropology of the particular. This is because the transcultural makes possible an overlapping of experiential horizons, where certain indirect and interpretive leaps of understanding can take place. It suggests a shift from general ethnographies, or studies of emblematic cultural events such as rituals, to studies of the experience of individual social actors in situations of wide cross-cultural relevance.

We can conceive of visual media contributing to a new field of *experiential studies* in anthropology—studies of the actualization of social knowledge—what might be considered a more broadly defined "anthropology of consciousness."[24] But if so, what might such a field consist of? How would it differentiate itself from psychology and sociology, or the forms they have taken in the work of scholars as varied as Goffman, Turner, Bourdieu, and Piaget? How would the transculturality of visual images be turned to good account in conveying experience *within* culture—that is to say, the particularities of negotiating between the personal and the cultural? Might such a field in the end turn out to be nothing less than the empirical arm of phenomenology?

As well as attending to the symbolic world of social practice, a redefined anthropology of concsiousness would study the passing flow of consciousness in everyday life, that mixture of sensory and cognitive experience that consciousness perceives as an integrated field. In this it would intersect with recent efforts in cognitive science to understand consciousness itself, a problem which has been approached from both a philosophical and neurobiological perspective.[25] It would also necessarily take account of the role of the unconscious in influencing the fabric of consciousness. Here the visual media may have a particular relevance. The experiential world that cinema creates is built upon a similar interrelation between perceptions (images, sounds) and the forces (cultural, social, biological) that organize them in various ways. This is reflected in how we view films as at once "real" and mediated, and in the often unaccountable intensity of our responses to them. The relation of this mediation to our film experience, rather than being considered merely as an underlying structure or set of pressures, can perhaps best be described as what Christian Metz (1982: 20) calls a *juxtastructure*—something "as it were *laterally engaged* with it" and therefore ultimately forming a part of it.[26]

If social experience cannot finally be translated, except by first being conceived linguistically, it can be *made perceptible* in images and sounds. But how well we perceive the experience of others depends upon fields of consciousness we share with them. This involves a transcultural process (now in the sense of crossing cultural boundaries) and a willingness to enter into a sympathetic contract with others, including the filmmaker or writer as intermediary. Consciousness includes the domain of tacit knowledge, evoked only in the interstices and disjunctions of what can physically be shown. Gaining access to this requires an awareness of what is absent. This kind of ethnography emphasizes, as Tyler puts it, "the cooperative and collaborative nature of the ethnographic situation in contrast to the ideology of the transcendental observer" (1987: 203). Thus, although the transculturality of images suggests universality, it in fact always operates locally.

At present we can only speculate on what an anthropology of consciousness might explore: the oscillations and relativities of subjectivity and objectivity, of meaning and non-meaning, of consciousness and "habitus," of cognition and action, of being and becoming—that we all to varying degrees experience. It may address fundamental questions concerning the *lebenswelt* raised many years ago by Wittgenstein, Sapir, and Whorf, as well as exploring questions of embodied experience raised more recently by Mary Douglas (1966; 1970) and Victor Turner (1967) in relation to the social role of symbols, and by Michael Jackson (1989), Gilbert Lewis (1980), and others in relation to the performative efficacy of ritual. As an anthropology of the particular, it is likely to be empirical as well as theoretical, and it may increasingly draw upon the particular expressive qualities of visual media.

The anthropological exploration of consciousness must begin with an exploration of our own conscious experience, for that is the only source directly available to us. However, our experience is not isolated but always conscious of others, and implicated in their consciousness. This is not to say that such introspection should ever dominate visual or written anthropology, but that we should take our own experience seriously as raw material and as a bridge to understanding the social experience of others.[27] We can aim to observe and express the fabric of consciousness as determinedly as linguists attempt to record the fabric of speech. It is clear that in this we are bound by our own expressive capabilities and cultural predispositions. We are approaching something like the observation of subatomic particles, in which our intention and our interference form an inescapable part of our means of understanding. The objective is ultimately to convey the relation of consciousness to social practice. If we were able to find a language to express even five minutes of our social experience in all its verbal, iconic, and kinaesthetic complexity, we should have made a major stride in this direction.

An anthropology of consciousness requires the gradual building up of a shared experience in the world with those we seek to understand. This is as much sensory as cognitive. Consciousness does not separate the experiencing of ideas and mental images from touch, vision, sound, and smell. Nor does it clearly separate the experiencing of others from the experiencing of self. In this sense, the subject of consciousness is not fixed but undergoes shifts between individual and shared subjectivities, as when one stands apart as an observer and then joins in a communal activity. These shifts cannot be reduced to simple engagement or disengagement but represent a wide spectrum of intensities and qualitative states. In another sense as well, the subject of consciousness is not static. Social actors are engaged in a constant exploration of their own potential, realizing new facets of themselves in new contexts. It is therefore important to regard social actors not as fixed personalities but as what Julia Kristeva calls "subjects in process": selves in a continual state of self-becoming, sometimes more rapidly (as in childhood and adolescence) and at other times more slowly. The discovery and creation of the self does not occur in isolation, but in relation to others and in interaction with them. This sometimes includes the anthropologist, and indeed the presence of an anthropologist (with or without a camera) can be a significant catalyst in altering people's awareness of themselves.

The consciousness of the observer is always subject to such processes as well. Most critics discuss the authors of films and anthropological texts in terms of an "authorial voice" that stands in solid contradistinction, often dialogically, to the ambiguous and often suppressed voices of others.[28] However, the concept of the author of a work as a stable center is illusory and seems more like the reification of one side of a structural or moral abstraction. In fact, our voices as authors are plural. At any moment we represent shards and fragments of a continuing social and cultural experience, in which those we film or write about form a crucial part. The author is never isolated but always a contingent being, and the author's "voice" is always constituted in relation to its object. Finally, no author is fully aware of what constitutes its voice—it speaks differently in different contexts, it undergoes shifting subjectivities with others, it is a ventriloquist for its teachers, parents, friends, and heroes.

To express how the world is experienced and shaped in social practice, an anthropology of consciousness must also take into account how the experience of its audience is shaped. In a world of implication and metaphorical richness, grounded in tacit knowledge, it must often speak metaphorically and by implication. This means drawing the viewer or reader into the historical and social space of an ethnography, just as one might introduce someone gradually to the geography of a new terrain. Consciousness is a multidimensional field in which gaps and elisions constitute much of the perceived world. Indeed, like the tonal and temporal intervals in music, they *are* the world. The unsaid is the common ground of social relations, communication, and ethnography. It is also the domain of the image.

[1998]

# Notes

1. Adapted from the *Oxford English Dictionary*, Second Edition (Simpson and Weiner 1989). The actual definition given is: "Transcending the limitations or crossing the boundaries of cultures; applicable to more than one culture; cross cultural."

2. It is, of course, possible never to refer to (or even think of) trees at all—by using such words as oak, elm, acacia, and so on. But although these words are more specific, they remain widely applicable until one gets down to the level of a known tree (e.g., "the Putney Elm"). If the languages of some societies seem more context-bound in certain categories than others, pictures seem more context-bound than all languages.

3. I accept, of course, that many visual images show only the face of a person, and that some living persons do not have two legs or two arms. My point is a general one.

4. Gilbert Lewis (1985) has pointed out the potential surrealism of isolated written details in ethnography. André Breton, Tristan Tzara, and other surrealists exploited this possibility in their poetry, and Michel Leiris drew up a glossary showing the suggestive power of words in isolation—e.g., "humain—la main humide." For James Agee the language of reality was "the heaviest of all languages" for its "inability to communicate simultaneity with any immediacy" (Agee and Evans 1960: 236–37).

5. Plate XXIV. F. D. Corfield was a District Commissioner in Nuerland and is described affectionately by Evans-Pritchard in the Preface to *The Nuer* as "*amico et condiscipulo meo*" (1940: vii).

6. Plate I.

7. The same argument could be extended to ideology as well. Photographs undoubtedly express assumptions about the subject held by the photographer. For example, a particular colonial discourse can be read in a group of photographs of a Nuba gathering made in 1929, the year before Evans-Pritchard began his fieldwork, as James Faris (1992) demonstrates. As this case suggests, ideological codes are more likely to emerge in a larger sample, such as the corpus of *National Geographic* photographs studied by Lutz and Collins (1993), than in a single photograph, such as Corfield's. But even when an ideological message is quite clear, as in a mocking or racist photograph, the integrity of the subject often undercuts or contests it. Thus we may say that a photograph is also physical and psychological before it is ideological.

8. These are matters that deserve fuller exploration than I can give them here. They involve such factors as the different contexts and ephemeral conditions of everyday vision and the probability that framing of any kind carries an intentionality that alters our conception of what is in the frame. The physiology of seeing may also be important in encouraging us to see photographic images as representing more generalized (and hence transcultural) meanings than what we see in everyday life or during anthropological fieldwork. Most recent studies of vision suggest that our impression of "framing" subjects with our own eyes (unlike the framing of cameras) is more psychological than physical, and that we actually see in a much more fragmented and impressionistic way, building up a mental sketch from very limited sampling and from what we *assume* to be before us. (But there is also counter-evidence in the prodigious visual feats of certain autistic artists such as Nadia and Stephen Wiltshire—see Selfe [1977; 1983] and Sacks [1995a].)

9. In his Preface to *The Intimate Enemy* (Nandy 1983: xvii).

10. See, for example, *Nisa* (Shostak 1981), *The Children of Sanchez* (Oscar Lewis 1961), and *Baldambe Explains* (Lydall and Strecker 1979). Earlier ethnographic life histories include *Baba of Karo* (Smith 1954) and *Worker in the Cane* (Mintz 1960).

11. .A number of people, and notably nonacademics for whom a Turkana camel-owner might be expected to be a quintessential "cultural other," have responded to seeing Lorang in the film *Lorang's Way* by saying, "He's exactly like my father!"

12. Geertz's paper on the cockfight (1972) is well known. Hastrup (1992) character-izes film as "thin" description compared to text, using the ram exhibition as an exam-ple. For a critique of Hastrup, see Taylor (1996).

13. This question was answered confidently by Clifford Geertz in the following exchange with Richard Shweder in 1980: "*Shweder*: What you're saying is that all cultural ideologies are available in all cultures, at least in an incipient form. That the Balinese or the Moroccan pattern is available in our system to both adults and children and that the question is how much we pick it up, amplify it, represent it, and enshrine it. *Geertz*: Right!" (Shweder 1984b: 16).

14. Recently, of course, the contrary view expressed in much postmodern anthro-pology—that all cultural boundaries are in fact fluid and porous—has achieved almost canonical status.

15. Admittedly, however, films may reinforce for some viewers more cultural boundaries than they challenge, through an emphasis on exotic elements that remain insufficiently contextualized in other aspects of daily life.

16. In much current writing, they already have. For a discussion of the history of challenges to the culture concept, see Brightman (1995).

17. They can, of course, also create and perpetuate stereotypes, but in the contempo-rary world photographic and electronic media appear to have played a greater role in spreading, and making evident the spread, of international popular culture (supported by transnational capitalism) than in promoting regional identities. Painting, literature in translation, and music (in the seventeenth and eighteenth centuries, for example) have played a similar transcultural and intercultural role, and continue to do so.

18. For an overview of these studies, see Lock (1993). Recent interest in this area includes works by Stoller (1989), Feld (1982), Taussig (1987), and Csordas (1993a).

19. Christian Metz provides a Freudian interpretation of such responses to films, arguing that one's satisfaction with a film "must stay within certain limits, must not pass the point at which anxiety and rejection would be mobilised." Otherwise the film may (in Kleinian terms) be thought a "bad object." After pointing out that films may be rejected because they are dull ("the id is insufficiently nourished by the diegesis") he continues: "But aggressivity against the film—whose conscious form in both cases consists in declaring that one has not liked it, that is to say that it has been a bad object—can result equally from an intervention of the super-ego and the defenses of the ego, which are frightened and counter-attack when the satisfaction of the id has, on the contrary, been too intense, as sometimes happens with films 'in bad taste' (taste then becomes an excellent alibi), or films that go too far, or are childish, or sentimen-tal, or sado-pornographic films, etc., in a word, films against which we defend our-selves (at least when we have been touched) by smiling or laughing, by an allegation of stupidity, grotesqueness, or 'lack of versimilitude'" (1982: 111).

20. This corporeal quality of the voice is emphasized in the following passage from E. L. Doctorow's *Billy Bathgate*: "I will say something more about Mr. Schultz's voice because it was so much an aspect of his power of domination. It was not that it was always loud but that it had a substantial body to it, it came out of his throat with harmonic buzz, and it was very instrumental actually, so that you understood the throat as a sound box, and that maybe the chest cavity and the nose bones, too, were all involved in producing it, and it was a baritone voice that automatically made you pay attention in the way of wanting a horn voice like that yourself . . ." (1989: 8).

21. The sound film is, of course, both a performance of looking and *listening*, and listening not only to sounds but to words. Films do not lack verbal expression, since this exists in the world, and we can respond to it with all the passion and intellect we possess. But words in a film remain very different from words on a page.

22. I am indebted to Ivo Strecker for introducing me to a number of the writers and concepts discussed in this section.

23. Historians, too, turn increasingly to first-person narratives in an effort to uncover neglected histories of feeling and sentiment. In his book *Return to Nothing: The Meaning of Lost Places* (1996), Peter Read explores the feelings people hold toward places they have lived by examining their experiences of seeing them destroyed, or being displaced from them. Histories of loss are also of necessity histories of attachment. In Peter Loizos's ethnography, *The Heart Grown Bitter*, a study of Cypriot war refugees, the anthropologist's interest in the experiencing subject is effectively joined with the interests of the historian.

24. There is already a Society for the Anthropology of Consciousness (a society of the American Anthropological Association) with its own quarterly journal, *Anthropology of Consciousness*; however, the work of this group has tended to focus on religious, mystical, and altered states of consciousness rather than consciousness as an aspect of everyday social experience.

25. These include the efforts of neurobiologists such as Francis Crick and Cristof Koch to explain consciousness through neuronal hierarchies, and the contrasting approaches of philosophers and mathematicians such as Daniel Dennett and David Chalmers. But even these scholars stop short of addressing the "harder" problems that lie beyond what Chalmers (1995) calls the "hard problem" of what, if anything, separates subjective experience from physical processes in the brain. For philosophers, at least, these include, but are by no means confined to, such questions as why consciousness appears at specific points in space/time (i.e., here/now) rather than being more broadly distributed throughout it, and why consciousness is necessarily linked to individual physical organisms (e.g., "me") rather than shared among an entire community or even all living organisms.

26. Metz borrows this term from L. Sève's *Marxisme et théorie de la personnalité*. See Metz (1982: 83–83 n6). It is not necessary to subscribe wholly to Metz's Lacanian view of the cinema screen as a mirror of the Imaginary to recognize that cinema reflects, and provides a way of exploring, the cultural and transcultural elements of consciousness. This was implicit in the Navajo film project of John Adair and Sol Worth, described in their book *Through Navajo Eyes* (1972). It has always been an aim of cognitive anthropology, where language rather than visual expression has provided the source materials and the "experimental model." In 1931, Walter Benjamin (1972)

drew an analogy between photography and the unconscious, but his was a rough one, for he meant only photography's ability to show us the normally inaccessible surface of the visible—details of movement revealed through slow motion, for example. The analogy would be more apt if we took it to mean that photography reveals the invisible world of thought and feeling through its expression in the visible, much as psychoanalysis seeks to show us the unconscious through its symbolic forms in our conscious life.

27. Certain recent anthropological writings exhibit such an approach and sensibility, including work by Michael Jackson, Anna Tsing, Jean Briggs, Leslie Devereaux, and Jean Lydall and Ivo Strecker. That the camera can be an expressive instrument of intersubjectivity is evident in the films of John Marshall and Jean Rouch, as well as in more recent work by such filmmakers as Gary Kildea, Eliane de Latour, and Lisbet Holtedahl. John Berger and Jean Mohr's collaborative projects involving photographs and written texts represent a similar initiative taken in another form.

28. Marcus and Fischer (1986), for example, take the anthropologist's voice unproblematically as a coherent entity or part of a dialogical pair. Bill Nichols (1983) distinguishes the voices "in the film" from the voice "of the film" (the author's), but leaves this latter term unexamined.

# Bibliography

Abel, Richard. 1984. *French Cinema: The First Wave, 1915–1929*. Princeton: Princeton University Press.

Abu-Lughod, Lila. 1991. Writing against Culture. In *Recapturing Anthropology: Working in the Present*, edited by R. G. Fox. Santa Fe, N.M.: School of American Research Press.

Agee, James, and Walker Evans. 1960. *Let Us Now Praise Famous Men*. 2nd ed. Boston: Houghton Mifflin.

Anderson, Carolyn, and Thomas W. Benson. 1991. *Documentary Dilemmas*. Carbondale: Southern Illinois University Press.

Anderson, Carolyn, and Thomas W. Benson. 1993. Put Down the Camera and Pick Up the Shovel: An Interview with John Marshall. In *The Cinema of John Marshall*, edited by J. Ruby. Chur, Switzerland: Harwood Academic Publishers.

Antoninus, Marcus Aurelius. 1891. *The Thoughts of the Emperor M. Aurelius Antoninus*. Translated by George Long. London: George Bell & Sons.

Appadurai, Arjun. 1991. Global Ethnoscapes: Notes and Queries for a Transnational Anthropology. In *Recapturing Anthropology: Working in the Present*, edited by R. G. Fox. Santa Fe, N.M.: School of American Research Press.

Asad, Talal. 1986. The Concept of Cultural Translation in British Social Anthropology. In *Writing Culture*, edited by J. Clifford and G. E. Marcus. Berkeley: University of California Press.

Asch, Timothy, John Marshall, and P. Spier. 1973. Ethnographic Film: Structure and Function. *Annual Review of Anthropology* 2:179–87.

Asch, Timothy. 1991. Das Filmen in Sequenzen und die Darstellung von Kultur. In *Jäger und Gajagte: John Marshall und Seine Filme*, edited by W.P.R. Kapfer and R. Thoms. Munich: Trickster Verlag.

Banks, Marcus. 1994. Television and Anthropology: An Unhappy Marriage? *Visual Anthropology* 7 (1):21–45.

———, and Howard Morphy, eds. 1997. *Rethinking Visual Anthropology*. New Haven and London: Yale University Press.

Barley, Nigel. 1983. *Symbolic Structures: An Exploration of the Culture of the Dowayos*. Cambridge: Cambridge University Press.

Barnouw, Eric. 1974. *Documentary: A History of the Non-Fiction Film*. 2nd revised (1993) ed. New York: Oxford University Press.

Barthes, Roland. 1975. *The Pleasure of the Text*. Translated by Richard Miller. New York: Hill and Wang.

———. 1977a. *Image-Music-Text*. Translated by Stephen Heath. Glasgow: Fontana/Collins.

———. 1977b. The Third Meaning. In *Image-Music-Text*, edited by S. Heath. Glasgow: Fontana/Collins.

———. 1979. Shock-Photos. In *The Eiffel Tower and Other Mythologies*. New York: Hill and Wang.

Barthes, Roland. 1981. *Camera Lucida*. Translated by Richard Howard. New York: Hill and Wang.

Bateson, Gregory, and Margaret Mead. 1942. *Balinese Character: A Photographic Analysis*. New York: New York Academy of Sciences, Special Publications No. 2.

———. 1977. Margaret Mead and Gregory Bateson on the Use of the Camera in Anthropology. *Studies in the Anthropology of Visual Communication* 4 (2):78–80.

Bateson, Gregory. 1943. Cultural and Thematic Analysis of Fiction Films. *Transactions of the New York Academy of Sciences* 5:72–78.

Baxter, P.T.W. 1977. The Rendille. *Royal Anthropological Institute Newsletter* 20:7–9.

Benedict, Ruth. 1946. *The Chrysanthemum and the Sword*. Boston: Houghton Mifflin.

Benjamin, Walter. 1968. The Work of Art in the Age of Mechanical Reproduction. In *Illuminations: Essays and Reflections*, edited by H. Arendt. New York: Schocken Books.

———. 1972. A Short History of Photography. *Screen* 13 (1):5–26.

Berger, John. 1980. Uses of Photography. In *About Looking*. London: Writers and Readers Publishing Cooperative.

Berry, J. W., and Elizabeth Sommerlad. n.d. Ethnocentrism and the Evaluation of an Ethnographic Film. Kingston, Ontario and Canberra: Department of Psychology, Queen's University and Department of Psychology, Australian National University.

Bloch, Maurice. 1974. Symbols, Song, Dance and Features of Articulation: or Is Religion an Extreme Form of Traditional Authority? *Archives européenes de sociologie* 15:55–81.

———. 1986. *From Blessing to Violence*. Cambridge: Cambridge University Press.

Blue, James, David MacDougall, and Colin Young. 1975. Conversation recorded January 5, 1975. Unpublished.

Blue, James. 1967. Jean Rouch in Conversation with James Blue. *Film Comment* 4 (2–3):84–86.

Bordwell, David. 1985. *Narration in the Fiction Film*. Madison: University of Wisconsin Press.

Brandes, Stanley. 1992. Sex Roles and Anthropological Research in Rural Andalusia. In *Europe Observed*, edited by J. de Pina-Cabral and J. Campbell. London: Macmillan.

Branigan, Edward. 1984. *Point of View in the Cinema: A Theory of Narration and Subjectivity in Classical Film*. New York and Berlin: Mouton.

Bresson, Robert. 1977. *Notes on Cinematography*. Translated by Jonathan Griffin. New York: Urizon Books.

Briggs, Jean L. 1970. *Never in Anger: Portrait of an Eskimo Family*. Cambridge, Mass.: Harvard University Press.

Brightman, Robert. 1995. Forget Culture: Replacement, Transcendence, Relexification. *Cultural Anthropology* 10 (4):509–46.

Brown, Penelope, and Stephen Levinson. 1978. Universals in Language Usage: Politeness Phenomena. In *Questions and Politeness: Strategies in Social Interaction*, edited by E. N. Goody. Cambridge: Cambridge University Press.

Browne, Nick. 1975. The Spectator-in-the-Text: The Rhetoric of *Stagecoach*. *Film Quarterly* 29 (2):26–38.

Bruner, Edward M., and Phyllis Gorfain. 1984. Dialogic Narration and the Paradoxes of Masada. In *Text, Play and Story: The Construction and Reconstruction of Self and*

*Society*, edited by E. M. Bruner. Washington, D.C.: 1983 Proceedings of The American Ethnological Society.

Bruner, Jerome S. 1964. The Course of Cognitive Growth. *American Psychologist* 19:1–15.

Buck-Morss, Susan. 1994. The Cinema Screen as Prosthesis of Perception: A Historical Account. In *The Senses Still*, edited by C. N. Seremetakis. Boulder, Colo.: Westview Press.

Burgin, Victor. 1982. Photography, Phantasy, Function. In *Thinking Photography*, edited by V. Burgin. London: Macmillan Education.

Caldwell, Erskine, and Margaret Bourke-White. 1937. *You Have Seen Their Faces*. New York: The Viking Press.

Capra, Frank. 1985. *The Name Above the Title*. New York: Vintage Books.

Cardinal, Roger. 1986. Pausing over Peripheral Detail. *Framework* 30–31:112–33.

Carpenter, Edmund, and Ken Heyman. 1970. *They Became What They Beheld*. New York: Outerbridge & Dienstfrey/Ballantine Books.

Carpenter, Edmund. 1976. *Oh, What a Blow That Phantom Gave Me!* St. Albans: Paladin.

———. 1980. If Wittgenstein Had Been an Eskimo. *Natural History* 89 (2):72–76.

Cavadini, Alessandro, and Carolyn Strachan. 1981. Two Laws/Kanymarda Yuwa, an Interview Conducted by Charles Mcrewether and Leslie Stern. In *Media Interventions*, edited by J. Allen and J. Freeland. Sydney: Intervention Publications.

Chakrabarty, Dipesh. 1993. Marx after Marxism: History, Subalternity and Difference. *Meanjin* 52 (3):421–34.

Chalmers, David J. 1995. Explaining Consciousness: The "Hard Problem." *Journal of Consciousness Studies* 2 (3) (Special Issue).

Clifford, James. 1986. Introduction: Partial Truths. In *Writing Culture. The Poetics and Politics of Ethnography*, edited by J. Clifford and G. E. Marcus. Berkeley: University of California Press.

———. 1988. On Ethnographic Surrealism. In *The Predicament of Culture*. Cambridge, Mass.: Harvard University Press.

Csordas, Thomas J. 1993a. *The Sacred Self: A Cultural Phenomenology of Charismatic Healing*. Berkeley: University of California Press.

———. 1993b. Somatic Modes of Attention. *Cultural Anthropology* 8 (2):135–56.

Dayan, Daniel. 1974. The Tutor-Code of Classical Cinema. *Film Quarterly* 28 (1):22–31.

De Brigard, E. 1975. The History of Ethnographic Film. In *Principles of Visual Anthropology*, edited by Paul Hockings. The Hague: Mouton.

de Heusch, Luc. 1962. *The Cinema and Social Science: A Survey of Ethnographic and Sociological Films, Reports and Papers in the Social Sciences No. 16*. Paris: UNESCO.

de Lauretis, Teresa. 1984. Desire and Narrative. In *Alice Doesn't: Feminism, Semiotics, Cinema*. Bloomington: Indiana University Press.

———. 1987. *Technologies of Gender: Essays on Theory, Film, and Fiction*. Bloomington: Indiana University Press.

Deleuze, Gilles. 1986. *Cinema 1: The Movement-Image*. Translated by Hugh Tomlinson and Barbara Habberjam. Minneapolis: University of Minnesota Press.

Dewey, John. 1894. The Theory of Emotion. *Psychological Review* 1 (1894):553–69, 2 (1895):13–32.

Dillon, M. C. 1988. *Merleau-Ponty's Ontology*. Bloomington: Indiana University Press.

Doctorow, E. L. 1989. *Billy Bathgate*. London: Macmillan London Limited.

Douglas, Mary. 1966. *Purity and Danger*. Baltimore: Penguin Books.

———. 1970. *Natural Symbols: Explorations in Cosmology*. London: Cresset.

Dumont, Louis. 1970. *Homo Hierarchicus: An Essay on the Caste System*. Chicago: Chicago University Press.

Dunlop, Ian. 1983. Ethnographic Filmmaking in Australia: The First Seventy Years (1898–1968). *Studies in Visual Communication* 9 (1):11–18.

Edwards, Elizabeth. 1990. Photographic "Types": The Pursuit of Method. *Visual Anthropology* 3 (2–3):235–58.

Eisenstein, Sergei. 1957. Methods of Montage. In *Film Form*. New York: Meridian Books.

Ekman, Paul, Wallace V. Friesen, and P. Ellsworth. 1972. *Emotion in the Human Face: Guidelines for Research and an Integration of Findings*. New York: Pergamon Press.

Evans-Pritchard, E. E. 1940. *The Nuer*. Oxford: The Clarendon Press.

———. 1956. *Nuer Religion*. Oxford: Oxford University Press.

———. 1962. *Social Anthropology and Other Essays*. Glencoe: Free Press.

Faris, James C. 1992. Photography, Power and the Southeast Nuba. In *Anthropology and Photography 1860–1920*, edited by E. Edwards. New Haven and London: Yale University Press.

Feld, Steven. 1982. *Sound and Sentiment: Birds, Weeping, Poetics, and Song in Kaluli Expression*. Philadelphia: University of Pennsylvania Press.

Flaherty, Robert. 1950. Robert Flaherty Talking. In *The Cinema 1950*, edited by R. Manvell. Harmondsworth: Penguin Books.

Forster, E. M. 1927. *Aspects of the Novel*. London: Edward Arnold & Co.

Fulchignoni, Enrico, and Jean Rouch. 1981. Entretien de Jean Rouch avec le Professeur Enrico Fulchignoni. In *Jean Rouch: une rétrospective*. Paris: Ministère des Affairs Etrangères—Animation audio-visuelle, et Service d'Etude, de Réalisation et de Diffusion de Documents Audio-Visuels [SERDDAV] du CNRS.

Furhammar, Leif, and Folke Isaksson. 1971. *Politics and Film*. London: Studio Vista.

Gage, Nicholas. 1982. *Eleni*. New York: Random House.

Gandelman, Claude. 1991. Touching with the Eye. In *Reading Pictures, Viewing Texts*. Bloomington: Indiana University Press.

Gardner, Howard. 1985. *The Mind's New Science*. New York: Basic Books.

Gardner, Robert, and Karl Heider. 1968. *Gardens of War*. New York: Random House.

Gardner, Robert. 1957. Anthropology and Film. *Daedalus* 86:344–52.

———. 1969. Chronicles of the Human Experience: *Dead Birds*. *Film Library Quarterly* (fall):25–34.

———. 1972. On the Making of *Dead Birds*. In *The Dani of West Irian*, edited by K. G. Heider: Warner Modular Publications.

Geertz, Clifford. 1972. Deep Play: Notes on the Balinese Cockfight. *Daedalus* 101 (1):1–37.

———. 1973a. *The Interpretation of Cultures*. New York: Basic Books.

———. 1973b. Person, Time and Conduct in Bali. In *The Interpretation of Cultures*. New York: Basic Books.

———. 1975. On the Nature of Anthropological Understanding. *American Scientist* 63:47–53.

————. 1980. Blurred Genres: The Refiguration of Social Thought. *American Scholar* 49 (2):165–79.

————. 1988. *Works and Lives: The Anthropologist as Author*. Stanford, Calif.: Stanford University Press.

Geffroy, Yannick. 1990. Family Photographs: A Visual Heritage. *Visual Anthropology* 3 (4):367–409.

Ginsburg, Faye. 1994. Culture/Media: A (Mild) Polemic. *Anthropology Today* 10 (2):5–15.

Goffman, Erving. 1967. *Interaction Ritual: Essays on Face-to-Face Behavior*. Garden City, N.Y.: Doubleday.

Goldschmidt, Walter. 1969. *Kambuya's Cattle: The Legacy of an African Herdsman*. Berkeley: University of California Press.

————. 1972. Ethnographic Film: Definition and Exegesis. *PIEF Newsletter* 3 (2): 1–3.

Gombrich, E. H. 1960. *Art and Illusion*. Princeton: Princeton University Press.

————. 1972. The Mask and the Face: The Perception of Physiognomic Likeness in Life and Art. In *Art, Perception, and Reality*, edited by E. H. Gombrich, J. Hochberg, and M. Black. Baltimore: The Johns Hopkins University Press.

Goodman, Nelson. 1968. *Languages of Art*. New York: Bobbs-Merrill.

Grandin, Temple. 1995. *Thinking in Pictures, and Other Reports from My Life with Autism*. New York: Doubleday.

Griaule, Marcel. 1938. *Marques dogons*. Paris: Institut d'Ethnologie.

Grice, H. P. 1975. Logic and Conversation. In *Syntax and Semantics, Vol. 3: Speech Acts*, edited by P. Cole and J. C. Morgan. New York: Academic Press.

Grimshaw, Anna. 1992. *Servants of the Buddha*. London: Open Letters.

Gross, Larry. 1981. Introduction. In *Studying Visual Communication, Essays by Sol Worth*. Philadelphia: University of Pennsylvania Press.

Gupta, Akhil, and James Ferguson. 1992. Beyond "Culture": Space, Identity, and the Politics of Difference. *Cultural Anthropology* 7 (1):6–23.

Hastrup, Kirsten. 1992. Anthropological Visions: Some Notes on Visual and Textual Authority. In *Film as Ethnography*, edited by P. I. Crawford and D. Turton. Manchester: Manchester University Press.

Hearn, P., and P. DeVore. 1973. The Netsilik and Yanomamö on Film and in Print. Washington, D.C.: Paper presented at Film Studies of Changing Man conference, The Smithsonian Institution.

Heider, Karl G. 1976. *Ethnographic Film*. Austin: University of Texas Press.

————. 1991. *Indonesian Cinema: National Culture on Screen*. Honolulu: University of Hawaii Press.

Henderson, Brian. 1970. Towards a Non-Bourgeois Camera Style. *Film Quarterly* 24 (2):2–14.

————. 1971. The Long Take. *Film Comment* 7 (2):6–11.

————. 1991. The Civil War: "Did It Not Seem Real?" *Film Quarterly* 44 (3):2–14.

Henley, Paul. 1985. British Ethnographic Film: Recent Developments. *Anthropology Today* 1:5–17.

Hinsley, Curtis M. 1991. The World as Marketplace: Commodification of the Exotic at the World's Columbian Exposition, Chicago, 1893. In *Exhibiting Cultures*, edited by I. Karp and S. D. Lavine. Washington, D.C.: Smithsonian Institution Press.

Hockings, Paul. 1975. *Principles of Visual Anthropology*. The Hague: Mouton Publishers.

Holland, Dorothy, and Naomi Quinn, eds. 1987. *Cultural Models in Language and Thought*. Cambridge: Cambridge University Press.

Horowitz, Mardi Jon. 1970. *Image Formation and Cognition*. New York: Appleton-Century-Crofts.

Houtman, Gustaaf. 1988. Interview with Maurice Bloch. *Anthropology Today* 4 (1): 18–21.

Hymes, Dell. 1972. The Use of Anthropology: Critical, Political, Personal. In *Reinventing Anthropology*, edited by D. Hymes. New York: Pantheon Books.

Jackson, Michael. 1986. *Barawa and the Ways Birds Fly in the Sky*. Washington, D.C.: Smithsonian Institution Press.

———. 1989. Knowledge of the Body. In *Paths Toward a Clearing*. Bloomington: Indiana University Press.

———. 1989. *Paths Toward a Clearing: Radical Empiricism and Ethnographic Inquiry*. Bloomington: Indiana University Press.

Jameson, Fredric. 1983. Pleasure: A Political Issue. In *Formations of Pleasure*, edited by F. Jameson. London: Routledge.

Jeanne, René. 1965. *Cinéma 1900*. Paris: Flammarion.

Jonas, Hans. 1966. *The Phenomenon of Life: Toward a Philosophical Biology*. New York: Harper & Row.

Kertesz, Andrew. 1979. Visual Agnosia: The Dual Deficit of Perception and Recognition. *Cortex* 15:403–19.

Knight, John, and Laura Rival. 1992. An Interview with Philippe Descola. *Anthropology Today* 8 (2):9–13.

Kracauer, Siegfried. 1947. *From Caligari to Hitler*. Princeton: Princeton University Press.

Kuhn, Thomas. 1962. *The Structure of Scientific Revolutions*. Chicago: University of Chicago Press.

Lacan, Jacques. 1977. The Mirror Stage as Formative of the Function of the I. In *Écrits: A Selection*. London: Tavistock.

Lakoff, George, and Mark Johnson. 1980. *Metaphors We Live By*. Chicago: Chicago University Press.

Leach, Edmund. 1961. *Rethinking Anthropology*. London: Monographs on Social Anthropology No. 22, University of London, The Athlone Press.

Leroi-Gourhan, André. 1948. Cinéma et sciences humaines: le film cthnographique existe-t-il? *Rev. Géogr. Hum. Ethnol.* 3:42–51.

Lévi-Strauss, Claude. 1966. Anthropology: Its Achievements and Future. *Current Anthropology* 7 (2):124–27.

———. 1974. *Tristes Tropiques*. New York: Atheneum.

Levin, G. Roy. 1971. *Documentary Explorations*. New York: Doubleday.

Lewis, Gilbert. 1980. *Day of Shining Red*. Cambridge: Cambridge University Press.

———. 1985. The Look of Magic. *Man (N.S.)* 21:414–47.

Lewis, Oscar. 1961. *The Children of Sanchez*. New York: Random House.

Leyda, Jay. 1960. *Kino*. London: George Allen & Unwin.

Lienhardt, Godfrey. 1954. Modes of Thought. In *The Institutions of Primitive Society*, edited by E. E. Evans-Pritchard. Oxford: Basil Blackwell.

Lock, Margaret. 1993. Cultivating the Body: Anthropology and Epistemologies of Bodily Practice and Knowledge. *Annual Review of Anthropology* 22:133–55.

Loizos, Peter. 1981. *The Heart Grown Bitter*. Cambridge: Cambridge University Press.

———. 1992. User-Friendly Ethnography? In *Europe Observed*, edited by J. de Pina-Cabral and J. Campbell. London: Macmillan.

———. 1993. *Innovation in Ethnographic Film: From Innocence to Self-Consciousness, 1955–1985*. Manchester: Manchester University Press.

Luria, A. R. 1968. *The Mind of a Mnemonist*. Translated by Lynn Solotaroff. Cambridge, Mass.: Harvard University Press.

Lutz, Catherine, and Jane L. Collins. 1993. *Reading National Geographic*. Chicago: Chicago University Press.

Lydall, Jean, and Ivo Strecker. 1979. *Baldambe Explains*. Arbeiten aus dem Institut für Völkerkunde der Universität zu Göttingen—Band 13 ed. 3 vols. Vol. 2, *The Hamar of Southern Ethiopia*. Hohenschäftlarn, Germany: Klaus Renner Verlag.

Lyon, Margot L. 1995. Missing Emotion: The Limitations of Cultural Constructionism in the Study of Emotion. *Cultural Anthropology* 10 (2):244–63.

Lyon, Margot L., and J. M. Barbalet. 1994. Society's Body: Emotion and the "Somatization" of Social Theory. In *Embodiment and Experience: The Existential Ground of Culture and Self*, edited by T. J. Csordas. Cambridge: Cambridge University Press.

MacBean, James Roy. 1983. *Two Laws* from Australia, One white, One Black. *Film Quarterly* 36 (3):30–43.

MacDougall, David. 1975. Beyond Observational Cinema. In *Principles of Visual Anthropology*, edited by P. Hockings. The Hague: Mouton.

———. 1978. Ethnographic Film: Failure and Promise. *Annual Review of Anthropology* 7:405–25.

———. 1981. A Need for Common Terms. *SAVICOM Newsletter* 9 (1):5–6.

Malinowski, Bronislaw. 1922. *Argonauts of the Western Pacific*. London: Routledge & Kegan Paul.

Marcus, George E. 1990. The Modernist Sensibility in Recent Ethnographic Writing and the Cinematic Metaphor of Montage. *Society for Visual Anthropology Review* 6 (1):2–12, 21, 44.

Marcus, George, and Michael M. J. Fischer. 1986. *Anthropology as Cultural Critique*. Chicago: University of Chicago Press.

Marey, Étienne-Jules. 1883. Emploi des photographies partielles pour étudier la locomotion de l'homme et des animaux. *Comptes Rendus de l'Academie des Sciences* 96:1827–31.

Marshall, John. 1993. Filming and Learning. In *The Cinema of John Marshall*, edited by J. Ruby. Chur, Switzerland: Harwood Academic Publishers.

Martinez, Wilton. 1990. Critical Studies and Visual Anthropology: Aberrant vs. Anticipated Readings of Ethnographic Film. *Society for Visual Anthropology Review* (spring):34–47.

Mauss, Marcel. 1973. Techniques of the Body. *Economy and Society* 2 (1):70–88.

Maybury-Lewis, David. 1967. *Akwe-Shavante Society*. Oxford: The Clarendon Press.

Mayne, Judith. 1993. *Cinema and Spectatorship*. New York: Routledge.

McNeill, David, and Elena Levy. 1982. Conceptual Representations in Language Activity and Gesture. In *Speech, Place, and Action*, edited by R. J. Jarvella and W. Klein. Chichester: John Wiley & Sons.

Mead, Margaret. 1975. Visual Anthropology in a Discipline of Words. In *Principles of Visual Anthropology*, edited by P. Hockings. The Hague: Mouton.

Mehta, Ved. 1980. *The Photographs of Chachaji*. New York: Oxford University Press.

Merleau-Ponty, Maurice. 1964a. The Child's Relations with Others. In *The Primacy of Perception*, edited by J. M. Edie. Evanston, Ill.: Northwestern University Press.

———. 1964b. Eye and Mind. In *The Primacy of Perception*, edited by J. M. Edie. Evanston, Ill.: Northwestern University Press.

———. 1968. *The Visible and the Invisible*. Translated by Alphonso Lingis. Evanston, Ill.: Northwestern University Press.

———. 1974. Indirect Language and the Voices of Silence. In *Phenomenology, Language and Sociology: Selected Essays of Maurice Merleau-Ponty*, edited by J. O'Neill. London: Heinemann.

———. 1992. *Phenomenology of Perception*. Translated by Colin Smith. London: Routledge & Kegan Paul.

Mermin, Elizabeth. 1997. "Being Where?: Experiencing Narratives of Ethnographic Film." *Visual Anthropology Review* 13 (1): 40–51.

Metz, Christian. 1974. *Film Language*. Oxford: Oxford University Press.

———. 1982. *Psychoanalysis and Cinema: The Imaginary Signifier*. Translated by Celia Britton, Annwyl Williams, Ben Brewster, and Alfred Guzzetti. Edited by S. Heath and C. MacCabe, *Language, Discourse, Society*. London: Macmillan Press.

Meyer, Leonard B. 1956. *Emotion and Meaning in Music*. Chicago: The University of Chicago Press.

Mintz, Sidney W. 1960. *Worker in the Cane: A Puerto Rican Life History*. New Haven: Yale University Press.

Mitchell, W.J.T. 1994. *Picture Theory*. Chicago: Chicago University Press.

———. 1995. Interdisciplinarity and Visual Culture. *Art Bulletin* 76 (4):540–44.

Moore, Alexander. 1988. The Limitations of Imagist Documentary. *Society for Visual Anthropology Newsletter* 4 (2):1–3.

Morin, Edgar. 1962. Preface. In *The Cinema and Social Science: A Survey of Ethnographic and Sociological Films*, edited by L. d. Heusch. Paris: UNESCO Reports and Papers in the Social Sciences 16.

Muybridge, Eadweard. 1887. *Animal Locomotion: An Electro-Photographic Investigation of Consecutive Phases of Animal Movements*. 16 vols. Philadelphia: J. B. Lippincott.

Myers, Fred R. 1988. From Ethnography to Metaphor: Recent Films from David and Judith MacDougall. *Cultural Anthropology* 3 (2):205–20.

Nandy, Ashis. 1983. *The Intimate Enemy: Loss and Recovery of Self under Colonialism*. Oxford: Oxford University Press.

Nichols, Bill. 1981. *Ideology and the Image: Social Representation in the Cinema and Other Media*. Bloomington: Indiana University Press.

———. 1983. The Voice of Documentary. *Film Quarterly* 36 (3):17–30.

———. 1986. Questions of Magnitude. In *Documentary and the Mass Media*, edited by J. Corner. London: Edward Arnold.

———. 1991. *Representing Reality: Issues and Concepts in Documentary*. Bloomington: Indiana University Press.

———. 1994a. *Blurred Boundaries: Questions of Meaning in Contemporary Culture*. Bloomington: Indiana University Press.

———. 1994b. The Ethnographer's Tale. In *Blurred Boundaries: Questions of Meaning in Contemporary Culture*. Bloomington: Indiana University Press.

Nichols, Bill, ed. 1976. *Movies and Methods*. Berkeley: University of California Press.

Oudart, Jean-Pierre. 1969. La Suture. *Cahiers du Cinema* 211 (April):36–39; 212 (May):50–56.

Paivio, Allan. 1971. *Imagery and Verbal Processes*. New York: Holt, Rinehart.

Parry, Jonathan. 1988. Comment on Robert Gardner's "Forest of Bliss." *Society for Visual Anthropology Newsletter* 4 (2):4–7.

Paulhan, F. 1930. *The Laws of Feeling*. Translated by C. K. Ogden. New York: Harcourt, Brace and Company.

Piault, Marc-Henri. 1989. Ritual: A Way Out of Eternity. Paper read at Film and Representations of Culture, September 28, at the Humanities Research Centre, Australian National University, Canberra.

Pinney, Christopher. 1990. Classification and Fantasy in the Photographic Construction of Caste and Tribe. *Visual Anthropology* 3 (2–3):259–88.

———. 1992a. The Lexical Spaces of Eye-Spy. In *Film as Ethnography*, edited by P. I. Crawford and D. Turton. Manchester: Manchester University Press.

———. 1992b. The Parallel Histories of Anthropology and Photography. In *Anthropology and Photography*, edited by E. Edwards. New Haven: Yale University Press.

———. 1995. Indian Figure: Visual Anthropology and the Anthropology of the Visual. Paper read at Visual Anthropology at the Crossroads, May 6–11, 1995, at the School of American Research, Santa Fe, N.M.

Polanyi, Michael. 1966. *The Tacit Dimension*. Garden City, N.Y.: Doubleday & Company.

Pratt, Mary Louise. 1986. Fieldwork in Common Places. In *Writing Culture: The Poetics and Politics of Ethnography*, edited by J. Clifford and G. E. Marcus. Berkeley: University of California Press.

Preloran, Jorge. 1987. Ethical and Aesthetic Concerns in Ethnographic Film. *Third World Affairs*. 461–79.

Pribram, K. H. 1970. Feelings as Monitors. In *Feelings and Emotions: The Loyola Symposium*, edited by M. B. Arnold. New York: Academic Press.

Rabinow, Paul. 1977. *Reflections on Fieldwork in Morocco*. Berkeley: University of California Press.

Read, Kenneth E. 1966. *The High Valley*. London: C. Allen and Unwin.

Read, Peter. 1996. *Return to Nothing: The Meaning of Lost Places*. Cambridge: Cambridge University Press.

Reddy, Michael J. 1993. The Conduit Metaphor: A Case of Frame Conflict in Our Language about Canguage. In *Metaphor and Thought*, edited by A. Ortony. Cambridge: Cambridge University Press.

Regnault, Félix-Louis. 1931. Le Rôle du cinema en ethnographie. *La Nature* 59:304–6.

Reichlin, Seth, and John Marshall. 1974. *An Argument about a Marriage: The Study Guide*. Somerville, Mass.: Documentary Educational Resources.

Reisz, Karel, and Gavin Millar. 1968. *The Technique of Film Editing*. 2nd enlarged ed. London: Focal Press.

Renov, Michael. 1993. Toward a Poetics of Documentary. In *Theorizing Documentary*, edited by M. Renov. New York: Routledge.

Rivers, W.H.R. 1906. *The Todas*. London: Macmillan.

Rollwagen, Jack A. 1988. The Role of Anthropological Theory in "Ethnographic" Filmmaking. In *Anthropological Filmmaking*, edited by J. A. Rollwagen. Chur, Switzerland: Harwood Academic Publishers.

Rorty, Richard. 1980. *Philosophy and the Mirror of Nature*. Oxford: Basil Blackwell.

Rosaldo, Michelle Z. 1980. *Knowledge and Passion: Ilongot Notions of Self and Social Life*. New York: Cambridge University Press.

Rosaldo, Renato. 1986. Ilongot Hunting as Story and Experience. In *The Anthropology of Experience*, edited by V. W. Turner and E. M. Bruner. Champaign: University of Illinois Press.

Rosenfeld, Israel. 1984. Seeing Through the Brain. *New York Review of Books* 31 (15):53–56.

Rosenthal, Alan, ed. 1971. *The New Documentary in Action*. Berkeley: University of California Press.

————. 1980. *The Documentary Conscience*. Berkeley: University of California Press.

Rotha, Paul. 1930. *The Film Till Now*. London: Jonathan Cape.

Rouch, Jean. 1971. Interview. In *Documentary Explorations*, edited by G. R. Levin. New York: Doubleday.

————. 1974. The Camera and Man. *Studies in the Anthropology of Visual Communication* 1 (1):37–44.

————. 1975. The Camera and Man. In *Principles of Visual Anthropology*, edited by P. Hockings. The Hague: Mouton.

————. 1981. Interview by Enrico Fulchignoni, August 1980. In *Jean Rouch: une retrospective*. Paris: Ministère des Affaires Etrangères.

Ruby, Jay. 1975. Is an Ethnographic Film a Filmic Ethnography? *Studies in the Anthropology of Visual Communication* 2 (2):104–11.

————. 1977. The Image Mirrored: Reflexivity and the Documentary Film. *Journal of the University Film Association* 29 (4):3–13.

————. 1980. Exposing Yourself: Reflexivity, Anthropology, and Film. *Semiotica* 30 (1–2):153–79.

————. 1989. The Emperor and His Clothes. *Society for Visual Anthropology Newsletter* 5 (1):9–11.

————. 1991. Speaking For, Speaking About, Speaking With, or Speaking Alongside: An Anthropological and Documentary Dilemma. *Visual Anthropology Review* 7 (2):50–67.

————. 1994. Review of *Film as Ethnography*, edited by Peter Ian Crawford, and *Innovation in Ethnographic Film* by Peter Loizos. *Visual Anthropology Review* 10 (1):165–69.

Ruskin, John. 1887. *Praeterita: Outlines of Scenes and Thoughts, Perhaps Worthy of Memory, in My Past Life*. New Edition, 1949 ed. London: R. Hart Davis.

Russell, Bertrand. 1912. *The Problems of Philosophy*. London: Oxford University Press.

Sacks, Oliver. 1984. *A Leg to Stand On*. London: Gerald Duckworth.

————. 1985. The Disembodied Lady. In *The Man Who Mistook His Wife for a Hat*. London: Picador.

————. 1995a. Prodigies. In *An Anthropologist on Mars*. London: Picador.

————. 1995b. To See and Not See. In *An Anthropologist on Mars*. London: Picador.

Sadoul, Georges. 1962. *Histoire du cinéma*. Paris: Flammarion.

Salmond, Anne. 1982. Theoretical Landscapes: On Cross-Cultural Conceptions of Knowledge. In *Semantic Anthropology*, edited by D. Parkin. London: Academic Press.

Salt, Barry. 1974. Statistical Style Analysis of Motion Pictures. *Film Quarterly* 28 (1):13–22.

Sandall, Roger. 1969. Ethnographic Films—What Are They Saying? *Australian Institute of Aboriginal Studies Newsletter* 2 (10):18–19.

Sapir, Edward. 1949a. The Emergence of the Concept of Personality in a Study of Cultures. In *Selected Writings of Edward Sapir*, edited by D. G. Mandelbaum. Berkeley: University of California Press.

———. 1949b. The Unconscious Patterning of Behavior in Society. In *Selected Writings of Edward Sapir*, edited by D. G. Mandelbaum. Berkeley: University of California Press.

Schwartz, B. J. 1955. The Measurement of Castration Anxiety and Anxiety over Loss of Love. *Journal of Personality* 24:204–19.

Selfe, Lorna. 1977. *Nadia: A Case of Extraordinary Drawing Ability in an Autistic Child*. London: Academic Press.

———. 1983. *Normal and Anomalous Representational Drawing Ability in Children*. London: Academic Press.

Seligmann, C. G., and Brenda Z. Seligman. 1911. *The Veddas*. Cambridge: Cambridge University Press.

Sherman, Sharon R. 1985. Human Documents: Folklore and the Films of Jorge Preloran. *Southwest Folklore* 6 (1):17–61.

Shostak, Marjorie. 1981. *Nisa, the Life and Words of a !Kung Woman*. Cambridge, Mass.: Harvard University Press.

Shweder, Richard A. 1984a. Anthropology's Romantic Rebellion against the Enlightenment, or There's More to Thinking than Reason and Evidence. In *Culture Theory: Essays on Mind, Self, and Emotion*, edited by R. A. Shweder and R. A. LeVine. Cambridge: Cambridge University Press.

———. 1984b. Preview: A Colloquy of Culture Theorists. In *Culture Theory: Essays on Mind, Self, and Emotion*, edited by R. A. Shweder and R. A. LeVine. Cambridge: Cambridge University Press.

———. 1991. Rethinking Culture and Personality Theory. In *Thinking Through Cultures: Expeditions in Cultural Psychology*. Cambridge, Mass.: Harvard University Press.

Simpson, J. A., and E.S.C. Weiner, eds. 1989. *The Oxford English Dictionary*. Second Edition. Oxford: Clarendon Press.

Singer, André. 1992. Anthropology in Broadcasting. In *Film as Ethnography*, edited by P. I. Crawford and D. Turton. Manchester: Manchester University Press.

Smith, Mary F. 1954. *Baba of Karo: A Woman of the Muslim Hausa*. London: Faber and Faber.

Sobchack, Vivian. 1992. *The Address of the Eye*. Princeton: Princeton University Press.

Solomon, Robert C. 1984. Getting Angry: The Jamesian Theory of Emotion in Anthropology. In *Culture Theory*, edited by R. A. Shweder and R. A. LeVine. Cambridge: Cambridge University Press.

Sontag, Susan. 1966. Against Interpretation. In *Against Interpretation*. New York: Farrar, Strauss & Giroux.

Sontag, Susan. 1969. The Aesthetics of Silence. In *Styles of Radical Will*. New York: Farrar, Strauss and Giroux.

———. 1977. *On Photography*. New York: Farrar, Straus and Giroux.

Sorenson, E. Richard, and Allison Jablonko. 1975. Research Filming of Naturally Occurring Phenomena: Basic Strategies. In *Principles of Visual Anthropology*, edited by P. Hockings. The Hague: Mouton.

Sorenson, E. Richard. 1967. A Research Film Program in the Study of Changing Man. *Current Anthropology* 8:443–69.

———. 1976. *The Edge of the Forest*. Washington, D.C.: Smithsonian Institution Press.

Spencer, Frank. 1992. Some Notes on the Attempt to Apply Photography to Anthropometry during the Second Half of the Nineteenth Century. In *Anthropology and Photography*, edited by E. Edwards. New Haven: Yale University Press.

Stanner, W.E.H. 1958. Continuity and Change among the Aborigines. *Australian Journal of Science* 21 (5a):99–109.

Stein, Gertrude. 1934. *The Making of Americans*. New York: Harcourt, Brace & World, Inc.

Stoller, Paul. 1989. *The Taste of Ethnographic Things: The Senses in Anthropology*. Philadelphia: University of Pennsylvania Press.

———. 1992. *The Cinematic Griot: The Ethnography of Jean Rouch*. Chicago: University of Chicago Press.

Stott, William. 1973. *Documentary Expression and Thirties America*. New York: Oxford University Press.

Strathern, Marilyn. 1987. Out of Context: The Persuasive Fictions of Anthropology. *Current Anthropology* 28 (3):251–81.

———. 1989. Comment on "Ethnography without Tears" by Paul A. Roth. *Current Anthropology* 30 (5):565–66.

Strecker, Ivo. 1988. *The Social Practice of Symbolization*, London School of Economics Monographs on Social Anthropology No. 60. London: The Athlone Press.

———. 1997. The Turbulence of Images: On Imagery, Media, and Ethnographic Discourse. *Visual Anthropology* 9 (3–4):207–27.

Sutherland, Allan T. 1978. Wiseman on Polemic. *Sight and Sound* 47 (2):82.

Sutton, Peter. 1978. Some Observations on Aboriginal Use of Filming at Cape Keerweer, 1977. Paper read at Ethnographic Film Conference, May 13, at Australian Institute of Aboriginal Studies, Canberra.

Swedish State Institute of Race Biology. 1926. *The Racial Characteristics of the Swedish Nation*. Uppsala.

Symons, A.J.A. 1934. *The Quest for Corvo: An Experiment in Biography*. London: Cassell.

Taussig, Michael T. 1987. *Shamanism, Colonialism, and the Wild Man: A Study in Terror and Healing*. Chicago: University of Chicago Press.

Taylor, Lucien. 1996. Iconophobia. *Transition* 6 (1):64–88.

Thomas, Nicholas. 1991. Against Ethnography. *Cultural Anthropology* 6 (3):306–22.

Thompson, Kristin. 1986. The Concept of Cinematic Excess. In *Narrative, Apparatus, Ideology*, edited by P. Rosen. New York: Columbia University Press.

Tillman, Frank. 1987. The Photographic Image and the Transformation of Thought. *East-West Film Journal* 1 (2):91–110.

Tolstoy, Leo. 1982. *War and Peace*. Translated by Rosemary Edmunds. Harmondsworth: Penguin Books.

Toren, Christina. 1993. Making History: The Significance of Childhood Cognition for a Comparative Anthropology of the Mind. *Man (N.S.)* 28 (3):461–77.

Truffaut, François, and Marcel Moussy. 1969. *The 400 Blows: A Filmscript*. Edited by D. Denby. New York: Grove Press.

Truffaut, François. 1967. *Hitchcock*. New York: Simon and Schuster.

Turnbull, Colin. 1973. *The Mountain People*. London: Jonathan Cape.

Turner, Victor. 1967. *The Forest of Symbols: Studies in Ndembu Ritual*. Ithaca, New York: Cornell University Press.

———. 1981. Social Dramas and Stories about Them. In *On Narrative*, edited by W.J.T. Mitchell. Chicago: University of Chicago Press.

Turton, David. 1992. Anthropology on Television: What Next? In *Film as Ethnography*, edited by P. I. Crawford and D. Turton. Manchester: Manchester University Press.

Tyler, Stephen A. 1978. *The Said and the Unsaid*. New York: Academic Press.

Tyler, Stephen A., and George E. Marcus. 1987. Comment on "Out of Context: The Persuasive Fictions of Anthropology" by Marilyn Strathern. *Current Anthropology* 28 (3):275–77.

Tyler, Stephen. 1987. *The Unspeakable: Discourse, Dialogue and Rhetoric in the Postmodern World*. Madison: University of Wisconsin Press.

Urry, James. 1972. *Notes and Queries on Anthropology* and the Development of Field Methods in British Anthropology, 1870–1920. *Proceedings of the Royal Anthropological Institute of Great Britain and Northern Ireland*:45–57.

Valéry, Paul. 1970. The Centenary of Photography. In *Occasions*. Princeton: Princeton University Press.

Vaughan, Dai. 1976. *Television Documentary Usage*. London: British Film Institute.

———. 1981. Let There Be Lumière. *Sight and Sound* 50 (2):126–27.

———. 1985. The Space between Shots. In *Movies and Methods, Volume II*, edited by B. Nichols. Berkeley: University of California Press.

———. 1986. Notes on the Ascent of a Fictitious Mountain. In *Documentary and the Mass Media*, edited by J. Corner. London: Edward Arnold.

Weakland, James H. 1975. Feature Films as Cultural Documents. In *Principles of Visual Anthropology*, edited by P. Hockings. The Hague: Mouton.

White, Hayden. 1980. The Value of Narrativity in the Representation of Reality. In *On Narrative*, edited by W.J.T. Mitchell. Chicago: University of Chicago Press.

Wikan, Unni. 1991. Toward an Experience-Near Anthropology. *Cultural Anthropology* 6 (3):285–305.

Williams, Linda. 1995. Corporealized Observers: Visual Pornographies and the "Carnal Density of Vision." In *Fugitive Images: From Photography to Video*, edited by P. Pedro. Bloomington: Indiana University Press.

Wollen, Peter. 1972. *Signs and Meaning in the Cinema*. 3rd ed. Bloomington: Indiana University Press.

Worth, Sol, and John Adair. 1972. *Through Navajo Eyes*. Bloomington: Indiana University Press.

Worth, Sol. 1965. Film Communication: A Study of the Reactions to Some Student Films. *Screen Education* (July/August):3–19.

Worth, Sol. 1969. The Development of a Semiotic of Film. *Semiotica* 1:282–321.

———. 1972. Toward the development of a semiotic of ethnographic film. *PIEF Newsletter* 3 (3):8–12.

———. 1981a. A Semiotic of Ethnographic Film. In *Studying Visual Communication*, edited by L. Gross. Philadelphia: University of Pennsylvania Press.

———. 1981b. *Studying Visual Communication*. Larry Gross, ed. Philadelphia: University of Pennsylvania Press.

Wright, Basil. 1971. Interview. In *Documentary Explorations*, edited by G. R. Levin. New York: Doubleday.

Young, Colin. 1986. A Provocation. *CILECT Review* 2 (1):115–18.

# Filmography

*À Bout de souffle*. 1960. Jean-Luc Godard. SNC (France). 90 mins.

*Akazama*. 1986. Marc-Henri Piault. C.N.R.S. (France). 80 mins.

*Allies*. 1983. Marian Wilkinson. Coral Sea Archives Project/Cinema Enterprises (Australia). 94 mins.

*An American Family* (series). 1972. Craig Gilbert. National Educational Television/Corporation for Public Broadcasting (U.S.A.). 12 episodes of 58 mins.

*L'Amour à vingt ans*. 1962. François Truffaut, Renzo Rossellini, Shintaro Ishihara, Marcel Ophuls and Andrzej Wajda. Ulysse-Unitec/Cinesecolo/Toho-Towa/Beta Film/Zespol Kamera (France/Italy/Japan/W. Germany/Poland). 123 mins.

*L'Amour en fuite*. 1979. François Truffaut. Les Films du Carrosse (France). 95 mins.

*Ananas*. 1983. Amos Gitaï. Les Film d'Ici/A.G. Productions (France/Israel). 73 mins.

*An Argument about a Marriage*. 1969. John K. Marshall. Film Study Center, Harvard University (U.S.A.). 18 mins.

*L'Arroseur arrosé*. 1895. Louis Lumière. Société Lumière (France). 40 secs.

*The Atomic Cafe*. 1982. Kevin Rafferty, Jayne Loader, and Pierce Rafferty. U.S.A. 92 mins.

*At the Winter Sea-Ice Camp, Part 3*. 1968. Asen Balikci and Robert Young. Educational Development Center (U.S.A.)/National Film Board of Canada. 36 mins.

*Au Hasard, Balthazar*. 1966. Robert Bresson. Parc/Athos/Argos/Svensk Filmindustri (France/Sweden) 94 mins.

*L'Avventura*. 1960. Michelangelo Antonioni. Cino Del Duca/Produzioni Cinematografiche Europee/Société Cinématographique Lyre (Italy/France). 145 mins.

*The Ax Fight*. 1975. Timothy Asch. Documentary Educational Resources (U.S.A). 30 mins.

*Les Baisers volés*. 1968. François Truffaut. Les Films du Carrosse/Artistes Associés (France). 91 mins.

*Baruya Muka Archival*. 1991. Ian Dunlop. Film Australia. 17 parts totalling 807 mins.

*Bataille sur le grand fleuve*. 1951. Jean Rouch. Centre National du Cinéma (France). 35 mins.

*Bathing Babies in Three Cultures*. 1954. Gregory Bateson and Margaret Mead. U.S.A. 9 mins.

*A Big Country* (series). 1968–91. Australian Broadcasting Commission. Over 350 programs, usually of approx. 28 mins.

*Black Harvest*. 1992. Bob Connolly and Robin Anderson. Arundel Productions (Australia). 90 mins.

*Blow-Job*. 1964. Andy Warhol. U.S.A. 40 mins.

*British Sounds*. 1969. Jean-Luc Godard and Jean-Pierre Gorin. Kestral Productions for London Weekend Television (G.B.). 51 mins.

*Cannibal Tours*. 1987. Dennis O'Rourke. Dennis O'Rourke & Associates (Australia). 70 mins.

*A Celebration of Origins.* 1992. Timothy Asch. Australian National University. 45 mins.

*Celso and Cora: A Manila Story.* 1983. Gary Kildea. Australia. 109 mins.

*Chachaji, My Poor Relation: A Memoir by Ved Mehta.* 1978. Bill Cran. WGBH Television (U.S.A.). 57 mins.

*Chang: A Drama of the Wilderness.* 1927. Merian C. Cooper and Ernest B. Schoedsack. Paramount (U.S.A.). 90 mins.

*La Chasse au lion à l'arc.* 1965. Jean Rouch. Les Films de la Pleiade (France). 69 mins.

*Chequer-board* (series). 1968–70. Australian Broadcasting Commission. 35 episodes of 30–51 mins.

*Un Chien andalou.* 1929. Luis Buñuel and Salvador Dali. France. 17 mins.

*Childhood Rivalry in Bali and New Guinea.* 1952. Gregory Bateson and Margaret Mead. U.S.A. 17 mins.

*Children of Fate: Life and Death in a Sicilian Family.* 1992. Andrew Young and Susan Todd. Friedson Productions/Archipelago Films (U.S.A.). 85 mins.

*La Chinoise.* 1967. Jean-Luc Godard. Productions de la Guéville/Parc/Athos/Simar/Anouchka Films (France). 95 mins.

*Chronique d'un été.* 1961. Jean Rouch and Edgar Morin. Argos Films (France). 90 mins.

*Citizen Kane.* 1941. Orson Welles. RKO-Radio Pictures (U.S.A.). 119 mins.

*The City.* 1939. Willard Van Dyke and Ralph Steiner. American Documentary Films/Carnegie Corporation (U.S.A.). 44 mins.

*The Civil War* (series). 1990. Ken Burns. Florentine Films/WETA Television (U.S.A.). 11 hours; 9 episodes of 62–99 mins.

*Coalface.* 1936. Alberto Cavalcanti. GPO Film Unit (G.B.). 12 mins.

*Cochengo Miranda.* 1974. Jorge Preloran. University of California at Los Angeles (U.S.A.). 58 mins.

*Cocorico, Monsieur Poulet.* 1974. Jean Rouch. Les Films du l'Homme/Dalarouta (France/Niger). 90 mins.

*Cogito, Ergo Sum.* 1989. Renita Lintrop. Studios Tallinnfilm (Estonia). 30 mins.

*Collum Calling Canberra.* 1984. David MacDougall and Judith MacDougall. Australian Institute of Aboriginal Studies. 58 mins.

*Coniston Muster: Scenes from a Stockman's Life.* 1972. Roger Sandall. Australian Institute of Aboriginal Studies. 30 mins.

*Contes et comptes de la cour.* 1993. Eliane de Latour. La Sept/CNRS Audiovisuel/Aaton/ORTN (France). 98 mins.

*Cortile Cascino.* 1962. Robert Young and Michael Roemer. NBC Television (U.S.A.). 47 mins.

*Cree Hunters of Mistassini.* 1974. Boyce Richardson and Tony Ianzielo. National Film Board of Canada/Department of Indian Affairs and Northern Development. 58 mins.

*A Curing Ceremony.* 1969. John K. Marshall. Film Study Center, Harvard University (U.S.A.). 8 mins.

*Damouré parle du SIDA.* 1994. Jean Rouch. France/Niger. 10 mins.

*Dani Houses.* 1974. Karl G. Heider. Educational Development Center (U.S.A.). 16 mins.

*Day after Day.* 1962. Clément Perron. National Film Board of Canada. 27 mins.

*The Day after Trinity: J. Robert Oppenheimer and the Atomic Bomb.* 1980. Jon Else. KTEH Television (U.S.A.). 88 mins.

*The Days before Christmas*. 1958. Terence Macartney-Filgate, Wolf Koenig and Stanley Jackson. National Film Board of Canada. 25 mins.

*Dead Birds*. 1963. Robert Gardner. Film Study Center, Harvard University (U.S.A.). 84 mins.

*Death and the Singing Telegram*. 1983. Mark Rance. U.S.A.. 115 mins.

*Debe's Tantrum*. 1972. John K. Marshall. Documentary Educational Resources (U.S.A.). 9 mins.

*De Grands évenéments et des gens ordinaires*. 1979. Raoul Ruiz. L'Institut National de l'Audiovisuel (France). 65 mins.

*Déjeuner de bébé*. 1895. Louis Lumière. Société Lumière (France). 40 secs.

*Diary of a Maasai Village* (series). 1985. Melissa Llewelyn-Davies. BBC Television (G.B.). 5 episodes of 50 mins.

*Dirt Cheap*. 1980. Ned Lander, Marg Clancy, and David Hay. Australia. 91 mins.

*Disappearing World* (series). 1970–. Granada Television (G.B.). Over 50 films of approx. 52 mins.

*Domicile conjugale*. 1970. François Truffaut. Les Films du Carrosse/Valoria/Fida (France). 97 mins.

*Don't Look Back*. 1966. Donn Alan Pennebaker. Leacock Pennebaker Inc. (U.S.A.). 95 mins.

*Drifters*. 1929. John Grierson. New Era for Empire Marketing Board (G.B.). 58 mins.

*Duminea: A Festival for the Water Spirits*. 1966. Francis Speed. University of Ife (Nigeria). 20 mins.

*8 1/2*. 1963. Federico Fellini. Cineriz (Italy). 188 mins.

*Emu Ritual at Ruguri*. 1969. Roger Sandall. Australian Institute of Aboriginal Studies. 35 mins.

*The Eskimos of Pond Inlet: The People's Land*. 1977. Michael Grigsby. Granada Television (G.B.). 55 mins.

*Essene*. 1972. Frederick Wiseman. Zipporah Films (U.S.A.). 86 mins.

*The Face of Another*, 1966. Hiroshi Teshigahara. Teshigahara Productions (Japan). 121 mins.

*Familiar Places*. 1980. David MacDougall. Australian Institute of Aboriginal Studies. 53 mins.

*Farrebique: ou les quatre saisons*. 1947. Georges Rouquier. L'Ecran Français/Les Films Étienne Lallier (France). 100 mins.

*The Feast*. 1970. Timothy Asch. Brandeis University Center for Documentary Anthropology/University of Michigan Department of Human Genetics (U.S.A). 29 mins.

*A Few Notes on Our Food Problem*. 1968. James Blue. United States Information Agency (U.S.A.). 35 mins.

*Finis Terrae*. 1929. Jean Epstein. Société Générale des Films (France). 86 mins.

*First Contact*. 1982. Bob Connolly and Robin Anderson. Arundel Productions (Australia). 54 mins.

*Forest of Bliss*. 1985. Robert Gardner. Film Study Center, Harvard University (U.S.A.). 91 mins.

*For Love or Money: A History of Women and Work in Australia*. 1983. Megan McMurchy and Jeni Thornley. Flashback Films (Australia). 109 mins.

*Frontline*. 1983. David Bradbury. Australian Film Commission/Tasmanian Film Corporation/Australian War Memorial. 56 mins.

*Funerailles à Bongo: Le Vieil Anai.* 1972. Jean Rouch. C.N.R.S. (France). 75 mins.
*The General Line [Old and New].* 1929. Sergei Eisenstein. Sovkino (U.S.S.R.). 90 mins.
*Good-bye Old Man.* 1977. David MacDougall. Australian Institute of Aboriginal Studies. 70 mins.
*Grass: A Nation's Battle for Life.* 1925. Merian C. Cooper and Ernest B. Schoedsack. Paramount Pictures (U.S.A.). 63 mins.
*The Great Depression* (series). 1981. London Weekend Television (G.B.). Episodes of 52 mins.
*Il Grido.* 1957. Michelangelo Antonioni. S.P.A. Cinematografica/Robert Alexander Productions (Italy/U.S.A.). 116 mins.
*A Group of Women.* 1969. John K. Marshall. Film Study Center, Harvard University (U.S.A.). 5 mins.
*Harlan County, U.S.A.* 1976. Barbara Kopple. Cabin Creek Films (U.S.A.). 103 mins.
*Henry Is Drunk.* 1972. John K. Marshall. Documentary Educational Resources (U.S.A.). 7 mins.
*Hiroshima, mon amour.* 1959. Alain Resnais. Argos-Como-Pathé/Daiei (France/ Japan). 91 mins.
*Hitlerjunge Quex.* 1933. Hans Steinhoff. UFA (Germany). 85 mins.
*Home from the Hill.* 1985. Molly Dineen. National Film and Television School (G.B.). 57 mins.
*Home on the Range: U.S. Bases in Australia.* 1981. Gil Scrine. Association for International Co-operation and Disarmament/Australian Film Commission. 56 mins.
*Hoop Dreams.* 1994. Steve James. Kartemquin Films/KCTA-TV (U.S.A.). 174 mins.
*Hospital.* 1969. Frederick Wiseman. OSTI (U.S.A.). 84 mins.
*House.* 1980. Amos Gitaï. Israeli Television. 52 mins.
*The House-Opening.* 1980. Judith MacDougall. Australian Institute of Aboriginal Studies. 45 mins.
*Housing Problems.* 1935. Arthur Elton and Edgar Anstey. Realist Film Unit/British Commonwealth Gas (G.B.). 17 mins.
*The Hunters.* 1958. John K. Marshall. Film Study Center, Harvard University (U.S.A.). 72 mins.
*Las Hurdes [Land Without Bread].* 1932. Luis Buñuel. Ramon Acin (Spain). 27 mins.
*Imaginero—The Image Man.* 1970. Jorge Preloran. Tucuman National University (Argentina). 52 mins.
*Imbalu: Ritual of Manhood of the Gisu of Uganda.* 1988. Richard Hawkins. University of California at Los Angeles (U.S.A.). 70 mins.
*India Cabaret.* 1985. Mira Nair. India/U.S.A. 57 mins.
*Indian Boy of the Southwest.* 1963. Wayne Mitchell. Bailey Films (U.S.A.). 15 mins.
*In the Land of the Head-Hunters.* 1914. Edward S. Curtis. U.S.A. Approx. 50 mins.
*In the Land of the War Canoes.* 1973. Edward S. Curtis. Burke Museum, University of Washington (U.S.A.). 33 mins.
*In the Street.* 1952. Helen Levitt, Janice Loeb and James Agee. U.S.A.. 15 mins.
*In This Life's Body.* 1984. Corinne Cantrill. Australia. 147 mins.
*The Intrepid Shadows.* 1966. Al Clah. Annenberg School of Communication (U.S.A.). 18 mins.

*Is What They Learn Worth What They Forget?* 1996. Lisbet Holtedahl and Mahmoudou Djingui. University of Tromsø (Norway). 45 mins.

*Jaguar.* 1967. Jean Rouch. Les Films de la Pleiade (France). 93 mins.

*Japan—The Village of Furuyashiki.* 1982. Shinsuke Ogawa. Ogawa Productions (Japan). 210 mins.

*Jero on Jero: A Balinese Trance Seance Observed.* 1981. Timothy Asch, Patsy Asch and Linda Connor. Documentary Educational Resources (U.S.A.)/Australian National University. 17 mins.

*La Jetée.* 1964. Chris Marker. Argos (France). 29 mins.

*Joe Leahy's Neighbours.* 1988. Bob Connolly and Robin Anderson. Arundel Productions (Australia). 93 mins.

*A Joking Relationship.* 1966. John K. Marshall. Film Study Center, Harvard University (U.S.A.). 13 mins.

*The Kawelka: Ongka's Big Moka.* 1974. Charlie Nairn. Granada Television (G.B.). 55 mins.

*Kenya Boran.* 1974. James Blue and David MacDougall. American Universities Field Staff (U.S.A.). 66 mins.

*King Kong.* 1933. Merian C. Cooper and Ernest B. Schoedsack. RKO (U.S.A.). 103 mins.

*The Kwegu.* 1982. Leslie Woodhead. Granada Television (G.B.). 52 mins.

*The Land Dyaks of Borneo.* 1966. William R. Geddes. University of Sydney (Australia). 38 mins.

*Larwari and Walkara.* 1977. Roger Sandall. Australian Institute of Aboriginal Studies. 45 mins.

*The Life and Times of Rosie the Riveter.* 1980. Connie Field. Clarity Educational Productions (U.S.A.). 65 mins.

*Listen to Britain.* 1942. Humphrey Jennings. Crown Film Unit (G.B.). 21 mins.

*Liu Pi Chia.* 1965. Richard Chen. University of California at Los Angeles (U.S.A.). 25 mins.

*Living Hawthorn.* 1906. William Alfred Gibson and Millard Johnson. Australia. approx. 15 mins.

*Lonely Boy.* 1962. Roman Kroiter and Wolf Koenig. National Film Board of Canada. 27 mins.

*Lorang's Way.* 1979. David MacDougall and Judith MacDougall. Rice University Media Center (U.S.A.). 70 mins.

*Louisiana Story.* 1948. Robert J. Flaherty. Robert J. Flaherty Productions (U.S.A.). 77 mins.

*Lousy Little Sixpence.* 1982. Alec Morgan and Gerry Bostok. Sixpence Films (Australia). 54 mins.

*Ma'Bugi: Trance of the Toraja.* 1971. Eric Crystal, Catherine Crystal and Lee Rhoads. Crystal-Crystal-Rhoads (U.S.A.). 22 mins.

*Madame L'Eau.* 1992. Jean Rouch. NFI/SODAPERAGA/Comité du Film Ethnographique/BBC Television (Netherlands/France/G.B.). 125 mins.

*Les Maitres fous.* 1955. Jean Rouch. Les Films de la Pleiade (France). 36 mins.

*Man of Aran.* 1934. Robert J. Flaherty. Gaumont-British Picture Corporation Ltd. (G.B.). 77 mins.

*The Man with the Movie Camera.* 1928. Dziga Vertov. VUFKU (U.S.S.R.). 90 mins.

*Maragoli.* 1976. Sandra Nichols. Document Film Services (G.B.). 58 mins.

*The March of Time* (series). 1935–51. Time-Life, Inc. (U.S.A.). Approx. 200 monthly releases of 15–25 mins.

*A Married Couple.* 1969. Allan King. Aquarius Films (U.S.A.). 97 mins.

*Marryings.* [1960—not completed]. John K. Marshall. Film Study Center, Harvard University (U.S.A.). approx. 60 mins.

*The Meat Fight.* 1973. John K. Marshall. Documentary Educational Resources (U.S.A.). 14 mins.

*Mein Kampf.* 1960. Erwin Leiser. Minerva International Films (Sweden). 122 mins.

*Memories and Dreams.* 1993. Melissa Llewelyn-Davies. BBC Television (G.B.). 92 mins.

*Men Bathing.* 1972. John K. Marshall. Documentary Educational Resources (U.S.A.). 14 mins.

*Miao Year.* 1968. William R. Geddes. University of Sydney (Australia). 61 mins.

*The Migrants.* 1985. Leslie Woodhead. Granada Television (G.B.). 53 mins.

*Moana: A Romance of the Golden Age.* 1926. Robert J. Flaherty. Paramount Pictures (U.S.A.). 64 mins.

*Moi, un noir.* 1957. Jean Rouch. Les Films de la Pleiade (France). 70 mins.

*Mokil.* 1950. Conrad Bentzen. U.S.A. 58 mins.

*Momma Don't Allow.* 1956. Karel Reisz and Tony Richardson. Experimental Film Production Fund (G.B.). 22 mins.

*The Mursi.* 1974. Leslie Woodhead. Granada Television (G.B.). 55 mins.

*My Family and Me.* 1986. Colette Piault. Les Films du Quotidien (France). 75 mins.

*N!ai, The Story of a !Kung Woman.* 1980. John K. Marshall and Adrienne Miesmer. Documentary Educational Resources/Public Broadcasting Associates (U.S.A.). 58 mins.

*N/um Tchai: The Ceremonial Dance of the !Kung Bushmen.* 1974. John K. Marshall. Documentary Educational Resources (U.S.A.). 20 mins.

*Naim and Jabar.* 1974. David Hancock and Herb di Gioia. American Universities Field Staff (U.S.A.). 50 mins.

*Nanook of the North.* 1922. Robert J. Flaherty. Revillon Frères (France). 75 mins.

*Nawi.* 1970. David MacDougall. University of California at Los Angeles (U.S.A.). 22 mins.

*Nehru.* 1963. Richard Leacock and Gregory Shuker. Time-Life Broadcast/Drew Associates (U.S.A.). 54 mins.

*Netsilik Eskimos* (series). 1963–68. Asen Balikci and Guy Mary-Rousselièrc. Educational Development Center (U.S.A.)/National Film Board of Canada. 9 films in 21 parts of 26–36 mins.

*Night Mail.* 1936. Basil Wright and Harry Watt. G.P.O. Film Unit (G.B.). 24 mins.

*North Sea.* 1938. Harry Watt. GPO Film Unit (G.B.). 24 mins.

*Nuit et brouillard.* 1956. Alain Resnais. Como/Argos/Cocicor (France). 30 mins.

*October [Ten Days That Shook the World].* 1928. Sergei Eisenstein. Sovkino (U.S.S.R.). 103 mins.

*Olivier Olivier.* 1991. Agnieszka Holland. Oliane Productions/Films A2/Canal+ (France). 109 mins.

*On Company Business.* 1980. Allan Francovich. Isla Negra Films (U.S.A.). 180 mins.

*Our Way of Loving*. 1994. Joanna Head and Jean Lydall. BBC Television (G.B.). 60 mins.

*The Path*. 1973. Donald Rundstrom, Ronald Rundstrom and Clinton Bergum. Sumai Film Company (U.S.A.). 34 mins.

*Paul Tomkowicz: Street-Railway Switch Man*. 1954. Roman Kroiter. National Film Board of Canada. 1953 mins.

*Un Pays sans bon sense*. 1969. Pierre Perrault. National Film Board of Canada. 117 mins.

*Les Photos d'Alix*. 1979. Jean Eustache. O.C.C./Médiane Films (France). 15 mins.

*Photo Wallahs*. 1991. David MacDougall and Judith MacDougall. Fieldwork Films (Australia). 59 mins.

*Police* (series). 1982. Roger Graef and Charles Stewart. BBC Television (G.B.). 11 programs of 50 mins.

*Portrait of Jason*. 1967. Shirley Clarke. Shirley Clarke Productions (U.S.A.). 105 mins.

*Pour la suite du monde*. 1963. Michel Brault. National Film Board of Canada. 84 mins.

*Primary*. 1960. Richard Leacock, D.A. Pennebaker, Terence Macartney-Filgate and Albert Maysles. Time-Life Broadcast/Drew Associates (U.S.A.). 54 mins.

*Public Enemy Number One*. 1986. David Bradbury. Australia. 58 mins.

*Pygmies of the Rainforest*. 1977. Kevin Duffy. K. Duffy (U.S.A.). 51 mins.

*La Pyramide humaine*. 1961. Jean Rouch. Les Films de la Pleiade (France). 90 mins.

*Le Quai des brumes*. 1938. Marcel Carné. Rabinovich/Ciné Alliance/Pathé (France). 89 mins.

*Les Quatre cents coups*. 1959. François Truffaut. Les Films du Carrosse/SEDIF (France). 94 mins.

*Queen of Apollo*. 1970. Richard Leacock. U.S.A. 12 mins.

*The Quiet One*. 1948. Sidney Meyers. Film Documents (U.S.A.). 67 mins.

*Red Matildas*. 1985. Sharon Connolly and Trevor Graham. Australia. 51 mins.

*Le Règne du jour*. 1966. Pierre Perrault. National Film Board of Canada. 118 mins.

*The Return of Martin Guerre*. 1982. Daniel Vigne. SFP/France Region 3/Marcel Dassault/Roissi Films (France). 123 mins.

*The River*. 1937. Pare Lorentz. Farm Security Administration (U.S.A.). 30 mins.

*Rivers of Sand*. 1975. Robert Gardner. Film Study Center, Harvard University (U.S.A.). 84 mins.

*Rocky*. 1976. John G. Avildsen. United Artists (U.S.A.). 119 mins.

*Rope*. 1948. Alfred Hitchcock. Transatlantic-Hitchcock/Sidney Bernstein (U.S.A.). 81 mins.

*Salesman*. 1969. Albert Maysles, David Maysles, and Charlotte Zwerin. Maysles Films (U.S.A.). 90 mins.

*Sans Soleil*. 1982. Chris Marker. Argos (France). 100 mins.

*The Scapegoat*. 1959. Robert Hamer. Guiness-du Maurier/MGM (G.B.). 92 mins.

*Seven Plus Seven*. 1970. Michael Apted. Granada Television (G.B.). 56 mins.

*Shoah*. 1985. Claude Lanzmann. Les Films Aleph/Historia Films (France). Part 1, 273 mins, Part 2, 290 mins.

*Sigui* (series). 1966–73. Jean Rouch. C.N.R.S. (France). 8 films of 15 to 50 mins.

*Sijainen: The Boy Who Never Smiles*. 1989. Antti Peippo. Verity Films (Finland). 23 mins.

*Sleep*. 1963. Andy Warhol. U.S.A. 360 mins.

*Soldier Girls*. 1981. Nick Broomfield and Joan Churchill. Churchill Films (U.S.A.). 87 mins.

*Sommersby*. 1993. Jon Amiel. Le Studio Canal +/Regency Enterprises/Alcor Films (France/U.S.A.). 117 mins.

*Song of Ceylon*. 1934. Basil Wright. Ceylon Tea Propaganda Board/GPO Film Unit (G.B.). 40 mins.

*Sophia's People—Eventful Lives*. 1985. Peter Loizos. London School of Economics (G.B.). 37 mins.

*The Spirit Possession of Alejandro Mamani*. 1975. Hubert Smith. American Universities Field Staff (U.S.A.). 30 mins.

*Stockman's Strategy*. 1984. David MacDougall and Judith MacDougall. Australian Institute of Aboriginal Studies. 54 mins.

*Stravinsky*. 1965. Roman Kroiter and Wolf Koenig. Canadian Broadcasting Corporation/National Film Board of Canada. 50 mins.

*A Stravinsky Portrait*. 1966. Richard Leacock. Leacock Pennebaker Inc. (U.S.A.). 57 mins.

*Sunny and the Dark Horse*. 1986. David MacDougall and Judith MacDougall. Australian Institute of Aboriginal Studies. 85 mins.

*Sunset Boulevard*. 1950. Billy Wilder. Paramount (U.S.A.). 111 mins.

*Tempus de Baristas*. 1993. David MacDougall. Istituto Superiore Regionale Etnografico/Fieldwork Films/BBC Television (Italy/Australia/G.B.). 100 mins.

*La terra trema: episodio del mare*. 1948. Luchino Visconti. Universalia (Italy). 160 mins.

*The Things I Cannot Change*. 1966. Tanya Ballantyne. National Film Board of Canada. 56 mins.

*Three Domestics*. 1970. John K. Marshall. Documentary Educational Resources (U.S.A.). 32 mins.

*Three Horsemen*. 1982. David MacDougall and Judith MacDougall. Australian Institute of Aboriginal Studies. 54 mins.

*Thursday's Children*. 1953. Lindsay Anderson and Guy Brenton. World Wide Pictures (G.B.). 20 mins.

*The Tin Drum*. 1979. Volker Schlondorff. UA/Franz/Seitz/Bioskop/GGB14/KG/Hallelujah/Artemis/Argos/Jadran/Film Polski (W. Germany). 142 mins.

*Titicut Follies*. 1967. Frederick Wiseman and John Marshall. Bridgewater Film Co., Inc. (U.S.A.). 89 mins.

*To Live with Herds*. 1972. David MacDougall. University of California at Los Angeles (U.S.A.). 70 mins.

*Touchez-pas au grisbi*. 1953. Jacques Becker. Les Films Corona/Del Duca Films (France/Italy). 94 mins.

*Tourou et Bitti: Les Tambours d'avant*. 1971. Jean Rouch. C.N.R.S. (France). 10 mins.

*Towards Baruya Manhood*. 1972. Ian Dunlop. Australian Commonwealth Film Unit. 9 parts totalling 465 mins.

*A Transfer of Power*. 1986. David MacDougall and Judith MacDougall. Australian Institute of Aboriginal Studies. 22 mins.

*The Transformed Isle*. 1917. R. C. Nicholson. Methodist Missionary Society of Australasia (Australia). 49 mins.

*The Trials of Alger Hiss*. 1980. John Lowenthal. History on Film Company (U.S.A.). 166 mins.

*Triumph des Willens*. 1935. Leni Riefenstahl. NSDAP (Germany). 120 mins.

*Trobriand Cricket: An Ingenious Response to Colonialism*. 1976. Gary Kildea. Office of Information, Papua New Guinea. 53 mins.

*Turksib*. 1929. Victor Turin. Vostok Kino (U.S.S.R.). 60 mins.

*21*. 1978. Michael Apted. Granada Television (G.B.). 105 mins.

*Two Girls Go Hunting*. 1991. Joanna Head and Jean Lydall. BBC Television (G.B.). 50 mins.

*2001: A Space Odyssey*. 1968. Stanley Kubrick. MGM (G.B.). 141 mins.

*Umberto D*. 1952. Vittorio de Sica. Dear Films (Italy). 89 mins.

*Under the Men's Tree*. 1974. David MacDougall. University of California at Los Angeles (U.S.A.). 15 mins.

*Valencia Diary*. 1992. Gary Kildea. Australian Film Commission/Australian Broadcasting Corporation. 107 mins.

*Vertigo*. 1958. Alfred Hitchcock. Universal (U.S.A.). 128 mins.

*La Vieille et la pluie*. 1974. Jean-Pierre Olivier de Sardan. C.N.R.S. (France). 55 mins.

*Vietnam: A Television History* (series). 1983. WGBH Television/ATV-Central Independent Television/Antenne-2 (U.S.A./G.B./France). 13 episodes of 55 mins.

*The Village*. 1969. Mark McCarty. Ethnographic Film Program, University of California at Los Angeles (U.S.A.). 70 mins.

*Waiting for Fidel*. 1974. Michael Rubbo. National Film Board of Canada. 50 mins.

*Waiting for Harry*. 1980. Kim McKenzie. Australian Institute of Aboriginal Studies. 58 mins.

*Warrendale*. 1966. Allan King. Allan King Associates/CBC (Canada). 100 mins.

*The Wedding Camels*. 1977. David MacDougall and Judith MacDougall. Rice University Media Center (U.S.A.). 108 mins.

*The Wedding of Palo*. 1937. F. Dlasheim and Knut Rasmussen. Palladium Films (Denmark). 72 mins.

*Week-end*. 1967. Jean-Luc Godard. Lira/Comacico/Copernic/Ascot Cineraid (Italy/France). 103 mins.

*Welfare*. 1975. Frederick Wiseman. Zipporah Films (U.S.A.). 167 mins.

*Why We Fight* (series). 1942–45. U.S. War Department. 7 films of 51–77 mins.

*A Wife among Wives*. 1981. David MacDougall and Judith MacDougall. Rice University Media Center (U.S.A.). 75 mins.

*With Babies and Banners: The Story of the Women's Emergency Brigade*. 1976. Lorraine Gray. Women's Labor History Film Project (U.S.A.). 45 mins.

*The Women's Olamal: The Social Organisation of a Maasai Fertility Ceremony*. 1984. Melissa Llewelyn-Davies. BBC Television (G.B.). 113 mins.

*The Women Who Smile*. 1990. Joanna Head and Jean Lydall. BBC Television (G.B.). 50 mins.

*Workers and Jobs*. 1935. Arthur Elton. Ministry of Labour (G.B.). 12 mins.

*The World at War* (series). 1974–75. Jeremy Isaacs. Thames Television (G.B.). 26 episodes of 50 mins.

*You Wasn't Loitering*. 1973. John K. Marshall. Documentary Educational Resources (U.S.A.). 15 mins.

*Zerda's Children.* 1978. Jorge Preloran. Ethnographic Film Program, University of California (U.S.A.). 52 mins.

*Zulay Facing the 21st Century.* 1989. Jorge Preloran and Mabel Preloran. University of California at Los Angeles (U.S.A.). 120 mins.

# Index